Wires, Wheels and Wings

Wires, Wheels and Wings
(A Wireless Mechanic's Diary)

by

Harry Reddin

Foreword by George Williams CBE

The Pentland Press Limited
Edinburgh · Cambridge · Durham

First published in 1994 by
The Pentland Press Ltd.
1 Hutton Close
South Church
Bishop Auckland
Durham

ISBN 1 85821 128 X

Typeset by Elite Typesetting Techniques, Southampton.
Printed and bound by Antony Rowe Ltd., Chippenham.

Dedicated to all my friends,
past and present, who served
with the Royal Air Force (1939–45)

Contents

Foreword

Meeting up again with Harry Reddin, after a gap of some fifty years, stirred my memory. A great flood of events came crowding back into focus: events involving my war service with the Royal Air Force in the Mediterranean Area, events which were happy and sad, successful and disappointing, memories of which had remained dormant too long.

Harry showed me an article he had written describing some of his experiences in Algeria during the time we both served there. I was most impressed both by his recall of detail and by his ability to record events in an amusing and readable manner. Consequently, I urged him to embark upon this, his autobiography, which I trust you, like me, will thoroughly enjoy reading.

I will comment only on the period when our paths crossed or, better expressed, adjoined, for indeed, I recollect only harmony and co-operation between us.

The greater part of my time was devoted to tackling the U-boat threat.

Firstly: as a pilot of a Hudson of 608 Squadron. On my second tour of operations from both Gibraltar and Blida I reported sighting, attacking and critically damaging a U-boat in November 1942. The vessel subsequently beached itself between Oran and Algiers.

Secondly: As a staff officer at NACAF (North African Coastal Air Forces) Headquarters in Algiers and later at 242 Group in Italy. During my time in Algiers I designed 'Operation SWAMP'. This, being approved by the Air-Officer Commanding, Air Vice-Marshal Hugh Pugh Lloyd, was used extensively and with considerable success. The operation commenced on the sighting of a U-boat or when a U-boat revealed its own position by attacking our shipping. By extending carefully planned air surveillance in co-operation with naval forces to cover the possible submerged endurance of the U-boat, it had no chance of surfacing for air and battery-charging without being sighted. Harry

Reddin made a valuable contribution to the planning of the elaborate communications procedures required for such an operation.

Thirdly: As the Commanding Officer of No. 36 (Wellington) Squadron operating from Algeria, Sardinia and Italy. This, my third operational tour, included not only U-boat hunting but an exciting diversionary manoeuvre. In co-operation with a flotilla of Motor Torpedo Boats commanded by Douglas Fairbanks Junior, a simulated landing on the southern French coast was contrived. Our aircraft dropped a continuous curtain of 'window' (strips of silvered paper) moving ever forward at some 8 knots for several hours as directed by the MTBs, which made sufficient noise on nearing the coast to deceive the Germans into believing that a major landing was imminent. The operation was deemed a great success.

Service in the Royal Air Force, as well described by Harry Reddin in the forthcoming chapters, is indeed worthy of recall. His accounts are not confined to achievement and disaster; they include chronicles of great comradeships and personalities.

George Williams CBE

Chapter 1

Sunday's Child

Life is purely, but not simply, a game of chance. My own game began on a Sunday. A week later my country was at war with Germany.

The two events – my birth and the outbreak – were quite unrelated. The joint effects of the two, however, brought about unexpected alterations to family programmes. Firstly, my father enshipped as an engineer in the Merchant Fleet, only just managing to stay around long enough to buy my first vehicle, a pram with wire wheels.

Mother was not cut out for the nursing profession in any form and quickly sought the assistance of my Grandmother in the art of bringing up a child. That necessitated the removal of Mother, myself and pram from Sowerby, the picturesque place of my birth, to South Shields. The arrangement showed promise. Grandpa Wase, a Chief Engineer of the Redhead line, spent most of his time at sea. The two ladies would be company for one another, at the same time providing amply for my welfare.

The possibility of enemy action from the air had not been taken into account. The Germans selected South Shields as a target for a raid by a Zeppelin. We, all three, entrained for the relative safety of the Yorkshire countryside and remained at Sowerby until the cessation of hostilities four years later.

Grandma Wase never returned to her home on Tyneside. It appears that incompatibility of temperament caused her to allow Grandpa to concentrate on his life at sea. I don't think they ever met again. The separation caused me no distress, for I was unaware of such affairs. To my mother it represented a dreadful stigma which preyed upon her to such an extent that, many years later, she suffered a most severe attack of dermatitis. A brilliant psychiatrist at York searched out the problem. A magician could not have cleared the inflammation more quickly.

Mother was an accomplished pianist and painter. She was also a very good cook but was so obsessed with hygiene that meals never appeared on time. So Grandma did the general cooking with highly satisfactory results. She played a major part in my upbringing at the same time, for which Mother was grateful indeed. Mother would put the finishing touches to my outfitting after Grandma had done the spade work.

Of course, I knew nothing of the difficulties of survival. At what age the vague realities of life began to implant any lasting impressions into my memory

1

I cannot know. I must have reached at least the push-chair stage when I became conscious of being hailed by groups of jovial adults dressed in pale blue uniforms. They were known by me as 'wounded soldiers'. We met them on the way to town.

The parish of Sowerby is an annex to Thirsk and in the market place of the mother town the parishioners were obliged to do their shopping. On our way we passed the Town Hall which had been adapted for use as a hospital. Whenever Grandma was my guardian she would be sure to stop and pass the time of day with the lads, so I became accustomed, at an undefined early age, to meeting grown men hobbling on crutches or sitting in wheel-chairs. They were a cheerful lot, yet Grandma persisted in referring to them as 'poor boys'.

I liked the wounded soldiers. From our meeting place I could see a huge and fearsome picture of a heavily moustached soldier pointing at me from the wall of the Trustee Savings Bank. I used to see this awful fellow staring at me when I had been told to go to sleep. As I grew up the face seemed to get bigger and more terrifying. Then I began to read letters and ask questions. Grandma explained that the picture was of General Haig. He was saying: 'YOUR COUNTRY NEEDS YOU!' I shall never forget the face, or the command. I began to worry about what my country would do with me when it got me. Maybe one day I would be a wounded soldier and wear a pale blue uniform and a red tie.

Of the processes of war I knew nothing. Such results of it which came to my notice seemed not distasteful. The wounded soldiers were not the only uniformed characters of my acquaintance. The German prisoners of war who enjoyed the hospitality of the local maltings frequently kicked a football over the wall onto our village green. The faces which appeared in the appeal for return of the ball were, to my young mind, kindly and friendly. Grandma said they were 'a bad lot'. It was no use arguing with Grandma.

Father's career at sea ended on 10 May 1917, when the SS *Broomhill* was torpedoed off Portland Bill. Of his return home in borrowed clothes I have no recollection. The following extract from his description of the action is preserved in the family scrap-book:

> . . . shells came through our sides. I thought at first there was a complete smash-up of the engines . . . On deck they must have had lively scenes. Two of the lifeboats were blown to pieces, derricks split, funnel riddled, chart room, wheelhouse, bridge all shot away. The Captain and the mates had a very near squeak. They just got off the bridge before the whole thing came down. Two men – brothers – trying to get the starboard lifeboat out were blown to pieces and another man seriously wounded. Others were slightly injured. The Captain sent the second mate to call me out of the engine room. We got off in one of the boats and to our surprise, the U-boat came close up to us. I should have

said the morning was hazy and we had not been able to see her before. The U-boat commander, in an excited flurry, ordered us alongside and the men were ordered on to the submarine, leaving four sailors in the boat to take two German sailors alongside our vessel. These men placed bombs forward, aft, amidships and in the stoke-hole, igniting them with time fuses . . .

Rescue came in the form of a British destroyer, the appearance of which caused a rapid departure of the U-boat. Father and his colleague watched the end of the *Broomhill* from the relative comfort of the destroyer.

Father spent the last year of the war as a munition volunteer, maintaining electrical machinery at the Rubery-Owen works at Darlaston. His left wrist, damaged during the *Broomhill* affair, troubled him to the end of his days but he never considered applying for compensation. He refused to read any book which tended to dramatise war. He was both pacifist and socialist at heart. Once the war was over he rejoined the family business to become the world's No. 1 workaholic.

Born at Church Stretton in 1885, to earn a reputation as leading practical joker of that tree-lined valley, my father thrived on action. At an early age he could handle the horse and trap which Grandfather used for delivery of groceries and wine from his delicatessen. When the family transferred to Hoylake he found employment at Boothroyd's of Birkenhead. He studied assiduously at night school and moonlighted for a local house-wiring contractor and a model engineer. Somewhere along the line he had learned to play flute and piccolo sufficiently well to supplement his income by performing with a theatre orchestra.

By the age of twenty-three my father had built up not only a reputation as an electrical engineer but also a nest-egg. In 1908 the family moved to Thirsk. The name of H. Reddin and Sons, boldly displayed on an enamelled plate, overlooked Thirsk Market Place for the next thirty-five years. In copperplate handwriting Uncle William kept the books of the prosperous ironmongery business which Grandfather supervised with rigid autocracy. My father set up an electrical department and ran a 'Regal' taxi based upon his workshop behind the Fleece Hotel.

Father's proficiency as an electrical engineer is exemplified by an article which appeared in a Thirsk and District newspaper during the year 1910:

. . . The oil lamp and candle, the use of which entails endless time and trouble and attended with the danger of fire, have been displaced by the electric light, which may be put into operation by the mere pressing of a switch . . . One cannot refrain from making special comment upon the appearance of the mills when fully illuminated . . . a splendid effect . . . The dynamo is driven from a four-post pulley . . . through differential gears from the main water wheel. The scheme is really enterprising. Its adoption will certainly effect a considerable saving in time and trouble, not to speak of the expense of lamp-oil and candles . . . Praise is all the more due to Mr. C.E. Reddin when it is considered that the whole installation was carried out entirely by himself with no assistance of any kind. He personally designed the switchboard and dynamo, which were built to his order by Messrs. Siemens Bros. at their London works . . .

Two years later, on 25 January 1912, a letter from Messrs. Rymer Bros., Millers and Corn Dealers of Thirsk, reads as follows:

To Mr. C.E. Reddin, Electrician, Thirsk:

Dear Sir,

It is now two years since you fitted us up with electric light. I thought you would like to know that, up to now, there has not been the slightest trouble with the plant. It is as good today as the first day it was started, which I think is in itself a proof of the excellence of the material and workmanship which you put into it. It has proved a great boon and my wife and I often say that if it had cost twice the amount it would still have been a cheap investment.

Yours truly

J. Rymer (Signed)

In spite of devoting enormous energy to the business my father did not neglect to practise as a flautist. He played in a small dance orchestra. When the pianist failed to turn up one summer evening the organiser appealed for a volunteer from the patient audience. A stately lady visitor came forward and played to such a degree of excellence that my father, ever searching for perfection, fell in love. They married in the spring of 1913, at South Shields.

Father's nest egg was put to good use in the purchase of Melrose House, Victoria Avenue for the sum of £230. It was there that I was born on 26 July 1914. Thus we arrive back at the beginning, of which I was not conscious.

When the war ended, officially at 11 a.m. on the 11th day of the 11th month of 1918, I was old enough to start building a visual memory. The victory parade in Thirsk Market Place was of such immensity that it forms the earliest pictures which I can recall in some detail. The whole family assembled on the roof of Central Buildings from where we surveyed the grand event. Beyond the town the green fields glittered in the sunshine, the backdrop of the escarpment formed by Whitestone Cliff and Roulston Scar, one of the grandest sights in all England, completing the stage.

Some of my friends in pale blue rode on the Model-'T' Ford ambulances, bands played, people cheered, Model-'H' Triumph motor-cycles puttered and scout cars scouted.

Auntie Lizzie got upset because Grandma wanted to serve tea on the roof instead of 'properly' in the lounge below. Everybody thought Grandma's tea-cakes were wonderful, everybody except Auntie Lizzie who liked to show off; she said they were overdone. I said I liked the browned edges and was told to keep quiet.

Uncle William had an arm in a sling. He said he had been swinging a 'prop' when the engine back-fired. Otherwise his war service had been charmed. Uncle Percy was even more fortunate; his country had not needed him, owing to a natural disability. He had acquired a 'safe' job in a bank and joined the golf club.

It was during the extensive celebrations that I first became aware of having a father. Hitherto, through no fault of his own, he had taken no part in my upbringing. Grandma Wase had played the principal upbringer and she had no intention of relinquishing the post. The scene was set for many a domestic upheaval.

Chapter 2

Melrose House

Victoria Avenue failed to comply with any acceptable definition of the meaning of 'avenue', except maybe as a 'means of access or attainment'. In the case of our 'avenue', four distinct building contractors had been involved, each one working to a different plan. The final objective, it could be assumed, was to have been to build two identical terraces on opposite sides of the roadway. The finished product would thus have conformed with normal Victorian practice. Had the builders agreed to start their work in the centre and work outwards the result could well have been architecturally pleasing.

For some reason each builder commenced work at an outer end and made towards the middle. Thus four separate terraces took shape. It was not to the entire disadvantage of the uprising generation that hostilities broke out in Europe and all four builders catered for other needs. They left, as a bonus to the local children, two village greens admirably suited to the playing of games. Chimney breasts made ideal refuges from storm as well as bases for hide-and-seek, goals for ball games and sites for surreptitious bonfires. The 'green' on the north side of the 'avenue' was known universally as 'The Pit' by virtue of the deep hole in its centre.

Even after the hole was filled the northern 'green' was termed 'The Pit'. Our elders ordered the sealing of the hole following the rescue of three kids who had fruitlessly descended by a makeshift rope-ladder in an effort to retrieve Ma Claxton's spaniel pup. The unfortunate animal had heedlessly chased a cat which cleared the hole with ease, leaving its pursuer stranded in mid-air. The rope-ladder had parted company from its ill-conceived anchorage to the dismay of the triad, not to mention that of the whimpering pup. The German prisoners of war had returned to their homeland, otherwise rescue of the whole party would have been achieved promptly. As it was the wails and whimpers went unheeded until a pedestrian chanced that way.

The announcement of the closing of 'The Pit' caused a wholesale turn out of domestic trash. Down the hole went brass bedsteads, fenders, chamber pots, rusted bicycles, armchairs which oozed horsehair and springs, push-chairs minus wheels and wheels without push-chairs, miscellaneous odds and ends which maybe today would reach surprisingly handsome valuations in an antiques roadshow.

6

It took years for 'The Pit' to settle down, for grass to grow over its final coverings. It remained a trap for the unwary. After successive mountainous bonfires had calcinated Guy Fawkes and numerous of his reproductions the charred circle warned would-be trespassers to our territory, the grass growing to extraordinary heights around the circumference during eleven months of the year. Victoria Avenue gained an enviable reputation for its bonfires. After neighbouring conflagrations had sputtered to a miserable glow ours flourished. Crowds from outlying districts gathered to watch the grand climax of our celebrations. Auntie Mercy handed round the parkin and Grandma dished out ginger wine. On one occasion Uncle William donated a half-crown box of fireworks, the contents of which included the biggest and best Roman Candle ever seen, the highest climbing rocket and by far the loudest thunderbolt.

Melrose House stood four doors up from the 'green', facing north. It glowed in the light from the bonfire and though it was a carbon copy of the adjoining houses, to my young mind it was the best looking by far. Its name in gold lettering on the glass over the front door was the distinguishing feature. Its Scottish connotation paid respects to Auntie Fanny, Grandma's sister who had married a wealthy gentleman over the Border and who contributed over the years to the welfare of us all. The arrangement suited my father admirably. He was enabled to add substantially to his nest egg without disclosing his assets to my mother, or to anyone else except his close ally who managed the local branch of The Yorkshire Penny Bank.

Compared with the modern so-called 'Town House' our residence in Victoria Avenue could well be described as capacious. From a well constructed pavement two clean stone steps must be mounted in order to enter the very substantial front door. Skilful use of the graining comb had put a touch of class to our door; further embellishment by a large brass knob and letter-box with knocker to match the gold-leaf on the fanlight satisfied my mother's one up-personship. Her tasteful choice of curtains at the bay window put finishing touches to the frontage.

Beyond the door came the 'passage' though Mother would persist in dubbing it the 'hall'. Ahead, the stairs pointed the way to the three bedrooms. To the right of the 'hall' was a door through which one might enter the front room.

The front room was Mother's show piece. Her upright piano stood behind the door. She was a good but not brilliant pianist. Her star turn was Sinding's 'Rustle of Spring'; then she would turn to Chopin and strive for technical excellence. She tried to teach me but soon ran out of patience because I failed to appreciate that the left hand was more important that the right. I never got to the end of the 'Primary Tutor'. The piano needed regular tuning because the north-facing room never warmed up except when the fire was lighted at Christmas time. On a later summer evening the setting sun struck our front room window obliquely just before it went down behind the timber yard at the end of the 'avenue'. It was at such times that Grandma might be seen sitting in the window seat keeping a look-out for passers-by. Otherwise the room was maintained in apple-pie order to receive special visitors such as Dr MacArthur or the vicar.

Behind the front room was the back room, sometimes referred to as the dining room. It was entered by a second door in the 'hall'. In the summer it collected quite a bit of heat from the mid-day sun when I found it useful as a retreat from the turmoil of the kitchen. It was too cold in the winter to be used at all except for very brief periods. The economics of the household did not allow for a fire to be lighted other than on Christmas day when the room assumed its dignified role as a dining room. This was about the only time of the year when the four of us sat down together for a meal.

At the end of the 'hall' or passage stood the entrance to the principal room of the house. The kitchen was always warm, once Father had got the fire going in the stove. As soon as he had stoked up, shaved at the kitchen sink and prepared and eaten his own breakfast he dashed off to work. Grandma was next on the scene. She drew up the fire to full heat, stacked on more coal, brought the oven to baking temperature, put the kettle on the fire and the business of the day began in earnest. She and I had a 'proper' breakfast. Mother never came down before all these preliminaries were completed. Her own breakfast consisted of a light snack based on her daily programme of 'Food and Inner Cleanliness'.

Our respective ablutions were carried out at the kitchen sink. Grandma would see that I washed behind my ears. When either of the ladies wished to undertake other than a superficial swill I was despatched from the presence.

Mother was not averse to cooking. She specialised in delicate dishes which she found it convenient to prepare during periods of her solitude, all too rarely possible, in the kitchen. Her tomato savoury was much sought after by organisers of sales of work, garden parties in aid of charities and meetings of the Women's Institute. When Mother set her mind to cuisine her artistic temperament showed in mouth-watering results. To achieve these she required to be left in peace for prolonged periods. It would have been quite impractical for her to undertake the day-to-day feeding of the household.

Grandma was ideally suited to the job of home-making in the practical sense. Diplomatic nicety was not her line. Her cooking was done in the grand style, good plain food and plenty of it. Rich smells rose with the steam, bread rose in tins before a glowing fire. Pricking the bread and tea-cakes with a fork was a task I might be permitted to perform under supervision. Add a few items of laundry to the clothes-horse to share the heat with the bakery and Grandma could settle down to half-an-hour of steady knitting in her armchair. Her morning's production was under control. Mother was upstairs cleaning, again, everything in sight.

The mid-day meal was dinner. Grandma would set the table and Mother would rearrange the settings. Father turned up at times to suit business conditions. Conversation between my father and his mother-in-law never went beyond a few carefully chosen courtesies, never breaking into open warfare. I was counselled frequently on the principle of 'little boys should be seen and not heard'. The possibility of my engaging in a man-to-man discourse with Father receded into a distant unattainable future. He couldn't get back to work fast enough.

Grandma washed up also in the grand manner with a great clattering of pans. After that would come a flurry of oven-door opening and closing, making up the fire, brewing tea and filling tins in the adjoining pantry before getting down to knitting again. Once a week she would drift off to town with the principal objective of replenishing stocks of wool. My disappointment on finding the rocking chair unoccupied when I arrived from school or play, struck deep beyond endurance.

I was not the only one to seek advice from the genius of the armchair in the kitchen. Grandma ran an IQ well into three figures. She could read a novel as she knitted; *Penny Plain* was her favourite but a close runner from her bookshelf was the timetable of the London and North Eastern Railway. Anyone contemplating a train journey would be well advised to consult Grandma in advance. Her range of subjects covered a vast field. I think of her as the forerunner of the present Citizens' Advice Bureau. Winter evenings in the kitchen frequently embraced a seminar with Grandma in the chair. Beneath the gaslight a small group of eager faces smiled in admiration of the words of wisdom freely dispensed by the hostess. On those occasions I might be permitted to sit up late so long as I remained silent.

Tea, served in the kitchen of course, was a substantial meal which Father found time to attend. It was the last recognised meal of the day, after which Father returned to the shop where there was always work to be done. Supper consisted of a cup of cocoa and a biscuit. For the first eight years of my life I was asleep in bed before Father finished work.

The back door opened directly into the back yard where a row of ferns, the common bracken variety, enhanced the base of the brick wall which divided us from our neighbours. A few steps down the yard was the wash-house where Mother spent one morning every week at another variety of her favourite pursuits into hygiene. Father would light the fire under the copper full of water before going to work. With precise timing Mother caught the water just before the boil and the first wash was on its way. Holiday times I liked to give a twirl on the dolly but it was hard work. Mother said I was more hindrance than help so I was obliged to leave her to the arduous task. She was a regular customer at the chemist's for Doan's Backache Pills.

The wash-house had other uses. It made a useful store for a multitude of domestic tools. On one substantial nail hung the zinc bath. In summer time the wash-house might function as a bathroom; winter time baths had to be taken on a system of rota in the kitchen.

Next door to the wash-house came the smallest room of Melrose House. This contained a highly efficient water-closet, maintained to a high standard of perfection by Father. The pipes were thickly lagged with sacking, the walls whitewashed every springtime. The wooden seat reflected any glimmer of light which touched its wax-polished splendour.

A small, pleasant garden, walled at either side and populated by perennials, separated the house from two further and important structures. The midden outclassed the modern dustbin in its capacity for accepting domestic waste by a hundred to one. A door, three feet above ground level, gave access for the ejection of rubbish into its interior. There was no limit to the variety of trash nor, it seemed, to the quantity which could be flung into the midden. Not only was it ideal for the amassment of junk, but it made a comfortable breeding ground for flies and a potential harbourage for rats. At regular intervals the 'dustmen' called, climbed through a duplicate doorway on the outside of the premises and shovelled the muck into a waiting cart. So, in fairness to the system, the timorous rats had no chance of making a permanent home. The adjoining building served as a coal store and tool shed.

A gate gave on to the back lane which provided a convenient access not only to the rear of the houses on the south side of Victoria Avenue but also to the timber yard at the western end. The disturbances caused by the timber hauliers were at least annoying and sometimes terrifying. The sight of four giant horses straining at a load of enormous tree trunks was impressive enough in the heat of summer, when dust clouds rose from grappling hooves and wobbling wheels. In winter when the lane was bogged and rutted the horsemen overused their whips to urge the poor beasts to exert more power. When wheels sunk to a standstill the steaming animals were allowed a short period of rest before the men lost patience. More violent cursings and whippings brought the horses, with heads down, to ever more effort. Protesting residents of the 'avenue' came to cry shame upon the men and their masters. There were times when a load would be left standing in the back lane all night, hoping fresh horses might succeed where tired ones had failed.

When the back lane became impassable for the timber trucks an attempt was made by the hauliers to use the front 'avenue' which was paved with loose cobbles. The suffering residents objected but not before lasting damage was done to the roadway.

In spite of these certain blemishes to its environment, Melrose House was a cosy corner of England. Cherished memories of life there during my first decade come crowding back as of yesteryear.

Chapter 3

Free-Wheeling

Following an absolutely unconscious period of transportation by perambulator I understand that I was transferred to a push-chair. Of this I have but vague recollection. During the push-chair stage, however, I experienced concurrently my first journeys on two wheels.

Mother and Father each owned a bicycle. On the cross-bar of Father's machine he fixed a small saddle and on the forward down-tube a pair of foot rests. Thus I was accommodated in some degree of comfort, for I could hold on to the handlebars and take a part in the operation of the vehicle. We covered a considerable number of miles in this manner. Mother carried her paintbox for she was expert in water-colouring. The sight of any river would cause us to halt whilst Mother sketched a landscape and touched in the major colours. Those were the chummy days before Father got too busy at work to bother with us.

My own first two-wheeler was a wooden scooter. Speed was impossible and journeys were limited to the confines of our back yard, to the detriment of a number of lilies of the valley and pride of London plants, not to mention shoe leather. A small pedal car was acquired in the interests of safety and economy but I soon grew out of that and a second-hand tricycle with rubber-tyred wheels brought me to a new dimension in transportation. The invigoration of speed brought in its wake more accidents to plant life and to myself. I was allowed to trike up and down the pavements of Victoria Avenue.

Such action set a precedent. Other trikers joined the fun. Where they came from I had no idea but I made friends fast. Unthinkingly we made enemies of a number of neighbours. Their wrath inspired the inauguration of speedway racing on the 'green'. At first the going was tough but as the grass wore thin we got down to stony ground. Speeds rose and so did the accident rate. Some of the accidents resulted in worse than superficial bruises and scratches. Competitive events were suspended in the hope of a rapid recovery but even after the removal of bandages by fond parents it was evident that our disabilities were long- rather than short-term. Anyone who has suffered scabbed knees will appreciate the problem. We decided to take up scootering, a sport which called for minimal bending of the knee.

My old wooden affair was useless on the grass track but I was fortunate in doing a swap with a smaller child whose scooter was far too large for him to handle. I executed my first deal in wheels.

John Fox, whose father owned a toy shop, turned up with a model on eight-inch-diameter pneumatic-tyred wheels. Nobody came anywhere near his lap times so we set up a handicap system based on wheel diameter.

We constructed a 3-in-1 ramp of wood, bricks, clay, and iron railings dug up from 'The Pit'. A 'ramp start' was introduced as standard, with J. Fox setting par for the course; that was the intention. Starting from the top of the ramp John entered the first bend at an uncontrollable rate, failed to recover from a front wheel skid and crashed into Mrs Crowther's garden wall. Damage to the wall was not worth reporting but the fallen rider yelled for five long minutes. His machine was withdrawn from future events pending replacement of the front wheel.

The remaining competitors were fairly matched. A system, later adopted by the ACU in the Isle of Man, of 'au pair' starting was inaugurated. Push starts added spice to the game. Riders stood with both feet on the machine, held vertical by a 'pusher' who imparted the initial impulse to his entrant. The first jab at the ground by a rider was not allowed until beyond the slope of the ramp. This encouraged the maximum effort from the 'pusher' who felt more responsibility to his team. It was hell or bust to the first bend but overshooting allowed the opposition to nip through on the inside; battle raged then for the second bend. Enthusiasm knew no bounds.

Regrettably, parental objectors did not fail to detect the inevitably serious deterioration of shoes. The operational foot performed the dual function of accelerator and brake. The end of the racing came when socks as well as shoes were holed to barefoot level. It became painfully obvious that whatever sport should be attempted next we must pay regard to parental economics. The solution to the problem came in fortuitous fashion, thanks to another life-saving movement on behalf of the Claxton spaniel.

In a last desperate dash along the back lane on his scooter, Snotty Johnson was attacked head-on by the dog. A deft move avoided harm to the animal but Snotty over-corrected his steering and smashed into the garden gate of No. 10. The gate had been hanging onto its rusty hinges for some time. It was overdue for major repairs. Not according to the owner who flared into a rage and declared that a perfectly sound gate had been ruined by hooliganism. A friendly carpenter made a satisfactory job of the repair, at a favourable charge. We promised to pay within a few days.

In consideration of fund-raising techniques we were surprised at our own ingenuity. A list of charges for work was drawn up: dog-walking could no longer be free; clearing of drain holes would be charged at one shilling, twice current rates; weeding, window cleaning, any odd jobs; all were entered in our lists. 'Bob-a-Job' week was a mockery compared to our scheme. Parents took an interest in our activities and offered moral support; we needed more than that. The aim of the plan, after paying the carpenter, was to purchase proper bicycles.

Parents were canvassed with the idea that their interests would best be served by discarding shoe-destroying scooters in favour of pedal-propelled machines. A surprisingly favourable reaction brought in a surge of business especially when an early arrival of winter brought with it a bumper crop of snow. To clearing it we went with a will. I opened my first account with The Yorkshire Penny Bank. Father found he could buy a 'Rambler' bicycle from a wholesaler for £4 15s. 6d. I set a target of £5 by the spring of 1922.

The winter hardened. The snow hardened so much that we could clear no more. On the 'all work and no play' principle the gang turned to sledging on the Castle Garth. The hill, a remnant of the original moat, is of very modest declivity but to a group of short-trousered little boys it served as a run down the Alps. Two wooden runners nailed to a plain board with string attached at the front made a proud substitute for a Santa Claus replica. Our launching drew the attention of envious, critical rival clans. Two boys sat aboard with feet tucked neatly out of harm's way. A third man pushed off, jumped aboard hanging on to the shoulders of the midshipman. The board split down the centre with a sickening crack, depositing all three on to the ice, much to the delight of the spectators.

Urgent repairs were necessary. We picked up the two halves and sought the advice of Fred Hutchinson. Fred was a master tinsmith whose value to the community could never be overstated. He could pick up a sheet of galvanised iron, place it on his anvil and, with half-a-dozen skilfully aimed clouts of a hammer, form the basis of a pig trough. Fred produced cake tins, buckets, funnels, milk churns, shovels, coal scuttles and a host of appliances for farm and home. He was famous for his 'Long Stands'. Many an apprentice boy had been sent to Fred for one of these. After a prolonged and tiring wait the unsuspecting child would venture to ask Fred:

'How long will it be, Mr Hutchinson?'

'Well, haven't you had long enough?' was Fred's stock question!

Our sled was transformed in no time. Fred shaped a couple of strong cross brackets, screwed the woodwork to them and fixed iron runners to the slides.

'How much, Fred?' I knew him well for he did a lot of work for my grandfather.

'Go on wi' yer!' he laughed and away we went to demonstrate just how successful sledging could be on a short course.

Came the thaw and we worked like beavers. We managed to sell off the scooters to the up-and-coming generation and launched ourselves into the countryside by bicycle. Our radius of operation was limited to that of the slowest rider who owned a second-hand bargain.

A favourite venue was Pudding Pie Hill, reputed to be stocked with bones of Saxon warriors. Certainly excavations had been completed with some success, the 'finds' being on display in York Museum for all to see. Our cycling activities caused no further unrest for we confined our wheeling to the recognised pathways up, down and around the tumulus. In proportion to the size of our growing bodies the dimensions of the hill appeared enormous, the steepness of its descents encouraging hair-raising, defiant speed. Its diminutiveness will be scorned by modern 'B-X Bikers'. It served for us another purpose; at Eastertide we rolled our paste eggs, hard-boiled and highly coloured.

A popular variation in our cycling routine was known as clay-fire stoking. A block of clay, rather smaller than a standard brick, was gouged out and a hole bored at each end. The cavity was filled with smouldering touchwood whereupon the apparatus was held aloft as the speeding cyclist pedalled for all he was worth, the resulting stream of smoke swelling in proportion to velocity.

Use of the bicycle broadened our minds considerably. We began to take an interest in trains. Already a healthy trading of cigarette cards featuring 'Railways of the World' had drawn our attention to the thrilling sight of the 'steamers'; now we could reach any of three viewing points in quick time.

The up 'Flying Scotsman' left Edinburgh at 10.00 a.m. at the same time as its corresponding down train left King's Cross. If both trains were spot on time they crossed over on the 400-mile non-stop run between the capitals at Beningborough at 2.00 p.m. This meant that we could station ourselves at Topcliffe Bridge at a quarter to two and be sure to see both trains flash along the 'galloping ground' at full speed during only a half-hour wait. When a firearm or driver acknowledged our cheers the day was 'made'. We learned every engine name and most of the numbers but none matched the vivacity of No. 4472 'Flying Scotsman' itself. Lovingly polished green, red and gold enhanced by a horizontal stream of clean, white steam; rods and wheels glinting in hurried rhythm ahead of an impatient train; a majestic splendour captured in many a photograph.

My world of wheels expanded its fascinations at a gathering pace. Every now and then a motor-car passed along Topcliffe Road. Any members of the younger classes playing whips and tops, hopscotch, taws, or pitch and toss were obliged to stand back to allow the monster to pass unhindered. A series of cigarette cards dealt with this growing craze of motoring. Smokers were pestered for the cards in which a healthy bartering developed within our circle. The trade suffered something of a setback when the Kensitas people started issuing coupons instead of picture cards. Prizes ranged from a modest fountain pen in exchange for a dozen coupons to an Austin 'Twelve-Six' for many thousands.

The Model 'T' Ford was proving itself to be popular with farmers and tradesmen, not entirely without criticism. Grandma hated motor-cars from the start, writing them off as noisy, smelly things. She was disagreeably surprised when Mr Thornton, our milkman, turned up half-an-hour late.

Thornton had served us faithfully and with great promptitude. From the five-gallon can which he carried in one hand he scooped, with an appropriate measure in the other, the required quantity of milk and poured it into the customer's waiting jug. Thus, prior to the introduction of pasteurisation, was bacilli tuberculosis delivered from door to door. As the master proceeded along the street his faithful horse, complete with appended trap, followed him in attendance, conveying the bulk stocks ready to hand.

When Grandma's strict routine was upset by such a thing as tradesmen deviating from schedule she was in no mood to be appeased:

'What's got into you to-day? Here's me waiting to get on with the bread.'

'Well, Ah'm sorry about it, Missus, but Ah've given up t'owd 'oss and got misen a motter-car an' it don't foller me like Nessy.'

'Well, you'll have to get up earlier,' remonstrated Grandma. 'We can't go on like this.'

'Ah'll see what Ah can do, then.'

'I should think so,' Grandma closed the conversation.

The next morning Mr Thornton was even further behind Grandma's expectations. When he did turn up, there was Nessy and the trap standing in the roadway. Thornton had one arm in a sling.

'Now what's the matter?' Grandma inquired. 'Has the horse kicked you out of spite?'

'No, it's that damned motor-car, Missus. It what they call backfired and t' startin' 'andle cum back an' brock mi wrist.'

'They should be done away with before somebody gets killed. That's going to happen. You mark my words,' said Grandma.

Though the motor-car business prospered in general my father was obliged to dispose of his taxi to George Green who was to become the local distributor for Morris cars. Father's services as an electrician were in such demand that he chose to concentrate on that means of earning a living. For transportation he used the trusty Triumph Model 'H' with sidecar attached. Weather permitting, on Sundays my mother would condescend occasionally to travel in the 'chair'. With myself perched on the pillion we ventured along the dales. Father refused to tackle steep hills for he was ever concerned about the slipping of the belt drive. We carried a spare belt; it was never used.

Whenever I was permitted a ride in the sidecar I spent the whole time watching the belt tugging away at the pulley. To my young mind it seemed a most satisfactory way of propelling the wheel.

From the age of eight I was permitted to accompany Father, outside school hours, on occasional visits to stately homes of Yorkshire where he had installed private generating sets. My favourite call was to Kepwick Hall where Charlie Scaife, the chauffeur, would allow me to sit in the driver's seat of the Rolls-Royce open tourer. Charlie was immensely proud of this great, dark-green monster over which he whisked a feather duster every time he passed it.

'The windscreen,' Charlie would say, 'should be so clean it is invisible. It's no good motoring unless you can see where you are going, is it?'

It was Charlie who first demonstrated to me how to check for sparks at the plugs, how to avoid a shock and how to get one. With every passing day I learned something of the world of electricity, of magnetism and motors.

Chain-drive motor-cycles were superseding belt-drive models. Not to be behind the times Father replaced the Model 'H' Triumph by a Monopole and sidecar. Made by the Coventry Chain and Cycle Company it was a fine example of the latest chain-drive outfit. Finished in green with red lettering the Monopole attracted a good deal of attention. Both aesthetically and mechanically it gave satisfaction. I think that only a few Monopoles were made. The marque disappeared in a welter of competition.

When my sister joined the family it was considered that more commodious accommodation should be available in the form of a motor-car. Father turned up with a Morgan 3-wheeler. Mother took one look at it and promptly directed its removal from the garden path. I was sorry about that. The twin, side-valve JAP engine projecting in the forefront of the chassis appealed to my artistic tendencies. Father took me for a ride and when we achieved 40 m.p.h. the thrill surpassed anything since experienced.

Our next vehicle was a two-seater Jowett with a dickey seat and a beautiful brass radiator. It chortled happily for many months, endearing itself even to Mother, when the hood and side-curtains were raised to protect her from the dust. She declared the car to be comfortable, there being 'far less jogging about than in the sidecar'. The secret of success lay in the load of cables and tools with which I shared the dickey. These 'kept the back down,' Father said and 'gave the engine something to work at.'

Jowett cars were in their ascendancy in more ways than one. A favourite testing ground was Sutton Bank, only forty miles from the Bradford factory. The 1-in-4 section of the climb brought many a more dignified vehicle to a shameful halt whereas the chuffing Jowett's seven horsepower would continue unperturbed, even after half a dozen enthusiastic schoolboys had, by invitation, supplemented the passenger list by jumping upon the running boards.

My tenth birthday present was a 3-speed gear for my bicycle. Thus, I was able to join the Sutton Bank Supervisors. This exclusive gathering of four members would park bicycles at the famous hairpin bend and observe the antics of the rapidly expanding motoring fraternity. We soon lost interest in under-powered failures on the deadly 1-in-4. Burnt-out clutches could not be repaired. We concentrated our attentions on the tactics adopted by drivers who succeeded in reaching the hairpin.

Once the 1-in-4 had been conquered, an encouraging stretch of almost level road prompted the unknowledgeable driver to change up a gear and dash into the left-hander with enthusiasm. It was an enthusiasm fired partly by his own ego and partly by the desire to show off in front of the eager spectators. Unfortunately the structure of the rock masses was such as to present, immediately after the apex of the bend, a short section of 1-in-3!

The best performers were the two-speed Scott motor-cycles. Close neighbours of the Jowett people, the Scott folk produced, if not the fastest, certainly the sweetest-sounding motor-cycle of the times. Having only two gears, it was difficult for the rider to choose the wrong one. For Sutton Bank he selected 'first' by the foot pedal and wound up the twin-cylinder two-stroke engine, adjusting speed by throttle control alone. Echoing from the limestone cliffs the song from the Scott mimicked a colossal swarm of bees.

We witnessed the commencement of divorce proceedings at the hairpin. It was on a bright and sunny summer afternoon. There hove in sight a BSA 'Square tanked' Vee-twin ridden by a well-clad and responsible looking gentleman of middle age. High up on the pillion rode his stately wife. With confidence, the 1-in-4 behind him, the rider changed up to 'second', nodded to us a 'this-is-the-way-to-do-it' acknowledgement of our presence and swept into the hairpin. Confronted by the 1-in-3 surprise he muffed the change to No. 1 and panicked. The whole ensemble made contact with the uncompromising rock face, husband clinging to the machine and holding it vertical, his wife toppling onto the road. Sutton Bank's first dressing of macadam was not due for several more years. Madam lay painfully in limestone granules.

Our gang of four was quick enough to the rescue. We received no thanks from the injured party. Upon restoration of herself to the vertical she pitched into the kindly gentleman with a vigour of language unbecoming of a lady of her apparent class. Expressing unequivocal distaste for motor-cycles and husbands she limped away downhill, being lost to sight as she began the descent of the 1-in-4. We assisted the rider in making minor adjustments to the handlebars. He thanked us before free-wheeling away, mentioning something about a 'difficult case'. Shortly, we heard numerous high-pitched phrases drifting from below our immediate horizon, then the starting of the engine but no renewed attempt to climb was made. Peace was restored when we saw the BSA disappearing, two up, towards Thirsk.

Descent of the bank was even more hazardous. Until 4-wheel brakes became universal equipment the norm for motorists was to go 'up Sutton and down Wass', the latter bank being much less steep. Cars fitted with 4-wheel braking carried a red triangle at the rear to warn a following vehicle that a very respectable distance should be maintained! It was not unusual for passengers to be invited to alight at the top of Sutton Bank and walk alongside a vehicle in descent in case additional braking became necessary.

Riding of cycles down Sutton Bank was decidedly dangerous, almost impossible without accident. If speed rose beyond control by the brakes it was advisable to select the softest tuft of vegetation at the roadside, land in it or fall off deliberately and suffer the consequent bruising.

One memorable descent resulted in the distressing loss of a large consignment of bilberries. I spent the whole morning in the company of Benjamin Foggitt and his brother William, the latter now famous as an amateur weather forecaster. There was no shortage of the delectable fruit on the moors. We had accumulated enough berries to fill a dozen pies. The plan for the descent was that Ben should carry the basket on his handlebars and walk down. Bill and I would free-wheel down as far as the hairpin and await his arrival.

At length Ben arrived at the meeting point to express displeasure over the arrangement. He had experienced severe difficulties in preventing the weight of fruit from carrying the bicycle away from him. Further, he declared his intention of riding the rest of the way and put forward a plan of load-sharing. We agreed to test the idea on the reasonably level stretch which lay between us and the 1-in-4 drop.

Ben and I rode our bikes one-handed, the basket, held by our free hands, slung between us. Bill would go ahead to warn on-coming traffic of our approach. The practice run passed off without incident. We dismounted for the 1-in-4, wisely walking that hazardous section. At the change in gradient to 1-in-6 we reverted to our master plan.

We had failed to allow for the halving of our respective braking capacities. With only one hand on the helm for steering and braking we very soon gathered uncontrollable velocity. There was only one thing to do – abandon ship! We dropped the basket and charged each to his own softest refuge. Personal injuries were as nothing compared to the total loss of the bilberries, now scattered over a large expanse of the highway. The loss of pride before our parents deepened with the admonishment given to us for 'riding down Sutton Bank!'

Sutton Bank's greatest, yet saddest, day came in 1926. The government declared the last of racing on public roads. Every vantage point was filled by spectators who enjoyed a feast of excitement and mechanical variety. Frazer-Nash took off with a great thrashing of chains and peppering of stones from spinning wheels. Marjorie Cottle set a new standard for neatness, the outside fly-wheel of her 'Velocette' sparkling in the sunshine. By the end of the day everybody and everything was covered in dust and reeked of Castrol 'R'. Thereafter, the road was labelled A170. Intrepid steam-roller drivers worked wonders for it to be accepted as a main highway to Scarborough.

Chapter 4

Scarborough

Grandma said everybody should have a proper holiday once a year. With the war safely out of the way she tackled the peace with planned force. Forty winks would be the limit of her daytime rest period between energetic knitting sessions. Jumpers, pullovers and socks poured off the needles and every penny she earned went into the holiday fund. She chose Scarborough as the venue, not without careful research. A reconnaissance of the place was arranged.

When news got around that Auntie Annie, as she was known to the neighbours, was taking a day excursion trip to Scarborough, several applications to join us were received. Organisation was left entirely to Grandma who insisted on rail fares and bus fares being paid in advance. Some preferred to save the sixpenny bus fare by walking to the station. Train fare was one-and-eight pence, children half price. Each party had to arrange its own catering.

Grandma always did things in style. The horse bus would collect us at Melrose House for an extra threepence per person, children half-price. Those who wished to board the bus there at 6.00 a.m. were welcome. Anyone late would be left behind. Grandma never went anywhere unless there was 'plenty of time on hand'. Auntie Mercy and Cousin George reported to the house at 5.45, in time for a last cup of tea to 'put us on our way'.

Excitement was now at fever pitch. George and I were instructed to 'go out the back and pay a last call' and then to proceed to the front door to look out for the bus. We walked to the end of the avenue from where we could observe the approaching vehicle as it turned the corner at Town End. That was the signal for our racing back to the house to announce the great news. There followed a last minute gathering of bags and umbrellas, a swishing of skirts and Grandma's final check that everything was 'all right'.

The bus did a U-turn outside the house. The rear door was pushed open by a passenger already seated in the plushly upholstered cabin. Grandma again checked that nothing, nor anybody, was being left behind.

The two horses were beautifully groomed. The light from the brass lanterns reflected off their shining rumps as well as from the harness trappings. Mr Elliott, immaculate as usual when driving, with bowler hat and huge moustache, wished us a pleasant day. The weather being mild he invited George and me to sit 'up top' with him and get 'a bit o' good mornin' air'. We jumped at the

19

chance and with the enormous travelling rug spread jointly over our knees we assisted in the geeing up of the horses.

At The Town End we picked up half-a-dozen more passengers who would pay the standard sixpenny rate. At six o'clock we galloped off toward the station, passing along the way a group of excursionists who, Grandma said, 'would rather waste shoe leather than pay sixpence for the bus ride.'

As we rumbled along, the spokes of the wheels sparkled in the lamplight. We maintained 'a nice steady pace' at Grandma's request. Besides, Mr Elliott explained:

'I only shodden t'osses yesterduh. They tek a day or two ter run in, so we'll tek it canny.'

Too soon, for George and me, we approached the station. On the steep descent to the station entrance Mr Elliott applied the hand brake and we ground to a halt. The stationmaster touched his hat to Grandma and conducted us along to the waiting room where a roaring fire climbed up the chimney.

Tickets had been paid for in advance. These were now delivered to Grandma for safe keeping until everybody was ready to board the train. This well conceived move avoided chaos at the ticket office window.

The party could now relax in wait for the excursion special. Cousin George, however, had a better idea. He was several years my senior and took me in his charge to a seat on the platform in hopes of seeing other trains pass through the station. We were warned by the stationmaster and ordered by Grandma to remain seated. The London express was due any minute.

The Darlington-York section of the LNER rightly deserved its title of 'The Galloping Ground'. At the sound of a warning bell the shutters of the W.H. Smith bookstall and of the little tobacco kiosk were slammed down and the stationmaster shouted:

'Stand back everybody!'

We peeped round the edge of the end wall of the platform to see the lamps of the fast-approaching express. Then came a wild scream as the driver gave a final warning of danger on the way. We saw briefly the flashing of con-rods and wheels as the scream rose to a frenzied climax and changed suddenly to the dying sounds of departure. Loose papers and feathers whirled madly in the slipstream as the guard's van vanished into the background, leaving us in an uncanny silence.

A discontented chuffing announced the pending arrival of the modest 0-6-0 tanker dragging our sedate 3rd-class-only carriages labelled 'Excursion'. Grandma made sure that everyone had a ticket and a seat, then secured for herself a place with her back to the engine. She never failed to fulfil this requirement when she travelled by train. If all the rear-facing seats were occupied already, she exercised her compelling powers of persuasion to have at least one position released for her use. She seemed to imply that if the request wasn't granted she was likely to become ill and that any non-compliant person would be responsible. Her reluctance to travel any distance by car must be attributed to the same inherent belief that it is safer to travel backwards as a passenger so long as the driver looks ahead.

To the accompaniment of a great hissing of steam and a purposeful scream of the whistle our train pulled out of Thirsk exactly on the advertised time. Grandma said we had made a good start. Dawn broke and we could see the Hambleton Hills clearly. The train clickerty-clonked along quite merrily until we made our first stop at Sessay to pick up more excursionists. Once they were on board it was anticipated that we would renew our journey. Disappointingly we were obliged to wait until a fast express had swept past us at great speed, before we could rejoin the main line. At successive stops we experienced unexplained delays and on more than one occasion we went into reverse. Grandma said it was always the same with these excursions. During a lengthy halt at Malton she dropped the window and spoke harshly to the nearest employee of the LNER who happened to be enjoying a few moments of rest. The hold-up was none of his concern but he understood that a truck had jumped the rails a mile ahead of us. Grandma shut the window and suggested that tea from the thermos flasks be distributed.

We reached Scarborough at 11 o'clock, when Grandma said 'half the day has gone'. She instructed her party to be back at the station by 6.15, bade its members a very good day, grabbed me by the hand and made sure we were first through the barrier where she remonstrated with the unrepentent ticket-collector over the lateness of the train.

Thus discharged of her responsibilities until 6.15, Grandma set sail with me in tow. I describe our gait, not facetiously, but with metaphorical sincerity. Grandma cruised effortlessly, erect as a guardsman. On all outdoor occasions she wore a spectacular navy blue straw hat, wreathed by a colourful floral arrangement. A somewhat ostentatious ornament, central to the garland, denoted the termination of the hatpin which secured the total ensemble to her snow-white hair.

The swishing of satin skirtings attended our stately emergence into the salty air of 'The Queen of Watering Places'. The imposing building of the Pavilion Hotel, home of the great actor Charles Laughton, stood sentinel over the station parade but to me the great glory of Scarborough manifested itself in its tramcars! Immediately spellbound, I decided that my future as a tram-driver must be pledged. I lost no time in declaring my intention to Grandma who offered nothing more encouraging than the stock answer: 'We'll see.'

Oh, the sheer frenzy of it all: wheels, wires and sparks galore, bells clanging, pick-up trolleys hissing and spluttering, drivers leaning out over the front of their cabs to poke a steel bar into the points, thus, with a satisfying clonk, changing the tram's direction. The scrumptious whirring of the wheels as the monster gathered speed was as music to my young ears. I wanted nothing more out of Scarborough than to watch the trams.

A firm grip was taken on my hand as Grandma dragged me across the road. I was compelled by electric tension to put a foot firmly on each rail as I was propelled unwillingly onward. We set course for Barwick Street where the Misses Limbert ran a miniature boarding house, on a self-catering basis.

The approach to the terraced house was made via an iron-clad gateway in a thick privet hedge. The idea of the hedge was to dampen the noise of the tramcars which ran on a single pair of lines along the middle of Barwick Street. At first sight the hedge appeared to be a grave disadvantage to me but when I learned that I was to be allocated to a small upstairs bedroom from which I could view the passing trams I approved the choice of lodgings. Terms were agreed for our residence during the last two weeks of August and the first of September. Beyond that date Grandma anticipated that the weather would 'go off'.

The next port of call was to Mr Holloway's delicatessen where, during certain hours of the day, alcoholic liquors might be purchased. 'For medical purposes' Grandma bought a half-bottle of top quality brandy at six shillings, excellent, Mr Holloway agreed, for 'bringing up the wind from round the heart'. I was told not to 'let on' to anyone about the brandy. She refused to buy the stuff at home where 'folks talk'. Having assured the genial Holloway of a substantial order come August we moved on to Westborough in which street the principal attraction was the dignified building labelled 'Rowntree's' in large gold lettering.

Rowntree's, I think of as a scaled-down version of Harrod's. Its carpeted walkways enticed potential buyers from one department to the next, always the smiling assistants ready to serve. Grandma said Rowntree's was for middle-class people, not for the riff-raff. At the materials counter Grandma established cordial relations with the staff. A chair was brought for her use while I was obliged to fidget about listening to talk on taffeta, tussore and tulle. Roll after roll of textile temptations were unfurled before a dress-length was selected and neatly parcelled. With that as protection for the brandy bottle we bade farewell to the ladies of cloth, promised more business in August and moved up two floors.

I was permitted a brief look at the Hornby train and Meccano sections before being urged through numerous departments which were of no interest to me, yet which to my guardian caused long and detailed interrogations of the attendants. Finally we descended to ground level and exchanged the scents of the store for sea breezes. Hopes of sighting the magical seashore were raised but immediately dimmed when Grandma announced it was time for a good lunch.

Not for us the packet of sandwiches and a pot of tea on the sea-front: we entered the Silver Grill in Huntriss Row. The neatly dressed waitress was addressed by Grandma as if she were manageress of the place. We received prompt attention to our requirements at the same time establishing for me a standard in 3-course lunches: tomato soup, plaice and chips plus treacle tart.

Grandma topped out with a small Scotch. The bill came to four shillings and ninepence the two, including orange squash, the threepenny tip to the waitress rounding off the sum to 25p. in modern money. At last we made for the seafront.

When we reached the cliff-top the appealing sign: 'Tram to the Foreshore' beckoned us to descend by funicular but Grandma had other ideas. I was whisked along St. Nicholas Street to enter the elegant store of Marshall and Snelgrove. We halted in the doorway to admire a photograph of a good-looking young man who Grandma thought was 'every inch a Prince' and would certainly be a great King. Herself an ardent Royalist to the end of her life, she was spared the disappointment of one of the shortest reigns in British history. Within the shop we stayed only long enough to examine garments beyond our modest means and to my delight take a couple of rides in the escalator.

We took the funicular to the shore, one penny down, children half-price. By the time we reached the bottom I had a fair idea of how the system operated.

The weather did not encourage more than a glance at the sweep of golden sands. Furthermore, as Grandma explained, the holiday season didn't start until Easter time. Things were pretty quiet. None of this bothered me. All that mattered was that the trams were running and I had been promised a ride.

We walked to the harbour of shouting fishmongers and salted trawlermen, braved the brisk breezes to the end of the pier, admired the castle on the hill, the far-reaching coastal view of bays to Flamborough Head, the fashionable Spa Buildings and the Grand Hotel, grandest in Europe, majestically overlording the waterfront. The War Memorial, at the top of Oliver's Mount in the background, stands sentinel over Britain's most charming seaside resort, where I was destined to spend a dozen successive annual holidays.

We boarded the tram at South Pier. Sadly, it was considered too cold to ride on top but I managed to secure a seat at the front where I could observe closely the operational antics of the driver. Oblivious of the passing scenery I maintained a careful watch on the rails ahead, taking note of the various controls. The route involved the climbing of the very steep Vernon Road. Grandma had convinced herself that it was safe enough to climb the hill but never to descend it by tram. There was some justification for this latter fear. Some years later a tram did run away down Vernon Road, overshot the right-angle corner at the bottom, crashing into the underground entertainment centre known as 'The Aquarium' and killing the driver.

All too soon we arrived at the railway station, but not before I had formulated my ambition to join the Scarborough Corporation as a tram-driver. As the train lumbered over the rail joints from one station to the next, darkness fell and I feigned sleep in a corner, mentally rehearsing the deft movements of the professional tramster: the firm stamp of the heel upon the pedal which causes the alarm-bell to warn jaywalkers of the approach of the monstrous vehicle, the determined winding of the great brake-wheel and the cautious notching of the motor control. I went over and over the motions in semiconsciousness, only vaguely aware of the reportings to 'Aunt Annie' of the doings of the day by our fellow excursionists. Cousin George recounted his adventurous donkey ride during which his unfortunate animal had paused to relieve its feelings before an appreciative crowd of onlookers. Stanley Armishaw bemoaned the loss of fourpence, his entire capital gone through a hole in his pocket. I heard of these tales of happiness and woe through a maze of tram-lines and overhead wires, eventually to be awakened by Grandma when the train exhausted itself to a halt at Thirsk.

With a fully laden bus behind them the two horses scraped up the slope from the station yard. Once on the level the hoofs clippity-clopped an awakening rhythm, the wheels rumbled and the lamps sent sprays of light dancing along the railings and hedges. 'Auntie Annie' appreciated the thanks bestowed upon her, acknowledging each by: 'Get away with you!'

Our August holiday began during the third week of that month when the 'season' was at its height. Numbers in our party varied according to circumstances but Grandma and I stayed the full course including the first week of September, even when the weather went 'off a bit'. A fair measure of stamina was required to keep up with Grandma's routine. Mother never enthused over games on the sands; she loathed defilement in any form, sand-between-the-toes being quite unacceptable. Father might appear for a few days during the second week, become worksick and dream up a convincing excuse to return home.

Heavy baggage had arrived in advance. Mother's first act was to open the large trunk and extract a freshly laundered and ironed duster with which she set about polishing the brass bedsteads and other furnishings of our respective sleeping quarters. Leaving Mother to her phobias, Grandma and I drifted up the street to place a substantial order with Mr Holloway, the most expensive item to be a bottle of White Horse at twelve shillings and sixpence. The amiable grocer apologised for the high price but guessed that excise duty accounted for at least fifty per cent of the total, his own profit being 'nowt but a few pence'. The general grocery order came to nearly £1 which included free delivery to our boarding house, a complimentary packet of peppermint creams and a 'Thank you' card.

Our comestibles were stored in the sideboard of our dining room, which was, in fact, the front room of the house. Mother would decide the menu for each meal, set the table and co-operate with the Misses Limbert to a small extent in food preparation. The system called for extremes in tolerance, a commodity in which my mother was under-stocked. When Grandma intervened in any dispute I knew it was judicious of me to step outside to watch the passing of the tramcars, a practice of which I never tired.

Over a period of time I established nodding acquaintances with the drivers, who operated quite unprotected from the elements except by their smart uniforms. When it rained they donned a complete sou'wester kit matching that of the trawlermen. This spartan aspect of the job increased my determination to take it up as a career.

Grandma and I could never get enough of Scarborough. We stretched the holiday out to three weeks. We sampled every form of entertainment which Grandma considered suitable for a young boy. I saw my first 'movietone' film at Scarborough in the Capitol cinema. It was *Showboat* with sound on disc. Every now and then the synchronisation of sound and film became dislocated much to the annoyance and sometimes amusement of the audience. A couple of days later we attended the Futurist cinema. The film there was *The Trial of Mary Dugan*. The Futurist had opted for the Western Electric System of sound-on-film. It was a vast improvement, setting the standard for years to come.

Every year we enjoyed a show at Catlin's, a first-class Pierrot theatre. At the Floral Hall we saw, over the years, most of the top music hall artists including Sir Harry Lauder and Joyce Grenfell, as well as some of the big bands. Surrounded by plants and flowers the setting of the stage at Scarborough's Floral Hall made it one of the most delightful theatres in the world.

I saw my first 'television' at Scarborough, a John Logie Baird apparatus. The face of a lady in an adjacent room was being scanned by a light, projected through the holes in a spinning disc. The audience paid sixpence each and joined a queue which shuffled along to see the screen, about four square inches in size. The picture was built up in 60 lines, that being the number of holes in the spinning disc next-door. It was a miracle.

Grandma said: 'Tut-tut, whatever next?' Some guy overheard and commented: 'I can't see that coming to anything.'

'Young man,' retorted Grandma, 'People used to say that about the steam engine! Now look at it – trains to anywhere.'

Grandma was prepared to enter into a discussion on any subject and with anybody. She would join a group of strangers on a cliff-top seat and within minutes be leading a friendship society. During such periods I was permitted to enjoy a favourite occupation of watching one or other of the funicular railways.

I could spend a whole morning gazing in wonderment at the successive ascendings and descendings of the cars on the South Cliff railway. This used an ingenious hydraulic system; a tank underneath the carriage at the top was filled with water, while the water emptied from the opposite number at the bottom of the slope. Once the passengers had boarded and the operator released the brake, the cars moved quietly and smoothly on their respective tracks. The only appreciable noises arose during the pumpings of the water, agreeable forms of swishing and gurgling. There were times when my enthusiasm for tram-driving wavered in favour of the more tranquil duties of brake-man on the South Cliff.

During August Scarborough exceeded its normal colourful self, in Carnival; it was then that the tramcars won my heart. They appeared in such flamboyant garb as: 'The Wedding Cake', or as pictorial representations of 'The House that

Jack Built', 'Hispaniola', 'Old Mother Hubbard's Shoe'. On the great day these splendid apparitions formed parts of the grand parade. Afterwards they reverted to their normal service still wearing, for the following week, their splendid regalia, at risk to the temperamental climate. Cloudbursts and brisk breezes but temporarily spoil the joys of Carnival Scarborough.

Grandma entered into the spirit of the place. With tremendous fortitude she tried to appease my appetite for looking into things mechanical. On just one occasion I persuaded her to accompany me to the 'Wall of Death'. The admission charge was sixpence (children half-price). From my half-a-crown pocket money I never failed to pay for at least one visit to the 'Wall'. Grandma would not believe that a young lady would earn a living in such dangerous pursuits until she saw one gazing up at her from the bottom of the pit.

'It's disgraceful. Such things should never be allowed. For a young slip of a girl . . .' but her words drowned in a voorumph and crackle as the lady in question started up a machine and roared around the bowl rising to within inches of the 'safety' rope around the perimeter. She made half a dozen circuits, descended, stopped and waved to Grandma. A new age of heroines was born. 'They say we have to move with the times,' said Grandma, 'It's never been the same since Emmeline Pankhurst . . .' but then another bike roared upwards, its rider carrying the young lady on his shoulders, waving nonchalantly as she was circled and whirled. Then came a pause in the performance when the leader announced that no insurance company would cover the team against accident. He appealed for contributions. Gladly, I threw down another threepenny piece and Grandma said it was worth every penny of her 'little extra' – 'just to think what would happen to that poor girl if she fell off; it should never be allowed.'

Mother would not entertain such outrageous adventures. She confined herself to examination of delicate china and fabrics in the better class of shops, the odd orchestral concert at the Spa or tea at the Corner Café which typified the seaside Palm Court. She worried through life, advocating not only external hygiene but inner cleanliness as well. Meal-times at the lodgings were preceded by inspection and polishing of crockery and cutlery. A major meal must be concluded by a Cascara Sagrada pill and a cup of tea. She was then obliged to wait indoors in case the potion 'worked', permitting Grandma and myself to push off in search of merriment.

When my sister was old enough to stand the rigours of a holiday at Scarborough she was firstly obliged to coexist with Mother's timetable. As the years went by I was made more and more responsible for the newcomer's welfare. Grandma began taking afternoon naps; she was 'feeling her age'. At the mature age of twelve years I took charge of the growing child and introduced her to the joys of riding on top of a tram, canoeing on the Mere, journeys on the miniature railway and flurries in speed boats. This last entertainment was frightfully expensive at two shillings per ride; it incurred severe reduction of all other enterprises; excepting tram rides.

Father's short and infrequent interventions in our Scarborough vacations brought some measure of relief to the financial stringencies of his offspring; he insisted on paying for all treats when he headed the party. His own favourite pleasures were in listening to the military bands which played on the island bandstand in Peasholm Park, a visit to the Corporation Fire Station and a cruise round the bay on the paddle steamer *Bilsdale*. The aesthesis of cruising was of no interest to Father who lost no time in establishing contact with the Chief Engineer of the ship.

'Would it be possible for this young lady and my son to see the engine-room?'

No engineer worth his salt would miss a chance of showing off his pride and joy to anyone genuinely interested. So we all trooped below to gaze upon the glistening pipes, pistons, rods and wheels. We children listened to puffings and hissings while Father chatted to the Chief. When the bell rang and the whistle blew and the cranks began to turn, still we stayed below deck until Father had taken his fill of reminiscence. Should he have stayed in the engine-room instead of in our boarding-house he would have enjoyed his holiday instead of suffering it.

Not even a severe decline in the weather could destroy my love of Scarborough. Gale force winds brought huge, towering waves crashing against the stalwart walls of the Marine Drive. The graceful curvature engineered into the walls ensured powerfully frightening entertainment by colossal sheets of violent water rising to great heights before collapsing on the roadways and footpaths. A popular sport was to stand near enough to the protective railings to risk a wetting, misjudgements being loudly applauded by more cautious by-standers. Truly Scarborough lived up to its title: 'The Queen of Watering Places'.

Chapter 5

Leeds

Refreshed by the sea air, Grandma fell with vigour into kitchen routines, adding such seasonable preparations as mincemeat, piccalilli and her special brand of chutney to stocks in the pantry. 'Aunt Annie's' chutney was in great demand at church bazaars as well by an ever-expanding circle of neighbours. It would qualify, today, as a major British export. Another ready 'seller' was 'Aunt Annie's' prune jam. This dynamic mixture would have use at Cape Canaveral as a propellant for the rockets. Regrettably, the recipe was a closely guarded secret but I recall that its chief constituents were prunes and senna pods. It was administered to us children on Friday nights. Of a consistency similar to that of Irish peat it tasted none too disagreeable, though in anticipation of stirring effects we chewed it under audible protest. Anything was preferable to syrup of figs and having been forcibly convinced that a 'good clean-out' weekly would enhance our chance of survival we took to prune jam as the least of evils.

Six dozen eggs were 'put down' in a large earthenware pot which was then topped up with isinglass. This made sound economic sense in view of the anticipated rise in the price of eggs beyond ninepence a dozen come the winter. A few jars of pickled onions were shelved alongside the vast array of goose-berry, strawberry and damson jams. All this additional activity did not inter-fere with Grandma's flow of thoughts of further amusements. As the knitting needles clicked she picked up the gist of news from the *Darlington and Stockton Times* and the *Yorkshire Post*, considered numerous attractions of-fered in the theatre world and always finished up by organising a trip to a Leeds pantomime.

The 'Royal for Fun' and the 'Grand for Scenery'; thus Grandma measured the merits of the two big theatres. Only once did we break faith with the Royal, but never was the decision taken lightly. A preliminary visit to Leeds to settle the detail was essential. This was taken at the tail end of November when the shops would be in full Christmas regalia. Though Grandma would book seats for a party of up to ten, this exploratory trip was unencumbered by no other than myself.

The horse bus transported us to the station, in foggy darkness, to catch the first train of the day. Immediately after leaving Thirsk the train rounded what was known as the Leeds Curve, a perfectly engineered right-angle climb. We seated ourselves in a carriage well back from the engine. Whilst this was another of Grandma's safety precautions it suited me to see the steam-puffing, spark-dispensing monster hauling us round the bend. At Melmerby we waited at the junction for passengers from the Northallerton train to join us. At Knaresborough daylight blessed the spectacular view of the River Nidd as the train slowly rumbled across the viaduct, a treat still available to travellers by rail, in spite of the excesses of Beeching.

My first visit to mucky Leeds shattered my ambition to sign on with the Scarborough Corporation Tramways. The Leeds trams were no less than twice the size, ran on two sets of four-wheeled bogeys and the drivers were protected from the dust-laden elements by veritable greenhouses. The top decks were fully enclosed. I made it clear to Grandma that the top of a tram must be paradise. She assured me that the day's routine would include at least two journeys by tram. Prospects of a pantomime faded to insignificance.

The statue of the Black Prince on his charger made a striking centrepiece to City Square. In the framework of moving trams passing to and fro in all directions I still visualise my favourite monument. Not only the Prince was black. In those days the whole of Leeds was black. The air was laced with soot. On a November day if the Prince could be seen from the front of Central Station visibility was considered reasonable; the only safe way of getting across the city was by tram. I remember standing, one afternoon, on the pavement in Briggate, hearing the clanging bell and the rumbling wheels of an unseen tram. Those were the days when mill chimneys belched cough-giving smoke and John Fowler built beautiful steam engines. It was years before I learned that black was not the natural colour of Bradford stone.

Our first call was at the Scotch Wool Shop where Grandma ordered up a replenishment of her stocks, to be collected later in the day. Next we visited both theatres and checked on the castings for the forthcoming pantomime season, with a bias towards the 'Royal for Fun'. When Cora Goffin was billed as principal boy that settled the matter. There were certain specific requirements: only front row dress circle seats at a February matinee. Grandma was of the opinion that the company would not have settled into its parts before the end of January. Come March the costumes would be showing signs of wear. Therefore the best time for pantomime was February and so we booked the required number of seats, paid for and collected the tickets. Grandma never took anything on tick: '"Take what you want", saith the Lord, "take what you want and pay for it."'

A visit to Schofield's store followed, after which I was introduced to the proprietor of the Model Shop in City Arcade. I made a pilgrimage to that interesting establishment every November until model trains ceased to amuse.

At 12.30 sharp we entered the White Horse Restaurant, a first-floor and first-class place in Boar Lane. Immaculate in white tie and tails the waiter offered the full three-course lunch at 1*s*. 6*d*. Tomato soup, plaice and chips, crusty bread and treacle tart as usual for me. Grandma selected the steak pie and had a word with the waiter about a little 'something' in a glass which was unsuitable for young boys, but I could have orange juice. The waiter would look forward to seeing us in February and we were off toward our next port of call.

A handsome pork pie was purchased from a specialist shop in Vicar Lane. With pie wrapped and placed flat in Grandma's capacious handbag we boarded a tram labelled 'Kirkstall'. The conductor received instructions to keep an eye on me upstairs while Grandma would travel in greater comfort below. We were set to visit an old lady (Grandma was old but didn't look it), some relation who lived alone in poor circumstances.

The house we entered was of the 'one-up-and-one-down' type in a long terrace of matching design. To the rear of the tiny living room was a miniature scullery equipped with a stone sink accompanied by a cold water tap. The back door gave access from the scullery to an alley on the opposite side of which stood a row of 'privvies'.

Entry to a 'privvy' was possible only by the use of a key, specially guarded by the appropriate householder. The practice of 'key-borrowing' was not encouraged generally. When I had reached an age of maturity Grandma recounted in my presence the following tale:

A passer-by, being taken short, popped his head into the open doorway of the barber's shop and asked:

'Can I borrow the key?'

'Who shaves you?' enquired the busy barber.

'I shaves mi'sen,' replied the passer-by.

'Then shit thi' sen,' said the barber.

Personally, I never plucked up courage to ask for the key. As soon as preliminary introductions were completed I excused myself from the company and took station at the end of the street to watch the gigantic trams. They were quieter, far faster than the four-wheeled Scarborough types and didn't lapse into an undignified yaw when cruising light. I prolonged my vigil long enough for Grandma to present the pork pie to Aunt Sally and exchange views on their respective pasts, over a cup of tea. I refused politely any form of liquid refreshment, thus avoiding any necessity for 'key-borrowing'.

The return tram ride to the city confirmed my desire to be a tram-driver. I confronted Grandma with the news that I had resigned my position with the Scarborough Corporation and would apply to Leeds. Grandma would hear nothing of such things. I began to wonder whether her sense of humour was slipping. She said there were better ways of earning a living. I asked what she had in mind: 'School-teaching,' she said. She would have a word with a friend of hers and get my 'name put down'. The decision sounded final. I finished the trip in a state of depression.

Chapter 6

School

'School days are the best days of your life'. With this ridiculous postulate I disagreed from the start. I look back on school days as a less desirable period of life. I enjoy the sound of screaming children at play but do not envy them the traumas of growing up, the disappointments of blighted love-affairs, the measles and chicken-pox, the fear of 'getting it wrong'.

Ivydene, my first school, was a private establishment run by the Misses Joll. Miss Bertha 'took' the infants, Miss Gertrude the seven-to-tens. Their students received a good grounding in the three R's. The dear ladies learned a whole lot about infant psychology.

The entrance to Ivydene by a single wooden gateway in a high brick wall gave into a gravelled playground in which students spent as much time as possible, weather permitting. In one corner of the playground an 'earth' toilet signalled its availability by emitting a strong smell of carbolic. Many an infant committed an accident *in situ* rather than visit the 'pooh-ha'.

Playtime allowed violent expressions of freedom by the pupils. At the same time the Misses Joll regained some degree of composure in preparation for the next session of pandemonium in the classrooms. At times both teachers and students might be reduced to tears. At worst Miss Bertha's pallid complexion turned red. She would call for assistance from her less corpulent sister. The pair of them would then set about restoring order by wielding substantial ebony rods. Meanwhile, the unattended class in 'the other room' would incite general mutiny. It was not unknown for a muscular 'seven-to-ten' to take possession of the batons, threatening to depose the administration in favour of anarchy. The usual outcome was early dismissal of students to the playground whilst tutors took to the aspirin bottle.

Smoking in class brought about a display of uncontrolled anger by our teachers. Francis Kirby had disposed of a week's pocket money by purchasing a packet of five Woodbines. He distributed the forbidden weeds among his immediate friends. During the temporary absence of Miss Bertha on comfort break we lit up. The dear lady was not slow to detect the smell of tobacco smoke.

'Who has been smoking cigarettes?' asked Miss Bertha.

The answer came not verbally, but in the form of thin wisps of smoke from the desks in the back row. One of us had failed to extinguish his fag, prior to stuffing it into his desk. Our desks being closely coupled, it was not possible to identify the exact source of the smoke. We covered the gaps in the woodwork with books, rulers and pencils. The smoke crept unquenched to alternative outlets. In spite of our combined pressure on the desk lids Miss Bertha revealed the supreme power of an elderly female in wrath. We were hauled from our seats. The source of imminent conflagration now being exposed we were dealt punishment unrestrained by any regulations against child abuse. Miss Gertrude swilled cold water over a smouldering *English Primer*, all girls under seven screamed. Total breakdown of discipline could be avoided only by despatch of all children to the playground.

An important advantage of the 'mixed' school system was the relief from parental responsibility of explaining basic gender differentials to the younger generation. The Misses Joll did not include the subject in their curriculum.

Curiosity could not go unsatisfied in close company. A major break-through came about when one young lady was treated, by her six-year-old admirer, to a demonstration of how to 'wee' at right-angles to the playground wall. The news spread like wildfire. A multiple exhibition was about to commence when our two perplexed guardians emerged from the school-house to investigate the cause of extraordinary jollification. Parents who inquired of their offspring the reason for a late home-coming were enlightened by the simple explanation that 'we were kept in'.

Rumour, spread undoubtedly by the 'under-sevens', reached the ears of our parents. Exaggeration of the extent of smoking in school and of ungentlemanly behaviour in the grounds brought inter-parental committees into being. Punishment became unreasonable in severity, not so much corporally as in the lasting aura of suspicion. My own pockets were emptied every day for the following week to ensure the absence of Woodbines and matches. During the rigorous searching of my private belongings a cherished copy of *The Blue Lagoon*, beyond the third page of which I had never progressed, was discovered. My mother who, I am sure, had not read the book, could go no further than tell me it was fit only for the midden, into which she flung it.

We miscreants were so offended by the unjustified suspicion which hung over us that we revolted against all authority by playing truant. We ventured upon an afternoon of train-spotting without a thought for concealing our identities. The 3.42 'up' had just left for York when Bill's Uncle Harold, in stepping from his dutiful position in the booking office, espied his wayward nephew and took further steps to dispatch us to a home-bound confessional. Regrettably, we had failed to agree a common excuse for our truancy. The length of time to live down the event was out of all proportion to the shortness of its pleasure.

Confinement to the house for long periods was not altogether unpleasant. Grandma never deserted me for more than a few minutes. She shared my sufferings and when, to my great joy, Father fixed up our first 'wireless', a crystal set, my life set a new course. The music or speech emanating from the headphones did not capture my imagination half as much as the fact that it was possible 'to get' anything at all. Scratching away at the crystal with the cat's whisker to find the 'best spot' gave endless satisfaction. No modern schoolchild can experience from his plasticated stereo hi-fi a fraction of the excitement of 'getting something' from a crystal set. Father said the secret was in the long high aerial wire suspended from a pole in the garden to the chimney of the house and 'a good earth'. A licence was required for authority to 'listen-in'. Beyond that there were no running costs; that meant I was allowed to indulge in this new hobby whenever opportunity arose. There was no switching on and off because no batteries were involved; simply pick up the headphones, listen and twiddle.

When the fortunes of the family improved by virtue of a legacy from Mother's rich relations we moved house. There we had not only an outside water closet but an indoor one as well and a huge bathroom. The crystal set was discarded in favour of a wireless set with valves and lots of wires. Batteries were needed to heat the valves. Whilst I appreciated the fascination of peering through the small metal grilles to see if the valves were glowing I was restricted, in the interests of economy, to usage during 'Childrens' Hour' only. However, after Father wired the house for electricity he added an 'eliminator' which dispensed with the need for high tension batteries whereupon my listening time expanded, so long as I used the headphones. Grandma objected to the noise from the horn loudspeaker except for 'getting' the news. Mother considered piano music to be too tinny and brass band music too rumbustious.

Secure and very private beneath my headphones I spent hours twiddling knobs. The valve set 'brought in' numerous European stations which encouraged an interest in map-reading.

At the age of eleven I was relieved to transfer from Ivydene to the local Secondary School. Mother charmed her aunt into paying the fees of three guineas a term, thus allowing Father to conserve his steadily rising 'rainy day' fund. Life presented itself in much greater variety. Outdoor facilities were no longer confined to a walled-in yard. In due season cricket, tennis, hockey and soccer provided welcome distractions from the classrooms. Even inside we learned carpentry and conducted alarming experiments in chemistry. We drew diagrams of 'the right way and the wrong way to load a wheel-barrow', how to double-dig a garden, how to plant potatoes and raise cabbages from seed; in good weather our theoretical knowledge was applied in the school gardens. For me an additional attraction was the nearness of the main road along which the odd motor-car, bus or lorry might pass.

Anything on wheels which passed by received at least a cursory glance. I knew the timetables of the buses and checked their validity. I could recognise every make of car, if not by sight, by sound. One of the most impressive vehicles I have ever seen called at the school during the General Strike of 1926.

The huge lorry with solid rubber tyres and an imposing brass radiator cleared the gateposts by only a couple of inches. Behind the appropriately sized steering wheel sat an equally appropriate driver. Beside him sat a policeman with truncheon at the ready. Each of the two gentlemen sported a moustache to match the immensity of their machine. They were served lunch in the girls' cookery department which maintained the service throughout the strike.

1926 was the year when the Lincolnshire Handicap was won by a local horse named 'King of Clubs'. Many shirts had been placed upon it when it started as an outsider at 100-to-1. One bookie committed suicide and several left the district in the hope of coming to some alternative arrangement. Thirsk developed 'King of Clubs' madness. Whist drives, balls, concerts, jumble sales and garden parties carried the title of the famous horse. Elliott's horse bus was replaced by a Model 'T' Ford chassis on which was mounted a wooden structure resembling a chicken house. Naturally enough, in large white letters, it bore the thrilling name.

Despite such diversions I plodded away at Latin, maths and history, French, English, botany and art. My own summary of my annual reports would have read: 'Works hard but doesn't get anywhere.'

At the crucial age of fourteen, when scheduled to tackle the School Certificate Examination, I fell victim to bacilli tuberculosis. The first symptom was a soreness in the region of a salivary gland. The doctor suggested that a few applications of iodine ointment might solve the problem. It didn't. When I passed out in 'prayers' I was despatched homeward. When the summer holiday began I was put to bed. July boiled hot. The nodule on my neck grew into a lump the size of a ripened Spanish tomato, ripe enough, the doctor said, for 'lancing'. The operation would be performed at the Lambert Memorial Hospital on the following morning.

Readily available ambulance services were for the future. Mother hated hospitals and couldn't stand the sight of blood. Father was at work and Grandma was indisposed. Still, my legs were long for I had grown quite a few inches during eight weeks in bed. I walked alone to the hospital where I was instructed to sit on a wooden chair in the centre of the 'Out-patients' surgery and 'wait for the doctor'.

Dr MacArthur arrived in customary style, clad in tweed knickerbocker suiting, propped his big Elswick bicycle against the garden wall and carried his little black bag to a table adjacent to my seat. From the bag he withdrew an evil-looking tool designed purposely to incise my over-sized abscess. The sight of that instrument has stayed with me. At the end of a metal bar the business portion had the appearance of a miniature cactus plant in steel. Three sharp prongs projected from a pear-shaped pod. With a deft slash the swelling was relieved of its putrid contents into an appended bowl.

'That's it. Bandage him up, Nurse,' said Doctor Mac who washed his hands and rode away with his little black bag swinging from the handlebars. In a state of thorough dejection I sat in silence whilst the nurse applied bandages under the supervision of the matron, whose whispered remark I did not fail to over-hear:

'That boy seems to resent everything that's done for him.'

In my fight to hold back tears I was in no mood to express gratitude. I walked home in fear of meeting anyone who might inquire of my misfortunes. I went back to bed for the cry of my life. Only thoughts of Scarborough and tramcars saw me through.

Unfit to participate in sports on my return to school I found my niche in the role of Hon. Secretary not only of the Sports Club but of the Philosophical Society. My knowledge of Yorkshire benefited immensely. My favourite away fixture for the football team was that with the Police Orphanage at Harrogate. The hospitality extended to us was not the only attraction. To and from the railway station we made use of the local bus service which employed an unusual type of vehicle.

The 'Tilling-Stevens' single-decker bus was endowed with most excellent powers of acceleration and hill-climbing. It took off in determined manner and soon reached its maximum speed of about 25 m.p.h. The electric motors main-tained the speed up-hill so that a good average around the town and surroundings was achieved and without too much noise. A small petrol engine tucked within the bodywork drove the dynamo which charged the massive batteries. These hard-working transporters served Harrogate for many years and appeared to be everlasting. Maybe the march of time may see a return of a successor to the 'Willing Tilling'.

Activities of the Philosophical Society broadened our minds further beyond our small-town heritage. Not only did we organise lectures on specialist sub-jects but visits such as the memorable one to the Dorman-Long Steel Works opened our eyes to possibilities beyond our green fields.

The wireless aided greatly our appreciation of life outside our native York-shire. The experiments of Sir Oliver Lodge and Sir Arthur Eddington stimu-lated discussions on the likelihood of thought transference across the 'ether'. Interest in music was aroused by the world's first 'Disc Jockey', Christopher Stone, who was permitted to give the title and number of recordings played by him. Lunch-time and tea-time music came from theatre orchestras and cinema organs. Those of us dedicated to the wireless knew the scheduled programmes by heart. Mad dashes home to hear our favourites were daily occurrences. Maybe it was Monday for Reginald Foort, Tuesday for Dixon, Wednesday was special when from the Commodore Theatre, Hammersmith we heard the com-bined efforts of Joseph Muscant and his Orchestra accompanied by Harry Davison at the mighty organ, Thursday for Patmann at the Brixton Astoria and Friday for Horace Finch, a close runner to Dixon at Blackpool.

We knew all the big bands: the two Jacks – Hilton and Payne, Ambrose, Jerry Hoey, Roy Fox and their singers by voice. The late night dance music was absorbed along with pages of Shakespeare, algebra and European history. Poetry I learned by the metre, retaining it just long enough to recite in class the following day, only the rollickings of Kipling, Masefield, Coleridge and Yeats making any lasting impressions.

School work itself became a burden to be endured. Ironically enough I received a rousing accolade at the Speech Day following my second attempt at the School Certificate Examination. I had Matriculated! – with no fewer than nine credits for nine subjects taken. One of my colleagues with a spectacular rating on the IQ scale won four credits and five distinctions. He didn't get anything like half as much applause – such is justice!

The upshot of my meritorious performance was the offer of a scholarship which entitled me to two years further eduction in the sixth form, free of charge, with the proviso that I took a place at Leeds University. This delighted my father who had avoided payment of any sort and relieved my mother to the tune of 15 guineas a year. I took up the challenge but after three terms in the 'sixth' I became bored with further education, fell victim to the world of wireless, took the step I have regretted ever since and forsook a University Education. What is more I was obliged to repay 15 guineas to the Authority, from my own savings.

Chapter 7

The Shop

The truth was that my guiding light sputtered out when Grandma died. Had she been able to battle on for another six months I would have stayed on course. She hated 'the shop' and so did Mother. When I announced my intention of entering into 'trade', some pressure was brought upon me to do as Uncle Percy did and work in a bank. I got as far as looking inside one of the banks in the Market Place and revolted at the idea of sitting behind a desk all day. I wrote off banking as a career. A new maths master expressed surprise that I should not join the family business and a deal was struck. I started at 10*s*. weekly. It was agreed that out of that fabulous salary I would pay Mother 7*s*. 6*d*. 'towards my keep', leaving half-a-crown for my luxuries. I understood that I should consider myself 'lucky'.

My intention was to devote the whole of my working time to the up-and-coming Wireless Department. My grandfather, principal of the business, had other ideas for the newly engaged member of the staff. I was given a key and instructed to open the doors at 8.00 a.m. sharp, place the mail on the office desk ready for his attention, sweep the floor, clean the windows and never to be seen idling at any time of the day. The shop would remain open until 6.00 p.m. weekdays or until the last customer had been served, should any remain on the premises beyond that time. The same rules applied on Saturdays when official closing time was 9.00 p.m. and on Wednesdays when doors were scheduled to close at 1.00 p.m. for 'half-day'.

Financially I was worse off on my 'steady wage'. Whilst at school I had indulged in spare-time construction of kit sets, accepting the odd honorarium from well-pleased customers. Now the 'firm' charged the customer standard rates for my services at sixpence per hour and absorbed the cash into the general revenue. I had established myself as an expert in the building up of kits marketed under the magic names of Osram 'Music Magnet', Cossor 'Melody Maker' and Lissen 'Skyscraper'. No soldering was involved, the whole of the wiring being connected by screws and nuts to the various components. My favourite was the 'Skyscraper' which included 'Spaghetti' resistors, ingeniously comprising a length of string on which a spiral of constantan wire was wound of sufficient length to provide the correct value of resistance. Neatly enclosed in a plastic sleeving, labelled to indicate its electrical value and with tag ends the 'Spaghetti' added a very decorative touch to a finished 'Sky-scraper' chassis. Anyone of minimal competence could assemble the kit. Happily there were those who preferred to pay me 5s. for professional skill.

A popular pastime for the keener type of amateur constructor was the following of 'Blue Prints'. To cater for this enterprising customer we stocked at the shop a wide range of components under such famous brand names as Ferranti, Telsen, Igranic and Bulgin. We offered headphones by S.G. Brown as well as a range of loud-speakers from the 'Sterling Dinky' to the 'Amplion Lion'. The 'Lion', housed in an elaborate wooden cabinet, retailed at £9.

Such were the economics of the day that the following account of customer service *par excellence* can be truthfully related:

A private individual in Falmouth had purchased an 'Amplion Lion' but reported to the manufacturer that 'no sound could be heard'. A representative was detailed to travel by rail from London to inspect the 'faulty' instrument. It was discovered that a well-planned aerial and earth system had been connected to the terminals of the 'Lion'. The customer was diplomatically recommended to obtain a wireless set for inclusion in the installation. No charge was made for the service!

My Wireless Department at the shop was confined to a small corner of the main emporium which stocked an enormous range of ironmongery and accessories for the farmer. We sold shotguns, cartridges, beehives, chicken feeders, pig troughs, drainpipes, nuts, bolts, screws and washers, curtain rails, pots, pans, buckets and spades, knives and forks, lawnmowers, wheelbarrows, paraffin lamps and paraffin, cut-throat razors, shaving brushes, wringers and dollies, garden seeds and trellis, door-knobs and nails, fireplaces, coal scuttles, paints, varnish, tools and twine. Half a mile of catacombs contained corrugated sheeting, wire-netting by the roll and barbed wire by the bundle. If 'Reddin's' hadn't got it . . . the impossible would be obtained as soon as possible.

Nails of all sizes, stocked in huge bins in the cellars, were sold by the pound. The painful task of weighing nails on cold days fell to the lot of junior members of the staff. My status as a relation did not exonerate me from such loathsome duties. The dreaded cry of: 'Nails!' struck at young hearts; Grandfather's wrath was incurred whenever he espied a nail lying wastefully upon the floor. 'There lies capital,' he would say. 'Even though only one seventy-fifth of a penny it is capital lying idle. Don't let me see it again!'

Grandfather seldom smiled behind his drooping moustache and never complimented me or any member of the staff on a seemingly profitable operation. On the other hand he showed kindness toward animals, particularly to his faithful Irish terrier, Tishy. Only once did I see Grandfather fly off into a rage. The railway company's dray pulled up in front of the shop. The horse displeased the driver who gave the poor animal a resounding swipe with a whip. Grandfather ignored the 'customer comes first' rule, leaving the one he was serving at the counter and charged outside to give the unsuspecting employee of the LNER the dressing-down of his life, a performance relished by an appreciative audience of parishioners.

Monday being Market Day the square was transformed from a picturesque, cobbled model of country tranquillity into a turbulent centre of commercial agriculturalism. Horses and traps converged upon the town, each one bearing farmer and wife, baskets of squawking chickens, boxes of free-range eggs, packs of creamy butter, rabbits and any other farm produce which could be sold to anyone prepared to buy. Horses were unhitched from the traps and taken into care behind the Three Tuns or Fleece hotels until it was time to return home. Auctioneers shouted their offerings, stallholders vied with one another on price and quality much to the chagrin of the local shopkeepers.

At H. Reddin and Sons we were well prepared to meet the demands of the farmers. One item, now an essential item of farmhouse equipment, was the 2-volt accumulator for the wireless. By six o'clock on a Monday I was involved in cleaning, topping-up and connecting to our charging boards hundreds of the things. Each week the farmer or his wife brought in an 'empty' and took away a recharged one. At sixpence a time, battery charging was very profitable. At the cost of only a few pence in electricity long rows of accumulators could be charged. The chore of caring for them was very much my acid-defying job. Any carelessness with sulphuric acid became evident within a few days when pink spots appeared in clothing, each spot eventually disappearing complete with the cloth, leaving a hole. Protective clothing was provided at the expense of Mother's house-keeping money.

By dint of careful management my personal account at the Yorkshire Penny Bank had grown to the extent of my ability to purchase a 'New Hudson' 3-speed racing bicycle. At £7 19s. 6d. it represented, in my eyes, the peak of excellence in gleaming engineering. It served me well on pleasure trips and carried me to my first professional engagement as a Wireless Serviceman.

The August sun burned with extraordinary power when Father dispatched me to attend to a faulty Kolster-Brandes Model '333' at the stately home of a retired naval Captain. In my tool-bag was my faithful little Pifco test meter, a set of three Cossor valves, a screwdriver and a pair of point-nosed pliers. A pocket knife completed my tool-kit.

The White Horse at Kilburn shimmered in the sunshine as I turned into the tree-lined driveway. Nervously but proudly I propped my bike against a post, collected my kit and whacked the great oak door with the highly-polished brass knocker. The prim little housekeeper recognised me immediately:

'Eeee-h, no need to tell me who you are. Takin' after your dad, eh? 'an you've cum to see t'wireless. Eeee-h, Captain will be pleased. It gave oop last night just as t'news were startin'. Eeee-h 'e does miss it an' all; I 'ope you can put it to rights.'

'Well, I'll do my best,' I said, as we walked along the polished oak floor of the hall. We entered the sunlit lounge, the most beautiful room I had ever seen.

Overlooking a splendid flower garden the bow window, framed by flowered curtains, made complete the ideal subject for a glossy magazine.

The Captain sat in a huge armchair, coverings to match the curtains, with his back to the window so that the light fell upon his copy of *The Times*. Visible over the top edge of the paper a sparsely populated cranium with snow-white trimmings was a fair indication that a number of years had passed since the reader commanded a battleship. He did not speak but nodded towards the object of my visit. The 'K-B' in its wood cabinet was perched on top of a cupboard to the left of the armchair. The horn speaker stood on the marble mantleshelf. I circumvented chair and occupant and began my inspection.

A slight fizzing noise from the loudspeaker and clicks when switching on and off signified that all was well in the output stage of the set and with the batteries which were housed inside the cupboard. I had to examine the internal workings. The plywood back of the receiver was secured by several wood-screws. These I removed and dropped, for safe-keeping, into an adjacent china bowl.

My luck was in; instinct told me that the first valve was faulty. My Pifco confirmed an open-circuit filament. I fitted a replacement Cossor SG215. The music which trumpeted forth from the speaker brought words of appreciation from the owner. I was happy as a proverbial sand-boy. Reaching for the bowl containing the screws, I was beaten to it by the Captain who picked it off the cupboard top, spat into it with some force and returned it to its place. The little screws were not in sight! Without my point-nosed pliers I would have been tempted to neglect the replacement of the rear cover; with them I fished around in the bottom of the spitoon and one by one recovered the screws. As quickly as possible I completed my duty, wished the Captain farewell and made for fresh air and freedom.

The housekeeper expressed some surprise at my hurried departure and non-acceptance of the offer of a cup of tea. Painted boldly in black characters on the great white gate I noted the appropriate name: Spital Hill House.

Father was pleased with my effort, considered that the screws would be in no danger of working loose; Uncle Billy said he would post off the invoice; Grandfather commented that the account was a good one. Thereafter my responsibilities multiplied. Life at the shop never flagged in its provision of new interests, lessons in common sense and general economics. Nor was it without humour.

At the end of a harrowing Market Day, when everyone wearily looked forward to closing time, the occasion for harmless leg-pulling could not be resisted. When a new apprentice boy from Batty Smith's outfitters emporium asked for a left-handed varnish brush he was fobbed off by our ever-alert store-keeper with sincere regrets for his inability to supply the exact requirement but suggested a half-crown back-hander might be a suitable alternative. After some thoughtful hesitation the boy sauntered back to his employer to report the findings.

Requests for reels of reversed thread, long weights, water sieves, spare holes for half-inch washers and variegated paint were dealt with in good spirit. My father instigated many a prank, the most outrageous of which took advantage of a new apprentice electrician. Bostock and Wombwell's menagerie was paying one of its infrequent visits at the time.

Father came rushing into the shop in customary 'can't afford to hang about' style:

'Howard,' he directed, 'take a two-foot rule. Go down to the main entrance to the menagerie; ask for Mr Carter and tell him you've come to measure for a sanitary pan for the lion.'

The young man did as he was bid and Mr Carter greeted him, rising to the occasion as forewarned:

'Ah, yes. Come this way, young man,' said the animal-keeper, making great play of selecting a very large key from a row of hooks.

When they reached the cage in which the lion lay cleaning a paw, Mr Carter inserted the key in the lock. Howard lost no time in beating a retreat to the shop where he failed to join the merriment of the reception committee.

My knowledge of the outer world broadened through my numerous meetings with commercial travellers, a breed of men for whom I developed admiration bordering on hero-worship. Through them I learned much about their different motor-cars, their dedication to the business of product promotion. Times were not easy and life on the road not without hazards. Unwholesome characters roamed the countryside causing travellers to take precautions against attack. One chap told me he carried an ammonia pistol!

These knights of the road were willing to talk on a wide range of subjects but always steered me back to their purpose. The psychology of salesmanship is best applied by establishing first an amicable relationship with the customer, a practice well described as 'selling oneself'.

One of my mentors who was experiencing a particularly thin streak in his business blamed the up-rising popularity of hire purchase. He predicted that if all such credit schemes were abandoned, trade would fall into deep recession for six months after which everything in the garden would remain rosy for evermore. I never met him again.

Chapter 8

Lessons in Finance

An Austin-7 tourer pulled up at the front of the shop. Its driver found me dusting the stock, introduced himself as a Mr Golightly and expressed interest in a K.B. 'Pup'. He had read an advertisement in a daily paper wherein Kolster-Brandes Ltd. announced a new and attractive hire purchase scheme, financed by that company, low deposit, no references required, ever so easy, opportunity not to be missed.

The 'Pup' was a 2-valve self-contained receiver housed in a modest wooden cabinet: price £4 17s. 6d. cash or only twelve-and sixpence deposit and the rest 'on the nod'. Mr Golightly was delighted with the demonstration and declared his wish to enter into a Hire Purchase Agreement. By this time I was acting and felt like the proverbial bag of nerves.

The subject of HP was anathema to my grandfather, father and Uncle William, all of who had gone home to tea. I sought the opinion of my great confidant, John Butterfield, the storekeeper. John would 'have nowt ter do wee it'. I was standing on my own two feet at last. I found an application form, completed it and Mr Golightly's signature was added. A deposit was paid in cash. My first HP deal was concluded.

At that point my father arrived, refreshed by his afternoon tea break. To my way of seeing the exchange of greetings, no mutual affection was evident. Father examined the agreement. Not wishing to ruin my first 'sale' he signed on the dotted line and instructed me to accompany the customer to his home and make sure the set was left in working order.

Mr Golightly, K.B. 'Pup', batteries, aerial wire, earth rod and myself piled into the little car. We disembarked at a modest house on the outskirts of town. The sun had dropped below the distant Pennines. The room where the set was to be installed contained two chairs and an upright piano. Sole illumination came from a candle which stood in a wax-filled saucer upon the piano. It was explained that the furniture had not yet been delivered from a previous address. Mrs Golightly was currently putting to bed two youthful offspring in upstairs temporary sleeping accommodation.

To the K.B. 'Pup' a respectable outside aerial/earth system must be appended. My intention of drilling a hole in the window-frame for the accommodation of a lead-in tube met with Mr Golightly's disapproval. It was agreed that, in the interest of quick results, the aerial wire might be trapped under the sash window. For an effective enough 'earth' the copper earth rod might be immersed in a bucket of water. The customer quickly delivered this whilst I set off in gathering gloom to tie an end of the aerial wire to a conveniently sited apple tree at the bottom of the garden. My actions excited the attention of the two junior members of the Golightly family who were now viewing my performance from the window of the upstairs room.

As I uncoiled the wire whilst walking backwards towards the house I became conscious of being the target of youthful chicanery. I had noted a projecting bracket above the downstairs window. This would suffice as anchorage for the inner end of the aerial. To reach this I called into use a step-ladder which thoughtfully had been placed to hand.

Such comments as 'Watch it, mister,' and 'You'll get wet if it rains, mister,' came gigglefully from above. Just as I reached the point of hooking the wire over the bracket a perfectly directed jugful of water swished over the back of my neck. Resulting from my loudly voiced objection it was clear that the invisible Mrs Golightly had entered the bedroom to admonish her sons severely in most unladylike terms. She was soon to be followed by her husband who administered corporal punishment of such force as to set up heart-curdling screams.

My dampness caused little discomfort; Mr and Mrs Golightly apologised for the misbehaviour of their descendants. Nevertheless, I was delighted when the K.B. 'Pup' made music. Profuse thanks for my services attended my departure.

I did not sleep well that night. Something worried me, something I could not identify.

Three days later a cheque from K.B.'s accounts department arrived. A new column was started in Uncle William's 'Payments Inward' book. All seemed well, but nobody said 'Well Done!'

A week went by and I looked forward to seeing Mr Golightly bring his accumulator for recharging. He didn't. I decided to call and see if all was in order with the K.B. 'Pup'. The place was empty and my aerial wire had gone!

Grandfather played hell with my father for not checking on the customer's credentials, Uncle William said it wasn't my fault, I said it was, father said it was a daft scheme anyway and destroyed all unused application forms.

The next person to enter the shop was a friend by the name of Bill Benbow. Bill drove a truck for a local removal company. He had been ordered to transport the belongings of the Golightly family to Manchester. On arrival in that city Bill requested payment as per Cash on Delivery terms already agreed. No cash being forthcoming he unloaded everything except the piano which he retained in lieu of payment.

'Did you supply the wireless?' he asked.

I admitted guilt to which Bill said: 'By, gow if Ah'd knowd that Ah'd a' browt that an' all. Ah warnt gonna git pianner off truck til Ah got brass. Onny road Ah didn't reckon thou'd be soft enough i't 'ead ter let that shifty lookin' sod 'ave tick!'

A week later we were notified that Kolster-Brandes Ltd. had withdrawn their stupendous non-recourse HP arrangement. Grandfather was well pleased with that announcement. He declared that hire purchase was unsuited to the British way of life. Henceforward all deals would be by cash or direct credit between retailer and his clients.

The rest of the country went its own way but my first venture into HP was the last one entered into at Central Buildings, at least while my family operated the business. The site is now occupied by a branch of the National Westminster Bank.

Chapter 9

New Terminology

My revolting against further formal education in favour of delving into the world of commerce coincided, quite fortuitously, with a remarkable change in the attitude of the public towards the miracle of the 'wireless'.

Throughout the twenties an aura of mystery encompassed the very subject. The thirties heralded the age of 'listening-in' as distinct from 'tuning-in'. The reception of music and speech from the box on the side-board came to be taken for granted. 'Radio' sounded rather posher in conversation than 'wireless', the latter term being a misnomer anyway. Especially battery-operated receivers were notorious for requiring a tangle of wires.

The friendly enthusiasts of the earlier decade considered themselves fortunate if they 'got anything'. Foreign languages were more than welcome; a subject of envy amongst the neighbours. 'Tuning-in' was an art which became less delicate with the demise of the crystal and cat's whisker. Nevertheless, the number of knobs on the front of a set was a measure of excellence in design.

With earphones clamped securely to his temples the ardent operator sought distant signals, twiddled numerous ancillary devices reputed to 'reduce interference', 'improve reception' and 'eliminate whistles'. Names such as 'Formo-denser' and 'Pix-adaptors' adorned the pages of popular magazines.

The vogue for enclosing the chassis together with the loudspeaker in a cabinet sounded the death-knell of the kit set. The radio trade joined the furniture trade; appearance became paramount.

The cream of the enthusiasts banded together in societies which remained aloof from the ordinary listener. The elite learned the Morse Code and established themselves in that exclusive breed of aristocracy known as 'Amateur Transmitters'; another misnomer, for many of them belonged to the upper reaches of technology, communicating with one another in idiomatic eccentricities. This noble band of international comrades serve a secretly useful purpose in collecting scientific data from outer space, often inadvertently. The chance reception of 'SOS' messages has many times resulted in the saving of life at sea.

The 'wireless' had come into such general use that its veils of mystery were being overlooked. The mechanics of receiver construction attracted those with an engineering turn of mind. The less erudite looked to the pages of *Practical*

Wireless for guidance in their hobby. The most respected magazine for the more learned was *Wireless World*.

To talk about 'radio' was not widely acceptable. An aura of snobbery confined the term to the upper echelons of scientific thinking.

The amateur constructor could no longer remain supreme commander of his religion. Weird and wondrous 'complete' sets came to the market. The heydays of the mass-producer were beginning, paving the way to over-production, cut-throat competition and numerous commercial disasters.

The 'wireless' appeared in shop windows as a box inside which was hidden a puzzling device not to be touched by other than a 'qualified' person. Nobody had defined the 'qualifications' – nobody ever did. The vocation of the professional Service Engineer grew up and flowered long before any formal training schemes began. We thrived on practical experience, frequently to the cost of the customer.

The self-made Service Engineer could not concentrate entirely upon understanding the subject of electro-magnetic radiation. He had to be carpenter, aerial erector, van-driver, customer relations expert, accounts collector, French polisher, instrument repairer, shop assistant, window-dresser, electrician, diagnostician and psychologist.

A tremendous boost to business followed the introduction to the market of the 'portable' wireless. A misnomer if ever there was one, it appealed to the very people who were unable to handle it. Frail ladies in retirement considered as a splendid idea a set which could be carried from room to room, needing no outside aerial, no external wiring of any sort. Unfortunately the early 'portables' called for the services of a healthy young neighbour to move it from point to point.

One thing the 'portable' achieved was an increase in the demand for Service Engineers. The internal aerial comprised a square frame around which numerous strands of insulated copper wire were wound. The frame fitted the inside perimeter of the cabinet, thus circumscribing the receiver chassis and its associated batteries. The HT battery was heavy but otherwise inoffensive. The 2-volt accumulator was heavy and far from inoffensive. 'Unspillable' and 'leak-proof' accumulators belied their respective titles. Successive re-charging caused splitting of seams. Acid attacked supportive woodwork; fumes corroded the wires of the frame-aerial.

Best reception was achieved by orientating the 'frame' to be in line with signals coming from the desired transmitter. Careful direction-finding could greatly improve results. The fitment of a turntable to the base of the instrument facilitated such adjustment. Turntables of such better-class portables as McMichael and Murphy sported ball-bearings. The ease of manipulation provided ample amusement for young visitors to households which enjoyed these luxuries. Many a good 'portable' crashed to the floor with disastrous consequences for set and carpet. A few days might pass before pink patches appeared in tapestries but inevitably the acid would dissipate itself into the fibres.

The 'suitcase portable' diabolically appeared on the market in an attempt to improve portability. It was a little easier to carry, a lot more likely to be damaged in the movement, certainly more prone to suffer the rigours of acid burns. The 'frame aerial' resided in the upper half of the 'suitcase', together with the loud-speaker. The chassis and batteries were contained in the lower half. Connections between the two halves must necessarily be flexible. Satisfactory flexible connections were beyond the confines of the current technology. 'Suitcase portables' constituted what could fairly be described as 'the ultimate disaster'. I don't think anyone 'bought another one'! In extreme cases of neglect the batteries dropped through the acid-soaked woodwork, crashed to the carpet, ruined the wearing apparel of the unfortunate carrier. Many an undisturbed insurance policy was invoked by the 'suitcase portable'.

Another monstrosity of the era, known as the 'Milnes Unit' appealed to stringent economists. It consisted of an assembly of test-tubes containing an alkaline solution into which were immersed metal electrodes. Sufficient of these tubes produced, by chemical reactions, something like 120 volts High Tension. Economy was achieved by recharging the cells, not by carting them down to the local charging station but at home. They were connected via a complicated switching system to a 6-volt motor-cycle battery. Furthermore, the inconvenience of taking the 6-volt battery to a re-charging station could be avoided: the Milnes people could provide a unit by which the batteries could be recharged from the gas main!

Though the word 'radio' appeared in the advertisements of most manufacturers, the public continued to talk of the 'wireless'. Just as all vacuum cleaners were referred to as 'Hoovers' so all makes of radio sets were classified as 'wirelesses'.

The number of makers proliferated. Competition raged, prices were cut, special offers abounded. Variations in cabinet design disguised the identity of the chassis inside. 'His Master's Voice' carried the world famous motif of a dog listening to a horn loudspeaker. The same dog, in a different kennel, appeared under the name 'Marconiphone'.

Out of the confusion arose the revolutionary Murphy Radio, backed by a national advertising campaign in which Mr Frank Murphy himself was pictured, either smoking his pipe or with his young daughter on his lap. A new standard of ethics in business unfurled. The red, black and gold banners of Murphy Radio flew outside one specially selected dealer in every town in the land: only one per town regardless of the size of the town.

Frank's personal approach captivated the nation. People bought newspapers to see what Mr Murphy had to say next. They flocked to 'Your Murphy Dealer' to examine the sets which were promised to be outstandingly good. They were.

It was no use blowing the Murphy trumpet unless the sound was good. The public, extremely fond of beefy brass band music. were well pleased. You could turn up the 'wick' of a Murphy to a loudness beyond normal domestic requirements without distortion of the sound. Brought up on listening-in to headphones, horn speakers and thin paper cones energised by balanced armature movements, the solid punch from the moving-coil speaker of the Murphy Model A3 was a revelation. Passers-by came to recognise the 'woomph' of a Murphy drifting from an open window. The bass was there and that's what was wanted.

Trade and public went Murphy mad.

Not only were the sets well built and the methods of marketing unique but organisation in the factory at Welwyn Garden City was exemplary. Personnel management held the welfare of employees at the head of its list of priorities. Compared with the rest of the industry wages were high, holidays longer. The five day week was a norm. Trade union leaders of the nineties might well look up the records of how the Murphy factory turned out quality goods in the early thirties, practising the techniques of employer-worker relationships then which are now being introduced by the Japanese as novelties.

At the age of nineteen I was imbued with Murphy madness. The Murphy banner rippled in the good Yorkshire air over the front door of Central Buildings. Had I been sliced through the middle I would have read 'Murphy' like a stick of rock. Sad was the day when Mr Frank Murphy personally gave the order that the Murphy dealership must be withdrawn from H. Reddin and Sons.

It happened thus: According to the terms of dealership agreement all Murphy sets had to be sold at the retail price laid down by the company. There were to be no discounts for cash, no splitting of discounts with any other trader. My father broke the rules. His confederate broke faith.

A Model A3 was supplied to a non-Murphy dealer on the understanding that it was to be passed on to a private individual in York. My father should have insisted that such private individual be directed to Cussins and Light Ltd., the dealer appointed to cover York. No such individual existed. The A3 shortly was to be seen in the window of a non-Murphy dealer in York, presented as a red herring to draw potential customers into the shop and thereafter be 'sold' a make of set from that dealer's own agencies. In short, a dirty tricks campaign was instituted but quickly nipped in the bud. Cussins and Light reported the sighting to Murphy who promptly took appropriate action.

The loss of the Murphy dealership caused me great personal distress. The dealership was transferred to Rex Thompson who guarded it well. I sought to transfer my own affections further afield. I applied for a job in Wales and got it.

'Young man to manage wireless department of furnishing ironmonger. Apply in writing to Coppage and Sons, The Struet Gate, Brecon, stating salary required.'

I required £2 5s. 0d. weekly. This was acceptable. I looked up Brecon on the map and prepared for an exciting train journey to a foreign country.

I was informed that lodgings at £1 5s. 0d. full board would be provided. Even after deductions I would have almost a whole pound for lavish living. Not for me a bank clerk's paltry wage; I was on to a good thing.

Mother supplied me with a substantial stock of some of her best products of cuisine plus a package of sandwiches and buns to be consumed *en route*.

She filled my portmanteau as neatly as only Mother could pack, meanwhile shedding the odd tear or two. I was not to be diverted and resolved never to recognise the malady known as homesickness. I was on my way to uncharted territory with visions of mountains of extraordinary beauty. In that respect I was not to be disappointed.

Chapter 10

Wales, Wheels and Wireless

Mother and Father 'saw me off' at York station. Mother shed tears; Father showed signs of delight at getting me off his back, emphasising the necessity of my gaining 'further experience'. I promised to write when I reached my destination and to post off my laundry at weekly intervals.

A sense of freedom enveloped me as the train steamed from York. I began to take stock. My most treasured possession was a brand new ten shilling note, a parting gift from my Grandfather. He had never before given me a ha'penny. He said it was to set me on my way. His contribution was so unexpected that I nearly kissed him. Deterred by the revolting appearance of his tobacco-stained whiskers, I settled for an excessive display of appreciation; verbally.

Enthralled by the exciting Pennine scenery I felt no need to unfold my sandwich pack until I changed trains at Crewe. Previous experience in train-spotting had been confined to merchandise of the LNER. Such a variety of machinery puffed and snorted in and out of Crewe station that I felt loth to leave this paradise. However, 'Clun Castle' headed my Cardiff-bound train. I climbed happily aboard for the next stage of my journey. I had been instructed by my father to pay particular attention to the scenery around his birthplace, Church Stretton.

The vale formed between the Long Mynd and Wenlock Edge continues to be a favourite in my long catalogue of visual memories.

At Hereford, a major outpost of England, it being only a few miles east of Offa's Dyke, I once again changed trains. A single terminal platform was devoted to the two-carriage train complete with tank engine which would deliver me to my destination. The compartment immediately behind the engine being quite unoccupied, I entered with a view of being best able to observe the peculiarities of single-line working. We, that is, the diminutive train, its driver, fireman and guard were to become firm friends by the time we reached Brecon, some forty-five miles and twenty station-stops from starting point. It seemed that few passengers used the line except on Market Days. Only rarely did a passenger undertake the complete trip from terminus to terminus. For this reason I was accorded exceptional courtesy and instruction in the operation of a railway system.

At Llanfihangel Tal-y-llyn I became acutely aware of my entry into a new style of life. Strikingly different from the broad dialects of my native York-

50

shire, the singing Welsh tones sounded delightfully humorous and friendly. The guard explained that Llanfihangel stood at a junction where the Brecon and Merthyr line merged with our own. My sight was directed to the towering Brecon Beacons, far higher than any peaks I had ever seen. I was directed to observe a trail of steam from a distant goods train making hard work of its climb toward the Torpantau tunnel. A scream of our engine's whistle carried wildly into the sunsetting scenery, startling birds and cattle alike to augment the rural music. The guard waved his flag, the driver accepted the staff. All the ritual required by law, for the safety of a single passenger. We puffed along with clickerty pace, non-stop to Brecon.

'You the young man for Coppage, then?' asked the ticket-collector.

'How did you guess?' I wondered.

'Well, nobody else on the train now, is there now?'

'So?' queried I.

'Well,' he said, 'my brother-in-law did tell me you were due in today. Billy Jones, his name. He do work for Coppage, see?'

The Welsh 'See?' does not require an answer, for it comes with an implication that the listener has sufficient intelligence to understand the foregoing statement. So I saw.

Instructions how to find my way to Ship Street followed.

'You'll be comfortable enough at Number Six, indeed. Friend o' mine digs there, see? Charlie Lloyd by name. Tell Charlie you met Tom the Ticket, that's me, see? 'an when you get settled in I want you to see to my wireless. Private like! No need to mention it to Coppage.'

Suitcase in hand, I descended the steep hill to the Struet Gate. Shops were closed but there stood the emporium to which I must dedicate my expertise: Coppage and Sons, Furnishing Ironmongers. They were not Murphy Dealers, for the banner of my favourite radio manufacturer hung limply outside another shop along the street.

Sunday was spent 'settling in', visiting Cathedral and City Centre. A ten-minute walk covered the latter. The band of the South Wales Borderers played in the Market Hall that evening. The soloist was a local house-painter, John Fullard. It was a privilege to hear that fine tenor before he sailed to make a name for himself in Australia. He never looked back.

Come Monday morning I learned to drive the firm's 1928 Austin Seven van, a most lovable vehicle, which started easily.

Gear lever to 'neutral', release hand-brake, push vehicle forward, jump aboard, declutch, switch on magneto ignition, engage second gear, slam door, drop clutch and away we go, all in one smooth well co-ordinated set of movements. The Austin and I understood one another.

The only luxury item of equipment provided was one windscreen wiper. This worked by courtesy of the vacuum in the carburettor intake. The vacuum, of course, diminished as the throttle was opened. Thus, the wiper stopped when climbing a hill but oscillated at a fine rate when descending. During periods when the wiper stopped through lack of breath the driver could call into effect the manual operating level, this being in such a convenient position over the windscreen that the hand of the operator obscured the view ahead. When not in use that handle projected lethally towards the driver's forehead upon which it contrived to deliver many a star-spangled jab.

Whilst it will be seen that hill-climbing in the rainy season was decidedly dicey, it must not be assumed that descent could be achieved safely. The speed of the wiper increased beyond all reason, partly obliterating the view ahead as effectively as the raindrops. In addition, the brakes of the Austin were designed to slow the vehicle rather than stop it, even in dry conditions. During heavy rain the water sought to lubricate the brake linings. Smart gear-changing to the first of the three gears became an essential art. The clutch was either in or out, nothing in between. The cross-cut gears took very unkindly to anything but double-declutching. After considerable practice and exercising great dexterity, a change directly from third to first could be negotiated without a crunch. Stopping with a full load aboard on a steep descent was impossible. A wary eye must be cocked for slip-road or soft banking.

The starting handle was a permanent fixture. What a great asset it proved on occasions of immobilisation in boggy terrain. Once wheel-spin set in, a wise driver would stop the engine, engage top gear and 'wind' the car forward on the starting handle.

An extraordinary situation developed on a rare visit to a remote farm, the only approach to which was via a steep and narrow gully. Farmer Jenkins rode a Fordson tractor on his daily trips to the main road where, at the farm gate, he would leave messages, milk churns and boxes in which tradesmen might deposit goods for collection. Once per fortnight he would place a substantial 2-volt accumulator for re-charge and I would leave a replacement which would suffice to keep his four-valve 'Chak-o-phone' wireless set going for two weeks. On this particular occasion I found a note asking me to call and fit new high tension batteries. He required two 'Super-capacity 60 volt' types which were clumsy and heavy to carry along with the accumulator. I might need my toolkit also. I decided to drive down the gully. The tracks gouged out by the Fordson were wider apart than the track of the Austin Seven. We made an angular approach.

In spite of lumps of tough mud, loose rocks and chunks of broken tree-branches, we parked safely beside a pile of manure in the farmyard. Mrs Jenkins called off the yapping sheep-dogs, I completed the operations on the wireless, enjoyed a cup of tea and a Welsh-cake, made peace with the dogs and prepared to ascend the gully. We started off very well, bumped along and were halfway up the hill when it happened.

We struck a rock with the off-side front wheel. With a sickening lurch we slewed forty-five degrees across the gully and made a three-point landing. This mishap precipitated the following geometrical problem:

The off-side front wheel embedded itself in the right bank of the gully, the near-side rear wheel was stuck in the left bank and the off-side rear wheel sat in the bottom of the gully. The near-side front wheel was suspended in air, that is, until I disembarked to size up the position. Relieved of my weight the little vehicle settled to a new arrangement of co-ordinates. The off-side rear wheel had risen above ground in sympathy with the near-side front wheel's descent. The vehicle was now delicately poised and could be rocked on the 45° axis with a gentle pressure.

In an effort to solve the problem I set about simple handmade road construction. By systematically layering stones and twigs in the mud I was able to establish equilibrium. Within half an hour, tired but hopeful, I swung the starting handle and was about to attempt take-off when who should arrive on the scene but Farmer Jenkins at the wheel of the Fordson. He saw the funny side of the circumstance, hitched my little buggy to the tractor and together we completed the ascent to the main road.

My thanks to the kind farmer expressed, I proceeded on my remaining calls around Pwllgloyw. By the time I had fulfilled all my obligations, cold darkness had fallen over the mountains.

Headlamps on the Austin consisted of two bowl-shaped protuberances. They cast a light commensurate with the modest performance of the tiny side-valve engine. Maximum attainable speed was about 45 m.p.h. on the level. An extra 5 m.p.h. was available going downhill, flat-out. At that rate road-holding depended on the quality of road surface. When that deteriorated to the point of discomfort then a speed limit of 40 m.p.h. was self-imposed by the vehicle in the interests of survival. At anything over that figure an automatic alarm system manifested itself as frightful vibrations of the bodywork.

In the absence of road-markings, a cautious 25 m.p.h. in the dark seemed reasonable. We had just breasted a sharp hilltop, my Austin and I, when we came to a sudden and uncomfortable stop. We were surrounded by a flock of sheep. I could feel one poor animal writhing underneath the van. Two half-witted shepherds, one carrying a lantern, appeared from the back of the flock. The three of us lifted the Austin's front end, thus releasing the sheep which shook itself and wandered off to join its brethren, apparently none the worse for its painful experience.

There followed some mild remonstration on either side but the two country-men discontinued their argument when I suggested that the lantern needed to be visible to be useful. The incident was reported to my superiors.

Nothing more was heard until the following Market Day when the owner of the sheep kicked up a fuss in the shop. He considered that the unfortunate sheep would suffer after-effects and might possibly die within the not too distant future. How about compensation in advance?

My boss supported my opinion that anybody who ushers sheep at dead of night along the highway not displaying warning lamps front and rear of flock must be short of savvy. Not only that, but he would be breaking the laws of Wales. That ended the matter.

Some of the farms were so remote from civilisation that calls on a regular basis were uneconomical. We recommended and supplied the largest possible batteries, thereafter calling when requested. Such a farm was Blaenbrynach. Fortunately, it was a bright, sunny day as I sighted the buildings from the main road to Hirwaun.

A rough, stony track fell steeply down to a fast-running brook. Beyond that I reckoned it would be at least half a mile to the farm. A track through the bilberries showed where horse and cart traffic passed infrequently. The challenge presented itself.

The crystal-clear water splashed over granite rocks. Halfway across the stream the engine conked. I climbed onto the off-side front wing, unclipped the bonnet, mopped up the water which surrounded the sparkplugs, shut the bonnet, leaned over the radiator, gave a sharp quarter turn to the handle and the four cylinders fired instantly. I settled back in the cockpit ready to complete the voyage.

The little old Austin clutch was not designed to be 'slipped'. The art of getting away had to be mastered if kangaroo starts were to be avoided. It was a question of matching engine speed to road and load. Taking off in mid-stream on loose rocks called for a handsome measure of throttle and a well-timed application of the clutch to set us again on dry land. Bumping and jumping the Austin arrived at the farm gate. We had disturbed the resident collies which yapped and snarled unwelcomely. Rather than risk a bite on the ankle I called for help by blowing the horn. This brought forth Farmer Williams who merrily passed off as remote the possibility of his dogs turning nasty. It appeared that my wee Austin was the first motor car to have penetrated the defences of Blaenbrynach. That is what had offended the dogs. Had I walked I would have been greeted with affection; so I was told.

My work on the wireless completed, I requested the company of Mr Williams as far as my van. He asked me to convey to my company a reminder that his cream separator needed servicing. The work was specialised. My colleague who undertook such work was a dapper little chap known as Dickie Robinson. He carried his tool kit on a round-tanked BSA motor bike.

When I saw Dickie off I warned him about the dogs. Not in the least worried: 'Gracious me,' he said, giving a twiddle to his sharply pointed moustache, 'I've been over that mountain often enough. Dogs don't trouble me. It depends how you approach them.'

Dickie visited the local hospital that evening; the treatment: five stitches in his backside plus the recommended injections. He must have had a painful ride back over that stony track. He told the story well:

'Both dogs came yapping round me as I parked the bike against the wall by the gate. Mr Williams came out of the house saying: "All right, Mr Robinson, don't worry about the dogs. They're friendly enough if you don't turn your back on 'em. That young fellow who came to do the wireless the other day, he was scared of the dogs. Don't you worry."

'Well after I'd fixed the separator I had a cup of tea and walked back to the bike. I bent down to put my tools in the bag and that's where I made my mistake. I had my backside to the dogs and one of them got his teeth right in there.' (He pointed to his starboard buttock.) 'I've learned my lesson,' he said, 'Never turn either cheek!'

Some of the wireless sets I serviced were beyond economic repair. In such cases it behoved me to sell a new one.

Two elderly spinsters of the aristocracy owned a 'Chak-o-phone', the switches of which were corroded, its rubber-covered wires sadly perished. The horn loudspeaker was in good order but such were becoming out-dated.

I demonstrated the latest GEC receiver with self-contained moving coil loudspeaker completely magnificent in a walnut-veneered cabinet. The ladies were intrigued by the modern dial and the ease of tuning.

Compared to the 'Burndept' horn loud-speaker the sound from the GEC was of a decidedly 'beefy' nature. I was careful not to turn up the volume beyond a pleasant level and the sisters appeared well pleased with the results. They would not, however, make up their minds to purchase immediately for they never made such a bold move without consulting first the vicar. I agreed to leave the set for his appraisal and would call again within a few days time to hear the verdict.

The vicar considered the change of set a sensible move but suggested that the old horn speaker sounded 'better'. The customers were satisfied by my connecting it to the new GEC.

The combination of old and new may seem incongruous to many readers but it is well to bear in mind that as the human frame ages the response of the ear to higher frequencies diminishes. The old horn could not reproduce the bass notes but sounded 'clearer'.

Chapter 11

Motor Cycle Mania

Easter Monday dawned bright and clear. The very top of the beacons invited the uninitiated climber. With a pocket full of rock buns I set forth. Within one hour the fascinating change of scenery became more enchanting with each upward pace. The top was invisible but I determined to reach it. Now on my hands and knees struggling through the stubby ling, grabbing tufts of any plant which offered leverage toward the peak, I feigned numerous collapses into the springy plantage; any excuse to idly scan the widening country. At last the top, views all round now, temptation to look beyond the Welsh horizons. From the height of nearly three thousand feet it seemed almost feasible to emulate 'The Flying Yorkshireman' and take off.

I must have wheels. The railway company delivered my 'New Hudson' racing bicycle to Brecon, quite undamaged, at a cost of only four shillings. Far from being homesick I developed travelitis.

First I planned to explore every road out of Brecon, limiting journeys to forty miles return. Then I extended my adventures to Swansea; every weekend I found a hundred miles to be a reasonable distance. The magnificence of the municipal buildings of Cardiff fired my desire to see more.

Not all was beautiful. The depressing sight of the derelict Cyfartha iron-works, the downcast unemployed in Dowlais, set me wondering at the contrast between town and country, agriculture and industry, wealth and poverty: How could it happen?

The renowned statement by the Prince of Wales that 'Something must be done about it' had sounded very promising. From what I saw on my first visit to Dowlais nothing seemed to have been done about it. I fell into conversation with three grown men who were sitting on the doorsteps of a defunct cinema. It was Sunday. They did not go scratching around the scrap heaps on Sundays. They were sharing a cigarette, passing it from one to another for a quick drag.

I think they regarded me as some kind of capitalist. Fine bike, how much was it? Where did I work? Any more jobs there? Could I spare a fag? I didn't smoke. I offered a shilling, trusting not to cause offence. 'Dieu, Dieu, bhoy, there's a friend. Offence, no fear. That's a packet of twenty.'

That was the day when I thought I had become a socialist. I had made a start at finding out how the rest of the world lived. I resolved not to stay too long anywhere.

Train rides were all very well. During two return trips to my native county I became acquainted with every station between Brecon and Thirsk but knew nothing of the towns they served. I made a momentous decision. I must have a motor-bike.

From Messrs. Fryer Bros. at the top of Ship Street I obtained a catalogue of Triumph motor-cycles. I learned every detail of every model pictured therein. I lay awake night after night learning and re-learning the art of starting and stopping. Relentlessly I compared performance figures and fuel consumption, tyre sizes and pressures. By the time I had plucked up sufficient courage to deplete my hoardings in the Yorkshire Penny Bank I could recite the gear ratios of every Triumph model in the book. I chose a 250 c.c. 'Mark 5'.

The total bill was a few pence over £55 for which amount I became the owner of a lavishly chromium-plated, purple-painted, twin-exhausted, four-speed masterpiece of Coventry engineering.

To my friend Don Morgan, nephew of the aforementioned Fryer Bros., I am indebted for my first lesson in motorcycling. With a tank full of National Benzole mixture we set off with myself as pillion passenger, intent on a good long running-in session. Just one mile along the road towards Abergavenny the engine stopped. We dismounted, looked in the tank, made sure it was full, tickled the carburettor, kicked the starter and away we went for another mile, only for a repeat performance.

We turned for home. Again the engine faded after one mile. After a short rest we decided to consult at the workshops of Fryer Bros., where again the engine stopped. The wily old mechanic said: 'Listen, can't you hear what's wrong?' Sure enough a hissing noise at the petrol filler-cap indicated an imperfectly drilled vent hole. With that small defect rectified, we rode away to complete our objective of 'running-in'. The Triumph never failed me again. I had learned a lesson in motor-bike maintenance, at the same time refreshing my memories of a chapter in the book of *Elementary Physics*.

Motor-cycling topped my list of priorities. By Triumph I explored the length and breadth, the mountains and valleys, the beauty spots and disasters of the industrial revolution, the magic and the miseries of Wales.

A favourite local attraction was the new reservoir at Talybont. Beyond that the old Brecon and Merthyr railway wound up a 1-in-38 incline to disappear at 1,300 feet above sea level into the Torpantau tunnel. The road consisted of loose shale, not without hazard. The reward came with the sight of a hard-pressed loco puffing its smoky way into the oblivion of the tunnel.

The scenic ride through the Elan Valley, to my mind, is one of the great sights of the world. In my early motor-cycling days the road from the top dam onwards to Devil's Bridge was a rough track but presenting little difficulty. Further north the connecting track between Lakes Vyrnwy and Bala was labelled distinctly 'Unsuitable for Motor Vehicles'. The reward for defying the notice by skilful negotiation of the rocky outcrops was the incredibly beautiful lakeland scenery. Now that these roads are macadamed, I trust the modern motorist may spare a few thoughts for the workers who toiled in the laying of the original tracks.

So economical was the Triumph that distance was no object. Where conditions permitted it would crackle along at 60 m.p.h. and consume no more than one gallon in a hundred miles. The tank held 2¼ gallons; a fill-up of National Benzole Mixture cost just over 4s. (now 20p). This meant that I could cover the return trip between Brecon and Thirsk, a total of 460 miles, for less than 50p, in modern money!

The petrol companies were up to all sorts of tricks to attract customers. As a staunch buyer of NBM I was reluctant to be persuaded by advertisement but when Esso introduced their 'Ethyl' and coloured it pink I broke with custom for a trial run. I set off from Brecon at midnight, with a full tank, determined on a non-stop run to Thirsk. I ran out of petrol in Halifax at three o'clock in the morning. By good fortune I met a couple of workers coming off night-shift. They directed me to an all-night filling station where NBM was on tap.

Subsequently I tried Cleveland 'Discol' and every other brand on the market, but always reverted to NBM. Sadly, it is no longer available.

All my spare time was taken up with motor-cycle riding, polishing, cleaning, maintenance and tuning. I became an avid reader of *Motor Cycling* and *Motor Cycle*. I studied riding styles of trials riders and road-racers. In the latter category I came to the conclusion that the greatest master of the craft was Irishman Stanley Woods of Norton, Velocette, Husqvarna and later of Moto-Guzzi fame.

Stanley once said: 'If there's any road left when you come out of a corner, then you weren't going fast enough.' The first time I saw Stanley in action I was thoroughly disappointed. The ACU had organised a race meeting at Donington Park to coincide with the National Rally, first of its kind, in 1934.

Don and I had entered the rally. He rode a nippy little 150 c.c. Triumph and I used my trusty Mark 5. We checked in at the Park after an all-night ride and by the time we walked down to watch the riders on the circuit, the 500 c.c. event was already nearing its end. Nobody could mistake the sight of Stanley on his 'Velo'. He went through the hairpin and under the bridge at a very leisurely pace with no other riders in sight.

'Oh, Lord,' I said to Don, 'Stanley must be in trouble.'

'Don't you believe it,' interjected an unknown spectator, 'He's a lap ahead of the rest and waiting to see if any of 'em can catch up!'

'Twas ever thus: the true expert makes his craft appear easy.

In those days personal riding styles were recognisable from quite some distance. Great was the variety of makes of machine, each with distinctive colours and mechanical peculiarities. The racing nowadays is, of course, much faster but far less interesting. The modern racing bike, encased in gaudy advertising material, ridden round corners at incredible angles with the rider's knee stuck out, is not a pretty sight. To see them chasing one another round and round the present Donington circuit is thoroughly boring compared with the exciting times of Woods, Frith, Foster and Daniel. There would have been some derisive comments in the press had those characters been seen doing the 'knees-out'!

Chapter 12

Public Address

Connecting accumulators to be charged from the 220 volt direct current (DC) mains of Brecon was anything but a hazard-free enterprise. The occasional thumping shock did at least provide relief from the boredom of the interminable task. Nevertheless, the need for change urged me to respond to an advertisement in *The Wireless Trader*. It called for a Service Engineer for a Murphy Dealer in Hereford.

I didn't bother to write but resolved to board the Triumph at the earliest opportunity and take a look at the place. It appealed to me. A short interview secured me the post with C.F. King and Co., at £2 10s. 0d. per week plus 1¼% commission on sales made in the shop. Fantastic, the sky the limit! Further, the company incorporated a motor-cycle sales and service department. I transferred my affections to the City of Hereford and entered upon some of the happiest periods of my life.

Battery charging, collection and delivery were not my responsibility except in association with the maintenance of 'Macaroni', with which piece of devilish instrumentation I suffered a love-hate relationship for two years. 'Macaroni' was the pseudonym of a monstrous public address amplifier manufactured by the Marconiphone Company. Charlie King, who was one of the great pioneers of public address work and very enthusiastic about the project, decided to do it in a grandiose manner. 'No job too big; no job too small; anywhere at any time!' Therefore, 'Macaroni' was powered by batteries and could operate far from electricity supplies. Any attempt to connect it to a mains supply would have caused a major disaster. It was transported from place to place in a specially adapted 20 h.p. Renault van and thoroughly resented ever being separated from its carrier.

'Macaroni's' ten valves were heated from a large 6-volt battery. Four hundred volts of high tension were supplied from four wet accumulators each of which weighed half-a-hundredweight. In operation after darkness had fallen, the C.F. King public address amplifier made an impressive sight, the valves casting a glow like unto a small bonfire and radiating heat in proportion to the luminosity. We performed at horse shows, galas, garden parties, gymkhanas, regattas, road races, sports days, grass tracks, scrambles, festivals religious and festivals hilarious.

For big events such as the Abergavenny Horse Show the practice of placing horn loudspeakers at intervals around the arena called for an early morning start. Each speaker was mounted on a pole supported by guy-wires and, being of the electro-magnetic type, required a 6-volt battery to energise its coil. All this gear weighed heavily on the old Renault, itself far from nimble.

Starting the 'Rennie' was simple indeed provided that the following routine was observed: raise the bonnet, prime the carburettor by 'tickling' the float, close the choke, take firm hold of the starting handle and turn the engine over twice. Next switch on the ignition, check the ignition lever is set to 'retard', give half-a-turn of the starting handle and the big flywheel would take over, the engine obeying its command with a satisfying 'chuff-chuff' of sound which counted out the revolutions.

Moving away called for an equally scientific approach. The clutch must first be 'freed' by treading the pedal to the floorboards, stirring up the engine a few more revs by judicious use of the throttle lever and repeating the operation, after which the first of the three gears might be engaged without fuss. Any slight departure from routine resulted in rude rumbles and mechanical mutiny. Once on the move the driver felt the responsibility of taking charge of a vibrant monster, all two tons of which creaked and groaned until, road conditions permitting, second gear might be engaged. Changing gear could not be hurried, double de-clutching being an essential group of movements: clutch out, select neutral, clutch in, allow engine speed to fall to a level gauged by experience, clutch out, engage second gear, clutch in and gather speed. On level going the third gear could be selected in like manner, by which time the first half-mile of the journey was completed.

Once in top gear the noise level fell dramatically and the crew could settle down to enjoy a roll-free ride at 25 m.p.h. Higher speeds were inadvisable for 'Rennie' took an inordinately long time over coming to a halt. Changing down a cog occupied more time than the changing up so when a substantial decline was sighted ahead it was necessary to give advance notice to the engine room in anticipation of the alteration. The lumbering flywheel was quite unresponsive to throttle 'blipping'. It was visible through a hole in the floorboards so a fair assessment could be made of the number of revolutions at which a sweet engagement of a lower gear might be achieved.

During the procedure of double-declutching, a not inconsiderable time elapsed with the gear level in the 'neutral' position. It was vital, therefore, to complete any changing down in advance of any descent, otherwise the effect of gravity upon the ponderous vehicle caused an alarming increase in speed. In the full knowledge of the inadequacy of the braking system the driver must allow for no margin of error in gear selection. It was my good fortune to be tutored in the handling of the Renault by Mr King himself. Charlie knew every contour of the surrounding countryside and had been brought up on cross-cut gears. He could change gear on the Renault without the slightest hint of a scratch from the machinery.

Successful public address engagements depended on a multitude of parameters such as an echo-free arena, a fine windless day or night, location of microphones out of the line of fire of the loudspeakers, an announcer amenable to tuition in the use of a microphone, a customer who knew what he or she wanted and equipment which never failed. Alas, the occasion when all these requirements were met at one and the same time was a rarity.

Once 'Macaroni' was set up and switched on, the custom of preliminary testing began with a tap on a microphone with the knuckle of a forefinger. A discreet 'Hello, hello,' called for a visual response from a colleague previously despatched to a listening point. Let there be no ear-offending howl from the loud-speakers. On a thumbs-up signal from the assessor we could confidently await instructions from the organising authority, be it the vicar, the President of the Horticultural Society, Chairman of the Parish Council, Secretary of the Sports Club or whatever.

I breathed a sigh of relief whenever I was asked to perform the task of announcer. It was, however, an axiom of business to bow to the customer's wishes. If a prominent member of the organising committee fancied his chance as a public speaker then the microphone must be handed over, trusting that a few moments of tuition might be accepted in good faith.

Public address systems are designed and built for the sole purpose of amplifying the human voice from its normal speaking level. It is both unnecessary and indeed inadvisable to shout at a microphone. It is very difficult to persuade some people not to do so. Many treat the microphone as though it were some kind of idiot who is incapable of understanding a foreign language. The resulting distortion must all too often be suffered by a captive audience.

Properly handled, 'Macaroni' could deliver as sweet a tone as ever came from a loudspeaker. Its reliability was suspect on two counts, both of them were inter-valve transformers the manufacture of which left much to be desired. Fortunately, the failure of a transformer could be forecast by virtue of an irritating series of intermittent crackles, gentle at first but increasing in volume before the final breakdown. Spares were carried. A rapid replacement by a routine operation could be completed in two minutes. It was incumbent upon the operator to arrange for a suspension of the event of the day whilst 'Macaroni' received corrective treatment. We never failed to see a show through to the end.

A memorable day with 'Macaroni' at its best found us at Kington where we played a leading role in the celebration of the twenty-fifth anniversary of the reign of His Majesty King George V. We received the fabulous payment of twelve guineas for the job. It was gone midnight when we packed up the kit. The vicar appreciated our efforts to such an extent that he pressed upon us a glass of port wine and a piece of Jubilee Cake. It was my first glass of port; it went to my head and I fell asleep in the passenger seat of the Renault. My companion on the occasion was Mr King himself. He had no problem in driving us safely back to Hereford where I awoke to the sound of crunching metal. The Renault halted within fifty yards of the garage doors where the left-side half-shaft broke. We needed a tow.

Charlie reversed his Vauxhall 'Twelve-Six' down the slope. Blearily I hitched a tow rope between the two vehicles. I took the driving seat of the Renault whilst Charles revved up the Vauxhall; the rope tightened. The Renault remained motionless as the rope parted from its company and was dragged along the ground by the Vauxhall which continued forward with engine revving merrily, its driver oblivious to the absence of a load. The expression on Charlie's face when he stepped out of his car and looked on the space where he anticipated seeing the Renault was something to behold. In the light from the great brass head-lamps my master cut a comical figure. At our second attempt both vehicles were locked away from possible harm. We repaired to our respective sleeping quarters as dawn was breaking, I with the sounds of 'God Save the King' still ringing in my ears.

'Rennie' was fitted with the last half-shaft available in the United Kingdom and we undertook to provide the public address system for Gloucester Regatta. For this we carried a crew of three including the gaffer. Only by a small margin of luck did we finish the day without a watery mishap.

The racing was held on the canal which carried coasters and barges on their business voyages to and from Sharpness. Our duties included the provision of field telephone communication between start and finish. These two posts, for geographical reasons, were located on opposite sides of the canal. Overhead wires were out of the question in case a high-masted vessel might pass. In order to sink a 'Don-eight' wire to the bottom of the waterway it was threaded through one of our steel scaffold poles. The pole and the drum of cable were loaded into a boat. We rowed across, dropping the pole mid-way, ensuring the cable could not become entangled with any form of water-craft. The wire was run out along the east bank and a telephone established at the distant starting point. The meeting was a great success, concluding at the initial stages of sundown.

Recovery of the telephone and land-line called for all hands, one to carry the instrument and the other two to carry the drum on a spindle and wind on the wire. We rowed across and moored the boat without problems, recovered the telephone and loaded the now filled drum into the boat. A group of onlookers assembled on the west bank, not in admiration of our boatmanship but clearly anticipating some amusement at our expense. The sun dropped below the Forest of Dean as we hove to in the centre of the canal and endeavoured to raise the pole. It was firmly embedded in Severn Vale mud. The wire was wet and try as I might I could not get a good enough grip to raise the pole. My fellow oarsmen made a hash of their attempts to steady the boat. As I pulled at the wire the danger of capsizing loomed imminent. We shipped water. Words of encouragement were shouted from the spectators on the bank where one stout fellow heaved on the wire attached to the Renault. The effect of this spontaneous gesture was to pull the wire from my grasp and transfer the tension rapidly to the heavy cable drum which lay firmly in the bottom of the boat. Thus the boat itself dipped to an alarming angle. Rapidly I paid out wire from the drum and yelled to the haulier to cease activity. We three in the boat became wet and worried. Much to the disappointment of the audience I directed the boat to the shore where we disembarked safely. With the aid of several volunteers we hauled on each leg of the 'Don-eight' and recovered the pole together with an assortment of bric-à-brac including samples of surprisingly agile animal life from the depths of the canal.

The old 'Rennie' had completed her penultimate assignment. Her final was made in Worcester. We were engaged by the Millers' Mutual Association which organised 'Bread Week'. It appears that the British consumption of bread was insufficient to suit the manufacturers of flour. I operated solo and mobile with the Renault and 'Macaroni' travelling around the streets of the city playing gramophone music and announcing attractions to be witnessed during the week. I never discovered why the citizens of Worcester had been selected for the treatment. Some of them objected to it.

One irate shift worker had settled down to a few hours kip when, disturbed by a rousing march tune, he emerged from his residence in pyjamas and dressing gown and thumped on the side of 'Rennie' with great force. He let me have his opinion of the Millers' Mutual Association in short crisp words. That street remained unmolested for the remainder of 'Bread Week'.

The indiscriminate use of loud-speakers in urban areas was largely responsible for the introduction of the Noise Abatement Act. I must confess to have been guilty of creating many a tumult.

On the fourth day of 'Bread Week' 'Rennie' revolted. The other half-shaft broke. She was towed into the Star Hotel yard, never to move again under her own power. As 'Macaroni' and 'Rennie' were inseparable they ended their service to mankind in a Worcester scrap-yard.

I kept faith with the MMA by playing music more quietly and making less resonant announcements through the firm's stand-by amplifier carried in an Austin 'Seven' van. I was not sorry to see the end of 'Bread Week'.

Chapter 13

Past Masters

My principal occupation as Service Engineer to the company was the repairing of faulty radio sets both old and new.

Our main agencies were for Murphy and Bush Radio. New sets from those two manufacturers were received in perfect working order. Many customers insisted on buying a set in its original packing case with unbroken seals. This was fair enough and we would accede to a request to deliver to the customer's home and unpack the new instrument before his very eyes.

With certain makes we contrived to take a second set in case the first one didn't work!

The normal practice was to unpack at the shop and test out each set before it was put on sale. We acted as the extra final test department for the manufacturer and in doing so saved ourselves and the customer a lot of trouble.

Frank Murphy ruled his company in the style of a benevolent dictatorship. The dealers were obliged to sell at the retail prices fixed by Murphy Radio Ltd., which allowed a lower margin of profit than normally acceptable to the trade. The dealers could only agree to such an arrangement if the products were reliable, which proved to be so. After-sales service on Murphy Radios, in the days of Mr Murphy, was minimal whilst pre-sale service was negligible. We were proud to be Murphy Dealers.

A valuable feature of Murphy sets was simplicity of design of cabinet and mechanism. There were no fancy and troublesome tuning indicator devices so popular with many other manufacturers. The customer could tune in by observation of a straightforward, numbered dial showing wavelengths only. Some makers went to no end of ingenuity to create a colourful dial with names, numbers and in some cases pretty lights moving up and down. There were strings, wires, bowden cables, gear-wheels, levers, bearings, pulleys and pointers all intended to attract a buyer. They represented potential trouble. Frank Murphy would have none of that.

Selling radio sets, still commonly known as 'wirelesses', was a seasonal business. Peaks in sales curves appeared in the run-up to Christmas, after which came a dreadful lull. Manufacturers dismissed production workers by the thousand, re-engaging them in the autumn, in preparation for the anticipated improvement in business following the annual exhibition at Olympia, when new models were announced.

Mr Murphy initiated measures to counteract this unsatisfactory state of affairs. He wished to maintain a loyal work force in continuous employment. New models were announced throughout the land around Easter time. What is Murphy up to now? – thought John Citizen. Murphy dealers had the new sets on demonstration and sales picked up enormously. More national advertising in conjunction with Radiolympia boosted autumn sales. Then followed the usual Christmas spending spree to keep the pot aboil. After that there was a potentially cheerless start to the New Year.

What did Murphy Radio do about it? They reduced prices and boldly proclaimed this new inducement to buy. This pleased everybody except the clients who had just purchased at the pre-Christmas prices. There were many grumbles and groans which had to be dealt with by the dealers. Murphy took action: when the new models were announced at Eastertide the whole policy was explained in the press to general acclaim. The overall sales curves settled down to a smooth line.

The public recognised a square deal. Murphy was established as a guiding light in the industry. Price tickets in the shop windows were clearly labelled with cash prices and Hire Purchase terms. Clearly there was nothing under the counter at 'Your Murphy Dealer'.

To the dealers themselves the service backing was exemplary. Any spare part required was available immediately. Technical drawings were the most comprehensive in the trade, and the regular publication of *The Murphy News* kept us on our toes with up-to-date details of modifications and business guidance. 'Murphy Madness' spread throughout the nation. Murphy ruled OK.

Then dear old Frank, thinking everybody understood his tactics, went a jump too far. He proposed the introduction of new price tickets showing explicit details of the price structure of Murphy products: manufacturing costs, dealers' commission, retail cash price and HP interest charges. Mr Murphy was just about fifty years ahead of his time. The dealers revolted. Tut-tut, dear boys: they did not intend disclosing trade secrets to an ignorant public. Discounts and commission figures were sacrosanct, to be mentioned only in whispers behind the counter.

It was not so much a clash of personality which brought about the divorce of Frank Murphy from Murphy Radio Ltd.; more a difference of intellectual standards. His thinking could not be understood. His controversial departure left a shadow over the industry. Murphy Radio never got out of that shadow; it had discarded its self-illumination.

So imbued was I with the principles on which Murphy Radio had been founded that I enthused over the marque well into the post-war era. Eventually, as will be seen by those who choose to pursue forthcoming chapters, I gave up in disgust. The Murphy label which may be seen on numerous foreign products is nothing but a mockery of its origin.

Meanwhile another great name came to the fore. The Bush Radio factory at Chiswick was administered under the direction of G. Darnley Smith. Rarely seen without a meerschaum, Darnley was a picture of contentment. Without wasting words he inspired confidence and friendship. He knew every employee by name. I never heard of anybody volunteering to leave his employ. No dealer would be daft enough to give up the agency once it had been appointed. Bush Radio prospered largely because of G. Darnley's undoubted charm.

That charm was very necessary to overcome the discontent engendered by the poor performance of the first models from Bush. They were no match for the Murphy sets but new models introduced at the Olympia show of 1935 rectified any shortcomings.

We at King's were proud to fly the Bush banner alongside the Murphy red, black and gold. The Bush motif represented an owl sitting in a tree. Soon to become household phrases were the slogans: 'It's a Wise Bird that settles on a Bush,' and 'There's nothing you can beat about the Bush'.

Competition was healthy. Customers had plenty of choice. As far as I was concerned the choice was between Murphy and Bush. Some other makes we handled were far less reliable though often of more attractive appearance. The customer made the decision. We guided but never pressed.

The age of fancy tuning dials was upon us. The antics which some designers got up to, in the quest for sales, were laughable to service engineers: laughable, that is, until it came to repairing the damned things. Moving lights of different colours became popular. Murphy and Bush lagged behind in this respect, thus retaining their reputations for reliability.

Philips went in for miniature 'Bowden' cable arrangements. They became the serviceman's nightmare. Not content with one tuning dial, some makes fitted two or even three. These involved pulley wheels and strings galore. In the absence of a service sheet for the particular model, it was almost impossible to reinstate a broken drive cord. Exchanges of information between service engineers on a friendly basis was widespread. Admittedly, the private trader fraternity kept at armslength from the 'multiples' such as Curry's and Stones'.

Many dealers would undertake only to repair sets sold by themselves. At King's we accepted anybody's troubles. I was prepared to 'have a go' at any make which came along. In this way a lot of experience was gained and a lot of goodwill generated. Many engineers refused to tackle any set which had already been mauled about by somebody else, often a well-meaning cowboy. That never deterred me; it presented a challenge and I must confess to a sadistic enjoyment of succeeding where others failed.

We were unable to find a perfect formula for pricing service work. A good, experienced engineer might locate and repair a fault in short time. If he charged working time by the hour the customer got a good job done cheaply. A second-rate so-called 'engineer' might take hours longer and charge more. The customer was always at the mercy of the trader.

Chapter 14

Trouble Means Business

Apart from replacing the odd valve, very little maintenance work was called for by owners of Bush and Murphy radios, which makes constituted the bulk of our sales. Plenty spare time was available for me to undertake service work on any make of set whether sold by King's Radio or not.

Perhaps only the family doctor became better acquainted with the inner workings of the British household than the radio service engineer. We served 'em all; large and small, rich and poor.

The majority of requests for service began with the stipulation that 'there can't be much wrong because it was working all right before we switched off!' I think the reason for this was the desire on the part of the complainant to persuade himself or herself that little expense would be incurred.

For my part I had every inclination to keep repair bills as low as possible and to provide a rapid service. We did not wish to earn a reputation for robbery. Many jobs were sufficiently straightforward to be completed in the home. Customers were very impressed by quick service on the spot, especially when they could be shown a faulty part or parts. I made a point of leaving these for examination by relatives and friends. A great camaraderie was built up between myself and our clients. There was no scarcity of hospitality on the part of the latter.

Frequent cups of tea or coffee were on offer. In many cases when a customer requested service by telephone, we would be advised where to find the key to the door should there be nobody at home when we called. On arrival I often found instructions to make my own liquid refreshment and where to find the biscuits! They were the days, of course, when house burglary was as rare as summer snow.

There were places where I would not take a cup of anything had I been paid for it. I well remember being driven by a colleague, Leslie Wheeler, to service a K.B. Model 333 mains radio at a council house on the outskirts of town. I was a non-smoker at the time but Les advised me to light up one of his Gold Flake cigarettes before going into the house. He knew every householder on the company's books. I took the advice and as soon as we got inside I realised the value of smoking in certain circumstances.

From the central ceiling rose hung the flex which carried the electric light bulb in its holder. In the lampholder was what was known as a '2-way adaptor'

68

from which was taken another flex to a picture rail, thus completing a rectangle with ceiling and wall. That rectangle was completely filled in by a curtain of dust-laden cobwebs.

The K.B. radio stood on top of a cupboard in an alcove by the fireplace. Set, cupboard and mantleshelf were laden with bric-à-brac from Barry Island, Weston-super-Mare and Blackpool. Each and every trinket was coated in greasy dust. No way was I going to try to service the set *in situ*.

As I summed up the situation an old hag appeared from an outer scullery. She had not washed for years. She looked up at the aforementioned rectangle and said:

'Eeeh, Aggie, we shall 'ave to get them cobwebs down one day.'

I said: 'Don't worry, missus, they're coming down now, all at once!'

With that, I took a deep breath, uncoupled the adaptor and pulled the flex away from the hook in the picture rail. A distinctly satisfying crackle sounded as pent up static charges relieved themselves from the weight of cobwebs. We cleared all the trashy ornamentation from the top of the radio, put them on the centre table, itself covered in filthy newspaper, and lifted the radio from the cupboard. We made our exit in double quick time, facilitated by virtue of there being no sitting-room door to be opened. It had been removed for firewood as had all other internal doors. Never did fresh air smell sweeter than when I left that house.

Back at my workshop the K.B. underwent special scraping and de-greasing before work could be started. The inside of the cabinet resembled a very grotty grotto. No fewer than six spider nests were dug out from the works and after that distasteful occupation the serious task of fault location could begin.

Considerable heat was radiated from the valves of mains operated wireless sets. This meant that dust was drawn into the bottom of the cabinet whilst hot air escaped from the top. A vacuum cleaner was a luxury item in the household, the brush and shovel being standard kit for daily tidying. Hence, the first job when a set came into my workshop was a thorough cleaning of the chassis. The difference between the amount of dust from a set where a vacuum was in use in the household and from a vacuumless home was very noticeable. The vacuum cleaner must surely have made a laudable contribution to the health of the nation.

In cases where the wireless dwelt in the kitchen the chassis collected dust which became congealed in grease. This called for special attention using trichlorethylene as a cleaning agent. In extreme cases where the set was located near a gas cooker serious corrosion of components containing copper took place. The cleaning process must be conducted with great care to avoid disposing of such parts altogether.

Whilst the majority of customers disdained any attempt to repair an ailing wireless set there was always the odd character who enjoyed a 'dabble'. One such owned a very powerful 'Pilot' set of American origin. I was called to investigate the cause of loss of entertainment. He treated me to a long harangue on the possibilities.

'I've had the chassis out,' he declared. 'I've tightened and oiled all the screws but still not a sound!'

'In that case,' I said, 'you've caused me a lot of work at your expense. Those screws are trimming capacitors and must on no account be moved, never mind oiled. Each one must be thoroughly cleaned and then re-set to a strict routine. I must take the set to my workshop for very special treatment. Meanwhile I will lend you a set to keep you going.'

As I left the premises with the 'Pilot' the lady of the house was heard to describe her husband as 'a damned fool'. That seemed to me a fair description.

It was customary for clients to ask the cause of failure of their radios. I never failed to advise them. After all, the set was their property and they had a right to know what they were paying for in the way of service. Conversation would proceed, for example, as follows:

'There you are, Madam. Just as good as new.'

'Oh, thank you. What was wrong with it?'

'The audio frequency coupling capacitor preceding the output stage broke down.'

'Oh, is that expensive?'

'No, but unfortunately that means that the output valve overheated and I have replaced that also, which does make it more expensive.'

'Oh, how much?'

At this point I would, by habit, display for examination the faulty parts. Always I left these with the customer. The effect was to save further technical explanation which it was obvious that few clients understood. More than that, it seemed to ease the pain of extracting the cash. When the master of the house returned home from his daily toil there were the faulty parts, his property, as proof of work done. The practice paid handsomely.

Another custom which enhanced my reputation as a service engineer was to treat each faulty receiver to a thorough course of hygiene. Particular attention was paid to the tuning dial and the glass window through which it was viewed, to the control knobs and finally to cabinet polishing. We tried to restore each set to nearly new condition, no matter whether it came from humble home or mighty mansion.

I was earning about £3 per week and a few windfalls came my way from satisfied customers. Overtime pay was unheard of in the trade. If there was work to be done I got on with it. I had no fixed hours for work. Though Thursday was an official half-day holiday, that would go by the board should a Public Address engagement arise. Any loss of holidays was compensated for by the feeling of freedom to take time off to suit one's convenience. I never counted the number of hours worked, nor the number of periods of relaxation. My happiest days were in Hereford on three quid a week with no rules or regulations.

Nevertheless, I began to think of broadening my technical knowledge. Absorption in correspondence courses was insufficient to satisfy my thirst for further understanding the intricacies of the modern super-heterodyne receivers. I regretted giving notice to King's to take up an appointment at the Kolster-Brandes factory at Sidcup.

Chapter 15

Mass Production

I signed on at the K.B. factory to work in the final test department which consisted of a row of half a dozen sound-proof cabins. My pay would be one and threepence per hour and an extra penny would be added in the event of my being required to work overtime.

Immediately I was assigned to a cabin, a sense of claustrophobia enveloped me. My accommodation measured about 4 feet by 6 feet. A window in the ceiling admitted a modicum of daylight. A peephole in the door allowed any outsider to ascertain whether or not the cabin be occupied. A flap beside the door permitted completed radio sets to be passed within for testing. A flap at the opposite side of the cabin was the exit through which tested sets were shoved into the packing department.

Lonesomeness was dispersed by the arrival of the genial Arthur Trowbridge, Chief Tester. He demonstrated to me how each set which appeared through the 'In' hatch was to be checked. A list of functions to be verified formed the basis of the work. If every condition met with my approval I was obliged to stamp indelibly my personalised number inside the cabinet. The procedure was stringent. It seemed impossible for a faulty K.B. set to reach the public. The Technical Director, however, did not have implicit faith in his testers. He made a practice of taking at random from the despatch department a completed set, cosily packed in its colourful carton, to his home where he unpacked it and tried it for himself! Any flaw detected he brought to the notice of the Works Manager in authoritative parlance. The WM then took up the matter with the Chief Tester in more emphatic terms.

Arthur commanded an extraordinary understanding of human nature. He could have coped with any post in the diplomatic service. He absorbed all manner of adversity and turned it to good account. Every mistake together with its subsequent correction was a welcome addition to the encyclopedia of experience.

Minor faults detected by us of the cabins must be eliminated. Anything of a more serious nature called for the attention of Arthur. Thus a constant flow of good sets to the packagers was maintained. The object of the exercise was to pass fifteen sets per hour through the 'Exit' hatch, thus allowing an average of four minutes per set. Arthur let three sets come into the cabin for a dummy run in order to ensure that I had understood his instructions.

Once my probation period ended I was a fully fledged tester. Within half an hour the flood gates opened. A never-ending stream of completed sets encased in skeleton cardboard protectors poured into the cabin. Arthur popped in every now and then to encourage, advise and deal with any 'sticky' fault which I was unable to clear within five minutes.

Arthur's whole body and soul was ingrained to the mass production system. He had been schooled in it, enjoyed every minute of it, inspired all around him. He had a thorough grasp of his job, knew every detail of the sets under production, thereby being able to diagnose faults in double-quick time. I have never met anyone else would could measure voltages, to a fair degree of accuracy, by application of a finger and thumb of the same hand between points of differing potential. As witness to his ability were tiny burns, like pin-pricks, on several fingers and the thumb was peppered with them. He would stick his thumb on an 'earth' point and swing the digit round from one high tension terminal to another saying: 'You should have sixty-five volts there, Harry mate. You've only got thirty.' He was right every time.

Whilst Arthur thrived on the environment it became evident that not every-one could stand up to the pace. A short break was allowed when the tea-trolley was brought round. Amongst my new-found colleagues one had just returned from treatment at a psychotherapy centre and two others were looking for alternative occupations. There were not too many alternatives around so it was a question of hanging on to the bird in hand.

I had been fortunate in finding comfortable lodgings very close to the factory in Footscray and could walk home to a leisurely lunch. The afternoon's routine was pleasantly broken by Lucy who propped up my 'Exit' hatch asking: 'Hello, what's your name?' She was a cheerful soul and of very pleasing countenance. She apologised for not having contacted me during the morning section but she had been overworked. She was my packer, who promised to keep in touch at regular intervals.

Lucy and I got on famously over the next few days. Eventually I got round to asking her if she fancied a spin through Kent on a motor-bike. Well, Lucy had not ventured on a pillion before but wouldn't mind trying. A rendezvous was ar-ranged at a clearly defined point and I arrived somewhat before the appointed time.

Now it must be appreciated that all I had seen of Lucy was her smiling face, topped by a very attractive permanent wave, through the frame of my 'Exit' hatch. When she appeared round the corner of the park I was astonished at the bulkiness of her main bodywork.

I had acquired a delightful but smaller motor-bike before leaving Hereford, a 250 c.c. 'S.O.S.' (So Obviously Superior) with a water-cooled two-stroke engine. It was not designed to carry other than a lightweight pillion passenger.

Lucy contrived to seat her ample form upon the none too spacious pillion seat whereupon I was conscious of the spreading of the rear tyre upon the roadway. Our first halt was at a near-by service station where I declared the necessity of taking on some engine oil. At the same time I took the opportunity of doubling the pressure in the rear tyre.

We took a very short ride into the Garden of England. We proved to be an unhappy combination. At every corner Lucy thought fit to take some part in the guidance of the machine. Each time I applied the brakes I fancied my passenger might roll over me and the handlebars. Each attempt at acceleration caused me to fear she might vanish over the rear number plate. At work we continued a happy relationship, confining our communications to niceties through the 'Exit' hatch. Without Lucy to cheer my life I am sure my term of duty in the cabin would have ended at a very early date.

An agreeable variation in the work came with a change of model, but with even greater relief I was promoted to work in the main hall as a production line diagnostician. My wages increased to one shilling and fourpence per hour. For the additional penny I put in about ten times the amount of energy. It was all go, all day.

Two parallel moving belts brought completed chassis at the rate of thirty per hour each. At the end of each line the chassis arrived at a dynamic test point consisting of four test rigs each staffed by a girl or woman of above average intelligence and of pleasant appearance and manner. My octet of beauty I was very proud and willing to serve.

At this stage of production the chassis was connected to the mains supply for the first time. If all was well the ladies performed routine adjustments to achieve certain results as indicated on instruments built into the test rigs. The chassis was then returned to the belt to pass to the stage of being fitted into a cabinet. I endeavoured to divide my time equally between the eight members of the beauty chorus, to supervise, encourage and help maintain a smooth flow. Infrequently a fault in a chassis might manifest itself by a puff of smoke and a minor explosion. Such occurrences called for great flutterings among the ladies.

I must confess to being encouraged by expressions of gratitude for my efforts. My function as a fault detector and rectifier required intimate knowledge of the chassis under production in order to locate faults with all speed. I must also be able to leap from one of the eight test points to another with the utmost agility, vaulting the lines many times a day.

The worst happened when all four testers on one of the lines held up hands in unison. That meant real trouble caused by a mistake at an assembly point. It came about when a storeman delivered components of incorrect specification to an assembly worker who might not notice the mistake. In appearance one small part may seem the same as another yet be of a quite different value. So all sets passing that assembly point arrived at the dynamic test as 'faulty', and all with the same fault. Until the error was located we could only stop production and pile up the chassis for attention in due course.

If Arthur's wet finger test failed, then a search must begin for an obscure defect. When the pile of 'rejects' had risen to alarming heights the Works

Manager would roar disapproval. Tempers begin to fray, especially when suggestions of 'trying to wangle overtime' were overheard.

Throughout such hallabaloo Arthur would ponder calmly over the problem, oblivious to all around. When finally the mistake had been identified, all the chassis had to be returned to the point of assembly where the operator had fitted the wrong component. There the corrected chassis would be set again on the moving line for its journey to final testing. Such delays were most unpopular with the accounts department.

A new model for presentation at Radiolympia of 1936 showed great promise. Production was stepped up to meet anticipated demand. The call for overtime was received with general acclaim. That week my wage packet contained only a few pence short of £5. The jackpot had been hit!

So the money was good. The luxury of a five-day week enabled me to enjoy some of the evening attractions around London. I could park the motor-bike at a mews behind Queen's Hall for sixpence and join the promenaders for a similar sum. Sir Henry Wood was very much in charge and Clifford Curzon was an up-and-coming young pianist.

Occasionally I would divert to Variety at the Holborn Empire or the Lewisham Hippodrome. Thursday night was 'Hammer' night at West Ham Speedway. Sundays I joined my motor-cycle friends in the traffic queues to and from Brighton or Hastings or grass-track racing at Brands Hatch. Life was a whirl, both inside and outside the factory. I found myself in the swing of South Country ways.

My landlady fed me well; she made me feel at home. My motor-bike would be better under cover so we went halves in the erection of a very substantial shed. The retired carpenter next-door built the shed at a total cost of £3. I was into property in Kent!

I first became aware of 'fiddles' in the factory when I borrowed a tome on the subject of motor-cycles from a colleague. At the factory gate that evening I was called into the security office and there obliged to open the book. The guard thumbed through the pages, found nothing unfavourable and returned the book. I asked what it was all about. He explained that a popular practice had been uncovered recently. The cutting of a substantial hole through all the pages of a book provided a sufficiently large cavity to accommodate a few valves. Thereafter I never took a book or newspaper to or from the factory.

Production of the new model proceeded apace. We had sorted out all the teething troubles. My young ladies understood what minor adjustments were required to turn out a 'good' chassis. I could draw the circuit diagram of the set with my eyes closed. I could 'clock-in' and 'clock-out' without losing 'time'. The monotony of the job was relieved by the good companionship of my fellow workers, particularly Arthur and the cheerful, chattering females. It seemed that I was locked into the mass production system.

When I received a letter from C.F. King and Co., telling me they were without a Service Engineer and asking if I knew of anyone who wanted the post I knew where my heart lay. I was paid by the hour at 'K.B.'. All I had to do was to collect my cards, settle with my landlady and despatch myself westwards. Over the Cotswolds the little engine of the 'S.O.S.' sounded happier than ever; in Herefordshire the great strong cattle grazed contentedly in lush green meadows between the hop-fields. I was home again.

There was no need to apply for my old job. It had been assumed that I would turn up and a pile of appointment cards awaited my arrival. Variety was again the spice of life.

Chapter 16

The Year of the Kings

That was 1936, that was. Three monarchs took turns at ruling the country.

King's Radio were called upon to install a temporary Public Address system in Hereford Cathedral for the occasion of a memorial service in honour of King George V.

We had acquired some very efficient 'Vitavox' horn-type loudspeakers. Two of these I decided to mount on a main pillar above the pulpit. I have always believed in grouping loudspeakers at one point, otherwise problems of echo are exacerbated. After all, the human voice is projected from one point and all that is required of a PA system is to amplify it, not multiply its outlets. Lack of observation of this elementary principle has ruined many a church service.

Our sole purpose was to amplify the sermon to be preached by the Bishop of Hereford. The microphone, suspended above the pulpit, would remain 'dead' until the Bishop raised a hand to indicate that he was about to begin his discourse. Therefore it was essential to establish the amplifying equipment at a point where I could see the pulpit and turn up the volume control to a pre-determined level, at the correct moment.

In anticipation of a massive attendance the placing of extra seating made it impossible for me to place myself out of sight of at least a few hundred people. I looked up to the pulpit and ahead into the north aisle which would be packed with eager worshippers.

Our new GEC amplifier had a nauseating habit of emitting farting noises during its 'warming-up' period, the cause being in the type of smoothing capacitors known as wet electrolytics. At first the fruity noises came in short sharp bursts, then gradually the frequency diminished. After ten minutes it was fairly safe to say that silence had been established.

No chances would be taken. I would switch on the equipment at least one hour before the first members of the public were to arrive. There could be no hitch.

A monitoring socket to which headphones could be connected enabled the operator to hear what sounds were being detected by the microphone without any sound coming from the loudspeakers. Half an hour before the service was due to start I was contentedly watching the congregation being ushered into place. The organ commenced the introductory which I was enjoying on the headphones when Charlie King tapped me on the shoulder, pulled up a chair, sat with his back to the people and grabbed the headphones to check if all was well. He was the boss so I couldn't argue but I would have preferred to retain full control.

Charlie listened in for a minute or two, nodded his approval but retained the headphones.

I knew the order of service; Charlie didn't. I sat and waited for the moment when the Bishop would ascend the steps to the pulpit. I knew this would be during a period of silence; Charlie didn't.

The service proceeded in immaculate order. The period of silence came.

It is well known that the majority of people who wear headphones raise their voices when speaking. Charlie was no exception to the habit.

I moved my hand towards the volume control, in anticipation of the signal from the Bishop. My movement prompted Charlie to whisper hoarsely:

'Has the Bishop gone up into the pulpit yet?'

My gesture to indicate to him that he had ruined my afternoon was misunderstood: he raised his whisper to a subdued shout:

'Has the BISHOP GONE-UP-INTO-THE-PULPIT-YET?'

The Bishop glared down at me from the pulpit steps. Those of the congregation in sight stared in my direction. I grabbed the headphones off Charlie's cranium, much to his surprise and I prayed that the tombstone over which I was sitting would open up and swallow the pair of us.

At this point I lost my nerve, overdid the volume setting which instigated a typical oscillatory howl from a badly manipulated PA system. The howl was short-lived as I throttled back the volume control. Murmurings of disapproval from the nave were sensed rather than heard.

The Bishop gave me a questioning glance. I raised an apologetic thumb in his direction. Thereafter the learned gentleman paid tribute to the late sovereign with uninterrupted eloquence.

Once dear old George had been laid to rest the nation experienced a period of tension and turmoil culminating in political upheaval. Whilst Edward VIII was dithering over whether or not to accept the crown, Stanley Baldwin prevaricated in his position of PM. Meanwhile Adolf Hitler was ranting and raving in Europe.

War clouds had gathered. In Spain they were about to burst. It was time to sharpen our swords. The local Territorial Army Unit organised a recruiting campaign on the beautiful Castle Green overlooking the River Wye. There is no more pleasant spot to spend a sunny evening. I welcomed the appointment to provide the Public Address system. A goodly crowd assembled. The TA put up a great show. I was able to hold the crowd's attention at the end by announcing that music would be played for dancing on the Green until midnight. There would be a charge of one shilling per person, the money to be a subscription to TA funds.

The crowd did not disperse but nobody wanted to pay.

Now it so happened that standing near the entrance were two very attractive young ladies one of whom I had often observed pedalling her way to her office at Bulmer's cider factory. Here was my opportunity. I said to the Major in charge of the show: 'Let us reduce the price to threepence and see what happens.' He agreed to this but still there was no movement. It was then I made my master stroke:

'You take the ginger one and I'll take the blonde,' I said.

So the first step to marriage was taken. My able colleague took over my job, played record after record, the dancers poured in, whether paid or unpaid I cared not. We danced until the batteries ran out. Then we had to wind in the cables and pack the equipment into the van. What could we do but offer the young ladies a lift home on top of the cable drums!

It so happened that I was in funds. An invitation to the pictures the following evening was accepted. We watched a George Arliss film from the back row of the one-and-threepennies at the Kemble cinema and got through a half-crown box of Black Magic. Lilian had never known such luxury and neither had I. We have been together ever since, even when luxuries were unobtainable.

The resignation of Prime Minister Baldwin caused a by-election in the Bewdley Division of Worcestershire. King's were instructed to provide mobile Public Address equipment, for use during the campaign, by the Liberal Party. The weather behaved itself right up to the last minute of the speech-making. It was Saturday. Lilian accompanied me in the van. We finished at Barnard's Green, Malvern, where Sir Richard Acland thrilled the crowd with a most convincing piece of oratory. We thought the Liberals were going to win.

We packed up the microphone and set course for home. The sun had dropped behind the Malvern Hills. Great black storm clouds assembled over British Camp. They burst when we were about two hundred yards from the top of the climb. The rain slopped all over the van and the engine stopped.

The uncomfortable interior of a Morris Twelve van laden with heavy electrical gadgetry, strong winds discharging gallons of water from over-hanging trees and pitch darkness beyond the limits of our side lamps was an unlikely setting for the advancement of courtship. I decided to have a look under the bonnet.

Checking that the van was in reverse gear I yanked on the hand-brake lever and hoped the vehicle would stay immobile on the 1-in-6 hill. I instructed my beloved how, should the van try to move backwards, to pull with all her might, using both hands on the lever.

I donned a dilapidated old mackintosh and stepped into the stormy night. Shining my torch under the bonnet I expected to find water swilling over the engine but it was perfectly dry. The ignition leads ran through a metal conduit and by good fortune I noted a black spot on one of them at the point where it emerged. I pulled it clear of the conduit, trusting the fault would be cleared. As

I closed the bonnet the van moved backwards just far enough for the front wheel to trap the toes of my left foot under the front wheel.

Throwing courtesy to the howling wind I yelled at my lady-love:

'Pull like hell on that lever.'

'I am pulling as hard as I can,' she shouted.

'Well, pull a bit harder,' I insisted, 'and don't touch that button on the end of the lever.'

'Oh,' she cried, 'Shouldn't I have done that?'

'No,' I said, 'you shouldn't. My big toe is stuck under the wheel.'

'Oh, dear,' she said, 'May I help?'

'Yes,' I replied, 'Just pull on that lever.'

'I can't pull any more,' came the reply, adding, 'It's no use getting excited.'

I wiggled and wiggled until I could feel my big toe release itself from the pressure. I bent down, oblivious now of the swishing rain, undid my shoe lace and extracted my foot. The big toe was still there though it felt numb. I entered the driving seat, allowed the van to run back a couple of feet, recovered my shoe and prepared to resume the journey.

Hey, presto – the starter brought the engine to life and in first gear the heavily laden van topped the summit. As we cruised down the west side of the hills the clouds cleared, uncovering a full moon. All was well with the world. Not disposed to tempt fate, we made haste to headquarters.

Chapter 17

Two-Strokes

My interest in two-stroke engines had been fired when I first observed Scott 'Two-speeders' buzz up Sutton Bank. I regret never having plucked up the courage to buy a brand new 'Flying Squirrel'. At £85 the cost was prohibitive. So I settled for the single-cylinder water-cooled 'S.O.S.'. I collected it from the 'factory' which turned out to be a back-street shed in Birmingham. The staff consisted of one man who assembled the bike from components imported from various sources. The engine was a Villiers, the petrol tank was made by 'Norton' and so on, the assortment being firmly secured to a very strong duplex frame.

I was delighted with the 'S.O.S'. The proprietor of the marque controlled the 'works' remotely from his headquarters in Redhill, Surrey. 'T.G.' Meeten, popularly known as Tommy, represented the hard core of the specialist motor-cycle manufacturer of the times. Always hoping that the high quality of their products might ensure success, they all slowly sank into the pre-war depression.

The 'S.O.S.' gave me an enormous amount of pleasure, certainly justifying the title of 'So Obviously Superior'. With patient tuning I could achieve a maximum speed of 64 m.p.h. and cruise comfortably at 50 m.p.h. for hours on end so long as a well-balanced mixture was fed to the engine. Should the mixture be weakened in the interests of good 'two-stroking' the piston was likely to seize in the cylinder, drawing the journey to a brief halt. After a few minutes the piston contracted whereupon the little engine could be restarted and the journey continued. Tommy Meeten described how he had conducted tests at Brooklands to prove that a Villiers engine could endure running without oil, so long as the petrol-air mixture was rich enough to promote 'cool' running.

It was Tommy who showed me the only safe way to empty a petrol tank. During the day he worked at Gatwick airport as a welder. (In those days one entered the airport by a wicket gate!) In the evenings he repaired motor-cycles in his workshop at Redhill. He was saving hard to begin 'Meeten's Motor Mecca' at Shannon Corner on the Kingston By-Pass. When the 'S.O.S.' sprung a leak in the petrol tank I rode over to Redhill for the fright of my life. I removed the faulty tank from the bike and handed it to Tommy who emptied the petrol into a bucket, placed the tank on his workbench, lit the welding torch and plunged the flame into the open neck of the tank. There sounded a dull 'plop'. My rapid approach to the emergency exit was halted by Tommy's shouting:

'Where are you off to?'

'I thought you'd gone stark raving,' I said.

'I do that every day at Gatwick airport,' he explained. 'The mixture is far too rich to explode. It simply burns gently as you have seen. How would you prepare a petrol tank for welding?'

'Well,' said I, gingerly, 'I think I would empty the tank and then wash it out with water.'

'You could not be sure of clearing all the petrol fumes. You may well have a highly explosive mixture and blow yourself to smithereens. Another dangerous method is to empty the tank and allow it to stand overnight. My method is safe; immediately after emptying the liquid set light to the rich fumes. After that there is nothing left to explode. Right?'

'Right,' I agreed. 'Lesson learned.'

Fortunately I have never been obliged to weld a petrol tank.

The 'S.O.S.' with its strong steel undershield lent itself to riding over rough terrain. In 1937 I was bold enough to enter a major competition: The Wye Valley Trial. To find my name listed amongst the famous of the day was a great boost to my ego. Len Heath, the highly successful rider of Ariel 'Red Hunter' machines, followed me over the Black Mountains. When we halted at the approach to Little Cwm, a notoriously difficult rocky ascent, my self-exhaltation received a set-back when Len made an uncomplimentary remark about my beloved 'S.O.S.'.

'That thing stinks like a poke of devils,' he said.

He was objecting to what I considered to be a most pleasing aroma resulting from the use of Essolube Racer oil, as recommended by the manufacturer – Tommy Meeten!

Anyway, I won the Pentiloe Cup which was awarded for the best performance by the rider of a two-stroke machine. There being no other two-stroke entry it seemed reasonable for me to accept the prize.

Sale of the 'S.O.S.' enabled me to pay my life insurance premium and retain £15 cash-in-hand. Though my lovely Lilian captivated most ardent affection I found myself unable to continue in life without a motor-cycle.

Brooker's of King's Lynn advertised in *The Motor Cycle* as follows:

'Scott' Flying Squirrel 498 c.c. 1928 model – road tested – £15.'

It must have been road tested by a one-legged man with a concrete backside. One foot-rest was tied to the frame by string. A vicious-looking piece of broken spring projected through the remnants of a saddle-cover. The engine refused to start and the whole machine seemed best suited to the scrap-yard.

My friend and ally at King's denounced my new purchase and set to work on its total dismantlement. Cecil Bowcott had served his apprenticeship under the eagle eye of Alec Bennett of TT fame. Within the hour my Scott became a collection of parts, each one to be examined with meticulous care. The strong duplex frame Cecil declared to be in perfect order. The serious work of reassembly could begin.

Reynolds of Liverpool advertised a remarkable service to Scott enthusiasts. To them the cylinder block was sent for reboring. Back it came complete with shining new pistons at a total cost of £2 including carriage! – all done within 72 hours. I lavished a few shillings on having the petrol tank painted professionally and a few more on a comfortable saddle cover. The first road test of the finished article verified the extraordinary skill of my colleague. After a running-in period my next step was to fit a respectable pillion seat and test my Lilian's ability as a riding companion.

A pillion rider should enhance the road-holding qualities of a motor-cycle, not ruin them. Extra weight over the rear wheel aids tyre grip but if the pillionist attempts to take over the steering by leaning the wrong way on corners there can be no harmony. My new pillion rider gave no cause for concern. We were in business for many years to come.

Our first ride together on the Scott was not without problems. A few miles from the City we halted to admire the scenery. On returning to the bike the rear tyre was flat. My tool kit did not yet cater for puncture repairs. The day was ending; the sun had dropped already into Wales and we were sure that mother would be getting worried for the safety of her valued daughter.

I recollected a story of someone stuffing grass into a flat tyre as a get-you-home-in-emergency tip. I tried it. It seemed to make not a scrap of difference but we managed to wobble at moderate speed as far as the firm's garage.

There I parked the Scott and in desperation borrowed the boss's new Vauxhall 12/6 to take my beloved as far as her garden gate where mother was waiting with anxious expression. My brief apologies for late arrival were accepted and I made haste to return the car to base.

The 'Twelve-Six' was a motoring revelation with independent suspension all round, leather seats, wooden dashboard, synchromesh gears and a general feeling of well-being for the passengers. Remarkable value for money at less than £250, the Vauxhall was a best-seller.

I had driven the Vauxhall several times and gloried in its smooth passage through the air. On the present occasion it struck me that the steering felt very much heavier than usual. I examined the tyres after parking in the garage. They appeared to be normal so I locked up and went to bed peacefully in the belief that my imagination had played tricks. I was unaware that the car had been, that very morning, in the hands of the local Vauxhall dealer for its 'first service'.

The following morning the car was required for an early start for London on the annual trip to Radiolympia.

Chapter 18

Vauxhallympia

We set off at 7.00 a.m. Charles took the wheel. Mrs King rode as front seat passenger, well equipped with packets of sandwiches. I took the offside rear seat whilst the other side was occupied by a very interesting lady who entertained me with stories of South Africa. She expressed no alarm at the distinctly wavering course which the motor-car seemed to be taking.

Charles never got the hang of a synchromesh gear change. He persisted in his long practised habit of double-declutching. It said a lot for Vauxhall gears, which stood up to mismanagement remarkably well though not without audible complaint. I had become accustomed to this but I was concerned about the excessive movement of the steering wheel even where the road ahead appeared to be quite straight.

My fellow passengers showed no concern so I held my peace. It was when we descended a short sharp hill, immediately prior to a bend a few miles beyond Ledbury, that all aboard expressed alarm. Whilst the road curved at a right-angle, the car only just managed 45°. Our nearside wheels mounted the grassy verges, ran along the edge of a deep ditch and exercised the independent suspension to its limits before we came to a standstill.

After a sharp exchange of words in the cockpit and a determined jerk into reverse gear we regained equilibrium and renewed our eastward progress. The suggestion that I might relieve the driver of his responsibilities was not well received. Our pilot declared himself quite fit, so onwards we sped. Charles was of short enough stature to enable him to see the road between the spokes of the steering wheel rather than over its rim. Therefore, at the steep incline by which the road from Ledbury makes its T-junction with the A38 he was unsighted on the morning mail van which was proceeding lawfully along that major road.

As far as our chauffeur was aware we were entitled to turn right onto a clear carriageway. I saw the white of the postman's eyes as the poor fellow hurled his van into his nearside gutter and skilfully avoided our rear end. In a cloud of dust the Royal Mail careered on its way to Tewkesbury.

My companion of the rear seat, at that moment, chanced the comment: 'That was a near squeak.'

Oblivious of any approximation to danger there was no response from the front seats. We negotiated the fair streets of Cheltenham and though our cornering techniques left a lot to be desired, owing to the paucity of traffic and the skill of other drivers we got through without a collision.

At Northleach we made our first coffee stop. By that time my nerves teetered on edge but a further offer to assist in the driving task was rebuffed. We continued as far as Beaconsfield where the coffee was called to action again, milk being dispensed from a separate supply. Inoffensive though a milk bottle may be it was to be the cause of our next fright.

We had resumed our motoring in the direction of the capital, as far as Denham. From that point the A40 climbs gently to what I have always called 'the Uxbridge roundabout', now a fly-over. At the time of which I write it was a single carriageway with no fewer than two lanes in either direction. Travelling westward downhill from the roundabout was only one vehicle, an outsize in furniture vans. It maintained a moderate speed in its nearside lane. We in the Vauxhall approached in our nearside lane. The reader will have gathered that there were two empty lanes between ourselves and the van. That was when the milk bottle toppled and Mrs King bent down in search of the blessed thing.

Charlie thought of joining the search and in taking his eyes off the road in favour of scanning the floor of the car he dragged the steering wheel clockwise a small degree. That action diminished our parallelism in relation to the line travelled by the furniture removers. We moved into lane number two with the oncoming van some hundred yards away.

The search for the milk bottle intensified. Both the King's heads were now bent over the passengers' footwell. Charlie's grip on the steering wheel did not relax.

Not only had our vehicle drifted into the third lane but it was so near the furniture van that I could see both its driver and his mate preparing to take evasive action. I didn't shout; I screamed: 'LOOK OUT!' which caused the following simultaneous reactions: The hitherto dignified lady who shared the rear seat with me appealed to her Almighty, Mrs King triumphantly held the milk bottle aloft for all to see but, most important of all, Charles fairly wrenched the steering wheel fully anti-clockwise and we made haste to the relative safety of a parking spot beside Lane No. 1.

Mrs King then spoke the wise words: 'Charles, now let Reddin drive.'

Without a murmur we changed places. As soon as the car moved forward I realised there was something radically wrong with the steering gear. My opinion was confirmed when it was announced that the car had been in the hands of the Vauxhall dealer in Hereford for a check on that very system.

As a service engineer myself, though in a different field, I had come to suspect anyone who professed to repair anything. There is always that possibility of human error, failure to tighten a screw or to leave it undone. I drove cautiously to the Vauxhall service station in Acton where a preliminary examination convinced the manager that we must leave the car for his attention. We continued on our journeys by Underground, the two ladies towards their shopping expeditions, Charles and myself to our hotel in Paddington and thence to Radiolympia.

Our annual pilgrimage to the Radio Show was thoroughly well organised. Charles was typical of the average British employer of labour. Wages must be held to a minimum, requests for increase in salary greeted by negative enthusiasm. Yet perks were distributed with gusto so long as they were considered 'good for business'. Charles did me proud on these expeditions. We enjoyed ourselves.

It was our practice to make a beeline for the Bush Radio stand. We reckoned always to be invited to a slap-up lunch in the excellent Olympia restaurant. The formality of introducing ourselves to G. Darnley Smith, admiring the new models and proposing to order some were preliminaries to our acceptance of a cocktail or two before we were taken to lunch by the worthy representative, Jack Davies.

Lunch was followed by a stroll around all the trade stands. Charles was so well-known in the business that there was no difficulty in fixing up lunch appointments for the other two days of our visit. Murphy did not throw their money about but it was certain we were not going to starve.

For evening entertainment Charles offered me a choice. I could not resist the temptation of renewing acquaintance with speedway racing at West Ham so Thursday's page of the diary was a standing entry. Charles insisted on his selection of Wednesday vaudeville at 'The Prince of Wales'. I must say that we saw some of the great entertainers of the day at that famous theatre as well as the eye-opening tableaux which evoked its fame. The third and final night of our Olympian revelry found us in the 'World of Radio' hall adjoining the exhibition.

A galaxy of entertainers appeared at Radiolympia in the forefront of which Louis Levy and his Symphony raised our spirits out of a world of cut-throat business, unemployment and rumours of trouble in the Rhineland. Radio, the wonderful communication medium, the amalgamation of the brotherhood of man, whereby nation shall speak unto nation, praised, lauded and glorified in a glittering array of stars. The grand finale went on and on until the stage was so full that the Dagenham Girl Pipers marched in the aisles. The sound of music mingled with the applause until one feared for the roof of the vast building.

Back to earth and to Acton the following morning where we collected the Vauxhall. The steering gear had been incorrectly assembled at Hereford but was now declared safe. Henceforward the car continued to give good service for many years.

Chapter 19

Murphy Madness

My introduction to the professional servicing of television receivers coincided with the visit of the Australian cricket team to England in 1938. Free courses at the Murphy Radio factory in Welwyn Garden City were available for dealers and their staff. So I had the privilege of viewing the great Len Hutton stroking his way to a total of 364 runs, a record unbeaten until twenty years later by Gary Sobers.

Reception from Alexandra Palace covered the London area only. Receivers were heavy by weight and price.

The extra high tension voltage required by the cathode ray tube was provided by a mains transformer of considerable dimension. Very necessarily it resided in the bottom of the console cabinet and was very properly labelled 'lethal'. Should testing, permitted by 'qualified persons only', be conducted with the set switched 'on' it was important to place one hand behind the rump as does a wine-waiter. At the same time both feet should be well insulated from 'earth'.

Cathode ray tube manufacture being in its infancy we 'engineers' took care to observe the rules. Tubes of greater than two or three inches in diameter were liable to implode. Therefore, it was thought that some of the internal parts of the 'gun' might be ejected at high speed as a result of the relief from vacuum. A story of the 'gun' which pierced the roof of Radiolympia went the rounds of the trade. Eye witnesses kept an invisible profile.

Nevertheless, precautions were customary. The cathode-ray tube was mounted vertically in its substantial cabinet. The picture could be seen to be inverted in the horizontal plane. The cunningly hinged lid of the cabinet, when raised, revealed a high-quality mirror which being set at a suitable angle provided a perfect reflection of the picture the 'right-way-up'. The audience viewed thus in 'safety'. Service engineers were advised to wear goggles.

Service manuals provided by Murphy were indisputably the best in the trade. As my own expertise improved so my reputation grew. Offers of greater financial rewards from competitors of my employer were rejected on grounds of loyalty. In search of higher income I moved to a more populous area.

At E.G. Bennett of Burton-on-Trent we sold only Murphy Radio. Television pictures from Alexandra Palace were unreceivable. Our 100% Murphy policy did not preclude our undertaking repairs to any other make of set nor of getting up to a few pranks in the furthering of Murphy Madness.

The Philips people introduced a most pretentious receiver advertised as the 'Monoknob'. It caught the public imagination to such an extent that E.G. Bennett displayed a sample in the shop window with a view to converting potential buyers to the Murphy fold.

Technically, of course, the Philips engineers had mastered their craft. Electrically their products, performancewise, measured up to any in the trade. Mechanically they represented the Dutchman's propensity to perplex. The Monoknob invited abuse by junior members of any household: up and down for the adjustment of loudness, sideways to alter 'tone', twiddle it for tuning the stations which were named on the extensive dial. A chromium-plated outer circle was thoughtfully fitted with finger grips to facilitate the changing of wave-bands. Potential buyers were instructed to admire the complexity of the network of 'Bowden' type cables which festooned the interior of the cabinet.

By accident or intent the Monoknob bore a £21 price tag, coinciding precisely with the price of Murphy's A21C, a much more substantial piece of radio engineering. It was easy enough to persuade prospective clients that their money would be better spent on the Murphy.

Murphy's outstanding pre-war achievement, the A80RG, retailed at £80. This superb radiogram with plate-glass tuning panel alongside the best automatic record-changer that Garrard could produce in quantity, was, arguably, the best and last word in pre-war radiograms. It surely must have been the heaviest.

Charlie Meekin's mother had borne three sons and an equal number of daughters before finding herself widowed. Five of the offspring were married and away from the tiny cottage in Gresley. Only Charlie remained in bachelordom, dedicated to caring for Mum.

When miners marry and leave home it is customary for them to stay within spitting distance of the parental base. Thus each and every member of the family will be in a position to observe the movements of others. It was no surprise that Charlie called at the shop to inquire which new Murphy model had been purchased by brother Tom. He cast a disdainful glance at the modest table model indicated by the ever-alert Sales Manager. 'Of course,' said he, 'your elder brother bought one of these.' He pointed to the magnificent A40 console with plate-glass panel at £40.

The facial expression of Charlie remained in unexcitable normality. Only the tiny beads of perspirational jealousy gathering beneath his eyes and upon the upper lip betrayed his inner feelings. 'Is aught better?' he mumbled.

The Sale's Manager stratagem had been perfected over long experience in a close-knit community. With subdued enthusiasm he called Charlie's attention to Murphy's masterpiece, the A80Rg.

'If that'll fit i' sittin' rum, Ah'll 'ave 'im.'

Sales of radiograms at £80 per one called for the very especial attention of the proprietor himself. The following morning he detailed me in the execution of delivery of the magnificent instrument to Charlie's cottage. The two of us just and only just managed to manoeuvre it into the firm's Ford 8 van. Carefully I drove the vehicle to Gresley, whilst Mr Bennett kept two watchful eyes on the valuable cargo, at the same time outlining our plan to clinch the sale. I was to remain silent unless called upon to agree with anything which he may have said.

The cottage looked like all the others in the terrace, identifiable only by its number. All pairs of net curtains testified to the loyalty of the villagers to the local Co-op textile department. Why should the curtains call for mention? Had they hung undisturbed they would have hung unnoticed, but they didn't. Our knock on the door of No. 14 drew attention to our little red van. A theatrical parting of curtains on both sides of the street signalled that our purpose in the course of duty was being scanned by numerous nosey parkers.

The hat-stand in the hall had to be moved to permit our ingress to the sitting room. My boss who chose to walk backwards whilst carrying his share of the weight was the first to see into the above-mentioned room. He directed me to lower the radiogram to the floor to allow his whole person to enter the inner sanctum in order to agree with the residents the most suitable place to accommodate the Murphy.

Though I was unable to see the actors in the scene their soft voices were audible enough. Mum inquired:

'Where are you goin' to put it, Charlie?'

Quite clearly Charlie didn't know.

Edgar Bennett had never been slow to suggest a solution to any problem concerning progress of business. On this occasion, as I stood in the hall with the door wide open because the radiogram was jammed against it, Edgar could only be heard thinking. After a long pause he said:

'Well . . .!' The intervening pause before he said: 'I know . . .' was shorter and more positive. 'There are only the two of you now, aren't there?'

'Yes,' agreed Charlie.

'Well,' repeated Edgar, 'you need only two dining chairs.'

'Yes,' agreed Charlie.

Following sounds of furniture on the move there appeared the four legs of a substantial chair, these beyond my reach unless I climbed over the precious radiogram. I waited and watched as Edgar emerged victorious, chair aloft, and edged it into the back kitchen along with the hat-stand. Charlie handed out the second chair to accompany the first.

Tactician Bennett came into his own at that point. From my post in the hall I appreciated the precision with which he directed the two remaining chairs to be stood on the table prior to the shifting of the table itself to one side of the room.

During the affairs of which I was no eye-witness Mum had been heard to chance mild protests. On each occasion she had been told quietly but firmly to ''old yer 'ush.' (That by Charlie, of course. Edgar supported the order telepathically.)

The stage was now set for the entry of the villain of the piece. I was relieved to feel that I could play some part in the sale. We raised the radiogram off the floor. Edgar reversed into the parlour. I shuffled forward with half the weight of the mighty instrument in my care and we tried to negotiate a left-hand-hard-down turn through the doorway. We got stuck. From the look of pain on the boss's face it was not difficult to understand that his funny bone had suffered a severe jab from a door jamb.

Though our inconveniences could no longer be observed by those 'over-the-way' peepers, a small number of adults and a large number of kids stood at a vantage point on the roadway. Edgar confided that the door should be closed in the interests of privacy. We lowered the Murphy to the floor. Much to the disgust of the onlookers I shut the door.

My breach of silence eased the situation. It gave Edgar a few moments for massage of his elbow at the same time as he nodded approval of my plan whereby he should first reverse into the kitchen allowing me to wedge myself and the other end of the radiogram into the parlour doorway. This allowed another inch of turning-circle.

I had failed to see that the clever move brought the face of the radiogram towards the wall against which it was destined to stand for demonstration. I could now see Mum. She was very concerned but seemed pleased to know that a real person had been concealed from her sight for the preceding quarter-hour. I think she viewed me as a possible ally who might tip the scales in favour of a more sensibly sized wireless to satisfy Charlie's craving.

Charlie was determined to go ahead. It was he who suggested that Mum should assist the operation by getting up from her armchair and making herself scarce for a minute or two.

Such was the configuration of the old furnishings at that juncture that it was impossible for the old lady to do more than stand upright. On the opposite side of the fire-grate stood Charlie's matching armchair. Into that we located Mum. Her own chair was lifted onto the table in conjunction with the two dining chairs. The extra space available enabled us to rotate the radiogram by 180° and stand it back to the wall. All was now set for restoration of Mum to her own chair, Charlie to his, and the table and two dining chairs to the only possible as well as practical positions. The fact that I was now imprisoned in the corner by radiogram and table presented an easily resolved problem.

Edgar moved the table away slightly from the radiogram from which I now removed its felt covering. I squeezed a way through the gap as Mum was heard to say:

'It'll be far too loud for this little place. All the neighbours will be up in arms.'

At that point I excused myself in order to reduce the over-crowding by twenty-five per cent. As I left the room I heard the Bennett *coup-de-maître*:

'Well, you see – the beauty of these very high-class sets is that the same quality of perfect reproduction is with you even at the very quietest level.'

With difficulty I kept expressions of amusement within my subconscious. As I fiddled about with items of the trade inside the van I was aware that observation from chinks in curtains was maintained. Then one of a pair of urchins, undoubtedly property of the local populace, inquired:

'Mr Meakin 'avin a new set, then?'

'Looks likely, doesn't it?' I countered.

'Aye,' said his mate. 'Big 'un, wurn't 'im?'

Thinking the question not to warrant a reply I ignored it. The intruders were not satisfied:

'Wurn it, Albert?' to his mate.

'Bye, aye, it wur, wurn it, mister?' – to me.

'Yes, it wur,' said I, falling into the lingo.

'Bet it cost a few quid, eh?'

It was Mum who relieved me of extended questioning.

'You two be off wi' yer,' directed Mum. Then turning to me: 'You mun coom in for cup tea, young man.' That too was a direct order so I went in.

A new atmosphere pervaded the sitting room. The great black kettle steamed away on the hob and the teapot was warming beside it. Charlie was silently engrossed in observation of the actions of the automatic record-charger. By pre-arrangement a number of Columbia 10" records of colliery bands had been assembled and these were in the process of being handled by the Garrard changer. The quality of reproduction was excellent but Charlie was oblivious to the sound of music. The magic of the machinery fascinated him. He took his cup of tea from Mum without looking away from the revolving turntable. Nobody dared to speak.

At length when the automatic mechanism had played the last record of the stack and switched itself off, Charlie grunted satisfaction.

Edgar took the opportunity to urge forward the selling process. 'Now allow me to show you the remote control,' he ventured. Charlie nodded assent, having no idea what was yet to come. The remote control unit fitted neatly into the front of the cabinet and could be used *in situ*. However, by extracting it from its nacelle it could be carried to an adjacent chair where the occupant could change stations by pressing one of the row of selection buttons. A volume control knob was included in the unit so that adjustments could be made from the armchair of both radio and record reproduction.

The Murphy remote control must not be compared with modern electronic systems for it remained connected to the parent by an umbilical cable. This cable was very special. It was flat, being composed of numerous thin and flexible rubber-insulated wires moulded together side by side. It was a potential source of trouble and must be handled with care.

However, for the present it served our purpose well. Mum was tickled pink with the idea. She still thought the set too big for the room but she made no attempt to deter Charlie from taking down from the top shelf an old Carr's

biscuit tin. From that he extracted an untidy mass of £1 notes. He counted out
forty of them and stopped, then handed them to my boss saying: 'Any discount
for cash?'

'No,' said Edgar, very firmly. 'The cash price is £80. Of course, if you want it
on Hire Purchase I can arrange it.'

'There'll be none o' that in this 'ouse so long as I'm alive! 'Ave another cup
tea, Mr Bennett?'

'I will that, thank you.'

'. . . and you, young man?'

The old lady reloaded all the cups and returned to her chair to change stations
by remote control.

'Eeh, I think this is a grand idea.'

'I'll gie yer 'arf now and tuther 'arf Sat'day,' Charlie offered.

'You'll do nawt o't sort,' Mum interposed, 'pay Mr Bennett now and 'ave
done wi' it.'

'Aye, s'pose I awt.' Charlie unfolded more £1 notes, slowly counted another
forty, handed them over and returned the tin to its storage place.

The deal was done. Edgar stuffed the notes into his pockets, made out a
receipt and thanked the customer for the business. The good salesman that
Edgar was, it followed that he extended the interview in order to avoid the
cardinal sin of leaving the impression that only money mattered. He asked
Charlie if there were any queries regarding the operation of the Murphy.

'Aye, about this thing on t'chair arm. 'Ow do t'cable go back in t'cabinet?'

'Oh, of course,' said Edgar, relieved to have some positive end to the happy
meeting. 'I should have mentioned that. It's very easy. You see the cable is
wound on a spring-loaded drum so you can pull it out against the force of the
spring and a brake locks the drum as soon as you stop pulling. Now to return it
you release the brake by pulling this little lever towards you. Just hold the
control unit while you do so and it will follow the cable back into the cabinet.'

Mum watched the operation with great interest. The remote control captivated her imagination. She joined the action:

'I'll see if I can do that,' she said as she grasped the control unit and yanked
it out to the full extent of the expensive cable.

Mrs Meakin was no weakling. The strength of the spring did not handicap her
traction. Fully extended, the cable was seen to snatch to a stop, jerk the control
unit out of Mum's hand and what happened next, happened in a flash.

Designed to be used in accord with guidelines laid down in the instruction
book, the machinery revolted against Mum's excessive pressure. The brake
jammed 'off'. The spring took command; with whiplash vehemence the cable
took the control unit hurtling to a sickening crash against the cabinet, scattering
cups, saucers and hot tea indiscriminately over furniture and persons.

Charlie's sole concern directed itself to the possible damage to the radiogram. After all, he had just separated himself from £80 and already rued not

sticking to his resolve to pay 'arf now and rest on Sat'day. Edgar assured him that any damage would be attended to 'under guarantee'.

Mum became mildly emotional in suggesting it was all her fault for being kackhanded. She thought Edgar's new shirt would 'wash out all right'. Edgar agreed and trusted that Mum's tablecloth would likewise survive.

The hot tea running down my own trouser legs was of no concern to anybody but myself. It occurred to me that the firm's insurance company might consider buying me a new pair.

Fortuitously, the BBC continued to provide soothing music via the Murphy during and after the excitement. It allowed a cooling-off period. There was no virtue in crying over spilt tea so all hands assisted in tidying up the premises.

Finally, British humour reigned supreme. We all had a good laugh. Edgar assured Charlie once again and felt that the superficial scratches to the rosewood veneer would polish into invisibility in course of time.

Tea-stained but cash-in-hand 'Your Murphy Dealer' and his service engineer watched the net curtains close as the van passed along the street.

Chapter 20

Three-Wheeling

As a dedicated optimist I scorned warmongering.

The Spanish Civil War was for Spaniards. Franco was a pompous little chap who must succumb to the wishes of the common people, especially as God was on their side.

Hitler made a lot of noise but we had our Prime Minister's word about the future: 'Peace in our time.'

I was on £4 per week at Bennett's, going steady with Lilian in Hereford and life insurance paid up to date. It was time I provided more comfortable travelling facilities for the light of my life. To the Scott I fitted a side-car.

My future mother-in-law had viewed with apprehension the sight of her only daughter setting off a-pillion. She considered a side-car outfit to be the essence of safety and gave permission on first asking for Lilian to accompany me on a tour of Scotland. It was Easter 1939. We took a week's holiday and £10 in cash between us to cover costs.

The first night of the journey north we stayed at Thirsk, taking advantage of free board and lodging at the home of my parents. By the time we crossed the border on Day 2, we had spent less than £1 in covering 400 miles.

At Ardlui we booked in for bed and breakfast at the Stationmaster's bungalow at five shillings per person per night. Lilian's bedroom was so close to the railway lines that two rows of potatoes were all that separated lines from bungalow. I opted for a camp bed in the parlour.

Readers born to the present period of popular promiscuity may raise eyebrows and questions why my beloved and I did not share a bed. Conditions laid down by our elders prohibited such comforts. The subject of sex was taboo in school and home. We were obliged to sort ourselves out from the confusions of hearsay. It was quite clear that if anything 'happened' we would have to face the consequences. Many of us had no idea what was supposed to 'happen' but disgrace must surely befall the whole family in the event.

Owing to the Stationmaster's absence upon another duty down the line, the Stationmaster's wife must attend to the business of running the station. Therefore, it was suggested that we should take our evening meal at the Ardlui Hotel across the road. Therein we ventured. The ambience implied upper class living.

The leather clad menu lay unopened on the table of the entrance hall. It remained in that position, for I would not have dared to indicate the unsuitability of the chef's offerings for fear of causing offence. There remained yet another hour to lighting-up time. Could we have late tea?

A prim waitress ushered us into the capacious dining room, tables set in splendid fashion. We drifted towards the large window through which we had a wonderful view down a becalmed Loch Lomond, its waters reflecting pictures of heather-clad mountains and pines.

'Would ye care for the afternoon tea with Scotch cakes? It's guid value at half-a-croon.' Our friendly young attendant was rallying to the occasion.

After all it was rare for the crew of a sidecar outfit to book in at the Stationmaster's bungalow, yet seek nourishment in a first-class hotel. Undoubtedly, our arrival had been monitored and our financial status analysed.

We trusted our appetites might be allayed if not satisfied. We need not have worried:

Within minutes our fairy godmother set down fine bone china and an extensive selection of shortcakes, scones, oatcakes, confections and, for starters, a plate of smoked salmon rolls. As Lilian poured the tea I unfurled the bill which the waitress had placed in its own silver serviette ring; it confirmed a total charge of five shillings.

It would have been impossible to clear the table but it must be admitted that a few extras were slipped into the inevitable handbag, for our late evening consumption.

Over the years we have feasted in hotels and restaurants in many countries. Foremost in our memories dwells 'tea at Ardlui'.

Whilst we regaled ourselves in stately surroundings the pace of Ardlui was temporarily disturbed by the steamy noises of the train which halted a wee while at the station. One passenger alighted. It was the Stationmaster. The last train of the day puffed on its way to Glasgow, the birds resumed their chirrupings. Ardlui resumed its normal tranquillity. A sixpenny tip supplemented our settlement of account. Profuse thanks having been dispensed on both sides we stepped guiltily on our way, shortbreads in handbag.

The tip of Ben Lomond retained a glimmer from the setting sun as we walked off the effects of our indulgence. The evening's entertainment rounded off in pleasant chatter with Stationmaster and his spouse. We learned a lot about how to make ends meet on parsimonious salary levels fixed by the railway companies and of the inner workings of the railway system.

One important piece of information was overlooked: the possibility of a train passing through Ardlui during the night. We fell in with the household practice of retiring early and slept like logs until approximately 2.00 a.m.

It was around that time I was awakened by a faint whistle. It broke the silence of the night from the direction of Glasgow.

Was this the original Ghost Train reincarnated?

The longest goods train in Scotland went by, slowly puffing and hissing and clonkety-clonking. Maybe my beloved in the adjacent room had been too heavily sedated by the Scottish ozone to be awakened. The walls trembled until the dreaded monster drew level with us whereupon the whole bungalow appeared to bounce. No screams could be heard above the thunderous thumps of metal wheels thudding into joints of rails. I started counting in pairs of pairs of thumps and by that simple method totalled sixty-five trucks had passed before the din changed to the diminuendo of retreat. The comfort of knowing the ordeal was over lingered on to be enjoyed the more the train distanced itself from the village. When at last it whistled its entrance to Glen Falloch the episode was ended.

Early morning tea, included in the price, was delivered in person by the Stationmaster's wife who apologised for neglect to warn us about the train:

'We never notice it, so we forget to tell our guests.'

Lilian had been as 'terrified' as in a thunderstorm at night. The appropriate avoiding action of diving under the blankets had mollified the shock.

By way of compensation, an enormous Scottish breakfast put us in a good frame of mind to continue our tour. Ardlui still ranks high in our list of 'favourite places'.

We were in no hurry to go anywhere. We examined the Bridge of Orchy, loitered by Loch Tulla and some unpronounceable ones as well, before entering the Pass of Glencoe. The busy buzz from the exhaust pipe of the Scott amplified itself time and again in echoes from the mountain sides. We stopped to admire the grandeur.

Once the echoes had died, the silence on that still and clear day, uncannily prompted us to restart the engine and scuttle off to reconnect with civilisation.

At the Ballachulish Ferry we renewed the art of conversation with our fellow men, introduced ourselves to Loch Linnhe and wondered at the tonnage of the vessels destined to be squeezed through the Caledonian Canal.

What with Ben Nevis to stare at and the tweeds in the shops to glare at, Fort William demanded attention. We dared not stay long for there was talk of Nessie having shown a leg by night if not by day. Our principal objective of the tour was to prove or disprove the existence of the monster. So onward we motored through the glorious scenery.

I choose not to bore readers with the impossible task of describing scenery. For those with stomach for such I recommend the Waverley Novels of Sir Walter Scott. We took a few photographs with the aid of my Kodak box camera, capturing some of the beauty and several quite astonishingly convincing pieces of evidence of Nessie in action.

Half a mile beyond Drumnadrochit we espied a tweedy character drawing on a huge meerschaum. He told us not to make a noise.

'That damned motor-bike of yours has just sent Nessie a-scudding. See the wash?' We did, by Gum, we did. 'What a shame,' he continued, 'got rid o' those interfering press people yesterday. She can't stand cameras clickin' away. No good; you've got to respect Nessie's rules. She'll not come up again the nicht.'

We apologised for the disturbance.

'Not your fault,' he said, 'That damned motor-bike.'

'It is a Scott,' I hazarded a pun.

'It's a damned motor-bike,' he persisted, 'Makes no matter. Ye'll no see Nessie the nicht.'

'Will she come up tomorrow morning, do you think?'

'With a smile on her lips and a tear in her eye.' That was all he said, so we left him to his sorrow.

We nipped back into Drumnadrochit, failed to find suitable accommodation and resolved to go on to Inverness. Our pipe-smoking friend had left his perch but about two miles along the road near Balchraggan we saw tell-tale puffs of smoke. We had seen no sign of a cycle by which he could have transported himself so quickly to his new vantage point. He did have a most elaborate walking stick with a built-in pouch below the handle. We assumed it housed a good supply of tobacco. Maybe it contained secret potions in aid of rapid walking. The fact was that he had moved mighty fast. His response was not unfriendly to our salute. Maybe we imagined his mouthing '. . . those damned motor-bikes.'

We booked in for a couple of nights at an address recommended by a member of the Inverness Police Force. Our landlady was not only a District Nurse but also a very good cook. The haddock had arrived by the evening fleet. Oven-cooked and delicately spiced, it lay temptingly surrounded by mushrooms which had been given 'just a wee touch of the malt' to bring out the flavour, and what a flavour . . . the creamed potatoes looked like snow and to crown the glory we completed the menu with my favourite . . . treacle pudd'.

The District Nurse could make coffee too. Her mother had been 'in service' and passed on the tricks. Talk over coffee came round to Nessie. There had been an unusual number of sightings in good time for the tourist season. Our pipe-smoking confidant was well known, was not Scottish but had come up to retire by the Loch. It was rumoured that his wife had been killed in an accident involving a motor-bike. The 'press' could not report further.

It was recommended that we should be at the Lochside not later than nine o' the clock. District Nursing called for an early start so after a trainless night's sleep we were up, had partaken of a handsome, 'full' breakfast to 'put us on our way' and were on the road by 8.30.

The Scott was placidly driven that morning, parked discreetly by the side of the narrow lane leading to Abriachan and then we walked. Scarcely a ripple fluttered on the Loch. We scanned the surface as we ambled along and had covered a mile when Lilian said: 'Look – smoke.'

Sure enough, a hundred yards away a pale blue whiff floated out towards Tom Bailgeann. We trod most quietly but the tweedy gentleman had sensed our arrival.

'I heard that damned motor-bike, you know. Sounds like a swarm of bees, but far enough away not to upset Nessie, I think.'

'Have you seen her?' Lilian whispered.

'Half-past six you should have been here,' he said.

'Do you think she'll come up again?'

'Not today,' he said, 'The cows are out. Hamish has let his damned cows out. Nessie can't stand cows; they moo too much. Cows and motor-bikes!' He re-lit the meerschaum, taking the tobacco from a pouch which resembled a lady's handbag. He put the pouch in his poaching jacket.

He said; 'Not today. Take care on the road.'

> We wandered and wondered all day:
> I cannot tell how the truth may be;
> I say the tale as 'twas said to me.

We turned south-east next morning, well 'put on our way' by virtue of a wholesome Scottish breakfast: porridge and outsize kippers. The District Nurse refused to take more than £1 for the two nights and we refused to argue. Next stop: Grantown-on-Spey in its setting so beautiful that my visual memory recalls the picture on the asking; on to Britain's highest town we went. Blowing more than a fair breeze here. We understood 'Ye Highland Whisky Store' to have on demand every known brand of whisky. This trivial information was recorded for future reference. Years later I was in a position to sample its wares on more than one occasion.

Through the Lecht Pass, then cruising down to see Balmoral Castle. This was all thrilling stuff for us on our initiation to international tourism. Rivers danced in all directions; difficult to distinguish Dee from Don; what was the difference between Burn and Brook, Bank and Brae? – and how many Burns make a Water? Glen Ey had Ey Burn but Glen Shee had Shee Water. All very puzzling, these Scottish terms, but maybe conditions are stabilising. What could it have been like when Sir Walter wrote:

> Your mountains shall bend,
> And your streams ascend . . .?

We determined to pay our respects at the monument to the great man. *En route* to Edinburgh the roads passed through pleasant enough country but we did miss the excitement of mountain scenery. The ferry crossing of the Firth of Forth afforded greatest wonder of the day by virtue of the spectacle of a passenger train rumbling across the river on the famous cantilever bridge.

Haggis appeared on the menu of the Guest House we chose for accommodation that night. We tried it, thought it less than appetising and vowed to avoid it in the future. There was much to see in Edinburgh. With guide book in hand we covered a lot of footpaths, but the mountains were calling.

From Scotland by Scott we moved to the foot of Helvellyn for our last night stop on the way home.

The Scott and sidecar served for only a few more weeks before they were separated. A good friend asked if he might borrow the outfit to transport himself and wife to Blackpool for the Whitsun holiday. He willingly took out a 28-days insurance policy for the occasion.

Stanley had not handled a sidecar outfit so I took him for a run to teach the special technique of steering one-handed. For a beginner it is most advisable to regard the right-hand handlebar as the rudder of a skiff. If both hands are used there is a strong tendency to oversteer and run out of road. Stan soon got the hang of it. Our test run finished with myself in the chair feeling very happy at being driven.

I was busy in my workshop the following morning when the 'phone rang. The caller was Stan, full of regrets: he'd forgotten the right-hand rule. The hedge had softened the blow but the outfit was in the ditch.

Within twenty minutes I was at the scene accompanied by an able mechanic friend. Both rider and passenger had suffered innumerable scratches but were in good spirits, thanks largely to the occupants of a nearby cottage who were accomplished in First-Aid. It had not been at all difficult to get Mrs Stanley out of the sidecar; it had disintegrated on contact with the hedge.

We hauled the wreckage out of the ditch. My colleague took one look at it and said:

'Ah well. You wanted a new radiator, didn't you?'

Before I could say 'Jack Robinson' he had severely dented the device with the aid of a hefty spanner. That was my first experience of seeing how insurance companies are swindled out of millions of pounds.

I was delighted with the result. The old Scott looked very smart with a new rad. I rode it solo until it gave up the ghost just a week before the outbreak of war.

The traffic lights were at 'red' in Sheffield. I waited for the 'green' with engine ticking over when without warning a loud knock from the crankcase region signalled a serious defect. However, the engine kept running and I drove gingerly onward to complete sixty miles of my journey to Thirsk. I made it. Just inside the garden gate a final crack told me the worst.

An admirable feature of the Scott design was the detachability of doors to the crankcase. I know of no other engine whereby examination of the big-end bearings could be made in a matter of minutes. By undoing one nut and removing a retaining bar on either side of the twin cylinder engine the vital parts were on view. The port-side crank of my old engine had sheared. My good and faithful servant had limped home for the last time. I sold it for scrap and put the money towards an engagement ring for Lilian.

A week later Neville Chamberlain cancelled his 'Peace in our time' forecast and announced: 'We are at war with Germany!'

Chapter 21

To War and to Wed

The Sunday morning was so bright and sunny that even the grim slag tips of Swadlincote sparkled. As the aged passer-by pulled his cap over his eyes to shield them from the sun he said:

'Well, it's the best thing that cudd 'appen. It'll all be over in three month, you see.'

'Do you think so?' I asked, quite seriously.

'Well, aye. Naught but a windbag, that 'itler fella. Burn 'imsel' out, you see. Won't last three month.'

That was my warning. If I didn't join up quickly it would all be over without my assistance.

The local paper of the following afternoon included an announcement which appeared to be my opportunity:

'North Staffordshire Regiment to form Anti-Aircraft Unit. Apply: Recruiting Office, Tutbury.'

I informed the boss of my urge to get the war effort moving. He granted permission for me to borrow the van and with minimum delay I was in Tutbury. I presented myself before what I took to be a Sergeant-Major.

'Sorry, lad,' he said. 'Sold out only ten minutes ago; all two hundred places gone.'

Until I purchased my weekly copy of *Motor Cycling* on the Wednesday, I had no clear idea what to do. Therein, Editor Graham Walker described a scheme ideally suited to my needs. Owners of motor-cycles were required to serve with their own machines as Despatch Riders in the Royal Corps of Signals. The application form was posted off that very evening. All I needed was a motor-bike.

By very good fortune a colleague on the staff of E.G. Bennett, 'Your Murphy Dealer', was on first-name terms with a local car dealer who hated motor-bikes. This man was temporarily embarrassed by having been obliged to take a motor-bike in part-exchange from a valued client. He wanted it off his premises quickly. Hence, I acquired a 350 c.c. Royal Enfield Bullet with only fifteen hundred miles on the clock at the knock down price of £20. I couldn't wait to join the RCS.

Meanwhile, the reparation of radio sets occupied the members of the service department of E.G. Bennett. When the air raid warning sounded we opened the windows and scanned the skies over Station Street in the hope of taking our first sight of enemy bombers. False alarm. Someone had inadvertently pressed the panic button.

Two weeks passed before I received notification that my application had been received. I was required to keep my motor-cycle in good trim and await further instructions.

Even though I was likely to be called to the colours at two-shillings-a-day Lilian agreed to my proposal of marriage. I found rooms to let in a new house at ten shillings per week, the owner being hard pressed to meet his mortgage commitment.

War-time rules forbade a white wedding. Thus I was saved considerable expense. My in-laws-to-be could manage only a token endowment. By whisking away their daughter I was depriving them not only of a tangible asset but also of a substantial portion of their weekly income.

I accepted the responsibility of providing a wedding feast, this also under government control. Sixteen persons in total were to be provided with a satisfying repast, by the proprietors of the Hereford Booth Hall, at a cost of £4 including a service charge.

The date was fixed for 30 October. It seemed inappropriate to turn up for my wedding on the Bullet and transport my bride by pillion. I made arrangements, therefore, to take an early morning train from Burton and had every intention of retiring in good time on the evening of the 29th. Purely as a matter of courtesy I accepted the invitation to join a few friends for a celebratory drink at the Constitutional Club, an establishment reputed to have first call on the best of Burton's principal product.

I was inexperienced in the art of drinking. Up to the time I entered the club on the evening of the 29th, my indulgence had never gone beyond the odd half-pint of shandy except on the very special occasion, shortly after my arrival in Burton, when I was taken on a conducted tour of the Bass brewery. Not only did I learn that the various buildings were served by seventeen miles of railway lines on which delightful little engines shunted fussily, collecting and delivering trucks and wagons, but we watched the coopers at work and stared in awe at the operational complexities of the bottling machinery. We sampled the beers.

For the duration of the tour I had been adopted by a team of rugby players from Birmingham. It had never occurred to me that beer-swilling could become a competitive sport in itself. Those boys taught me a lot.

Our guide's knowledge of the trade and of the geography of the site was profound. He had joined the firm after leaving school and ascended through the ranks. At something like retirement age he was a walking advertisement for Bass, his colourful features bearing ready testimony to its excellence. His working day consisted of two guided tours; his daily consumption was seventeen pints. The members of the Birmingham rugby team were hard pressed in trying to emulate his habit. Whilst my own intake was limited to sampling in small quantities, by the time we had completed the rounds I became less and less aware of what our guide was telling us. I came to the conclusion that beer was not my drink.

Hence, when called to the bar at the Con-club on the 29th and being invited to partake of a pint I declined politely and scanned the shelves with the aim of selecting a modest alternative. I chose Barley Wine. It sounded more genteel. I noticed how carefully the expert barman handled the bottle. With loving care he poured the rich, golden liquid into a goblet. When this process reached completion he raised the glass to the light, nodded satisfaction with his work and passed the vessel to me, very gently in order not to disturb the thin creamy froth. It looked good; I took a sip; it tasted good. Barley Wine would be my drink. It was not to be rushed; it must be savoured.

At the pouring of a second bottle I examined the label more closely. It read: 'Bass No. 1'.

I had chosen the best of Bass. An unprecedented warmth spread through my body. I radiated a new bonhomie over my fellow-men. One more Bass No. 1, before I set out towards a promising future, overflowing with goodness. My friends congratulated me yet again on my forthcoming marriage, wished me Good Luck and Goodnight at the steps of the Con-club.

Light of foot, I aimed to find the bus station. Five minutes later I was back at the steps of the Con-club. Burton-on-Trent seemed to have changed its shape in the black-out. My friends put me on the bus for Woodville and the conductor was kind enough to drop me off outside my digs. I had not noticed that one of the other passengers was my landlady's grand-daughter. That young lady reported to Grannie that I had entertained my fellow travellers by singing songs throughout the four-mile journey. Of that I remembered nothing, nor of the night through which I slept like the proverbial log. I woke up fortified against any pending problems and caught an early train to Hereford and wedlock.

A surprising number of friends and relations assembled at St. James's Church. Train timetables were yet to be seriously upset by bombs or the business of war.

My mother and sister had arrived from Yorkshire leaving father at home charging his batteries and caring for his beloved fire-engines. I got me to the church on time.

Lilian looked more enchanting than ever in a new blue outfit which must have strained the family resources to the limit. My Montague Burton suit, in a similar shade of blue, at £4 made-to-measure was representative of their upper price range. The pair of us were starting out fairly well dressed to face new ventures.

As we stood hand in hand before the altar the seriousness of the situation suddenly became apparent. All those nice people with whom I had been joking and chatting gaily were now sitting in the pews behind me watching out for any mistakes. It was they who worried, not I.

Edgar Bennett had said that at the age of twenty-five I couldn't know my own mind. Yet here I was publicly about to declare that I did. Lilian was only twenty-one; did she know her mind? We hadn't questioned one another on the subject, yet here we were standing before witnesses. No man had 'known cause, or just impediment' and I couldn't think of anything. Not only were friends and relations watching; the parson said 'we are gathered together here in the sight of God . . .' I must pay more attention.

'I require and charge you both, as ye will answer at the dreadful day of judgement when the secrets of all hearts shall be disclosed . . .' Well, there had been other girl friends but none of them could ride pillion as well as Lilian. Surely nobody was going to show 'any impediment' at this stage of events . . . 'Wilt thou have this Woman . . .?' Well, that's the whole idea of being here, really and Lilian isn't a Woman, she's a lovely girl. Yes, I would. Would she have 'this Man?' I hope she'll say Yes after all this performance . . . 'Wilt thou obey him, and serve him . . .?' It is getting very serious indeed; she would. 'Who giveth this Woman to be married to this Man?' Good old Dad – he wouldn't let me down . . . What about the ring – has Kenneth got the ring? My friend had never let me down yet. Not yet. First we hold hands and 'say after me . . .' '. . . have and to hold from this day forward . . .' I liked that phrase. '. . . to love and to cherish, till death us do part . . .' Remember I've promised to join the Royal Corps of Signals . . . The ring – Oh, good, he's got it. '. . . I thee worship, and with all my worldly goods I thee endow . . .' not much, my love but I am serious. 'Let us pray.'

At that point the vicar did a 180° turn to face the altar. He sank to his knees, his feet pushing his skirts aside. He'd been gardening. His shoes were filthy and one sole was worn right through – and the sock. His bare foot looked ever so clean in its frame of damp leather. I squeezed Lilian's hand; she squeezed mine. We were wed in Holy Matrimony. Together we had seen the light and would never forget.

The minister next spake unto the people, telling them what had been witnessed.

Finally we were blessed, reminded of our duties according to the Scriptures and called upon to sign the register.

The vicar shook hands cursorily at the vestry door, thereafter disappearing within to divest himself prior to rushing back to his gardening.

A reporter from the *Hereford Times* took notes. The photographer took pictures which, in due course 'came out very well'. Whenever we see ourselves as recorded in the family album, we wonder if our smiles are responding to the cameraman's request for 'cheese' or to the recollection of a pair of mucky shoes protruding from out the canonicals.

The wedding reception exceeded all expectations in merriment, liberal dispensation of Bulmer's Pomagne on empty stomachs being a contributory factor. I hoped that would not come as an 'extra' to the account, but the best man assured me that an anonymous benefactor had supplemented the funds. I had no need to worry. Everybody said Pomagne was every bit as good as Champagne. Never having sampled either I was unable to judge. One thing I did know was that compared to Barley Wine it was quite disagreeable. Ample supplies of fish-paste sandwiches, fairy cakes and Chelsea buns satisfied appetites, ensuring that a minute portion of wedding cake was enough to befittingly terminate the feasting.

At the railway station everybody was talking at once, bubbling over with Pomagne. Some thoughtful person stuck a 'Reserved' label on a compartment and we were moving off to our new life together. The last words, distinguishable from the confusion of voices, I thought to be in bad taste in the presence of ladies: 'If you can't be lucky, be careful!'

Quite untutored in the important obligation in life, oblivious to all possible hazards, that railway compartment was our refuge as far as Birmingham. From Snow Hill we handled our considerable baggage through the churchyard to New Street station. We could not expect to get, nor did we enjoy, a reserved compartment on the next stage of our journey to Burton. As things worked out it was to be many years before we found such splendid privacy as we experienced between Hereford and Birmingham.

The novelty of settling into 'rooms' was our honeymoon. The first night in bed was, naturally enough, the highlight of the exercise. Our bed had been 'prepared' by friends who were well-enough acquainted with our landlords to gain access to our quarters. After detection of such causes of discomfort as combs and hair brushes, we considered it wise to strip the bed and remake it. Countless items of cutlery and crockery were removed before we could establish ourselves in blissful luxury.

Subsequent activities were not entirely to our satisfaction. As novices in the art of love-making we began to consider that we should have taken some advice before marriage, or even done a few dummy runs in contravention of the families' ethics. Finally, tired out after the exciting events of the day, we fell asleep, consoling ourselves that improvements would come in time.

Our first day in residence being Sunday we set about arranging our apartments to our liking, bearing in mind that the principal items of furniture belonged to the Archers, owners of the house and co-residents therein. We displayed proudly our collection of pictures, glassware and ancillaries, some of which were wedding presents and some from the traditional 'bottom drawer'.

The time passed rapidly because of our activity being interrupted by well-wishing friends who called to offer help and advice. Everything in the new-fangled way of life appeared rosy. Our Sunday dinner was prepared jointly by my bride in close co-operation with Mrs Archer. In anticipation of a regular ten-bob a week towards the mortgage payments she made a great effort to be polite and agreeable in the sharing of kitchen facilities. It struck me that her pleasing demeanour was not spontaneous.

Culinary discord sounded its first alarm on the second day of our tenancy. I had returned to my service work at 'Your Murphy Dealer', trusting that my darling wife would have enjoyed a day of total independence. She had indeed occupied herself, during the morning, in letter-writing. It was over the procedure of preparing for a modest lunch that certain regulations would be laid down for the most economical use of the electric cooker, a miniature device which had been installed at an inconveniently low level near the kitchen floor. It was suggested that notice be given whenever cooking was to be undertaken so that joint use of the valuable heat might be made in the interests of the national economy. The kitchen was not designed to accommodate more than two people in standing position. If one of the two adopted a crouching posture, in order to make possible the visual examination of contents of the cooker, then the second person must be incommoded to the extent of desisting from lateral movement until the examination was completed. Should both cooks decide it was necessary to conduct a joint examination of the doings inside the cooker, then the situation became ripe for differences in temperament to erupt.

My Lilian operated on a short fuse. She had blown. So when I arrived home, my reception lacked something in joviality. Communication with the kitchen was out of the question until such time as the air might clear. Thoughts of a hot and tasty meal conjured up dreams of fish and chips, but it was Monday, traditionally a no-frying night.

We made do with beans on toast cooked on the open fire. The fireplace was of the modern tiled type which disposed of most of the heat up the flue. However, we were blessed with a good supply of Derbyshire 'Brights' in our own coal bunker. Toast done over a glowing coal fire is far superior, both in taste and appearance, to any which pops out of an electric rack. We enjoyed that meal and settled back in our cosy room determined to make ourselves comfortable for at least a few weeks before I was called to military duty.

The weeks dragged on into months. The war seemed to be confined to actions at sea. Food became scarce and petrol was rationed. I used the Bullet sparingly but whenever I could persuade the local petrol station proprietor to let me have an extra gallon we would take a weekend trip to Hereford. That helped Lilian over her spasms of homesickness. Meanwhile the winter turned exceptionally cold and after Christmas it became colder than that. Road conditions throughout January were sometimes quite hazardous in daytime and after dark almost impossible.

News filtered through from France of the death of a volunteer motor-cyclist on the icy roads. Meantime I still heard nothing from the RCS. What is more, business was becoming difficult for E.G. Bennett, 'Your Murphy Dealer'. Murphy Radio Ltd. was called upon to switch production facilities to military requirements. Dealers were surviving on service work alone. I became anxious to join the fighting forces. I heard from my old friend Len Gunn, ex-manager of the shoe shop next door, who was already established in the army complete with his 500 c.c. Rudge. His first assignment with the Royal Ordnance Corps, following his initial training course at Harrogate, was to escort a convoy of a dozen or so vehicles on a cross-country route. Len mis-read his map and succeeded in conducting his charges into a vicarage garden. It took more than an hour to get the convoy back on the road by which time, it appears, the poor vicar's lawn was churned to mud and his ecclesiastic dignity sorely corrupted. I became conscious of a feeling of guilt.

One evening at the conclusion of work I offered a lift on the pillion to a young assistant. The four mile journey was achieved with extreme difficulty in about half an hour. Rain had fallen during the afternoon, then the moon came up to a clear sky, the temperature dropped and the roads were converted into perfect ice rinks. Arthur's weight over the rear wheel improved the bite of the tyre and with careful use of throttle we were clear of the town and over Trent Bridge before the fun began. The extra touch of power required to climb away from the river was not acceptable. The rear tyre spun, down we went and found it extremely difficult to get up again. We sought some grip in the roadside gravel and reinstated our dignity. I steered along the gutter, thus making some progress homeward before a cyclist emerged from a side turning. Evasive action was necessary. The change in direction caused loss of front wheel adhesion. Down we came again and so did the cyclist. Now the three of us couldn't remount. The situation took on the semblance of a variety act. A kindly pedestrian joined in. He tried to aid the cyclist to his feet but he went down. Wholehearted laughter brought several householders to our assistance but they too were taken by surprise. They had not realised that ice had formed so precipitately around their homes. The more people came to our aid the more people slipped and fell.

The guy with the bicycle brought the party to renewed paroxysms. When he put his left foot on the pedal in the orthodox manner of mounting, the back wheel flew, frictionless, out of control. Bike and man went down again slithering into the gutter.

Grim determination got Arthur and me to our destinations. By releasing pressure from both tyres a trifle more tractability enabled us to complete the last couple of miles with no more than a few involuntary dismountings.

When, at length, I parked the Bullet in the garage at the end of the road my thoughts turned to my lovely wife who would be worried sick because of my unpunctuality. I was somewhat bruised and even shaky after the ordeal of the past half-hour. I relished the thoughts of a welcoming kiss, a blazing fire and a hot meal cooked on the open fire.

As I approached the house I was horrified to note that the black-out curtains were improperly closed. A chink of light was more than enough to attract the attention of an Air Raid Warden, if not of a German bomber. I hastened my step, gave three sharp raps on the window, that being my customary signal of the arrival of the bread-winner and rounded the corner to the front porch. There she was. Huddled, frozen and soaked in tears, the light of my life was near extinction. She had drawn the curtains and nipped outside to check upon the efficiency or otherwise of the 'black-outness'. The door had slammed shut. Mrs Archer was enjoying her weekly visit to her mother-in-law. What was a girl to do but cry?

As luck would have it, my own key was in my pocket and we entered the unhappy home. A further disaster caught my eye immediately on entry to our parlour. Just prior to stepping out to examine the black-out, my enthusiastic housekeeper had placed a pair of choice steaks in the frying-pan on the open grate. They were to be done to a turn in time for my home-coming. They were done to several turns and looked like knobs of Derbyshire Brights. The pan itself had undergone a change of shape.

Some gentle massage and numerous cuddles slowly restored circulation to my cold, cold wife. Through the sobs I recognised a serious inquisition:

'Where have you been? – Why are you so late? – The door slammed. – Can we go home this weekend?'

I promised a trip to Hereford. She could stay as long as she liked. She didn't want to stay away – just a few days. Gradually normal communication was renewed, sobbing subsided and she said:

'Oh, by the way – on the BBC they announced a new trade in the RAF. They want volunteer Radio Mechanics at five-and-six a day, plus marriage allowance!'

That sounded as a fortune compared with two-bob a day in the Royal Corps of Signals. I resolved to apply.

A week later I was at Hanley recruiting office where I met the son of a local doctor who was named, appropriately, Sparks. We were given a simple trade test by a Warrant Officer who wrote adeptly upside-down, a skill which I practised and found very useful when later I found myself administering trade tests.

The test used on that occasion was a hoary old puzzler: 'Draw the circuit of a full-wave rectifier.' Though it may be quite simple, an examinee under pressure can find himself in quite a tangle over it. It appeared that anyone who could succeed in this basic exercise was a candidate for the position of Leading Aircraftman (Radio Mechanic). Sparky and I satisfied the examiner who then chatted freely with us on his life in the Royal Air Force.

Above the office was an Army Recruiting Centre. Whilst we sat talking, several volunteers looked in with a view to joining the RAF. Any likely looking lad was received courteously and invited to wait for interview. Any applicant who didn't meet with the Warrant Officer's approval was directed upstairs!

At last I was to join His Majesty's Forces of War. For E.G. Bennett the supply situation made it impossible to continue in business. We parted company the best of friends. Lilian was happy to return to her home in Hereford until further notice.

Chapter 22

'Stand by your Beds'

It was early in March 1940 when I linked up with Sparky at the enormous recruiting station at Cardington. Numerically I was Sparky's senior. Ahead of me by the space of one digit was Sidney, henceforward known as El Cid. We formed a musketeer-like alliance during our first few weeks of service. We were determined that nothing would get us down. It turned out to be a very useful maxim. Consultation before commitment helped us over several hurdles and brought many benefits.

Our trio was easily distinguishable in the throng. Sparky may not have been as lofty as my six-foot-one-and-a-half but he had a wonderful head of ginger hair. El Cid shuffled along at about five-foot-five topped by an unruly mop of blond curls. RAF stores never found a suit to fit him. No matter how we urged El Cid he was always half a step behind and deep in thought.

When it came to queuing, however, it was necessary for El Cid to be pushed forward in case we lost him. Queues proliferated at Cardington. It was always wise to inquire into its purpose whenever one was sighted; otherwise one might miss a treat, such as a buckshee film show or a clandestine boxing match.

Official queues were not to be avoided, of course, and were good for a laugh especially when El Cid was asked for his credentials. Our numbers being sequential, El Cid was first of our gang to answer questions. Unfailingly the first requirement was for name, rank and number, then home address, then: 'Next of kin?' In response 'El Cid' would start: 'Miss E. –'

Clerk: 'Missus?'

El Cid: 'No. Miss. I'm illegitimate.'

An astonished clerk would look up in amazed embarrassment. El Cid would go on with a cheeky smile: 'Haven't you ever seen one before?'

Eating at Cardington was hazardous. Essential tools issued from stores were well described as 'mug and irons'. Armed with these one learned to tackle anything. The first breakfast was an object lesson in the art of balance. First a brown liquid was drawn into the mug from a huge metal container. We were not sure whether the brown colour was due to the stewing of tea leaves or to the heavy content of bromide. It did not taste like what we had known as tea at home but we would get used to it, no doubt.

108

Wading through spilled tea was a preliminary to collecting a plate of porridge which was best placed on top of the mug. The practice had two advantages: it helped to keep the tea warm and the heat from the tea helped to warm the porridge. At that stage it became clear that the irons were best carried in a pocket. That meant freedom for the left hand to collect a plate of sausages and rare-done bacon. The next move was to clear the queue and find a place to sit, not always easy because of the general and indiscriminate traffic passing to and from the garbage bin, which was constantly being topped up for the benefit of the local pig farmer and his pigs.

In the mêlée many an aspiring airman was jogged at the elbow, causing loss of balance, sausages and porridge. The tea was seldom lost in entirety, thanks to the handle of the mug. To avoid such an accident it was vital to look ahead for the purpose of dodging arm-joggers. At the same time it was advisable to look down for fear of paddling through pulps of sausage and porridge.

Sparky, El Cid and I made a practice of travelling the dining-hall floor in triangular formation. Thus we found a pathway ahead being cleared. El Cid looked down while Sparky and I from our greater heights could locate space for three at a table, even a dry space. It was quite revolting to find only table space which carried layers of left-overs. One soon learned to smuggle in a sheet from yesterday's newspaper with which to mop up when necessary. I had prepared my attitude to military life with a view to accepting a culinary standard well below that set by Mother. I must confess I was obliged to stretch my sense of humour beyond its normal limits to see the funny side of mass-eating in the mess, alternatively known as 'mess-eating in mass'. El Cid persisted in the belief that we would 'get used to it'.

Of prime importance in our sojourn at Cardington was the issue of uniforms, one for work and one for 'dress'. There was no difference except that one was to be kept clean and the other must be kept cleaner. Numerous aids to good airmanship came with the uniforms: clothes brush, hairbrush, button-stick and a 'house-wife' or hussif. This last was called into use by us Radio Mechanics immediately. Of an elite class, we spent only one day in the Royal Air Force as common or garden AC2s. That one day of service on the bottom run of the ladder satisfied a certain rule in the extensive Air Ministry Handbook, a tome never to be completed by virtue of an endless stream of amendments.

In view of our promotion on the second day to the rank of Leading Aircraftman we were obliged to bring into use needle and cotton from the hussif. Neat cloth badges depicting a propellor, six in all, were to be sewn on our sleeves, two on each jacket and two on the great-coat. Our embroidering came under the surveillance of lesser mortals who had to remain on the lowest rungs until such time as the powers that be recognised meritorious perform-ance. Some of the regular airmen who passed our way took umbrage at our rapid advancement. That was understandable. On inquiry we were informed that many a Leading Aircraftman had waited ten years to gain that lofty rank. It was not our fault that we found ourselves classed as geniuses but over the next few months we did meet some resentment. To quote El Cid: 'They'll get used to us' . . . and they did.

Life at Cardington was far from boring. Once in uniform we had to be inspected, presumably to satisfy the inspecting officer that we would be presentable to the public. Inspection was no haphazard affair. First we were taught how to get 'fell in' and how to become arranged in more or less a straight line. This was known as being 'on parade', at first a convivial gathering, soon corrected into an exercise in taciturnity, except for the parade commander who might be a Sergeant or Corporal of limited vocabulary but forceful persuasion. It was understood that penalties would follow unwillingness to obey.

A parade was followed by a march to another parade which had a particular purpose. All semblance of privacy was relinquished at the next parade, which the authorities did have the decency to hold indoors. Having achieved a straight line we were ordered to 'Stand Easy'. Even the drill Sergeant relaxed, drifting away to the end of the hall to engage in light-hearted conversation with a colleague. It was at that point we established a system of sub-audio communication. Its success was so remarkable that no drill commander ever twigged. It developed rapidly and spontaneously into a superior type of bush telegraphy which fostered outrageous rumour-mongery.

Information came down the line that the present parade awaited inspection by a medical officer. That seemed unlikely because we could not have been accepted for service unless we had been passed fit for it. Speculation ended when the Sergeant brought himself to attention violently and yelled:

'Attention!'

We followed his example. Then:

'For Medical Officer's inspection: Drop trousers!'

Well, I thought he must be joking, but he wasn't.

'Come on, now: drop 'em.'

Things were getting serious. A rustling of clothing masked the undercurrent of rumour coming down the line.

'We've nothing to lose,' one wag was heard to say. 'Speak for yourself,' said another. 'It's a Vee-Dee check,' said Sparky. 'What's Vee-Dee?' somebody asked. Another thought castration was imminent; somebody fainted.

'Stand easy,' bawled the Sergeant. That made more sense. Dropping trousers whilst standing to attention was difficult. I thought he must have made a mistake in his routine.

The MO strolled along at a discreet distance pausing in front of each man while he summed up whatever he needed to sum up.

'What's he look for?' I whispered to Sparky.

'Spots,' he said.

'I've got spots,' I said, 'born with 'em. You don't think . . .?'

'What colour?' He daren't look.

'Brown, moles I call them.'

'That's all right,' comforted Sparky, 'not to worry. Mine are ginger to match my hair.'

The MO passed along in silence. All clean in our party.

After re-hoisting of pants we were marched off to join another queue, the front of which inched towards the doorway of an unmarked hut. The rumour filtered back down the line: '. . . inoculations . . .!'

Inoculation was confirmed by the first recruit who emerged from a second door, rubbing his upper left arm as he passed us. One by one the recipients of whatever was being injected came out of the building registering pain or indifference. One chap grimaced and voiced the warning:

'Avoid No. 2. There's a hook on the end of his needle.'

Somebody fainted. It was the same chap who had succumbed to the threat of castration; a big well-built fellow he was, too.

At the end of a day of strenuous queuing, marching, stating name, rank and number, being issued with this and fitted for that, we repaired to the NAAFI. Here we found dart-boards fully occupied, shove ha'penny slates engaged, cribbage table booked and dominoes all in use. We three musketeers drew a pint of tolerably good beer each and resorted to conversation for our entertainment. A few other freshmen, bearers of 'props' on sleeves, joined us. They were all Radio-Mechanics-to-be and with that much in common we fell to conjecture upon our future.

One bright spark had it all worked out. We would be whisked away secretly within a few hours to a closely guarded RDF station. Our extraordinary skills were required urgently for work of the utmost importance. Not for us the tedium of drills and firearm practice. We were an elite group due for special treatment and should not fraternise with the common mob. I considered him a worthless gasbag, drank up my ale and declared myself ready for bed. Sparky and El Cid followed my example.

Our barrack room was warm and comfortable enough. We turned in to our respective beds and reviewed the day's work. El Cid had secured a corner site, with Sparky between the two of us. My other neighbour arrived a few minutes later, rather the worse for beer. He was a tough-looking customer, the possessor of few teeth and those which he had were blackened by smoke deposits. He announced himself as Bert, hoped we'd be chums for ever more and had we got away with the Vee-Dee test?

Without waiting for a reply Bert launched into an illiterate harangue on the subject of sex, considered it an overrated pastime. A butcher himself, he declared that just as much satisfaction could be had from a lump of fresh liver as from a prostitute, so why go to the expense? I said I would take his word for it and asked him the whereabouts of his butchery. He told us he had entered the RAF as a cook. We trusted we might avoid his kitchen.

The Corporal in charge of our quarters occupied a private room at the end of the building. We were relieved when he called, 'Lights out.' We concluded our day with a prayer for Bert who snored like a pig, but 'we got used to it'. It seemed no time at all before the Corporal shouted: 'Wakey-wakey!'

It is surprising how washing and shaving in cold water jollies one up in the morning. We worked up an appetite for breakfast, laid the foundations with undercooked porridge, topped it off with tinned tomatoes and fried bread and lubricated it with the inevitable bromide tea. Thus, we were prepared for another day of parades and queues. Our stay at Cardington did not last long and when we Radio Mechanics were called to a special meeting we wondered whether the garrulous comrade of the NAAFI would be proved right.

Certainly we were to be moved. We queued at the cookhouse. Each of us received a packed lunch, not to be opened until entrained. Kitbags were loaded into one truck and another truck was loaded with Radio Mechanics. Where now?

We boarded the train at Bedford, bound for Usworth. The craze for secrecy had not yet developed beyond a casual warning not to tell anyone anything. Nobody had heard of Usworth so any pretence of secrecy would have been irrelevant. Lunch packs were opened before we reached York. The Spam sandwiches were acceptable enough but the Lyons fruit pies at twopence apiece were one of the great successes of English provending, stuffed with fruit and attractively presented in decorated packets. (They don't make 'em like that any more.) News filtered through the train that Usworth was an aerodrome near Sunderland and that was where we disembarked.

Jogging along in another Bedford truck we were informed by the driver that Usworth was an Initial Training Centre. Radio Mechanics through and through, we jumped to the conclusion that now our serious war work would begin. We conjured up thoughts of arrays of modern test equipment with cathode ray tubes, direction-finding antennae and at least a look at some aircraft. Our disillusionment spanned several weeks.

Alas! – the aircraft at Usworth were no concern of ours. We entered immediately on an intensive course of drill, PT and Discipline with a capital D. Kitbags were unloaded and collected by individuals under the watchful eye of Sergeant Robertson who quipped over every name on every kitbag. He was a quick mover who imbued us with a necessity to follow his example. We were 'fell-in' complete with kitbags, numbered off, told which huts we were to occupy and given cursory instructions to be followed during the next hour, all at high speed.

The barrack room was spotlessly clean and warm. We three musketeers were fortunate to stay together. El Cid took to himself a corner bed as usual, Sparky and I settled for the same order as at Cardington. The whole company consisted of budding Radio Mechanics. There was no danger of my being lumbered with another sample of a 'Bert'.

We had been allowed a space of time for wash and brush-up for which we were thankful, especially as hot water was available. The meal provided was of excellent quality, served efficiently in a clean dining room. Usworth, it was obvious, must be under the strict supervision of a disciplinarian. It was not long before we met him.

Warrant Officer Dixon, henceforth known as 'Dizzy', had no peer in the craft of ordering men to do as they were told. The Station Commander was a delegator. To Dizzy he delegated full responsibility for discipline and Dizzy gloried in it. Immaculately turned out himself on every occasion, he was quite unable to tolerate the sight of an untidy airman. Whilst Sergeant Robertson and an equally sharp-moving Corporal trained us in parade ground drills and PT the eagle eyes of Dizzy were known to be watching.

We were 'sprogs'. Dizzy hated us. In all the weeks I spent at Usworth I never heard a kind word from him. He struck terror into every rookie who came into his sights. And we all came into his sights on our first evening at Usworth.

The meal had gone down very well. We sauntered back to our huts. It was the last time we sauntered at Usworth. A piercing scream rent the evening air:

'Get your hands out of your pockets, shoulders back and swing your arms!' Dizzy worked all hours.

We were learning fast that life at Usworth would be no picnic. The whole camp was a model of antisepticism. We newcomers were destined to maintain the condition. Our instructions to that end came to us the following morning at a general parade immediately after breakfast. This was Dizzy's party-piece, well rehearsed and delivered in clear, crisp sentences composed of carefully chosen words. He set out his standards which could only be a fanatical interpretation of the Air Ministry book of rules.

First question: 'Any complaints about the food?'

Nobody but an idiot would have stuck his neck out so there were none. In all fairness to the great man he knew the food at Usworth was good because he insisted on excellence in the cookhouse as elsewhere. God help the cooks should they turn out rubbish.

He outlined the leave pass system whereby airmen might visit Sunderland, using the public bus service. Severe penalties would be administered against skivers or unofficial leave takers. Daily Routine Orders were posted at numerous points throughout the camp. It was imperative that all airmen make a habit of reading them before breakfast, understand and obey them.

'I am now going to inspect every one of you.'

He inspected not only face values but rear view to include hair-styles. Enough customers to keep the camp barber busy for an hour were given orders, to be followed by further batches by rota.

Next we were divided into squads by barrack-room number.

'From each hut, I want a volunteer for permanent room orderly.'

I put my hand up!

'What's the matter with you, Lofty? Want to leave the room, do you?'

'No, Sir,' I ventured, 'I was volunteering for room orderly!'

'Well, you don't stick your hand up, son. You are at attention. Now wait for it!' He looked along the lines to make certain all were at ATTENTION, then said:

'One volunteer for room orderly, permanent for each hut . . . Two paces forward – March!'

I stepped smartly forward and was approved. I have made many mistakes but that move was not one of them. Though I had been counselled by an old soldier not to volunteer for anything the idea of looking after my own barrack room appealed to me.

Dizzy explained:

'Each and every airman is responsible for making his own bed, keeping his kit in order and laying it out for inspection in an approved manner. Permanent room orderlies will polish floors, clean windows, maintain stoves in new condition and keep adequate supplies of coal on hand in case it gets cold in the night. The reason is not to make you soft but to be sure nobody reports sick due to catching a chill. Anybody reporting sick must have a very good excuse indeed.'

Permanent room orderlies were dismissed at that point. We marched off with sufficient virility as not to cause Dizzy to criticise our conduct.

I took stock of the hut. It was reasonably clean but I dealt with ashes around the two stoves, topped up the coal hods, swept through and set to work with the 'bumper'. For the uninitiated in the skill of 'bumping' I should describe the tool provided: a very heavy, rectangular block, the under-surface of which is well endowed with stiff bristles. It may be thought of as a giant shoe-brush operated by a broom handle. For best results a good wax polish is spread in thin patches on the linoleum, never on the bristles. The block is shoved to and fro until a good shine is produced. The secret is to apply polish sparingly and 'bump' steadily away until satisfied with the results.

Next I turned attention to the windows and by 11.00 hrs. the place looked spick and span. I saw no reason why I should not commence my reading.

Over the preceding six or seven years I had disposed of several correspondence courses in Radio and Electrical Engineering. I had enough letters after my name to fill a visiting card. None of them counted for much and I resolved to rectify the situation by tackling the examinations set by the Institution of Radio Engineers. The duty of room orderly was far from arduous, allowing me at least one hour each day for quiet study. The Handbook of the Radio Society of Great Britain (RSGB) I found invaluable, not too cumbersome to carry in the kitbag and certainly full of useful text and data.

At 11.15 hrs. footsteps were heard heading in the direction of my hut. With fair warning a voice called:

'Orderly Officer: stand by yer bed.'

First appeared the Orderly Sergeant, owner of the voice. My book had fitted neatly into my little bedside cupboard. I stood to the best attention I knew as the

Orderly Officer himself appeared. It was none other than Dizzy. The acid test was upon me. I glanced at my polished lino. It glistened. Dizzy took a good look at it, scanned the stoves, the windows and finally me. He never batted an eye-lid but the Sergeant did; not until he had opened the door for his superior to pass through. Then the Sergeant nodded and winked very gracefully. It made my day. Dizzy had honoured me with his supreme accolade – no comment.

I continued to enjoy my privacy until 13.00 hrs. when all the other occupants of Room 10 returned to the hut for collection of mug and irons for dinner.

'You crafty bugger,' said El Cid. 'We are on our knees, and here's you in luxury.'

Tales of woe described gruelling work around the camp. The parade ground was swept of every vestige of soil, gardens weeded, windows cleaned, kerb stones painted white and manhole covers black. I had chosen well.

However, after dinner I was required to attend a general parade in which Sergeant Robertson put us on the right lines to qualify for entry to the Guards Brigade. His use of four-letter words seemed to be an outlet for his own frustrations, maybe brought on by working under Dizzy's extraordinary directivity. Adjectival expletive was used by Robertson more prolifically and more cunningly than by any parade commander I was destined to meet. He produced such wonderfully flowery phrases as: 'You, Shorthouse! That's not standing to fuckin' attention; you are droopin' like a daffo-fuckin'-dil.' On every parade ground there is always the odd character for a drill commander to target with his humour. One such was addressed by Robertson as: 'My wall-bloody-flower!'

Then came PT conducted by an acrobat. He radiated good health and quickly succeeded in convincing all of us that we needed exercise. There were parts of us which had been unused in civilian life. He knew just how to indicate painfully where they were. We needed time to relax.

Each airman was allowed the afternoon off twice a week. Leave passes must be carried in order to get past the guardroom. At the first opportunity, Sparky, El Cid and I procured the necessary pieces of paper with a view to visiting Sunderland. A couple of 'erks' were ahead of us by fifty yards on our way to the guardroom outside which, standing in customary vertical precision, was none other than Dizzy. Now we had all been drilled in the art of saluting: 'Longest way up and the shortest way down.' It was known as 'popping one up'. One of those nameless erks 'popped one up' to Dizzy who promptly exploded:

'You do NOT salute a Warrant Officer, boy! You have not listened to your instructor. I carry the King's Warrant but not the King's Commission. Get it?'

'Yes sir.'

'. . . And your buttons are unclean. Back to your barracks and polish them!'

So ended one lad's half-day, before he got as far as the guardroom. We three straightened our demeanours, looked straight ahead, had our passes inspected by a guard and through the camp gateway we marched unmolested.

Already a group of airmen were standing at the bus stop. They had been informed of the misfortune which had befallen their colleague and were counting their blessings. Three of them had made a passless exit via a secret hole-in-a-hedge and were thankful for not having been detected.

When the bus arrived it was half filled with civilian passengers. We airmen climbed aboard and took up most of the remaining seats but the bus did not start immediately. It appeared that the driver was ahead of schedule. We waited a minute or two with engine thumping over, until the reason for our delay in taking off became evident. From the direction of the camp gates strode Dizzy at a cracking pace. He boarded the bus, renewing acquaintance with the driver before taking a seat.

The bus stopped about three miles out from Usworth. Dizzy stood up and crisply demanded: 'Hold up your passes.'

The three passless miscreants were ordered off the bus with strict instructions to walk back to camp and report to the guardroom on arrival. Dizzy had demonstrated his power and settled down to savour the thoughts of a martinet.

As we rounded a corner in a major street of Sunderland El Cid excelled himself by 'popping one up' to the green-coated commissionaire outside the Odeon cinema. The gentleman was so intrigued by the gesture that he ushered us into the best seats at half-price.

After three weeks at Usworth we began to wonder whether we had joined the wrong outfit. I thought of Lilian at her home in Hereford thinking about her husband risking his life at war, of the Enfield Bullet languishing in my father's garage at Thirsk and of all the radio sets I could have profitably repaired instead of polishing lino.

Fitter we were, no doubt, but a mutinous feeling was spreading. A Council of Radio Mechanics was formed in the NAAFI. Leading Aircraftman Ward was appointed Chairman. A mode of attack was drawn up and action would begin the following morning on Work Parade.

Dizzy supervised as usual. At the conclusion of Sergeant Robertson's harangue came the same old question to which no reply, by custom, was expected: 'Any complaints?'

The usual deathly hush lasted only a couple of seconds when LAC Ward took two very smart steps forward, crashed his heels together in exemplary fashion and said: 'Sir.'

'So?' said Dizzy. He stared straight at Ward who, from our view of his rear, seemed not to flinch.

'Sir, we of this squad . . .' (At that point Dizzy raised his eyebrows. He had encountered individual complaints but this sounded like mutiny.) '. . . are objecting to employment on menial tasks. We volunteered to help prosecute the war as technicians.'

'What trade are you?'

'Radio Mechanic.'

'Ah! So you'd know something about transmitters.'

'Yes. Sir.'

'Corporal Brown!' Like a flash the junior NCO snapped to attention. 'My compliments to Flight-Sergeant Williams at the transmitting station. Ask him how many Radio Mechanics he can employ on a wiring party. Bring me the answer – at the double.' Corporal Brown vanished.

Addressing Ward again, Dizzy inquired whether Radio Mechanics would understand electric lights.

'Oh, yes,' said Ward. 'Anything in that line. We feel we'd be doing something useful.'

'Right! Sergeant Robertson. My compliments to Sergeant Johnson at the Hospital. Inform him that a party of technicians will be along shortly to deal with the electrical work he mentioned.' The estimable sergeant clicked away. I thought his grin indicated a thorough understanding of his task. 'Room Orderlies! Di-i-issmiss!'

I was on my way rejoicing in the comfortable anticipation of another round of 'bumping'.

At 13.00 hrs. I put my book away for fear of annoying my room-mates. I knew they envied my life of luxury. Sounds of their approach told me they were unhappy.

The wiring party showed scratched and bloody hands. Their task had been to arrange barriers of barbed wire around and over the building. They were 'brassed off'. The electrical work at the Hospital had involved removing all the lamp shades and bulbs, washing and replacing them. The 'electricians' were 'brassed off' too.

There were no complaints at work parade thereafter. We had made our protest. Dizzy reigned supreme. Under his guidance we became highly disciplined airmen. We learned to fire a rifle and at least hit the card. We could slope arms, shoulder arms, wear a gas mask, pack a gas mask, mark time and kill time. We were lectured on VD and how to avoid it, but there was no mention of Radio and how to Mechanic it.

After four weeks of us I think Dizzy became short of ideas to keep himself amused by our reactions. Like any human being he must have had a soft spot behind the sadistic façade. Behind the scenes there was concern, undoubtedly. One of our number had written to his MP questioning whether the war could continue without his active participation. Usworth had not been established to function purely as a high class correction centre. What is more, a rumour rustled through our ranks that there was a surplus of Radio Mechanics. A coastal RDF station had been bombed by the Germans, the very station near Whitby to which we were to be allocated. We had become redundant before we'd started.

The next Work Parade ran wild with rumour. Something was afoot. So it was not surprising that six members of the party including myself were called forward for special duty on 'Crash Guard'. That sounded frighteningly important. We felt important, too, as we were marched off for briefing. When we found ourselves being issued with rifles and bullets to fit it could only be concluded that our chance to defend the realm had come.

Corporal Brown took us in care and directed us to climb into a Bedford 15 cwt. truck. The Corporal sat in front with the driver and off we drove at a leisurely pace to a secret destination.

From the cliff tops at Seaham Harbour the Corporal pointed to the object of our attentions: in the gathering twilight we saw, on the beach below, a Hampden bomber. It appeared to be in one piece. We imagined the crew disembarked unscathed, having beached on running out of petrol. No explanation was given to us. As trainees it was our simple duty to be sure that no unauthorised person might be allowed to approach the aircraft.

Our instructions were that we must not approach the aircraft ourselves. There was no danger of this because of the sheer drop from cliff-top to cliff-bottom. We must stroll up and down the cliff-top, bayonets fixed, and to any intruder, call: 'Halt! Who goes there?'

The challengee must identify himself as an authorised person before being allowed to pass. Failure to do so would incur our displeasure.

Turns of duty would be in pairs, two hours on and four off, to be continued until relieved by another party. For those on rest a shelter was available in the form of the weigh-bridge office, a functional adjunct to a stone quarry.

The night-watchman welcomed our presence which enabled him to sleep all night whilst we performed the double function of guarding quarry and Hampden. Sleep he did, too. He lay flat on his back on a wooden bench and snored loudly enough to scare off any likely trespasser.

A substantial supper hamper had been provided by the Royal Air Force. The quarry office was well equipped for tea brewing. The job appealed to us. The moon came up and shone upon the North Sea, illuminating the lapping waves which gently licked our bomber, a machine of war in idyllic setting.

The two-on and four-off plan was subjected to modification. I was not alone in finding sleep impossible. The watchman's snores vibrated the building and though our palliasses contained ample straw the only space available for them was upon a large metal plate bearing the raised letters: 'W.T. Avery and Co. Ltd.' No matter which way I turned I was conscious of being stamped with at least one letter on at least one part of my anatomy.

We settled for four-on and two-off, quaffing numerous cups of tea during the 'on' turns. The Hampden was guarded well. We put the fear of God into the Corporal when he dropped in to check if we were awake.

On return to camp the next day we could feel a distinct change in the atmosphere. It was better than a rumour; it was pukka gen that Radio Mechanics were to be given the option of hanging on at Usworth, in hope for the best, or changing trade to Wireless Mechanic with immediate posting to a squadron.

'On parade!' Sergeant Robertson's voice shook the camp. Once we were fell-in and lined up the news was confirmed. 'Two paces forward, all what wants to change!'

I couldn't wait to join the real RAF, with aeroplanes. I joined the queue at the head of which a clerk was taking name, rank and number, by tradition. A further question being asked was simply: 'Where do you want to go?'

My objective in volunteering for service was to take pot-luck in being directed to wherever I may be needed. I reckoned the odds were on being despatched overseas at some time. I would prefer a warmer climate if I had a choice. The news of wet weather in France raised horrors of Ypres and Somme. I asked if I could go to Egypt.

'You can't do that here,' said the clerk. 'Don't you want to go near home?'

'Put "No preference". I'll take a chance.'

El Cid had opted for Dishforth, working on the assumption that he would find it a convenient base from which to visit his girl-friend in Heckmondwyke. His number being only one ahead of my own I think the clerk saved himself trouble by bracketing us together so I, too, went to Dishforth.

I had joined the Air Force to see the world. There I was, six miles from my home town.

Chapter 23

'Shiny Ten'

Dishforth is a pleasant village south-west of Thirsk. In my schooldays a favourite cycle ride would take me through the village and past the airfield. By setting a leisurely pace I was able to observe some of the activities around the aircraft. As soon as the war got going a 'No Through Road' sign went up, traffic making towards the Great North Road being diverted away from the entrance to the aerodrome.

Dishforth was well established as a standard Bomber Command Station with two squadrons of sixteen aircraft each.

El Cid and I were posted to No. 10 Whitley Squadron, known proudly as 'Shiny Ten'. We were not made wholly welcome. We were still designated as Radio Mechanics officially, until such time as written orders came along to convert us into Wireless Mechanics. Our sleeves bore the two-bladed propellor badges which rubbed it into the 'regulars' that we had jumped two steps of the promotion ladder. We were eyed with suspicion.

At the Orderly Room we gave the usual name, rank and number plus El Cid's little next-of-kin joke. The next move was to our accommodation which pleased us immensely. We took over two beds in an upstairs barrack room with highly polished wood floors. El Cid was fortunate in gaining a corner position though with the disadvantage of being just inside the doorway. Traffic must pass by the foot of his bed.

Most of the residents were out at work but one or two of those off duty greeted us and offered information. We learned that numerous trades were represented among the occupants but at least a third of the number were cooks. That knowledge seemed insignificant at the time but it will be seen to have a bearing on our fortunes.

A metal wardrobe was provided for the storage of our Sunday Best, a bedside table for odds and ends. Following initial arrangement of our belongings we were pointed in the direction of the Signals Section of 'A' Flight hangar, whither we made our apprehensive approach.

The Flight-Sergeant or 'Chiefy' as Flight-Sergeants are better known, was a likeable soul who made an effort to make our lives tolerable. As a father figure he negotiated an uneasy peace between ourselves and the 'regulars'. It was evident that both the Sergeant and the Corporal of the Signals Section resented the intrusion of a couple of jumped up inexperienced 'sprogs'. Corporal Whitty had spent twelve years of his young life in climbing to his exalted rank. He questioned our integrity: Had we 'done' the ten-eighty-two and ten-eighty-three? No, we hadn't a clue. What were they? The estimable Corporal was astonished to know that we had received no technical training whatsoever. It was obvious that he had no intention of enlightening us. Why should he let us into the secrets of intimate association with ten-eighty-twos and ten-eighty-threes? Sergeant Rowe concurred in this restriction of edification. We were classified as 'jumped-up fuckers'! 'Chiefy' recognised a way out of the impasse: The Royal Air Force administration had, in its wisdom, employed a number of civilian technicians in various trades. The idea may have come from political origins. Ostensibly the number of members of the armed forces was lower than reality, possibly to fox the enemy, possibly to fool the tax-payer or maybe just to hold a more flexible nucleus of technical expertise.

Whatever the reason for their presence the fact was that two civilian radio experts were useful adjuncts to the squadron. Arthur Yates was a Ripon lad. Subsequently his name shone in bold letters from over his radio emporium in the Market Place. 'Smithy' and I had met in civilian life during a few days I spent under tuition at the Kolster-Brandes service department at Newcastle-on-Tyne, in 1933.

El Cid and I were indebted to Arthur and Smithy for a period of instruction in the servicing of radio equipment in Whitley bombers. The 1082/1083 combination of transmitter and receiver was a very simple affair compared with that in modern aircraft. It was easy to understand, beautifully constructed and almost trouble-free. The snags which arose in the aircraft were more often than not a result of accidental damage or ingress of water. Broken leads on headphones and sockets could be expected at any time.

We raw recruits were not to be trusted to operate without supervision. That seemed reasonable enough. After all, aeroplanes don't come cheap, nor do the men who fly them. What we did resent was the allocation to us of menial tasks such as carrying accumulators round the airfield, finding ourselves getting an unfair ration of guard duties and on one occasion being conveniently denied leave passes.

The standard practice of rectifying a faulty transmitter was to replace it with a new one from stores, the dud item to be returned to a maintenance unit (MU). As an experienced service engineer I was annoyed at the denial of interesting diagnostic work. El Cid and I were underemployed. Sitting around waiting for the next tea break did not suit us.

By a turn of fortune 'Stores' had run out of spare transmitters and a faulty one lay on the bench before our very eyes. When everyone else had gone to tea we decided on a surreptitious look into the works. We knew the valves were in order for they had been checked as OK. (Valve replacements were not 'out of bounds'!). The circuit was so simple that a description of symptoms of the fault, as reported by the Wireless Operator on the aircraft, were enough to lead us to a quick diagnosis.

A faulty capacitor was removed from the transmitter and placed on the bench beside it. When 'Chiefy' appeared the culprit was shown to him. He indicated that we 'didn't ought to have done that' but took a chance on his further action, in view of the difficult circumstances. No air force likes to have aircraft grounded. He made out an order and a new capacitor was obtained from stores. He fitted it himself and took the responsibility, very generously, of passing the transmitter as fit for service. The matter was quietly dismissed and we continued as before, functioning as odd job men.

My maxim that life is nothing but a string of coincidences has proved invaluable throughout the years. Coincidence brought El Cid and me to fame on a sunny afternoon in May 1940.

Our plod round the airfield with accumulators ended at 'G' for George. We fancied a snooze, lay down in the shade of the starboard wing of the aircraft and dropped off to sleep. All was peace except for the swish of infrequent vehicles passing along the Great North Road and the twittering of birds in the hedges. How long we slept I had no idea but when we woke up we were being watched, caught in the act! A young and handsome Flight-Lieutenant grinned down at us and we prepared ourselves for a rocket. Much to our pleasant surprise he said:

'Want a flip, you two? I must do an air test and I haven't a full crew, so you're welcome.'

My only experience of flying had been on a ten-bob circuit in a bi-plane piloted by Captain West of Sir Alan Cobham's Air Circus and a short trip in a D-H 'Rapide' on the same day. I had not anticipated flying with the RAF at such short notice.

We were ushered aboard and I chose to take the tail turret position. All I knew about a tail turret was that the headphone socket must be checked daily and that could be done without climbing into the turret. One opened the little swing doors inwards to the fuselage and from a kneeling position examined the socket. Now here I was getting into the turret and taking the seat, pulling the little swing doors behind me. I didn't know how to lock them.

Before me and pointing downwards to the grass were the four machine guns. A bewildering tangle of pipes, cables, magazines of bullets, levers and knobs confronted me. I sat still, not daring to touch anything. Vibrations told me the engines had been started; I saw the grass being blown by the wind created by the propellors; we were moving. We gathered speed, the grass was being flattened by the wind. I looked left and saw the starboard tail-plane. I looked right and saw the port tail-plane. I looked down and saw the grass was further away. I looked straight out between the guns and saw sky. I was airborne with the Royal Air Force, painlessly airborne, untrained except as a square-basher, yet flying within three months of joining. This was the life; fantastic.

I was on my own in this turret, seemingly detached from the mainframe. I looked left and saw the starboard tail-plane. I looked right and saw the port tail-plane. So I must be attached to the fuselage. I glanced down to the left inside the turret. I took note of a little handle attached to a pinion which engaged with a rack running round behind my seat and fixed to the mainframe. It was patently clear that by turning the handle the turret could be made to turn through 180°. That was not for me. I was content to have a free ride straight ahead though with a view to the rear! It did not occur to me that the small latch beside the handle was a lock to prevent the turret from moving when the aircraft banked into a turn.

I looked right and I saw the sky. I looked left and saw inside the fuselage. I looked straight between the guns and there was the starboard tail-plane. We were banking steeply and I knew exactly where we were banking. I looked behind me. There were cows grazing in the field beside the River Ure at the bottom of Salem Bank. The two little doors were open. Between me and the cows was fresh air. Turning my head almost 180° I could see the port tail-plane so I knew I was still attached to the Whitley! Oddly enough I could feel no draught but I took the precaution of hooking an arm around the gun stalk, taking particular care not to trigger off any fireworks. We were flying level again but the turret still remained at right-angles to the fuselage. I turned the little handle and was relieved to find the turret moving. The starboard tail-plane began to move out of my sight. The half-door to my left closed automatically as I turned the handle and when I reached half-way back to normal I was able to pull the other half without effort. I have never worked out why the doors didn't blow off and never dared ask anyone.

When I could again see both tail-planes by looking right and left respectively I pushed open the little doors behind me and satisfied myself that the fuselage was still there. Then I squirmed out of the turret and lay down on the floor in a state of palsy.

I knew nothing of the landing except the rumblings of the wheels on the grass. When we disembarked there was El Cid beaming like a demented search-light. He'd enjoyed wonderful views of the Yorkshire Moors, of Ripon Minster and the River Ure.

'Did you see the cows grazing by the Ure?' I asked.

'No. I didn't notice any cows,' he said.

We thanked the pilot for a very enjoyable ride, expressing the hope that we join him again, if convenient. Then he realised we were new boys, recently from civvy street and he asked the question which transformed our lives:

'Do you know anything about the Link Trainer?'

We confessed that we had never heard of such a thing but were prepared to learn. We were at his service.

'I am the Link Training Officer for the Station,' he went on, 'and whilst the machine works well enough I can't talk to the pupil, because the microphone is u/s.'

We hopped into a Hillman shooting brake which dropped us off at the Link Trainer building. Inside we were introduced to the flight simulator known as the Link Trainer.

A trainee sat in the box-like model aircraft and shut himself inside. He then 'flew' by instruments under the instruction of the Training Officer who sat at a control table on which was drawn a flight plan. Instructions should have been given over the microphone-headphone system which was now faulty. The training programme had come to a halt.

The Station Signals Officer had been informed, his Warrant Officer had agreed that a fault had developed, the Flight-Sergeant considered it was a job for the manufacturer. A signal to the manufacturer had been acknowledged and a service engineer would be sent as soon as available, probably within ten days. Our pilot friend was dissatisfied. He took a chance in the invitation to El Cid and me to fiddle with this valuable piece of equipment. He gave us a short description of the *mode d'emploi*, found an instruction manual and left us to investigate.

In the back of the manual was a circuit diagram of the whole electrical system. The microphone, of the carbon granule type, needed an independent source of low voltage electricity and it didn't take us two minutes to see that somewhere was a battery, a nine volt battery. Where was it? Wrongly we assumed that it would be of substantial size and quality to match the excellence of the expensive machine. A diligent search around the control desk covered all likely accessible positions. We were baffled to the extent of our logic. So we went illogical. El Cid, being of moderate stature, lay on his back and felt around ledges under the desk and struck not oil, but a gooey mess which *had* been a PP3 battery.

We prepared an unofficial modification to the Link Trainer. First of all a replacement battery must be purloined from RAF stores. Normally it was possible to obtain a replacement only by submitting the faulty part but our PP3 had gone beyond the stage of recognition by any store-keeper. In any case it was not an Air Force catalogue item and we were illegally servicing equipment outside the jurisdiction of the squadron. I borrowed a 9 volt grid bias battery from squadron stores knowing that I could replace it the following day, after proving we had cleared the fault in the apparatus.

New connections to the battery were made and a far more satisfactory mounting looked very professional. The microphone system worked perfectly and within half an hour El Cid and I were well on the way to qualifying as stunt pilots.

When the Training Officer returned he was, naturally enough, tickled pink. He sent for the Station Signals Officer, who sent for the Warrant Officer who came with the Flight-Sergeant. The general opinion of these immaculately uniformed gentlemen was that the Link Trainer could be passed as fully serviceable. A signal would be despatched to the manufacturer to cancel the need for a visit by a qualified Service Engineer.

El Cid and I achieved instant notoriety. Our services were demanded from unexpected quarters. The Group Captain's radiogram was troublesome. It received our prompt attention and was repaired at minimal cost. Technically our future looked rosy. Even Sergeant Rowe thought we might be of more use than appearances suggested. We were permitted to include in our duties the testing of the detonator circuit of the secret IFF (Identification of Friend or Foe) boxes in the aircraft. The test was simple enough but if a mistake was made a sharp explosion preceded the issue of a pall of blue smoke from the now ruined blackbox. So highly regarded were our qualifications that when El Cid did blow one the incident was passed off as an understandable error.

Domestically our life at Dishforth was not entirely untroubled. Resulting from one unfortunate incident we were losing a lot of sleep. Not every night were we disturbed. It depended on which cooks were on night shifts.

Mention was made earlier in this chapter that a number of cooks shared our dormitory. Their inherent generosity brought about our share of discomfort. El Cid and I had worked extra hard at the shove ha'penny board and taken in more than enough of NAAFI beer. We were in a very heavy sleep when at 03.00 hours the night-shift cooks entered our sleeping quarters, carrying a large can of tea. I opened one eye to see a cook bending over El Cid's recumbent shape, shaking it and asking politely:

'Want a cuppa tea, chum?'

El Cid's reply was straightforward enough: 'Fuck off!'

Thenceforward whenever those cooks were on night duty they never asked whether we fancied a cuppa but they never failed to rattle the cans to excess. Furthermore, daytime slumbers following our own night duties didn't go unbroken. There were Crash Party, Signals Party and the odd Guard Duties to be undertaken outside normal working hours. It was desirable to take a few snoozes after breakfast on the morning after. Those cooks took a sadistic interest in our inactivity.

We cut our teeth at Dishforth. It was not a case of all work and no play. I was allowed to keep the Royal Enfield Bullet on the camp so whenever a leave pass was forthcoming I could quickly and easily visit my parents in Thirsk. On more than one occasion my Lilian came to stay with them so we did enjoy a modicum of married life in spite of the war.

My mother's cooking abilities enabled her to present food rations at table in tasty disguise. I was able to spend a little time at H. Reddin and Sons effecting repairs to any radio sets which my father had been unable to handle. Apart from working in the business he was very much involved in keeping his Fire Brigade in trim. His efforts were to pay dividends in efficiency, displayed during many fire-fighting episodes throughout the war.

This was not the first war my parents had experienced and I could depend on their stoic approach to the present one. Ironically enough, the first bomb of any kind to drop in the district fell in the allotments at the rear of their home. It was supposed to be an incendiary bomb but it didn't 'go off'. The filthy oil it contained splashed a neighbour's bungalow and made a mess of the cabbage patch.

It was anticipated that the German bombers would attempt to assault the aerodrome at Dishforth. A decoy 'flare-path' was set up on the North Yorkshire Moors, some of my electrician colleagues playing a part. They enjoyed the change of air but were pleased to leave the site in the care of non-technical airmen when the time came to switch on the lights. The ploy met with some success.

Our own Whitleys of 'Shiny Ten' made frequent excursions over enemy territory. They were not very spritely, flying uniquely nose-down, but we were proud of them. Because they took their time it was customary for daylight take-off and there was never a shortage of ground staff to wave them farewell. With a maximum speed not much over 200 m.p.h. the Whitley would have been easy game for a German fighter had it not been for the rear-gunner's fire power. At so modest a speed an enemy bomber could follow it to base. A false flare-path might well prove attractive to the hostile bomb-aimer.

During my short stay at Dishforth no bombs were dropped but it was there that I experienced my first taste of one of the horrors of war. 'Shiny Ten' was engaged in the laying of mines in Dutch estuaries in the hope that German shipping might be damaged or sunk. It was an operation calling for a high degree of skill on the part of our crews. If weather conditions didn't permit pin-point accuracy then the mines would be brought home, returned to the bomb store and defused until again required. It seems that an error was made inside the store and the poor chap who made it must have suffered not at all. The explosion was heard in Thirsk, by my mother who was hanging out her washing at the time. We of the Signals Section saw a thick cloud of black smoke containing pieces of debris rising a hundred feet. It was a shattering experience, bringing home to us the seriousness of our occupation. Talk in the NAAFI that evening was very subdued.

Every RAF station constitutes a close community with all the sorrows and joys which happen along. A pleasantly thrilling interlude in our normal activities was provided by a visiting Squadron-Leader who dropped in for lunch one day in a Westland Whirlwind. None of us on the station had ever seen one before. It caused tremendous interest. It was so very different from our dear old lumbering Whitleys that almost everyone examined it at close quarters. Forecasts of the Whirlwind becoming a leading fighter plane were rumoured. When the pilot returned and started the twin engines an eager throng gathered to watch the take-off. It was spectacular. Then came a low-level salute before the sleek fighter turned away and out of sight behind the hangars but the real thrill was yet to come. With a rush of wind the Whirlwind cleared the tops of the buildings by a few feet, almost brushed the grass in the centre of the field and climbed as near vertically as made no matter, before disappearing into cloud, leaving the audience bewildered.

Of all the air shows and stunts I have seen nothing has been as impressive as Whirlwind day at Dishforth. Though several squadrons of Whirlwinds played a part in our defences the Spitfires and Hurricanes were already set to win the Battle of Britain.

News came that 'Shiny Ten' was on the move. Maybe now I would see foreign lands. Move we did: to Leeming.

Chapter 24

Leeming Bar

Motorists who travel along the A1 today may not be aware of the existence of the RAF station, important though it is. Leeming Bar and the village of Leeming are both by-passed but in 1940 passers-by had a first-class view of the Whitleys dispersed around the field, a huge expanse of grass.

Tarmac runways were coming into fashion, at far greater expense and inconvenience than they could have been built before the war. 'Shiny Ten' settled in at Leeming while Dishforth was modernised. Metalled runways were under construction at many aerodromes including Catterick, from which fighters were diverted to Leeming every evening. Alternating with Spitfires were Blenheims. They parked in readiness for our defence against enemy air-raids.

One bright and sunny evening I was sitting in comfort, legs outstretched, reading the *Amateur Radio Handbook*, on a windowsill of my barrack block. I enjoyed an open view across the airfield and I was not surprised to see a twin-engined aircraft flying east to west at about 200 feet. Blenheims were due in about that time and I thought nothing of it until a stream of bullets spattered across the building just below my window ledge. I fell into the room, ducking below window level and waited a second or two. Four of my colleagues were playing cards around a folding table. They were seen to be surprised at my antics but before they found words in comment a loud bang prompted evasive action. The four of them dived under the little card table, scattering cards, tea mugs and legs, human and chair, in all directions. I dashed through the doorway to the top of the staircase while several more bombs fell.

The staircase was jammed with airmen in various states of dress, making for the air-raid shelter. I had no time to plough through the mass. I took a flying leap, still clutching the *RSGB Handbook*, landed softly among a tangle of erks, dropped the book, spotted it under somebody's foot, grabbed it and was swept along into the shelter. A hell of a racket was in progress above ground, a goodly proportion of it to the credit of a gallant colleague who fired off more bullets from his Lewis gun than he had ever been permitted to let loose in practice. He was highly commended by the Station Commander once the panic was over. His account of the battle was much sought after in the NAAFI. Whether he scored a hit on the Heinkel he couldn't be sure because the enemy got away from our district and no report reached Leeming of a triumph. The incident seemed to confirm that the RDF station near Whitby was not functioning.

The only casualties of the bombing were a few unfortunate cows which happened to be grazing in a field adjacent to the aerodrome. Bovine survivors were seen to be nibbling away quite contentedly at the grass, showing no concern for the corpses of their late companions.

Rustic though our surroundings may have been, realities of war were crowding upon us. Fairey Battles loaded with frightened soldiers and airmen landed at Leeming, themselves laden with cigarettes fortuitously gathered from abandoned canteens in Belgium. They brought tales of the evacuation of our forces from France and the Low Countries, of fellow men wading into the seas desperately grasping at any small boat which might bring them back to Britain. The leading question was: 'Why does the Luftwaffe reign supreme?'

El Cid and I had no answer to the question. Our job, allocated to us, continued to be the care of our beloved Whitleys. We had been accepted as Wireless Mechanics, though still on the books as Radio Mechanics. Along with our electrician, armourer, fitter and instrument mechanic friends we carried out our daily inspections and listened to Vera Lynn whitewashing us with 'We'll meet again', knowing that we might never see our air crews return from their next assignment.

Arthur and Smithy, our erstwhile tutors, had been absorbed into the uniformed service and were no longer with us. We were trusted employees of His Majesty, did what was asked of us and thanked our lucky stars that we were still alive and kicking.

Not that we were denied excitement, for there were those among us who entertained us by accident.

Our Whitleys persisted in trying to lay mines in the deltas of Holland. It was one of Winston Churchill's fads that they should keep at it. The mines were cuboidal in shape and so large that the bomb-doors could not be closed over them. That did not assist in enhancing the air-speed of the Whitley, but it did mean that when an aircraft returned to base without having discharged its deadly weapons, these mines were clearly visible between the open bomb-doors. Therefore, when we members of the ground staff trudged or were transported out to dispersal points intent on doing our 'DIs' it was common sense to note whether the aircraft was still loaded with mines.

Each mine was fitted with what was called a 'spinner', a device to be set only by an armourer. It had the appearance of a metal four-pointed star, in one point of which was a hole to accept one end of a wire, the other end of which was firmly fixed to the aircraft frame. The idea was to safeguard aircraft and personnel until the mine was well clear of the aircraft. Once the mine was released it dropped from its housing, still inert until it reached the limit of the length of wire. At that point the 'spinner' unscrewed and the mine fell ready to explode on impact with ship or barge.

One of the checks listed on the DI sheet of an electrician was 'Bomb release switches'. I was busy doing my DI on an aircraft parked on the side of the airfield remote from the hangars. Fitters, instrument mechanics and electricians swarmed all over the Whitley checking this and testing that.

It was possible for me to feed into the intercom system a broadcast programme from the BBC, then tour round all the headphone sockets to ascertain perfect function or otherwise. I had noted that this particular aircraft was carrying mines, also that an electrician by the distinctive name of Oddy was seated in the position of co-pilot. He had borrowed a pair of headphones and was listening in to my radio. In common with many of his comrades Oddy was addicted to the sounds of Glenn Miller's orchestra. Absorbed as he was 'In the Mood' he checked the bomb switches.

A sickening, dull thud preceded a shout from the Sergeant Fitter: 'Beat it!'

In haste, I ducked out of the wireless compartment, head down, instinctively reaching out with my right hand to steady myself with a hold on the Elsan. Somebody had left the lid open and I plunged my right arm into the bog. Dripping with creosote I shot out of the side door to witness airmen setting up times for the mile not to be bettered by Roger Bannister fourteen years later. The Sergeant was on his bike, the Corporal stood on the back axle of a tractor, arms round the driver, urging the poor chap to put his 'bleedin' foot down'.

Credit was due to Oddy who stayed with his craft, viewing with alarm the rapid dispersal of airmen to all points of the compass. He lived to tell the tale, of course, because the wires attached to the mines were much longer than the distance between bomb-bay and ground.

In the course of time, when the Sergeant and others had recovered breathing facilities, they removed the mines to safe storage and dealt with AC Oddy.

I was obliged to complete my disinfection by a dry-cleaning process, leaving the Sergeant to guess how his beloved Whitley had become spattered with creosote.

I experienced my next bomb scare at Thirsk. With El Cid on the pillion of the Bullet I paid my weekly visit to my parents. After tea we attended the Picture House and halfway through the film the building was shaken by the blast from a bomb exploding on Thirsk racecourse. A regiment of soldiers was billeted in the grandstand and at least one man was killed. The cinema was cleared to the sound of the air-raid siren. El Cid and I were grateful for having survived our temporary venture into civvy street.

Great was the jubilation when El Cid and I were sent on a course of training in the use and servicing of Lorenz Beam Approach equipment. For this we spent a most instructive and interesting week at Boscombe Down. We enjoyed the experience but it signalled the end of our association. On our return to Leeming, where there was no Lorenz installation, we found our postings to diverse parts.

Chapter 25

Stirling Days

The Royal Enfield Bullet was garaged safely at Thirsk. I caught the 8.00 p.m. train for Peterborough. There I finished off the night's sleep in the YMCA building. On 16 November 1940, I booked in at No. 7 Squadron, Oakington.

The squadron was being equipped with the RAF's first four-engined monoplane bomber, the Short Stirling. With its 100 feet wing span and long-legged undercarriage this machine stood with stately arrogance. When it took to the air it flew level, considerably faster than the dear old Whitley, promising to carry the war much further into enemy territory. 'Dinosaur reincarnated' was a fair description.

When new aircraft arrived from the factory they required final inspection and testing. As a specialist in Lorenz Beam Approach equipment I was accepted into the squadron family. There were to be no more snide remarks about 'jumped-upness'. More and more we volunteers were evident in all trades. No. 7 thrived on friendship.

Christmas at Oakington was enjoyable, if not hilarious. By tradition, dinner in the airmen's mess was served by the officers, a most excellent idea for the dissemination of good will to all men. It was during that dinner that I struck up a lasting friendship with an Instrument Mechanic named Don Hall. Don related splendid stories of the famous racing greyhound 'Mick the Miller'. This remarkable animal had been known, when unable to get ahead of the opposition, to stop and sniff the ground. In compliance with a simple law of nature, the other dogs stopped for a sniff while Mick re-started to finish at his own pace.

Don had made a fortune 'at the dogs' by following a simple mathematical truth: At eight out of ten meetings at a track, one of the traps wins three races. Therefore by conserving one's betting until one of the traps has won two races the risk is reduced enormously. Why had Don discontinued so prolific a form of income? After marriage, he told me, his wife had objected to the company he was keeping!

Another close friend at Oakington, a fellow Wireless Mechanic, partnered me in a clandestine radio repair business. Albert Pearson, proprietor of a small radio shop in Doncaster, joined me in supplementing our meagre salaries. Our services were in demand both on and off the premises. We established a relationship with a genial giant named John Bull, who ran a small cycle shop in Histon. Inevitably he received inquiries from owners of ailing radio sets. All the local radio servicemen had joined the forces! Using a bench in John's cycle shop Albert and I worked up a connection amongst the local populace. We bought valves and spare parts from King and Harper's shop in Cambridge where further offers of employment were discreetly rejected.

By great privilege I came under the spell of Flying-Officer R.W. Cox. Only recently elevated from the ranks following his apprenticeship as fitter-engineer, Reggie devoted his life to the adoration of the Stirling. A perfectionist if ever there was one, he saw the Stirling through its multitude of teething problems, later took command of No. 7 and was awarded the DFC, even flying this gigantic machine in Master Bomber escapades with the elite Pathfinders.

Reggie Cox possessed that most remarkable of human characteristics: the ability to persuade others to do his bidding without apparent pressurisation. His aircrew worshipped him, showing a distaste for flying with any other skipper. The ground staff unprovokedly applied that little extra spit and polish to his aeroplane. He took a keen interest in the Lorenz Beam Approach system, never failing to 'try the beam' on every flight. On the arrival of a new aircraft from the Rochester factory Reggie would call on me at the Signals Section:

'I'm taking 'N' for Nuts on air test, Lofty; we shall do a beam approach on Mildenhall. I'd like you to be with us to make sure we've got the hang of it.'

Hardly an order but an invitation not to be refused. Had he said we were to cross the enemy coast I would have been just as delighted to join him; he inspired confidence to that extent. Reggie loved flying because he understood how to handle an aeroplane. Exaggerated tales of his abilities added spice to life at Oakington.

New Year's Day was celebrated by No. 7 Squadron in most impressive fashion. For the first time in history a formation of Stirlings flew over the airfield, a sight which all the ground staff turned out to see and which must have heartened the patient residents of Cambridge and district who had so far in the war had precious little to cheer. London was burning and German bombers were reaching and ranging over inland Britain.

My own New Year's gift came from the Royal Air Force in the form of a beautifully built teak bench on which was mounted a complete Lorenz aircraft system. This enabled me to test individual units in the workshop uninterrupted by the army of fitters and mechanics who swarm inevitably over a large aircraft when it is being serviced on the ground. Further, I used it to good effect when called upon to lecture members of air-crews on the principles and functions of Lorenz. Thus, I made friends among the flying boys, many of whom were understandably apprehensive of the suggestion of a 'blind approach'. Flight-Lieutenant Cox insisted that every pilot should become conversant with the art of using the 'beam'. I was more than pleased to have the opportunity of flying almost every day.

As each new aircraft was brought up to standard I joined the crew on a test flight to include a beam approach to Mildenhall. New pilots were 'converting' to a four-engined monster from a small aircraft, whatever that may have been. Some of the landings by the learners were quite spectacular. A heavy thump on the grass was taken care of by the extra long undercarriage shock-absorbers which sometimes resulted in our being catapulted upwards. So long as Reggie was up front to correct the errors I had no cause for alarm. The sight of a hangar alternating with a view of the sky provides a fair measure of excitement. I confess to being relieved when the master-craftsman took over; a smooth landing could then be expected even during a snowstorm.

Snow it did in the January of 1941. It snowed on the 16th when Their Majesties George and Elizabeth visited Oakington. Majestic enough stood the Stirlings, covered in fresh snow. The royal couple examined one in the comfort of a hangar.

During this bitterly cold spell I learned of a facility known as a 'Living-Out Pass'. I lost no time in locating accommodation with a family in Histon. With all speed I set off for Hereford to collect my sleeping partner. On 19 January I arrived at Gloucester too late to catch the last train to Hereford. One other traveller joined me in the waiting room where we managed to keep warm enough to enjoy a series of bleary-eyed catnaps. At 02.30 hrs. a great banging of doors caused us to venture into the snow-covered station yard. The driver of the Royal Mail Van, destined for Ross and Hereford, welcomed our company. My new companion fell soundly asleep amongst the mail-bags. The old Morris 'Commercial' purred through the muffling snow, laying the first tracks of the day.

My early-rising father-in-law greeted me with freshly-made tea. Suitably refreshed I enjoyed a few hours of bliss alongside my lady-love before normal reveille.

Though snow continued to fall over the ancient City I paid respects to my former employers at C.F. King and Co. There I was prevailed upon to carry out urgent repairs to a number of defective radio sets, each one declared to belong to some poor soul in need of wartime comfort. Owing to shortages of this, that and the other as well as qualified service personnel I sensed the beginnings of what became widely known as 'the black market'. My skills could have been employed to considerable financial gain.

My yearning for 'civvy street' diminished. I had sold myself to the Royal Air Force where comradeship thrived in relative poverty.

In good health my joyful wife and I reached Cambridge on the following day by devious railway routing. The journey was accomplished in ten hours including calls at Oxford, Bletchley and Bedford. Frozen to our marrows we stepped off the bus at Histon where the thoughtful driver stopped opposite the fish and chip shop. The friendly proprietor, by a stroke of good fortune, had received a special delivery that very day. No better way for an English couple to celebrate the start of another temporary home.

Before the expiration of my leave pass there was time for a morning in Cambridge. A hurried introduction of my wife to its architectural splendour preceded lunch at Lyons'. On our return to Histon I bought a quality bicycle from John Bull for twelve-and-sixpence, kissed my spouse goodbye and pedalled back to my beloved Stirlings.

N.3636 was the first and most photographed Stirling of all. She had been tested extensively before entering active service, flew smooth and straight, was everything a good Stirling ought to be. It was to be expected that complex machinery turned out hastily in preparation for war would suffer teething troubles.

N.6003 arrived full of mysterious snags. The Lorenz set refused to tune up willingly, the intercom squeaked, hummed and crackled. The flight mechanics wrestled with their own problems and we got in one another's way. Rude words emerged from persons normally tranquil. The British public wanted to hear of action by Bomber Command. Stirlings were required for a raid on the U-boat at Brest. Pressure was brought to bear upon the ground staff to prepare every available aircraft. I worked on N.6003 until 02.00 hrs. Once the fitters were out of the way I could work by torchlight.

The battle against moisture in the numerous junction boxes was won by diligent mopping and drying. Prolonged study of circuit diagrams disclosed an incorrect connection. As if by magic all spurious noises vanished once the fault was cleared. I left the aerodrome in happy mood. My gentle tap on the bedroom window was the signal that I wished to join my wife in bed. Lilian was quickly to adapt herself to my irregular hours.

When N.6003 finally took off for air-testing the whole ground crew turned out to watch, praying, caring, hopeful. The Lorenz and the wireless performed impeccably. When she landed the engineers were still swearing at the poor thing but they got her ready for the expedition to Brest. With Reggie Cox at the helm she played the leading role. After take-off I went 'home'. Lilian and I attended a dance at Histon College that evening, February 1941.

During the small hours of the 9th we heard the unmistakable purr of the four Bristol engines of a Stirling making repeated circuits of the air space around Oakington. Nothing seemed amiss with the Bristols. Eventually came the change of tune prior to a normal landing, then silence.

At daybreak whilst cycling to the airfield I peered over the hedge to be horrified at the sight of N.6003 lying flat on her belly, deep in the mud. Blessedly, the crew had been rescued in spite of being overcome by fumes from the batteries which had burst on impact. The struggle to lower the jammed undercarriage had proved fruitless. With typical imperturbable skill the Captain brought N.6003 to rest in repairable condition. She was transported to a hangar for extensive operations. While she lay unused I borrowed vital parts from her Lorenz kit to make serviceable another aircraft which had arrived from Rochester incomplete.

My involvement with Lorenz deepened. Pilots raised complaints that in certain circumstances the receiving of signals from the ground stations faded badly. The conclusion reached was that the receiving aerial, being sited on top of the fuselage, was being screened by the wings when the aircraft steeply banked in a turn. A civilian of great flying experience came from the Royal Aircraft Establishment at Farnborough to investigate the problem. Frank King turned up in a Singer sports car; we became firm friends. He was accepted immediately as an additional boarder at our temporary home in Histon. Bad weather prevented flying. Lilian and I jammed ourselves into the passenger space in the Singer and the three of us drove into Cambridge to see Wallace Beery in *Twenty Mule Train.*

An improvement in the weather allowed us to take off in N.6041 with Reggie Cox in charge and Frank King in the co-pilot's seat. We flew up and down and across the beam at Mildenhall losing signals from time to time. Frank asked the skipper if he might take the controls. When Reggie looked apprehensive, Frank assured him:

'Oh, yes, I have a licence: spent a few years with Imperial Airways popping across to Orly, then flying boats to Corfu on the Indian route; happy days.'

He pronounced the Stirling to be a very nice aircraft to handle. We executed several 180° turns before deciding where the antenna should be mounted in the future. He must report accordingly to Farnborough. I was thankful that the master regained control before landing.

The day ended with a game of nap in the bungalow at Histon, its owners joining the fun. During the far-ranging conversations Lilian remarked that she was feeling a bit off colour. Frank looked at her and said there might be a very good reason for that. Lilian blushed in embarrassment; it was not many days before our doctor confirmed that she should expect to deliver a baby in November.

It was now 14 February. I had served in the RAF for just eleven months, still listed as 'Radio Mechanic'. Now, on St. Valentine's Day, I was officially remustered to the trade of 'Wireless Mechanic'. There would be no difference in my pay nor would it make any change in my duties on the Squadron. Life was both interesting and reasonably lucrative. Lilian acquired a congenial job in the office of the building department of Chivers', the renowned jam manufacturers. Her work put an end to daytime boredom as well as niggling upsets with our landlady.

Still my only formal training had been the one week's course at Boscombe Down, specialising in Lorenz.

Albert and I were entrusted with servicing radio transmitters and receivers, intercoms and Lorenz equipment. Flight-Sergeant Fawcett kept an eye on us and even introduced a few 'private' radio repairs for our attention in off-duty periods. Life at Oakington was very full. I continued studying; the RAF maintenance manuals were a joy to read. New designs in radio transmitters and receivers, notably the T.1154/R.1155 for aircraft, were a welcome change from the rustic 1082/1083. Albert and I introduced ourselves to their complexities.

They represented a revolution in communication equipment for airborne usage, serving both coastal and bomber commands right through the war.

Visitations by German bombers to Cambridge and Newmarket districts were becoming more frequent but did not deter Lilian and me from a weekly cinema show in Cambridge. We were lucky in getting seats at the Regal to see Charlie Chaplin in *The Great Dictator*. When we came out it was snowing heavily and it snowed all next day. We saw a Heinkel peep between clouds, take a look at the snow and turn back for base.

Frank King turned up with an experimental aerial to be fitted underneath the nose of the Stirling. The fitting called for close co-operation with the engineering branch of the squadron. Woe betide any humble Wireless Mechanic who dared to drill a hole in an aircraft. I left Frank to observe the work himself.

Meanwhile, I collected a 48-hour pass and route form, destination: West Drayton; purpose of visit: trade test. By starting at crack of dawn I made West Drayton by 10.30 hrs. The trade testers were anxious to evaluate me as suitable or not for promotion. In view of the paucity of my training in matters RAF, apart from the square-bashing sessions, I was surprised at the kind reception my answers received. At least I was not asked to demonstrate skills on the parade ground for I had done no parades except pay parades since leaving Usworth.

By 16.00 hrs. I was back at Paddington. Determined to gather some idea of what my fellowmen were suffering in London, I walked to Marble Arch, took a tube to St. Paul's, then walked to Liverpool Street. I saw enough bomb damage to persuade me that there was greater expectation of life at Oakington than in the big city.

I set to work with renewed vigour in the prosecution of war. Stirlings had rained bombs on the naval base at Brest for the third time. New aircraft were arriving from Shorts almost daily. Some were delivered to Wyton to which station I was one day driven with my test gear. I omitted to read the vital Daily Routine Orders before leaving. Had I done so I would have spent a happier day. It was cold and wet. I was pleased when the Dodge truck collected me. When I arrived back at Oakington I was greeted with the news that, following my trade test, I was promoted to the rank of Acting Corporal unpaid!

Though amongst my colleagues I might now be classed as 'jumped up' the sour grape feelings experienced at Dishforth were not evident. For one thing, the number of volunteers now matched the number of regulars. We were all pulling our weight. Another enormous boost came by telegram from the British Institution of Radio Engineers. During my Dishforth days I had been granted a short leave of absence in order to attend Manchester Technical College where the entrance examination was held. The telegram confirmed that I had passed the examination for Associate Membership and won the President's prize! A letter followed to inform me that I had been recommended for a Commission in the Royal Air Force (Signals Branch). Things were looking up, indeed.

Meanwhile, teething problems associated with new aircraft kept Albert and me extremely busy. Some of the most elusive faults had the simplest of origins. An unforgettable phenomenon came to our notice when N6037 was hauled out of the hangar at the conclusion of a major inspection by the engineers. We set about the testing of all the wireless mechanics' responsibilities. The aircraft stood some 200 yards distant from the control tower. It was when tuning the TR9 short range transmitter for maximum aerial current that a serious defect became apparent. We received the voice of the aerodrome controller loud and clear. He said we were barely audible to him. Our aerial was common to both transmitter and receiver. Nevertheless we tested the aerial for insulation and found it perfect so we changed the whole transmitter/receiver unit. Results were identical.

We checked all connections again and replaced the lead-in wire which passed inside the aerial support mast. We were completely baffled. By very good fortune a stranger hove in sight. A Flight-Lieutenant, bearing pilot's wings and DFC medal ribbon, plus a New Zealand accent, inquired into the cause of our obvious distress. He listened patiently to our tale and then asked for a pair of wire-cutters. What madness was this? Giving us a wry smile he cut both the guy wires which supported the aerial mast and said: 'Now try!'

We did, and all was well. Flight-Lieutenant Larney then told us he was a keen amateur radio operator, a member of the Radio Society of Great Britain and had recognised the problem from a past experience. On close examination a thin layer of corrosion was seen to have built up between one guy wire and its anchorage to the airframe. By a freak circumstance the guy wire, thus insulated, had formed a tuned circuit in liaison with its opposite number and absorbed the power from our little transmitter. After replacing the guys, paying careful attention to the bonding, the Stirling was again serviceable. Albert and I appreciated the lesson in wave-form theory. F/Lt. Larney was on rest from operational duty. He proved to be a great friend while temporarily attached to our Signals Section.

N.6037 could now be declared serviceable as far as the wireless equipment was concerned and would be taken on air test. In preparation for take-off the engineers were about to run up the engines. Just as I was disembarking through the side hatch a throttle was opened and a blast of air whipped my spectacles away at high speed. They smashed into a thousand pieces against the tailplane. I had worn spectacles from the age of eight. My next stop was at Sick Quarters, to inquire into the procedure by which I might be supplied with new ones.

Within 48 hours I was whisked off to the RAF Hospital, Ely. A specialist declared that I needed spectacles no longer. I saw through the war without them!

By the end of March we had so many Stirlings around the place that Newmarket racecourse was adopted as a dispersal point. There the ground was chalky and wonderful to walk on. Even when it poured with rain we could still drive our truck around from one aircraft to another, without wheelspin.

April came in wet and windy, making life difficult around our scattered dispersal points. We spent a lot of time trucking across to Newmarket and Wyton. Extra duties came my way, curbing somewhat my sleeping-out privilege. I took my turns at Hangar Guard, Orderly Corporal and Crash Party Duty as well as 'night flying' wireless mechanic. This last was most important to me because it meant direct involvement with members of the aircrews, prior to operations, and receiving any complaints when they returned, God willing.

No. 7 was reaching towards full operational strength. Tensions were beginning to rise. The glorious days of test flying took on their true purpose. We were getting set to clobber the Germans. At the same time the Germans were paying more attention to ourselves. We got the feeling that our big four-engined birds were stirring up passionate retribution aimed directly at Oakington. It became very noticeable in the early hours of a morning when Lilian and I were cosy in our bed at the bungalow in Histon.

The hum of the odd aeroplane overhead did not disturb us normally; this one did. It throbbed. The Germans made a habit, so it was said, of desynchronising propellors in an effort to upset the direction finders of the Royal Observer Corps and the searchlight brigades. Whether the practice ever saved a member of the Luftwaffe from an untimely end will never be known but it seemed worth trying. Our present intruder did throb and did drop bombs; eight of them. The first we heard as a dull puff, the second a less dull puff and the third as a puff. The spacing between first and second equalled the space between second and third so we knew how long before the fourth would sound a bit nearer. The fifth followed in equal time and we guessed the sixth would be louder. It was; and it sounded uncomfortably close. Lilian was under the blankets when the seventh shook the earth. I said that was no good and when the eighth dropped we were both under the bed and the bungalow convulsed. We kissed one another good-bye but the Hun had exhausted his stocks. After an embrace of thanks to the One higher in the sky than the bomber we emerged from our shelter to join the other members of the household in the sharing of a pot of tea.

Our Stirlings on operations suffered a lot of flak on that same night; N.6011 didn't return at all. So there was a blank space in dispersal points and gloom fell on No. 7. I was more than pleased to find myself due for a week's leave.

It was Good Friday when Lilian and I entrained at Cambridge for the 9½-hour journey to Hereford. My services at C.F. King and Co., in clearing a backlog of radio repairs, absorbed most of Easter Saturday. In the Cathedral on Sunday morning the youthful voices in the choir, inspirational as ever, set me wondering: why war? What happened to the crew of N6011? Then my mind wandered: there were the cornices on which I had balanced the loudspeakers for the King George V memorial service. How did I manage to get them up to that height? Would I come back to Hereford after the war?

We thought not of war on Easter Monday. We saw Basil Redford in *Crook's Tour* at the Odeon in Hightown. The holiday ended with a few drams of Scotch whisky at the Garrick and a seven-hour train journey to Cambridge on the Tuesday.

Lilian was due back at Chivers' on the Wednesday morning. I walked with her as far as the office and then we offered more thanks to the Almighty. Jam hung like stalactites from trees. Shattered timber lay around. A huge hole in the ground represented the air-raid shelter where my Lilian would have been had the factory not closed for the Easter holiday. The office itself remained operational. I left my lady-love, to continue my leave by hitch-hiking to Thirsk.

The principal objective of my journey north was to recover my Royal Enfield Bullet from storage. It started up immediately and after an oil change it was ready for the road.

With a day to spare I was able to enjoy some of my mother's culinary specialities. It was incredible what she conjured out of dwindling resources though it seemed that a couple of soldiers she had befriended knew where to pick up a few extra rations. Inevitably I had to cast an admiring eye over father's immaculate fire station where all was set to go into instant action at the firing of a maroon. I called in at his workshop to repair a few radio sets.

On my final day of leave I visited the Church Army canteen to say farewell to my sister who busily served the troops with tea and wads. Then, with petrol coupons in hand, I enjoyed a fast run back to Histon in good time to take Lilian to see George Formby in *Spare a Copper* at the Victoria.

Ownership of a motor-cycle proved to be advantageous in many ways. My time between camp and living-out digs was reduced to five minutes. Off-duty journeyings to Cambridge and its environs no longer incurred waiting for buses. We used to joke about carrying three on the Bullet because Lilian was now three months advanced into the glorious state of reproduction, so I drove steadily, avoiding potholes. On the camp I made extensive use of the bike during daily inspection routines around the dispersal points.

The most remote of the dispersal points was very popular with those of us who possessed petrol driven vehicles. The very thoughtful Flight-Sergeant fitter had concealed an open-topped oil drum into which 'dirty' aviation spirit was discarded. Though of very high octane value we reckoned that when mixed with ordinary 'Pool' petrol no damage would be done to our engines. 'Pool' had been increased in price to 2s. 0½d. (i.e. 11p. in modern currency) per gallon and was strictly rationed. A drop of illegitimate juice we welcomed. Aviation petrol was used by the fitters for cleaning down engines but once the dirt had settled down in the bottom of the drum a good clear and potent liquid could be siphoned off for domestic purposes. Of course, the aviation spirit was coloured sea-green, making it easily detectable by any inquisitive policeman. This did not deter its use because the Sergeant of RAF Police was a regular user!

Whether we owner drivers were insured for use of private vehicles on Air Ministry property never occurred to us. Such delicacies of protocol seemed irrelevant in wartime. On more than one occasion I took Albert on the pillion seat to dispersal points, even to Newmarket racecourse. No questions were asked so long as we completed our tasks, which multiplied with the arrival of more Stirlings in need of finishing touches.

I had been allocated my own parachute and was always prepared for a test flight. I was more than delighted when Reggie Cox telephoned the section requesting that I accompany him in N.6006. When I arrived at the aircraft I congratulated him on his promotion to Flight-Lieutenant.

'Thank you, Lofty,' he said. 'Now, you see, I'm level with you; two stripes!'

He was in great form. I think N.6006 was his favourite kite. He handled it as if it were a fighter. It was the one he took on a daring daylight raid on the Cruiser *Scharnhorst*, during which a group of Messerschmitt 109s intervened. Not only did the Stirling evade them but the rear gunner, Sergeant Capell, shot two of them down!

I felt now that I was making a substantial contribution to the prosecution of war. It was all work and no parades, except pay parades. I was too fully occupied to have given any thought to my application for a commission. The call to interview by the Station Commander came as a complete surprise. It was clear that my Squadron Commander had approved my application and I am sure that Reggie Cox had put in a good word, as had Flight-Sergeant Fawcett who himself was being commissioned. Anyway, the Group Captain indicated that I would be called for a final interview at Air Ministry in due time.

Three days later I was up before Group Captain Adams on another matter which I felt surely must jeopardise my chances of a commission. The matter was so serious that I have never been able completely to eliminate the stigma caused by the course of events. Resulting from my negligence a colleague was killed. Had I read the Daily Routine Orders of the day the tragic accident could not have happened. It was incumbent on all airmen to read DROs. My name was entered in error as Corporal-in-Charge of the Crash Party. At the end of a busy night in the Signals Section I cycled to the bungalow, assuming that I would not be called for another night duty. Had I read the notice, as I should have done, it would have been a simple matter to call at the Orderly Room and have a substitute appointed.

During the night whilst I slept soundly in my private quarters a squadron of Wellingtons was diverted to Oakington owing to foul weather affecting their home base. This called for the alerting of the Duty Crash Party, which must observe the landings of the visitors. In my absence a substitute was hurriedly sought. The unfortunate Corporal to be selected was an off-duty cook, a pleasant chap with whom I had enjoyed the odd game of darts in the NAAFI. I doubt whether he had ever been nearer to an aircraft than when seeing one fly overhead.

It may sound incredible to a stranger to Air Force custom that a quite untrained person should be called to perform any duty on the airfield. But this was wartime and many of us were novices. The duties of Corporal-in-Charge of the Crash Party had not been defined to anyone. A good guess was that physical assistance might be needed by unfortunate victims of accidents. At least I had some experience of aircraft movements and maintenance. My substitute had none.

All the Wellingtons landed safely and were directed by well-ordered signals to dispersal points around the airfield perimeter. The unwary Corporal who had been called from slumber watched with uninitiated interest, in the grey light of dawn, the stirring sight of war-planes coming to rest. One bomber taxied directly towards him. As it came to a standstill he observed a pair of legs projecting from beneath the nose of the aircraft. The bomb-aimer was anxious to disembark. My colleague, believing the fellow needed help, ran forward quite unaware of the yet-rotating propellors. Death was instantaneous.

The charge against me was: 'Failing to report for Crash Party Duty'. Once more I appeared before the Station Commander believing that my chances of a Commission must belong to history. I was relieved to hear him pronounce the simple words:

'I reprimand you.'

Truly remorseful, I was marched away by the Station Warrant Officer, not knowing whither next. The wise fellow counselled me to take particular note of DROs in future and forget the past. Unfailingly I observed the first part of his exhortation.

'Chiefy' Fawcett and my immediate associates in the squadron jollied me along and work proceeded at an ever-increasing pace. The weather took a turn for the better to cheer us up and good old N.6003 came out of the hangar to fly again. Using yet another experimental aerial I joined Squadron-Leader Seale's crew. We verified good beam approaches at Wyton, Mildenhall and Honington to make sure.

If ever I was alarmed in a Stirling it was during a flight in N.6032. Had not the skipper been F/Lt. Cox I might have invoked the first line of Psalm 16. An ominous sign may have shown when the driver of the truck which took us to the dispersal bay handed my parachute to me by the handle! A rapid visit to the parachute section for a re-package was necessary. When I arrived back at N.6032 a fault on the intercom was reported. That was soon corrected. We were airborne at teatime. As I would have no useful part to play until the crew had completed all their mechanical tests, I lay on the comfortable bed behind the wireless cabin, listening to the technical jargon via the intercom.

I gathered that we had achieved a height of 12,000 feet in good time, but that the starboard inner engine was showing signs of distress. That didn't worry me because the other three engines were more than enough to see us home. It had been reported along with other Coxian myths that this pilot *extraordinaire* had put a Stirling down at Turnhouse with all engines stopped but I never heard confirmation of that! So I lay there quite contentedly enjoying the quiet analyses of the experts, until I noticed an unusually strong smell of shellac. When I opened my eyes I saw blue smoke gracefully curling from under my bed. I pressed the switch on my microphone and spoke:

'Lofty here, Sir – smoke rising and it smells hot.'

'OK, Lofty. Someone will come and look.'

'Chalky' White, the engineer, appeared promptly, ran his hand over the heater pipes and said: 'That's fuck-all – just a bit of hot oil coming down the heater from the duff engine!'

So that's what it was!

Captain's voice over the intercom:

'All right, everybody, we're going back to base.'

That was the best news I'd heard for a long time. The smoke thickened but I decided to stick it out where I was in case I interfered with the work of the essential crew members. I heard the whirring of the motors which wind down the undercarriages. Then:

'Tail wheels stuck. Go and see what you can do, Chalky.'

Chalky passed me on his way down the fuselage carrying an axe, of all things. Whatever he did sounded desperate. He came back, coughing through the smoke saying: 'That's fixed the bastard. You'd better come up forrard now or you'll choke to bloody death. We'll be landing in a few minutes.'

And land we did, safely enough with fire engines and reception committee at the ready. We'd been up 1½ hours; it seemed like a whole day; surprising how time flies!

It was midsummer when Hitler switched his main offensive to Russia. Raids on Britain became less frequent. The RAF took advantage of the comparative lull by mounting raids day and night. Our Stirlings specialised in maritime targets: Kiel, Borkum, Wilhelmshaven and Boulogne were some of the harbours we humble mechanics of the ground staff heard about via members of the crews, whose snippets of information had to be put together with BBC news bulletins. The flying boys were reluctant to talk of their exploits except to the Intelligence Officers. However we could not help but get the feeling of success or failure from casual remarks, especially if there was anything wrong with the machinery. Tell-tale bullet holes often indicated how near to disaster they had been. The ones which didn't return at all could never be filed in the 'no news is good news' category. We would stand at a vacant dispersal point and remember the friends we had wished good luck a few hours earlier.

Then another new Stirling would be flown in to be parked in the vacant spot, a new crew to be introduced to the squadron, each member a young man full of hope. Their hope was that they would fly out, drop bombs and return. My hope was that by describing the Lorenz Beam Approach system they might find it a useful aid to their return. Nothing pleased me more than to hear a pilot tell me he had homed on the beam.

Theoretically it was possible to bring off a blind landing but it called for exceptional faith in the altimeter, which instrument was of doubtful accuracy below 50 feet. If the inner marker beacon, which signalled its position by emitting strong 'pips' at the immediate approach to the runway, was flown over at 25 feet, then any pilot would look for landing lights before final touch-down. However, I am sure there are those who made a genuine blind landing so long as the second pilot was doing a 'visual', providing an on-the-spot 'talk-down'.

Some of the pilots enthused over Lorenz, seeing it as a stand-by method of getting home without breaking radio silence. There was always the possibility of the wireless being shot-up or the operator himself injured. The Lorenz set, which was pilot-controlled, may well have survived. The beam at six different aerodromes on the east coast offered alternative emergency get-you-home services.

Of course, there was always the possibility of an enemy bomber doing a run along our own runway. That was one of the hazards of war. Flying control officers had the means of switching off the beam at discretion!

Beam or no beam, the Germans took a fancy to Oakington on more than one occasion, but only once during my sojourn did a bomb plunge into the airfield itself. I was on night duty. Having seen our aircraft depart on a mission I slept soundly on a camp bed in the Signals Workshop, an integral part of 'A' Flight hangar. If an air-raid siren was sounded I did not hear it; neither did I hear an aircraft overhead. All I remember was standing vertically beside my bed. The hangar was still vibrating. A hundred yards away was a very deep hole in the grass and the remains of a tent used by the Crash Party. The German must have had the odd bomb left in stock and with it scored a magpie on our headquarters.

Lilian was getting nervous of living at Histon, had crossed swords with our landlady and thought it was time to return to Hereford. The final decision came when she was sick at the gates of St. John's, foretelling the procreation of another academic. If it were to be a boy it would be named John, if a girl, Valerie. I collected a weekend pass and we entrained immediately.

On my twenty-seventh birthday I found such a pile of radio sets awaiting repair at C.F. King and Co. that I felt obliged to select half-a-dozen which belonged to invalids and fix them. The ranks of radio service engineers in civvy street were sadly depleted; hence faulty sets accumulated all over the country. New sets were not available until the government introduced the famous wartime 'Utility' receiver. This was manufactured in various parts of the country by Murphy, Cossor, Philips and others. It operated on medium waveband only. The powerful Droitwich transmitter on 1,500 metres had been closed to deny its use by the enemy as a beacon.

Lilian and I spent a lovely English Sunday afternoon on Hereford's beauteous Castle Green, still one of the best public parks in the country. When the time came for me to return to the arms of the Royal Air Force a flow of tears fell into the River Wye, enough, I feared, to raise the summer level.

On arrival at Histon I collected the Royal Enfield, rode to camp and re-established myself in 'F' Block. It was good to be back in full-time residence. Albert was on leave and a number of 'private' radio repairs awaited me in the Section. There was additional work of an official kind, too. The Austin Motor

Company was involved now in the manufacture of Stirlings. A group of engineers from that company studied the wireless and Lorenz installations under my guidance; an interesting exercise.

Further excitement was added to my test flights when No. 7 took to dive-bombing, of all things. After checking the Lorenz at Mildenhall or Wyton we would beetle off to Berner's Heath for practice bombing and Lakenheath for gunnery. Some of the pilots became very expert. Although I was unable to see everything that was going on I soon found myself making secret judgements, from my prone position on the bed!

The Stirling was the first of our four-engined bombers. It must have presented a terrifying sight to anybody in its firing path. I think our reputation caused Oakington to be singled out by the Germans for more attacks. The only damage during August was to the railway line.

Life on the camp continued undisturbed. ENSA did us proud in the way of concerts. I was delighted in particular when Jerry Hoey and his Band, of Piccadilly Hotel fame, entertained us. When his microphone amplifying system broke down I was able to rectify the fault. That cost him a pint of beer. In addition I obtained his autograph for onward transmission to my young sister, a keen collector of signatures.

My life at Oakington came to an abrupt close when the Squadron Adjutant notified me that I had been granted a Commission in His Majesty's Service. I sold the Bullet to a Sergeant Fitter, collected a leave pass and despatched myself to George the Tailor in Cambridge.

Mr George specialised in uniforms for RAF officers. He was proud to provide almost the whole outfit for slightly less than the official allowance of £45. Everything was of top quality; it comprised:

> 2 – Suits
> 1 – Greatcoat
> 1 – Ceremonial cap
> 1 – Glengarry
> 2 – Shirts
> 4 – Collars
> 2 – Ties

Initial measurements completed, away I went on leave yet again. At Hereford I purchased raincoat, gloves and oddments not included in Mr George's package. That done, I was at a loss to fill in my time. It was all very well being in the company of my loved ones but I didn't half miss my aeroplanes. I became very weary of answering the questions put by acquaintances:

'Where are you stationed now?' and 'When are you going back?'

The days of leave began to drag. I was delighted to present myself eventually for final fitting. Mr George pronounced his satisfaction. I reciprocated. The venerable tailor, with a great flurry, presented me with seven-and-sixpence change out of my £45 allowance!

Completion of my clearance certificate at Oakington was like taking a passport to another world. I had enjoyed my work and the comradeship there. After an extended round of farewells my Stirling days ended.

Had chance come my way, I think I would have returned to Oakington in 1944. Wing Commander R.W. Cox DSO, AFC, took command of No. 7. As things turned out I did find another world. Meanwhile, my favourite pilot went on to distinguish himself, happily to survive the war and retire as a Group Captain in 1962.

Chapter 26

'Now, Gentlemen!'

On first sighting the large barrack blocks surrounded by high walls, broken only by enormous iron gates, I feared I might have been mistakingly directed to a prison. Numerous documents were to be signed before I was allotted my bedspace in Room 4, 'Somme'. The very name chilled the spine. My father-in-law had been in the area in 1918 and gave a very poor opinion of it. Nevertheless, he appreciated the friendships which had helped him to endure hardships. So it was at Uxbridge. We were in for a drilling, much of it 'at the double', but good humour saw us smile through.

I was one of a very small minority of entrants to the Officer Training School who had come up from the ranks. The vast majority were direct from civvy street: accountants, musicians, teachers, chemists, dentists and many recent graduates from a diversity of colleges. At first I felt somewhat inadequate amongst so many academics but I found myself to be the object of inquiry into my eighteen months experience in the service. I was regarded as an old hand. There was one very much older than myself, a veteran of World War I, whom I met on my first evening at Uxbridge and for whom I developed great respect.

All entrants were classified Acting Pilot Officer-on-Probation. Our uniforms were identical outcomes of the £45 allowance, except for that of Mr Philippi. *His* uniform was a product of Savile Row, unmistakably of superior quality. He wore a row of medal ribbons including that of the Military Cross. My curiosity got the better of me. Philippi had flown Nieuport Scouts of 60 Sqdn. of the Royal Flying Corps. On 26 September 1916 he shot down a hostile kite balloon over Bapaume, and was himself wounded in the attack. It was obvious that the man was very well connected, as it is said, so I did not question why he wore the rings and epaulettes of a Flying Officer. The thicker rings seemed to suit his general appearance better than the thin ones displayed by the rest of us. It was an error.

My next-door bed neighbour on my starboard side was 'Doc' Probert, an executive of the Roche Chemical Company, and on my port side a teacher from Ormskirk who was a keen amateur radio transmitter. Altogether some twenty of us occupied Room 4 of 'Somme'. Such widely varied interests engendered good conversation.

My introduction to the Officers' Mess revealed a new standard of service. After the queuing and clattering to which I had become accustomed, I enjoyed the relative silence and a more intellectual level of discussion. I had leaped a good many steps up the social staircase.

Our first morning on the barrack square served as an introduction to the basics of discipline, the difference between standing to attention and standing at ease. Next came a lecture on 'Care of the Feet'. This proved invaluable in the weeks to come, especially for those of us who were of sedentary occupation in civilian life. It soon became clear that the Royal Air Force did not intend its officers to spend overmuch time in an office.

Rain poured over the square on our second afternoon when I spent a couple of hours in the excellent camp library. As an ex-ranker I was excused attendance at the grand inoculation ceremony. Sunday was devoted to leisure activities, allowing serums to soak in where applicable.

Any ideas we may have dreamed that Uxbridge was to be a centre for relaxation were dispelled by an extremely noisy Drill Sergeant. At 06.30 hours on the Monday morning we awoke to a Tyneside accent: 'Come along now, gentlemen. Rise and shine!'

Doc Probert had risen already, partaking of his first round of pills. He required more time over ablutions and dressing than the rest of us. After a light breakfast, together we assembled on the parade ground. The real business of the course was about to begin. Four squads of trainee officers, each under the direction of a raucous Sergeant, occupied the four sides of the square. It was very necessary to tune the ear to one's own Sergeant. Many an hilarious incident arose when a trainee mistook a command emanating from the core of an adjacent squad.

The elementary rules of marching in step, turning and halting were explained. With such a variety of human structures to be tutored our dapper little instructor showed remarkable patience. It was clear that many of our number had never learned to walk, never mind march. Mr Philippi was willing enough but his elegance showed distinct signs of bending with age. The Sergeant's first attempt at compromise was a dreadful mistake. He put Philippi at the tail of the column as we set off marching west to east along the south side of the parade ground. Whilst Mr Philippi fell slightly behind, at least he did not impede the rest of us. That is, until the Sergeant ordered the 'About Turn'. Our turn was executed in orderly fashion. The front of the column now faced the venerable Philippi, who had not picked up the command. He continued in the easterly direction. The westerly moving line diverged slightly to absorb him into the midst of swinging arms whereupon he made a belated turn and formed a singleton.

The Sergeant brought the ensemble to a halt and took a few breaths in gaining composure before addressing his elder in kindly terms: 'You are having difficulty, Mr Philippi.'

'I am afraid so, Sergeant.'

'Do stand upright on parade, Mr Philippi.'

'I will indeed,' he replied, bending forward to emphasise his sincerity.

'I think it is better that you stand out here beside me and watch the performance.'

We had taken to our little Geordie instructor and did our best to show good results. He informed us that the next parade would be a formal inspection by the Station Commander. For that we assembled in two lines, having paid extra careful attention during a break to such details as fingernails and toecaps. We made sure that Mr Philippi stood erect in the front row and he responded with natural grace.

The Group Captain, accompanied by the Station Warrant Officer, examined carefully each and every uniformed trainee, finding no fault with the turn-out and making scarcely a comment until he stopped in front of the veteran of the squad. The CO was both impressed and intrigued:

'I appreciate that you are an old campaigner but I don't think you are entitled to wear the insignia of a Flying-Officer. How did it come about?'

'I am afraid I put too much faith in my tailor, Sir. He considered the thinner rings to be out of proportion. I will have the correction made as soon as possible.'

That very evening a Rolls-Royce pulled up at the barrack gate. It was driven by a lady of fashion who welcomed Mr Philippi as a passenger. Grapevine information disclosed that overtime work by a Savile Row tailor rectified his error. The same source revealed that the Group Captain's schedule of entertainment was being adjusted as a matter of urgency.

When Mr Philippi reappeared among us he did so as an Acting-Pilot-Officer-on-Probation. His personal charisma radiated the aura of a Commander-in-Chief. He communicated with us very little because of our reluctance to ask questions, certainly not because of his aloofness. He listened attentively to the numerous lectures on subjects ranging around Air Ministry Instructions. He gracefully avoided excessive activities on the Parade Ground and paid scant obeisance to the PT instructor's exhortations to flex unused muscles. Whilst many a tortured body creaked and groaned over press-ups, Mr Philippi limited his exertions, without complaint, at the back of the class.

By the end of the first week the Sergeant had broken us in to something like the shape he envisaged. Following a relatively peaceful weekend we practised firearms drill, shooting on the range by rifle and pistol. Whilst results varied tremendously we had achieved a degree of efficiency sufficient to move on to squad command. This was designed to prove whether the officers were capable of controlling their men. All one was required to do was to emulate the function of the Drill Sergeant. The results varied from exemplary to absolute chaos.

In fairness to those trainees who lost control of their squad it should be remembered that four different squads carried out similar exercises at any one time. Ideally each squad would confine its movements to one quarter of the square and not encroach upon neighbouring zones. There was ample room for the standard manoeuvres with which we had all become familiar. Troubles arose when two squads were found to be approaching each other and the commander of one or the other, or both, forgot or omitted the 'Ay-bout Tu-rn' order. This omission sometimes resulted in a rather neat transfer of the two squads to alternative command.

A clever method of avoiding the head-on situation was attempted by one trainee who endeavoured to move his squad at right-angles to the on-coming party. He called out clearly enough:

'Squad . . . Move to the right . . . RIGHT TU-RN.'

His squad obeyed the order and turned south without mishap. Unfortunately for Squad 'B', its members understood the order to apply to themselves also, whereupon they turned north and set off over the grass bank which forms the northern edge of the Uxbridge rectangle. It should be mentioned that the square is inclined towards the grass bank, which in turn falls steeply to a roadway. Therefore, any person stepping determinedly over the bank is likely to do so in a state of acceleration. Squad 'B' demonstrated the effect *en masse*.

Errors made by individual squad commanders can best be attributed to 'nerves under stress'. To be taken from the security of the serried ranks of the squad and placed before those very comrades with whom you have marched to orders, is a chastening experience. A good squad commander must bring forth from his deeper self a measure of sadism; there must be at least a forced enjoyment of making one's fellow-men jump to it. Amongst us were those natural leaders who gloried in power. They got the best results and were complimented by the instructor. There were some gentlefolk for whom the giving of orders was uncharacteristic. Results ranged from hilarity to total paralysis.

Doc Probert, whose early morning pill-taking never failed to wake us before the Sergeant's call to arms, would not say 'boo' to a goose, never mind a squad of satirical A/P/Os. Of Pickwickian rotundity, Doc took station in front of his friends and froze. Moments passed before his mouth opened to a large 'O'. No sound came forth, the mouth closed and Doc took a nervous step backwards. Once again the 'O' formed, closed and then: the one-step. Now, the steep grass bank at the bottom of the parade ground was close behind Doc and whispers of speculation rippled through the ranks. The Sergeant watched in keen anticipation of minor mishap. Doc released a very subdued: 'Squa . . . o . . .', and took two steps backwards. Not only did he roll down the grass bank but he continued into the entrance of a built-in air-raid shelter.

Happily, Doc's well upholstered body prevented damage to his bone structure. A few words of encouragement from the Sergeant restored his equilibrium. The next move by our ingenious instructor gave Doc confidence to continue his task. He walked him to the rear of the squad from which aspect he stood higher up the slope of the ground and looked down on our hindquarters. The next thing we heard was: 'Squa . . .d, Ay-bout-turn . . .' When we had completed this cleverly conceived movement there in front of us was dear old Doc smiling all over his chubby face and in complete command.

We entered our third and final week at Uxbridge fitter and wiser. The days were filled with drilling, firing practice, lectures and PT. In the evenings small groups of us would drift off for a pint at a local pub. The wartime beer, controlled in strength and price, was very acceptable; it acted as a spur to walk further afield in spite of a hard day on the square. We were fitter indeed.

Our final squad-taking tests satisfied the staff. Those of us with any inclination to perform upon the stage took part in a Grand Concert in the mess. We paid our mess bills – mine was slightly less than £3 for the three weeks – and then came announcements of our postings to operational stations.

It was at that point that I met a new and famous friend: Dr Leslie Paul FRCO. The pair of us had been listed under: RAF Station, Wick. Les possessed a well maintained Hillman Minx coupé. He had ascertained that he could obtain petrol coupons for the journey. Would I care to join him as passenger? I was more than delighted to accept the invitation.

Good wishes proliferated until late at night. Everybody wanted to know where everybody was going: Smith to Shawbury, Jones to Jarrow and Robinson to Rissington. Jolly good show chaps and isn't Mr Philippi fortunate in being posted just around the corner to Stanmore?

The little Hillman started up first tweak of the switch. By mid-morning of Friday 12 September we were heading up the Great North Road at 50 m.p.h. destined to stay the night at Thirsk. My parents had been warned to expect two guests. The family piano had no idea that it was about to perform the greatest act of its life. It was in good tune, for my mother was an accomplished pianist who took care of the instrument. Leslie approved its qualities in running through a couple of Percy Grainger's pieces and promised further entertainment after dinner.

Though the meal provided by mother must have caused a slimming of ration books it was understood that the butcher had found a bit extra in honour of my visit. Vegetables grown in the wonderfully fertile Vale of Mowbray cannot be bettered in quality. Neighbours had supplemented produce of our own garden. A good feast was had by all. Then came the real treat.

Leslie played a few of his favourites to begin a concert which extended into the small hours. Mother requested Sinding and Schubert, Father stuck to Mozart and plenty of him. Neighbours joined the company until the little house could contain no more. They never forget the night that Leslie D. Paul performed at Thirsk.

The Minx ran perfectly again on Saturday. We were obliged to erect the hood when rain started to fall at Edinburgh. It was pouring down when we reached Perth where we found a welcome at the Salutation Hotel. It was my first experience of a good hotel. Though I have sampled many a hotel since that memorable journey my affection for the Salutation never lessened.

On a leisurely final day we lunched at the 'National' at Dingwall, took tea at Lybster and a fine supper was spread for us in the mess at Wick. We were sufficiently relaxed to attend a gramophone recital after which Leslie obliged with a few tunes to shake up the mess piano. His skills were roundly applauded and much sought after during the time I stayed at Wick. He enhanced the musical education of all who were fortunate enough to serve at that northerly station in September 1941.

It was a privilege indeed for me to share a billet with so distinguished a musician for a whole month.

Chapter 27

Coastal Command

Never in my wildest dreams did I imagine that I could enjoy myself more than I had done at Oakington. At Wick, as a supernumerary Pilot Officer in the Signals Section, I was about to embark upon what was tantamount to a holiday. I think the remoteness of Wick engendered an especial closeness of companionship. We contrived our own entertainments. When Leslie Paul played the piano everything else stopped.

As new boys we were welcomed by a genial Adjutant and despatched to our respective sections, Leslie to Flying Control and myself to Signals. It was my very good fortune to be taken under the wing of Flight-Lieutenant Reg Lawes, an old hand at the game, an extremely competent Signals Officer from whom I learned both the principles and the practices of running a Signals Station in Coastal Command. Reg was a dynamo of a man, always on the move but never failing to find time to teach and help others. To him I owe many of my successes and none of my failures.

I arrived on the scene just as a fault had developed at the MF/DF (Medium-Frequency Direction Finder) station. The operator on duty reported variations in bearings taken on a few check points. Pilot Officer Lewis, another supernumerary, knew his way around the environment.

The pair of us were despatched to form an opinion. It was my first sighting of a MF/DF system at first hand. I had read up W. T. Keen's *Wireless Direction Finding*, the best book then, and maybe still, on the subject. To see the textbook coming to life was fascinating.

The weather had been somewhat inclement and the Corporal Wireless Mechanic, on the strength of his insulation tests, thought that a good polish to the aerial insulators at the bottom of the masts might clear the fault. Lewis took to this idea because he saw it as an excuse for getting his uniform dirty. Though a 'VR' like myself he suffered from a not uncommon form of inverted snobbery. Scruffy uniforms were supposed to indicate long service by the wearer. His scratching around and using his cap as a polishing cloth got us nowhere. Insulation on two of the four aerials was below standard.

Back at the Signals Office we reported our findings to F/Lt. Lawes as instructed. He asked me what I thought should be done about it. I said I would like to dig up the feeder cables and examine them. At that point my first lesson in decision making began:

'First of all,' he said, 'you must obtain a second opinion from your immediate superior – that's me!'

Off we drove to the MF/DF where Reg satisfied himself that the two feeder cables were leaking.

'Now; do you still want to dig up the cables?'

'Yes.'

'I say, No! The very first thing we must do is to notify Group Headquarters that this MF/DF is out of commission. They will do two things: No.1, inform all appropriate operational stations via their respective commands. No.2, instruct a Maintenance Unit to carry out repairs. It is not our job to repair equipment, only to operate it. That is the rule. As an Officer you do not start digging holes except in a grave emergency. Let us hope you never find that necessary.'

Having despatched the relevant message to Group HQ we despatched ourselves to the mess for lunch.

'The MF/DF is somebody else's problem now. Let's have a beer and a game of shove ha'penny.'

Lunch, as all other meals at Wick, was a wholesome one. We were far enough from the direct effects of the war not to be concerned about food rationing. The catering staff knew all the local farmers and producers by name. The fishermen were only too pleased to have a market expansion on their quaysides. A favourite evening ride was to purchase fresh crabs and lobsters at Keiss village. Wick was a great place to be, for friendship, comfort and interesting work.

Various forms of Radar systems were coming into use. An aircraft arrived from Farnborough with some ASV (Air-to-Surface Vessel) equipment to be installed in one of our Whitleys, for experimental purposes, in conjunction with a miniature transmitter to be carried in an Air-Sea Rescue rubber dinghy. Wick was the ideal place for such trials. We were unlikely to be molested by enemy aircraft and September usually favours those northerly latitudes with calm weather.

On the same day as I enjoyed my first outing in an RAF Rescue Launch, Leslie Paul made his first flight on convoy escort duty. We both thanked our lucky stars for our posting to Wick.

Our skipper of the Hants and Dorset high-speed launch was Flight-Lieutenant Spikin, a bemedalled old sea-dog. He had spent many years at sea and gave us a few tips on avoiding sea-sickness. He had never suffered the malady, he told us, but understood it could be quite distressing. Although the sea was dead calm the launch stirred up the water as it accelerated at an inspiring rate, cocked its prow and fairly danced out of the harbour. I observed the Captain's advice and danced with the boat. Enjoy moving with the boat, he said, and you won't ever feel sick.

Ten miles out we stopped and unshipped the rubber dinghy into which F/Lt. Lawes and a Flight-Sergeant Pilot climbed, complete with the emergency transmitter. They cast off and we moved slowly away leaving them, lonely figures in the little rubber boat. Then the porpoises took an interest in them, a whole school of the creatures. What a wonderful sight it was: the orange boat on the still blue sea ringed by dorsal fins cutting the surface like knives, dozens of them, scarcely disturbing the water.

As we drew away the gurgling of our motor seemed to delight the dolphins who left the dinghy and followed us. Reg Lawes and the Flight-Sergeant became a speck on the horizon. We stopped engines. The dolphins seemed to take offence at the abrupt discontinuation of the conversation. They flurried away amidst a great commotion of the sea. The mini-waves lapped soothingly against the hull of our launch which began to rock slowly and gently. I joined the crew in silently gazing over the side, at minor fish catching flashes of sunlight on their scales. Peace, perfect peace. Then from the stern of the vessel we heard significant retching sounds. Flight-Lieutenant Spikin was vomiting!

Condolences were not well received by the ancient mariner but a more important diversion prevented a reversion to our former reveries. The ASV-equipped Whitley was heard, then seen to be making straight towards our colleagues in the dinghy. The experiment was a success. Search time had been reduced to a minimum.

Nor was I to be denied additional flying experience. An assortment of aircraft included an Anson of the Communication Flight. It was in that old favourite I flew with F/O McAdam to Stornoway on the Isle of Lewis. We had it on good authority that kippers of exceptional quality were obtainable ready boxed for transit. To buy a load was the main purpose of our visit.

F/O Chandler, the genial assistant Signals Officer, took charge of the wireless. Like myself, Chandler was a VR but he had passed through the Signals Course at Cranwell, to which I was destined following my probationary period. Unlike him, therefore, I was not a qualified operator. That gave me the advantage of sitting alongside the pilot, thus getting a far superior view of the Scottish countryside. When we sighted Cape Wrath, instead of making a bee-line for Stornoway we turned sharply south-westward. The reason was that the alert McAdam had sighted the enormous convoy of which he had been warned. Steaming north up the Minch, headed by minesweepers and accompanied by an assortment of ships of the Royal Navy, was the largest collection of merchant vessels I could have imagined.

I saw the flash of light calling for identification. Mac said: 'Give him the letter of the day.'

Feeling very important I picked up our Aldis lamp, took aim at the destroyer which had called. I flashed 'M' and received prompt acknowledgement. Nevertheless our cautious pilot had no intention of flying over the convoy. 'They're a trigger-happy lot,' he said. 'We'll fly round 'em.' And so we did. We sighted Loch Ewe before Mac deemed it safe enough to turn north for Stornoway.

We took tea in a hotel which served as Officers' Mess and gathered that we would be wise not to wander round the streets. English sightseers were not all that welcome. There was strong anti-Anglo feeling among the population, especially on that day. It appeared that on the previous evening an RAF aircraft had dropped a string of practice bombs on the beach for the purpose of putting the wind up the locals, some of whom were inclined to regard Nazism with affection. Proprietors of the fishmongeries showed no animosity as they pocketed our money and we loaded the Anson with numerous boxes of kippers.

From Wick station I despatched a box of kippers to Thirsk. Included were instructions to retain half the consignment locally and to forward the remainder to Hereford. Unfortunately the duration of the second part of the journey was more than the kippers could withstand. Burial of the offensive remains was the only sensible method of disposal. Within the course of time, my father-in-law reported a record crop of potatoes over the burial point!

My success with the Aldis lamp spurred me on to take renewed interest in learning the Morse Code and to study Signals Procedure. It was at Wick that I recognised the vital importance of communications and economy of use of its various channels, particularly of the telephone. A Signals Officer is empowered to dictate rules, even to his Commanding Officer, on how to make best use of channels. (I have yet to learn how to restrict use of my domestic telephone to essential business.)

The Meteorological Officers were among the worst offenders in wasting communication facilities. A trained Wireless Operator manned the Met. channel, taking down endless 5-figure codes which the Met. men swallowed. From those figures they compiled their charts and then what? They would telephone their neighbouring stations to compare results and come up with a compromise forecast, always hedging their bets with a few probables and possibles! On top of all that expense a Spitfire would go up to a great height every day, take a look around and see, first hand, what weather was on its way.

RAF Wick rejoiced in versatility. Apart from the regular convoy escort duties, continuous stand-by for Air-Sea Rescue, Met. flight, Communications Flight, a watch was kept on enemy activities around Norway. The distance to Bergen is about 400 miles. Quick, twin-engined aircraft were used on these reconnaissance flights. I think the De Havilland Mosquito was the quickest by far and what a beautiful machine it was; sad to say that, being built of wood, the British weather played havoc with it. The pilots who undertook those sorties gathered intimate knowledge of towns. Of course they studied maps but after a few trips they learned on which buildings the enemy had fixed machine guns and which streets to avoid. It was an education to hear them mentioning such details as the names on the shops!

The Germans didn't reciprocate. During my stay at Wick our social life was unmolested. Snooker, billiards and table tennis games were popular but if Leslie Paul took his seat at the piano everybody gathered around to listen. His repertoire seemed endless. I think he responded to every request. Occasionally he would conclude a sonata by slapping his brow and apologising for a mistake. On one memorable occasion he was heard to say:

'Oh, dear. I omitted a whole phrase from the second movement. My brother Reginald has a wonderful memory!'

Nobody but the maestro himself had detected any omission.

One evening Leslie and I walked down to Wick town. He wanted to try out the church organ in preparation for a service at which he had been invited to play. The occasion would be the baptism of the baby of a Wing Commander and spouse. Leslie approved of the organ. The dust was shaken from some of the hitherto unused pipes. I was unable to attend the service myself but reports told of the rebirth of a church organ. The congregation was uplifted by the music to such an extent that its most important members ascended skywards. Piloted by father, a Wellington took off carrying mother, baby, organist and numerous guests on a trip round the bay before celebrating in more orthodox manner. That was one evening when our star pianist did not entertain us. I found him fast asleep, fully clothed, on his bed. There he stayed for several hours. When he did wake he asked me whether I had enjoyed the Bach minuet, which he had played 'for fun'. He was disappointed that I had been unable to attend the service. I asked him how he had enjoyed his flight. He couldn't recollect having been on one!

I took advantage of an invitation from P/O Unwin to fly with him in the Anson to Sumburgh in the Shetland Islands. The sea was dead calm and blue, not a cloud visible. The sun was about to dip into the horizon as Unwin took us very low over the water on our return flight. I thought he was flying low just for the fun of it but he was preparing for us a special treat. F/O Chandler was called forward from his position at the wireless. We were told to look straight ahead at the horizon. Just at the right moment the pilot pulled back the stick and there from the sea, orange bright in the sunshine, rose the Fair Isle, an unforgettable surprise. Set in the sparkling sea, a few white gulls circling around the lonely rocks, a more appropriate name at the time might have been 'Fairyland'.

Chandler returned to his wireless in a flash when we heard our call-sign. Wick warned us of enemy aircraft approaching. We were quite defenceless but our fears were needless. When we landed a smiling Reg Lawes welcomed us: 'You got my message all right, boys?' His joke had been shared by all members on duty in the Signals Section.

Though good humour prevailed, the business of war had taken a very serious turn when Hitler swung a massive attack against Russia. Efforts must be made to supply our new allies by sea via the North Cape. That called for additional air cover of convoys. More aircraft and their crews converged on Wick. Suddenly accommodation on the camp was overloaded. To make room for the essential elements somebody must move. Leslie and I, along with a few other trainee officers, took up temporary residence in MacKay's hotel in the town, which is about 300 feet below the aerodrome.

Alongside the road between town and aerodrome is a narrow footpath, broken only at intervals by entrances to a number of cul-de-sacs which serve rows of cottages. At the end of each row is a chimney stack which abuts into the footpath at base and rises straight upwards to terminate in a chimney pot, a favourite perch for Wickian seagulls.

I left MacKay's after a late breakfast because I was not on duty until 10.00 hrs. My companions had all gone ahead. Alone I set off up the steep and narrow footpath. The morning was cold, damp, foggy. I wore my spotless blue rubberised waterproof coat and my equally new glengarry. I was truly proud of my Royal Air Force uniform. Two young members of the 'Waaf' walked out of the swirling fog. At a suitable distance they saluted smartly. The timing of my return of salute coincided precisely with the discharge from the bowels of a corpulent cormorant. It was a direct hit. I was conscious of the stifled merriment of the two Waafs as they continued down to town. The bird flew off seaward giving a gutteral gloat of relief. Uncomfortably I passed the Guardroom with raincoat inside out and folded over my arm and returned the salute of the guard who stared askance at my polluted cap. I made a beeline for the nearest toilet facilities.

It was an ignominious ending to my term at Wick for I was shortly to be despatched, for further experience, to Leuchars, before going on to the Signals School at Cranwell. My mentor, Reg Lawes, thought the school would be a waste of time and proposed to Group HQ that I should be excused the course. He considered that my experience in the ranks as a Wireless Mechanic, my technical knowledge garnered from civvy street, plus a month under his watchfulness at Wick, were sufficient qualifications to enable me to handle a junior posting at an operational station. Group HQ didn't agree and neither did I. Having foregone a University training I looked forward to a six-month course at Cranwell; an opportunity not to be missed.

As events turned out I think Lawes was right. I would have learned a lot more on a station than I ever picked up at Cranwell. However, as will be seen, I made good friends and nearly saw the King.

Meanwhile, I took leave of my companions of Wick, stepped aboard 'The Highlander' *en route* for Leuchars, via Perth and Dundee plus a ferry-boat ride across the Tay.

From the wooden huts of Wick it was a big up-market step to the relative magnificence of the Officers' Mess at Leuchars. I found it heavily populated by Dutchmen who operated a squadron of Hudson aircraft. The crew members were nearly all ex-KLM staff who were notable for hogging the enormous fireplace. As they had joined us ostensibly as guests they were respected as such but the idiom: 'You can't see the fire for Dutchmen' built itself into the general description of RAF Leuchars.

My new chief, F/Lt. Hall, was quick to describe the vast selection of signals facilities under his control. He was most anxious that I familiarised myself with everything of technical interest and beyond that he introduced me to Scottish Reel Dancing. The Town Major played the fiddle with tremendous gusto and his young son skirled the bagpipes to match. Twice a week we reeled to their rousings.

From Leuchars I had no chance of a flight. All our aircraft were operationally involved so that sightseeing was out of the question. I did take the opportunity of examining the Bendix radio equipment in a Hudson and thought it looked like a display of Cartier's jewellery as compared to some of our old-fashioned gear. Even our latest TR.1154/55 appeared clumsy in comparison with the Bendix which set new standards in communications equipment.

My rounds of duties kept me away from aeroplanes but I did manage to cadge a lively trip from Tayport by high speed launch. On board I learned at first hand the use of direction finding gear. The skipper described a few of the many hazards of Air-Sea Rescue operations. All these experiences added to my broadening knowledge of the intricate network of RAF communications.

A Lorenz system was being installed. I was delighted to be present at the commissioning. Another novelty came under examination at the HF/DF station which was equipped with a Plessey cathode ray tube system. When an aircraft called up for a course to steer, the operator swung the goniometer until the signal from the aircraft was a maximum, when the line on the CRT gave a direct visual reading for the recommended course to steer. Thus, time was saved over the conventional earphone method whereby the operator had to measure for a 'dip' in the signal and check for polarity before broadcasting the result. As well as saving a couple of seconds, the possibility of error was reduced.

A diversion from the Signals Section: I was detailed to assist in the umpiring of a mock invasion of the aerodrome; good cloak and dagger stuff. Indeed, the secrecy was such that I never understood what I was supposed to do. My accomplice was a much bemedalled Flight-Lieutenant, a new arrival at the station, enjoying a rest period from operational flying. We came under the instructions of an aged Colonel who was planning the invasion. We umpires were to decide whether his Army broke through the cordon of RAF Regimental defence, or were repulsed. It struck me that the old chap didn't have a clue about modern warfare, but as I had none either I sat and listened in the hope that my new found colleague would grasp the import of the underlying strategy. I had, of course, heard the word 'Blitzkrieg' used in news broadcasts. The old gentlemen went on and on at great length to describe his version of what it meant, presumably, what we were to expect. Whether he thought we were inattentive I am not sure but suddenly he broke from his tedious monologue and snapped: 'Do you follow me?'

I froze, but my fellow umpire didn't. He said:

'Well, Sir, when I was in Crete . . .'

The Colonel's face changed colour.

The invasion went off like a damp squib. Few people knew it took place. Certainly some members of the Home Guard were found drinking in the airmen's canteen after dark. In the Officers' Mess a group of invaders joined the Scottish reels and the Colonel showed us how the Highland Fling should be flung.

My education received further enhancement by a visit to the Royal Observer Corps post at St. Andrews and to Regional Control. A Post Office Engineer described the responsibilities of his vast organisation in providing the telephone and teleprinter networks.

I was an integral part of the Signals Branch of the RAF. Our talk was of Groups and Commands, frequencies and channels, transmissions and receptions, beacons and bearings, codes and ciphers. Our intercommunications were with other RAF stations. Towns and cities were places to pass through on the bus or in the train on the way to another RAF station.

The call to Cranwell came early in November. By ferry to Dundee to catch the train for Edinburgh. On the way the great thrills of crossing the Tay Bridge and the Forth Bridge. Then came the equally exciting crossing of the Tyne and on to Darlington where I took the 'local' for Thirsk to spend the night at the conclusion of a twelve-hour adventure. It was not too late to take my mother to see *Arise My Love* at the Picture House and then to find my father still at work. I helped him burn some midnight oil, repaired a few wireless sets in an effort to keep the Home Service going, caught up with the latest news, treated the folks to a drop of Scotch and slept well.

Father took me to Thirsk station in the Jowett van which was going as well as ever in spite of its juddering clutch and rattling bodywork. I vowed that when the war was over and done I would buy for myself a brand new Jowett car. The family saloon cost £150 in 1939. I thought that would just suit my pocket.

I caught the 9 o'clock to York.

Chapter 28

No. 10 War Course (Signals)

My college days at Cranwell began on 7 November 1941 and continued until 7 May 1942. In those six months we students were expected to absorb the contents of a course which in peacetime spanned two and a half years!

Academically I was outclassed by my fellow students, many of whom were fresh from universities. A number of schoolmasters, professional chemists and accountants made up the six dozen members of the course.

Our domestic quarters were located on the north side of the north airfield. This necessitated our marching twice daily to and from the wooden-hutted Signals School. Our marches through biting winds became less dignified when snow descended. Thankfully, the ample comfort of our greatcoats saved fractured limbs when falling and maintained respectable body temperatures in the classrooms.

No. 10 acquired the reputation of being the least disciplined of any course to date. Our isolated messing facilities did engender a freedom denied those fellow students on concurrent courses who shared their lives with hardened disciplinarians. A couple of less attentive students spent a great deal of time in building an elaborate model aeroplane, much of the delicate work surretitiously performed beneath desk level, within a few feet of the hardworking instructors. After the product of their labours smashed to pieces on its only flight, an improvement in class behaviour was appreciated by students and tutors alike.

Our accommodation in detached houses provided comforts far superior to normal communal barrack-type buildings. I shared a room with a brilliant mathematician who helped me to achieve a respectable mark in the introductory assessment examination.

On 8 November, in the lounge of our villa, a group of us discussed the results of our tests. Sealed against the biting winds, room temperature rose, oxygen content diminished. Whatever the cause, I collapsed in my seat at precisely 9.00 p.m. My friends revived me by enthusiastic application of elementary first-aid.

On the morning of Monday 10th, a telegram arrived at the Adjutant's Office. Its contents:

'Son born 9.00 p.m. Saturday. All's well, love, Lilian.'

The leave pass permitted me to visit mother and son over the following weekend. The return journey could be achieved by becoming thoroughly involved in the problems of wartime communications. Bus company and railway employees put forward individual suggestions on how best to move forward. The 48-hour pass enabled me to spend 24 with my family and 24 on foot, bus, train or taxi. The stoic humour of the people infused determination to keep going; nowhere were voiced thoughts of defeat by the enemy.

Following the discomfiture of wartime travelling I returned to the relative security within the Signals School. Lessons were conducted in leisurely fashion. The urgencies of war seemed quite irrelevant.

The most popular instructor was a Flight-Sergeant with many years of service to his credit. He amused us with tales of life in the Far and Near East and Malta. His anecdotes kept our attention far better than boring descriptions of elementary electrical machinery. He responded to our applause by describing the visit of a senior naval officer to an aircraft carrier. The unfortunate admiral was passengered in a light aircraft which missed the flight deck and landed on the water close to the carrier. The aircraft being raised by mechanical hoist became suspended alongside when the hoist jammed. Successive attempts calling for raising and lowering of the aircraft caused serious depreciation of goodwill between naval and air forces.

Our remarkable civilian instructor in Morse and Signals Procedure demonstrated another faculty of the human brain. He could carry out a normal conversation with a pupil at the same time as he transmitted a message in Morse Code and received another one on an adjacent channel. At the Signals School messages over the public address system came in Morse Code. Mr Wyatt could read such messages whilst transmitting a message by semaphore.

Lectures on basic radio and electrical theory in a blackboard setting were boring. I saw no virtue in copying out the circuit diagram of the R.1082 when faultless copies were readily available. Nothing ever went wrong with a 1082, anyway. It was built to exacting standards and unless someone blew a valve or two it could remain sealed for life.

The mathematical expertise of many of the graduates nearly but never quite matched that of F/O Pride, our Stornowegian tutor. They tried to baffle him but he always came out on top. The deathly silence which followed each challenge intrigued me. Pride remained cool and calculating, mentally working out the answer and writing it down on the blackboard. With a great flourish the final 'equals' sign appeared as a short railway track, followed by the result and a whacking big full-stop which broke the chalk. Not a word passed his lips; his eyes said everything.

Experienced mathematicians sat in awe, knowing full well that Pride would win, but unlike myself they could follow the arguments. One such character was Powell Tuck, mathematics master at Penarth Grammar School until joining the RAF. Tucky and I shared a room in the house, for which arrangement we were equally grateful. He spent hours showing me how to make maths exciting. I am sure there must have been a high rate of passes in the subject at Penarth.

He played the equations of James Clerk Maxwell's theory of electromagnetic propogation like a conjuror shuffles cards. As he wrote down the successive lines of expressions it was clear that he translated them in his mind's eye into curves as easily as a skilled translator of languages switches from one to another. In return for his patient guidance I showed Tucky how to solder professionally, rewind a transformer, recentre a moving-coil loudspeaker and a host of other practical skills which could well be useful to him in the service.

We were not too far divorced from the Air Force. On our daily marches to and from the school we witnessed activity on the airfield. The Signals School had its own fleet of light aircraft in which we would take eventually our examinations in Morse and Signals Procedure. Enviously we watched these machines flying around, sometimes struggling against strong headwinds. Amongst the collection of older aircraft was a Vickers Virginia which was seen, on one occasion, to make negative progress into the wind.

On one of our morning marches an unusual aircraft took off before our very eyes. Several of our number thought it lacked propellers. Some thought it was a captured German machine. A few suggested that the strength of the beer served in our mess had been increased beyond the limit set by the government. Distortion of vision could not account for the very different noise of the departing aircraft. Maybe the jet-propelled aircraft had proved to be practical after all. We completed our march, assembled in the classroom and waited for signals over the bush telegraph. We had seen E.28/39, forerunner of the Gloster Meteor.

Another major event in our lives at Cranwell was a visit by His Majesty King George VI. For that occasion aircraft were impounded, thoroughly cleaned down with petrol, lined up in the hangars and polished. Hundreds of officers in brand new uniforms at £45 per outfit, lined the route; thousands of airmen and Waafs in slightly cheaper uniforms stood in formations around the camp. Estimated time of arrival came and went. Rumours of accidents on the road crept through the lines. It began to rain. Maybe 'they' would let us take cover. The rain intensified; our new greatcoats doubled in weight. We must be ordered inside. The King would be here any minute now. I felt sure he would not like to think we were catching our deaths of cold. Whispers passed along the lines: 'My shoes are leaking. Do you think it would be all right if I stamp my feet? Try it. No, you try it. I'm going to sneeze. My sleeves are running up. Anybody got a St. Bernard? He's coming. He's at Sleaford. The rain will do the gardens good. I'm soaked right through. Day in bed tomorrow. He's here.'

The Daimler swept along the corridor of dripping uniforms. Through the blue tinted windows and running rain His Majesty was barely visible. The limousine stopped outside a long, low building. A few minutes later could be heard wet strains of the National Anthem. The recording scratched through two verses. Someone spoke a few words, audible only to the chosen few inside the building. The multitude was dismissed peremptorily. As an ardent Royalist, as indoctrinated by Grandma, I like to believe it had been His Majesty who spoke those few words which could have sounded like: 'Who the bloody hell ordered all those poor sods to stand out in the pouring rain? Dismiss him and them!'

The next day dawned bright and clear; just as well, for the Sick Parade stretched as long as a runway. The cold weather set in and our pipes froze. In the interests of preservation our directors inaugurated a series of route marches under the management of Warrant Officer Burrell. This gentleman knew how to get the best out of us. He looked every bit the disciplinarian but his infectious goodwill encouraged us to do his bidding as a return of gratitude. He enjoyed his work and we enjoyed his leadership. He was a big fellow, yet light on his feet. We marched out to Bristol Wood at a lively pace and when we fell out for a breather Mr Burrell changed character from militarist to humanist. He invited questions, was showered with them and answered every one sincerely. In this informal meeting we gained a broad insight into the vagaries of military bureaucracy and how to survive it with equanimity. This man must have endeared himself to many thousands of young people seeking their way *per ardua ad astra*.

January continued bitterly cold. Coughs and sneezes proliferated but our discomforts were not to be compared with those of our compatriots in the Far East where the war went so badly against them. We continued our preparations, yet trusting we might not suffer worse than our present inconveniences.

Diversions from our technical studies took shape in gas exercises, lectures on the devastating effects of different chemicals, first-aid, PT, swimming, Ensa concerts, cinema shows and other tests of endurance. On one occasion we spent a couple of hours down an air-raid shelter wearing gas masks. That exercise encouraged determination to end the war with all speed.

Mercifully, the big thaw came on 25 January. Everyone with any experience of plumbing was called upon to quench the multitude of waterfalls. Within three or four days normality was restored and then the snow fell in a very big way. Mid-course examinations were taken and a very welcome week's leave began. On the 31st a wealthy colleague offered lifts in his Austin Twelve as far as Grantham. The idea of over-loading the car to improve the rear wheel grip on the snow was only partially successful. The real advantage of carrying surplus passengers enabled a select few to remain aboard in comfort while some of us heaved the car out of snowdrifts.

On its winter schedule, The Flying Scotsman stopped at Grantham. I boarded at 15.45 for the one-stop (Peterborough) dash to King's Cross. At Paddington, inquiry revealed the next train going in the direction of Hereford would be the 00.55 for Newport. With time in hand I wandered down to the Regal at Marble Arch. The film was of no interest to me but Jack Payne and his Band performed on the stage and that was something I could not miss. Ravel's 'Bolero' was Jack's favourite piece of music and his boys gave it full justice. The haunting melody accompanied me through the tedious journey to Hereford where I found mother and son in good spirits and the garden deep under snow.

I considered myself to be more useful to the war effort whilst on leave than at school. I cleared a stack of radio sets awaiting repair at C. F. King and Co., fixed numerous electrical devices for neighbours and gave a talk on Radio Direction Finding to the kids at a local school. While the in-laws 'baby sat', Lilian and I saw at least one film at every cinema in town.

With no enthusiasm at all I entrained at Hereford at 17.45 on Sunday and managed, by devious route, to join an unhappy band of warriors in the Church Army Canteen at Grantham in the early hours of Monday. Regaled by tea and wads the cold, cold train to Sleaford was endured, thence to an icy arrival at Cranwell in time for a wash and brush up before school at 09.00 hrs.

We opened up with drill on a frozen barrack square, transferring later to 'out-stations', in which we transmitted messages in Morse Code to 'in-stations'. This proved great fun, especially to those of us who were amateur radio transmitters of civilian origin. There were three such specimens. Finding themselves fortuitously practising their old hobby at His Majesty's expense, they took the liberty of lapsing into colloquial language, but failed to consider that their exercises were being monitored by the staff who brought certain indiscretions to the notice of the Commanding Officer. That gentleman was in most aggressive mood having just heard the news of the loss of 42 of our aircraft in the action against the battleships *Scharnhorst*, *Gneisenau* and *Prinz Eugen* in the Channel. He let the three trainees know, in stern warning, that unseemly behaviour would not be tolerated. The incident was unpleasant but it did much to remind us of the seriousness of our schooling.

Though thoroughly bored by the lectures I became enchanted by militarism. The ceremony of hoisting the flag at 08.30 hrs. was impressive in itself but much enlivened by the bugler. When I took my turn as Orderly Officer I caused some embarrassment to the Orderly Sergeant, a professional NCO, by looking unusually interested in the fare offered to the airmen in their mess. Having witnessed the usual: 'Any complaints? – Right, carry on', routine I determined not to rush things. I took a good look at the menu and chatted to some of the lads. Apart from being regarded as somewhat eccentric I gathered useful experience in officer/airmen relationship, formulated a few new ideas in catering and began to relish my newly found position of authority.

Another most enlightening part of our training programme came at a rehearsal of a Court Martial. The procedure seemed very fair to the accused. From it I learned a good deal about tolerance and human understanding.

I enjoyed too the pomp and ceremony of a big Church Parade. In short I was addicted to Air Force life but was itching to get back among aeroplanes. Great was my joy when, attending the camp cinema to see Gordon Harker in *Once a Crook*, the news reel showed Stirlings of No.7 Squadron at Oakington. Even greater joy to see Reggie Cox had received promotion to Squadron-Leader. For the first time in my life I felt homesick.

A sharp reminder that the flying of aeroplanes is a hazardous business came when, on 18 March, a Whitley struck the main building of the RAF College. The fearsome blaze, in the gathering darkness, reached for the sky. Fatalities there were and the firemen could do no more than play their water jets upon surroundings which were not burning. For most of us this was the first terrible sight of an aircraft on fire. Even more terrible now is the thought that some of us 'got used to it'.

The penultimate month of our schooling included 'air-operating' exercises in Percival Proctors and D. H. Rapides. Our proficiency in Morse was considered satisfactory if we could cope at 12 words per minute in airborne conditions. I had struggled to achieve a maximum of 18 w.p.m. in the classroom and that after several hours extra curriculum. There seemed to be no relationship between IQ rating and ability to learn Morse. One chap, reputedly the smartest mathematician ever to graduate at Hull, got stuck at 4 w.p.m. He was so expert in all other aspects that the authorities turned deaf ears to his exams in Morse!

The flying programme passed all too quickly. Even when unsuitable weather prevented take-off we found diversionary excitement in parachute packing, rifle and pistol practice, sniffing tear gas and gardening.

Air Commodore 'Daddy' Probyn dropped in to see us in our little North Airfield Mess one bright evening. A most likeable character, he was quick to correct an extraordinary anomaly. One of our number, A/P/O Cunningham AFM, wore a winged bullet on his sleeve. 'Daddy' inquired into its origin. Cunningham had been a Wireless Operator/Air Gunner in the Auxiliary Air Force. That entitled him to wear a W/Op badge and a brass winged bullet. He transferred the latter to his uniform after being commissioned. 'Daddy' considered that out of order. Henceforward Cunningham would sport the 'AG' brevet. That looked more in keeping with his AFM badge which he had been awarded in recognition of flying duties over France in 1940. He told me the following story: 'I was a Sergeant W/Op A-G. We flew Ansons. We'd dropped our load and were on our way back home. I had been bending over my log book, taking down a message and at the end of it I leaned back to stretch my back and shout to the skipper when a piece of shrapnel came up through my log book and out through the roof. Three seconds earlier it would have got me between the eyes!'

After final exams came a farewell dinner and off we all moved to Cambridge for a week of grilling lectures at the Post Office Training College. The Royal Air Force depended for its intricate network of landline communications on Post Office Telephone engineering. Anybody who thinks of a telephone as a gadget connected to another gadget by a pair of wires would be disillusioned by a visit to even a village telephone exchange. Just one day at Cambridge was enough to convince me that 'GPO Telephones' was populated by an unusually high percentage of boffins. Their business called for exceptional mathematical skill. It was beyond my own ability to absorb transmission line theory so I concentrated on more assimilable and practical subjects such as the teleprinter network and its associated machinery.

'Rennie' at King George V Silver Jubilee celebrations, Kington 1935.

Les Wheeler and author awaiting orders during Bewdley by-election caused by resignation of Stanley Baldwin (1937).

Brecon County Show at Builth Wells 1933.

In the Brecon National Park with the 1934 Triumph 250 cc. Mk V and Don Morgan on the 350 cc. 'Bitza'. (Note: crash helmets not required!)

With the 16H. Norton at Bologna, 1945.

1960: A40 'Somerset' – useful, reliable. Drive carefully.

1936: With the 250 cc. S.O.S. (water cooled Villiers engine) at Vowchurch, Herefordshire.

Christian leadership course outside S. Maria Maggiore (Rome 1945). Author 2nd row, 2nd from right.

Blida airfield 1943: 'Struggie' chatting with Trenchard through car window. Wellingtons of 36 Squadron in front of hangar. The aircraft with three fins is an Albemarle.

Marshal of the Royal Air Force Trenchard conversing with Group Captain Strugnall on steps of HQ Blida (1943). Note the military canes carried exclusively by these two officers of the RAF.

Chapter 29

Work in Sight

The day Cranwell relieved itself of No.10 Signals (War) Course six dozen promising officers looked forward to making good use of their new-found knowledge, in prosecution of the war. Ended was the tedium of the classroom. The model aeroplane manufactured clandestinely by a consortium of Acting Pilot Officers of the front bench had been completed in time for the end of Course celebrations. It took off, circled with a starboard list and crashed into the railings which surrounded Northfield Mess. A write-off.

Our postings to diverse parts of Britain were discussed. Condolences and congratulations preceded futile promises to 'keep in touch'. My own posting to Headquarters 12 Group sounded frighteningly important but prior to taking up the appointment a further spell of ten day's leave was to be undertaken.

Lilian and son had arrived already at Thirsk where we spent half of my leave. There was work to be done. In between pram-pushing I tidied up the garage, sorted through my library and assisted Father at the shop. I repaired more radio sets in two days than I had seen in the previous month. Lilian and I managed to squeeze in a visit to Leeds. We saw Noel Coward's *Blithe Spirit*, caught the 6.10 from Leeds and arrived back home to find that Michael John had behaved himself like a gentleman. We 'should have stayed longer,' Mother said.

Completion of my leave at Hereford included a spell at my old workbench fixing radios. It seemed to be a noble war effort. Everybody was anxious to keep up to date with the news as administered by the BBC as well as chuckling over the exaggerations of Lord Haw-Haw.

In my anxiety to commence proper employment as an officer in the service of His Majesty I made the mistake of travelling to 12 Group on a Sunday. The train to Birmingham suffered from a shortage of coal. I made it in time for lunch in the station canteen. All ranks amassed for tea and wads. Northbound trains were not expected to operate within the foreseeable future. I deposited my heavily laden trunk with a reliable-looking porter who promised to send it forward. A small subscription to the porters' benevolent fund insured prompt delivery. I headed a small group of assorted servicemen to the 'Midland Red' bus station. Thence we moved at a steady rumble to Burton-on-Trent where another smoke-hazy canteen enveloped us in a further fight for tea and Lyons' fruit pies. At Derby it was recommended that I revert to the railway. By that method I arrived at Kimberley station in the late evening and was lucky to find RAF transport standing by to pick up chance arrivals. I was at least 12 hours ahead of ETA. There was no spare accommodation. I slept well enough in a cosy corner of the mess anteroom, undisturbed by the comings and goings of officers of the watch. Snippets of conversation on the subjects of bandits and angels indicated that I had entered yet another world.

The Group Operations Room represented that other world. An enormous map of that portion of England watched over by 12 Group of Fighter Command plus its approaches was known as the plotting table. It was surrounded by plotters, placed at strategic intervals. Each airwoman or airman plotter wore headphones over which information received from outside sources was translated into movements of flags on the table. The whole exciting scene was supervised by a Controller whose job it was to direct aircraft; to be alerted or stood down as required by his assessment of enemy movements. The Group was divided into Fighter Sectors, in which aircraft came under the direct control of the Sector Controller. The whole system depended on an intricate network of communications.

The vast number of telephone cables which converged upon HQ 12 Group entered the underground filter room via a tunnel reminiscent of a London tube station. The scale of the complex was overpowering. I was pleased to be directed to domestic affairs. There being no room for me on site I found myself billeted out in private digs on the outskirts of Nottingham. Again I lived a double life, half in and half out of the service. My good friend the porter of Birmingham had kept his word. With my trunk unpacked I felt quite at home at No.37 The Boulevard.

I spent only one week at 12 Group, almost entirely as a passenger, observing and learning, watching and waiting. The occasion when I sat beside the Controller in the Ops. Room until 03.00 hrs. 'seeing' enemy aircraft approach and being dealt with brought home to me the importance of immaculate signalling.

I was whisked around in a Humber Utility car in the company of the Group Signals Officer to Cranwell, Digby, Kirton-in-Lindsey and Hibaldstow where we inspected the Havoc aircraft. On another journey, by Hillman Minx, an official of the GPO showed me the ins-and-outs of the telephone complexities at Church Fenton, a Royal Observer Corps centre the insight into which furthered my rapidly expanding understanding of the responsibilities of a Signals Officer in Fighter Command. All the while, however, I was feeling more supernumerary than ever, wondering whether I should resign myself to becoming a rather highly educated telephone operator.

My daily contact with civilian life allowed me to indulge in a matinee performance of *The Brontes of Haworth Parsonage* by the Lyric Players at the local Repertory Theatre. The acting was sincere enough to arouse a latent interest in amateur stage work, which I had scarcely revived since my schooldays portrayal of Butters in J. J. Bell's *Thread o' Scarlet*.

Meanwhile, I meted out my last day at 12 Group by swotting up 'gen' on telephones. The subject had become an obsession. I was delighted to learn of a major diversion. A vacancy for Assistant Signals Officer had arisen at Digby Fighter Sector and to that post I was driven in a stately Vauxhall Fourteen.

My boss at Digby was Flight-Lieutenant Rawlins, a slow-running dynamo of a man, ex-Warrant Officer, immensely proud of the Royal Air Force. It was his life and he did much to make it mine. It was natural enough that so experienced a campaigner would eye with some distrust a VR raised via the cramming course of Cranwell to a rank achieved by himself after many years at the grindstone. We summed up one another in a few short sentences of conversation. When he learned that I had indeed served some little time in the ranks he breathed a sigh of approval. From that moment we worked well together. It was the moment when I was appointed to my first definite task as a Royal Air Force Signals Officer. The job was to organise the telephone operators' schedule!

That, I imagined, would be a simple arrangement of rosters, a task assigned to the new boy to keep him out of harm's way. Rawlins knew what he was doing. Given that a switchboard is to be staffed by four operators plus a supervisor on each of three shifts then simple mathematics dictate a requirement for twelve operators plus three supervisors: QED.

The reason for a re-schedule was the arrival of some new recruits. I thought it a splendid idea to mix new with old. There being thousands of ways of mixing twelve people I failed on one human factor. A high proportion of the operators were ACWs. When the Warrant Officer examined my schedule he forecast trouble with tears. He pointed out that certain females were tied by love-knot to airmen who themselves worked on watch systems. It had been the practice to match their respective off-duty periods.

'Of course, you are in charge, Sir, and if this is the way you want it done, Sir . . .'

'In the interests of happy relationships I am quite prepared to make some adjustments. Let me have your recommendations by tomorrow morning.' I was not prepared to start chucking my weight about at this early stage and wished for peace in time of war.

Our Fighter Sector Control HQ occupied Blankney Hall and constituted a closely knitted community, remote from any airfield. Our aircraft were represented by flags on the plotting table. A lot of people were involved in the purpose of placing accurately those flags on the map, in response to information received from Direction-Finding Stations and Royal Observer Corps posts. Harmony amongst the staff was a prime requirement. In the Operations Room itself pin-drop silence reigned for much of the time, the Controller himself being the only person to break that silence. Messages to the plotters were received by them over headphones.

The telephone exchange which connected us to the outside world was a separate unit in a soundproof chamber. Post Office engineers maintained the equipment. The Station Signals Officer was responsible for the smoothness of operation. Contented operators performed smoothly.

When Rawlins asked me to show him my completed telephone schedule I presented the product of many hours of jugglery.

'I think that, with Warrant Officer Lambert's kind assistance, I have pleased all of the people most of the time,' I said.

'Have you pleased Kathleen?' he asked.

'And who, may I ask, is Kathleen?'

'Lambert's girl friend,' he said. 'It is not so much your technical expertise which counts in this outfit but your diplomacy. You have just completed your first exercise.'

Rawlins' ability to delegate surpassed belief. He knew just how to get people to do things for themselves. Certainly he taught me how to study a problem for myself before calling for a second opinion:

I was reading from Air Ministry Instructions whilst carrying out the onerous task of sticking in Amendments. I came across a passage of some depth which I found difficult to understand. I interrupted Rawlins' concentration on his own reading:

'What does this mean?' I asked, quoting from the big book.

He looked out of the window for a few seconds, turned to me and said: 'What it says.'

I read the passage again. He was quite right.

Telephone calls going beyond or coming in from beyond the station exchange were necessarily to be accounted for financially. Private 'fiddles' could not be tolerated. Tape-recorders were instruments of the future; keeping records meant writing notes in log books. Examination of log books constituted part of my duty. I was in danger of becoming chairbound.

Meanwhile, bomber command sent 1,132 aircraft to hammer Cologne on 30 May and 1,032 to Essen on 1 June. I yearned for a return to the Stirling days but was committed to serve a more sedentary life for the next three months.

Rawlins had the Signals Section so well organised that he was able to take leave or visit outstations whilst I kept my eye on the shop. Any technical hitches were promptly attended to by the excellent Corporal Ambrose. Sergeant Nicholls managed the Traffic Office, Warrant Officer Lambert smoothed out most of the personnel problems. I waited to sign chits. My periodic turns as Duty Signals Officer in the Operations Room, on nights especially when enemy aircraft were plotted, came as an interesting diversion from tedium. I found it fascinating to observe the variation in methods used by different Controllers in handling an interception. Tensions built up to the 'highly strung' category, to be tightened even more at the 'Tally-ho' cry from one of our Spitfires, or to be slowly eased off should the enemy evade their hunters.

Tucky phoned from Shawbury to tell me he was to be posted to Combined Operations HQ as a Flight-Lieutenant. Some people are lucky, I thought, as I set course on my rounds as Orderly Officer. I had been issued with a bicycle and seemed settled into a peaceful routine at Blankney Hall.

Such was the degree of peace in the Digby Fighter Sector that the Derby was run at Newmarket on 13 June, uninterrupted by enemy action. Maybe the clouds acted as a deterrent. It rained all day. The going suited Harry Wragg and his winning steed, Watling Street. The weather turned up trumps for Digby Sports Day on the 20th. I entered the slow bicycle race and the 3-legged race for Officers and won neither. Tea was served in the gardens while General Rommel renewed pressure on Tobruk and the Russians were besieged at Sebastopol.

Whilst I cycled to Lincoln on the 23rd to discuss telephone business with the GPO manager Tobruk fell to Rommel. 28,000 British prisoners were taken and the Germans pushed on towards Egypt. News from Russia continued to be depressing. I was delighted to be appointed to a Trade Test Board for Wireless Operators at Digby. That kept me busy for a few days at the beginning of July before resuming my routine work as a rather superior office boy.

During a week's leave at Hereford I felt like a fish out of water. It was good to see Lilian and to play games with our son but attendance at an 'Aid to Russia' meeting in Hightown set me wondering what the hell I was doing about it. I consoled myself and, I hope, helped my audience, by giving a talk to an enthusiastic group of Army Cadets. After the talk I accompanied them on a map-reading exercise. I hoped, too, that such a nice bunch of kids would never be called to the fighting front.

A few days after my return to Digby the BSA Squadron of the Air Training Corps visited us. It was my pleasure to talk to them about Signals in Fighter Command. They were as keen as mustard to see the end of their school days and join the service. 'Aid to Russia' by them must wait.

Our life of relative tranquillity at Blankney Hall continued. Rawlins took a week's leave while the Germans advanced on Stalingrad. As soon as he returned I took another week in Hereford. During that week news came through of the terrible losses of men and aircraft suffered in the infamous raid on Dieppe. In the Mediterranean area Rommel was probing defences in Egypt; Malta could hardly be expected to take any more hammerings. There was no good news.

Yet Lilian and I saw *Reap the Wild Wind* at the Odeon, I fitted in a few service calls for C. F. King and Co., and strolled by the Wye a-pushing the pram, all very civilian. A letter arrived from F. J. Cox, ex-No.10 Course, announcing that he was about to board a troopship, destination secret, although he may have known; some people were having all the luck. I returned to my duties at Blankney Hall.

Then suddenly things perked up in the form of a signal from Group HQ. It ordered me to report to White Waltham where I would join 302 Mobile Signals Servicing Unit as second in command with the rank of Flight-Lieutenant (Acting). I couldn't get there fast enough. A friend at 'Group' wished me luck and hoped I 'wouldn't suffer too many privations'. I supposed the fellow meant well. My only concern was to get moving and there was every promise that at last I might be resuming technical activities.

On the last day of August I bid farewell to Rawlins and Blankney Hall. I moved to White Waltham where my accommodation in a Nissen hut seemed more fitting for an officer on active service. At the same time General Bernard Montgomery was taking over his caravan in Egypt. The end of the beginning of the war was in sight.

I spent the first day of September stooging around the Wing Commander's office and on the second day of September I was dispatched on LEAVE! Imagining that I was about to depart the old country within the next week I decided to spend a day at Thirsk. I arrived at 22.30 hrs. to hear the air-raid siren wailing and to see flares and incendiaries falling. Father dashed away on his fire-engine, not to be seen again until the following afternoon. Rations were running low in the larder but the Fleece Hotel provided a respectable lunch for mother and son. I looked in at the shop, repaired a couple of radio sets, called in at the Church Army canteen where my sister served tea and wads, said goodbye to all and caught the 8.32 p.m. for King's Cross. There I joined the masses for more tea and wads until the 'Underground' reopened. By that means I arrived at Paddington to catch the 06.32 to Maidenhead, thence by bus to White Waltham. I reported to the Adjutant at 08.30 to be handed a 48-hour leave pass for Hereford!

From professional office boy I had moved to professional leave-taker. However, on returning to White Waltham my unit was found to be at full strength under the command of Squadron-Leader Cecil Page, ex-bank cashier, ex-Auxiliary Air Force, amateur to the business of training for service overseas.

Chapter 30

Whiling at Wilmslow

At White Waltham, wireless wizards wondered what would happen next. We were joined by 301 MSSU commanded by Squadron-Leader Chapman. The whole assembly was addressed by Wing Commander McLaren who told us we were about to embark on an operation which 'can't fail'. We were to be prepared to repair, replace and resuscitate radio and radar gear damaged in action in the field. That sound right up our respective streets. We itched to move to embarkation.

Three days we languished at White Waltham. Refresher courses were improvised as a means of warding off boredom. One useful exercise in which we became thoroughly expert was the erection and dismantling of 75' aerial masts. After we had got the hang of this dangerous task we organised the operation as a disciplined drill. We surprised ourselves at the speed achieved. There was always a gathering of spectators to cheer along the different crews. By the time we had finished everyone knew exactly what to do. Even the cooks and MT drivers became adept at mast erection.

From White Waltham we took possession of a special train bound for Wilmslow, well known as an embarkation centre. The journey north took a whole day in which we cemented mutual acquaintanceships and shared our rations, favourite ingredients being the famous Lyons' fruit pies.

A remarkable phenomenon was witnessed during the journey. Our train had halted in Shrewsbury station, on a central line without platforms. We were not to be let loose on Shrewsbury. A more important train pulled up at the platform of a neighbouring line. The 'Pacific' type locomotive stopped parallel to our carriage. All of us became railway enthusiasts, admiring the great, steam-squirting monster at close quarters. Our slow 'special' must wait until this important express would go ahead of us. A group of our boys in an adjacent compartment struck up conversation with the driver and fireman who decided to show off their mastership of power. Their train was heavily laden. Easing in the pressure to the cylinders caused the mighty driving wheels to slip on the rails. The train refused to budge. Full throttle was applied and not only did the huge wheels spin, with sparks flying from the rails, but the whole gigantic engine shook from buffers to footplate. The structure broke into resonance, rivets were seen to work in the boiler casing and paint around them to crack. In a few

180

terrifying moments we thought the whole mass of machinery was about to explode, within a few feet of us. The crew took rapid life-saving action by slamming closed the steam valve. A few seconds elapsed allowing the restoration of normal steamy noises. Then with more judicious application of pressure and delicate wheel-slipping the long train departed.

We booked in at Wilmslow in the evening of 11 September, were appointed bedspaces in wooden huts, got a welcome night's sleep and paraded as ordered at 09.00 hrs. on the 12th. The CO read solemnly from an instruction sheet: '302 MSSU will take 5 days' leave. Rail warrants are to be issued at 10.00 hrs. Report back here before midnight on the 17th. Don't be late.'

I renewed my place in the family circle at Hereford in time for tea. For the next few days I kept a low profile, not wishing to be faced with questions concerning my war service.

On the morning of the 18th a move towards embarkation seemed imminent. We received our ATT injections. The afternoon was devoted to recreation. My mother was visiting friends in Manchester, where I met her. We took seats in the Palace Theatre to see Arthur Askey among others in a variety show. Arthur was at his best. Mother was highly amused by his joke about the woman who inquired the price of brassières.

'Three guineas,' said the saleslady.

'Three guineas!' exclaimed the woman, 'I'll see 'em swing first!'

Whilst mother enjoyed the joke, I laughed with her, felt hot and bothered and fainted in my seat. At least I had proved the fallibility of the suggestion that any after effects of injections are purely 'psychological'. On future occasions when that particular serum was injected I never failed to pass out within 24 hours.

On each morning of the following three days we held an after-breakfast parade, followed by dismissal to pursue our own diversions. The parade was necessary to keep a check on physical presence of our numbers. On each of the three mornings one man failed to answer the roll-call. That man was LAC Allen, transport driver. An NCO would be dispatched to the billet and a tired Allen would be aroused from his bed and brought before the CO. Full of apology, Allen would take his place in the ranks, returning to his slumbers after dismissal. The CO and I agreed not to commence formal charges against Allen, but to let him off with a promise of strict treatment in future. In truth, neither of us wished involvement in paper work in these, our temporary HQs. Throughout our sojourn at Wilmslow the enigmatic Allen was allowed a long length of rope. I marked him down as a likeable rogue for whom somebody provided cover. My time would come.

On 22 September orders came from above that a kit inspection would be made immediately. Business at last, it was rumoured. This must be the final check-up to ensure that we were fully fitted for foreign travel. False alarm; kit inspection completed we were to proceed on leave and report back on 25

September. At Thirsk I found a radiant sister had acquired her first driving licence; she piloted me around a few service calls in the family Morris 8. We took tea at The Fleece and saw *The Foreman went to France* at the Regent. I bade farewell again to friends and relatives and arrived back at Wilmslow ready for action. After lunch in the Officers' Mess there was just enough time for me to collect another rail warrant and catch the 13.48 for Hereford to celebrate Lilian's birthday on the 26th.

Having omitted to set the old alarm clock correctly I missed the earliest train on the 28th. I panicked all the way back to Wilmslow in case the unit had embarked without me. The worry was needless. We were on 'stand-by' and began an intensive course of square bashing.

One of the boys limped along, unable to keep up with the squad even at moderate pace. When I announced the intention of starting a series of marathon runs he declared boldly that he considered himself unfit for overseas service, owing to a club foot. I passed the buck to the Medical Officer at HQ, with the notion of relieving the unit of an embarrassment. The MO examined the chap, agreed the diagnosis of a malformed foot but in view of the fact that his trade was that of Driver (MT), passed him fit for duty anywhere in the world. Squadron-Leader Page adopted him as his personal driver and he did a good job at least during my own period with the unit.

After ten days of route marches and cross-country runs we imagined we were fit for strenuous campaigning. Splendid entertainment in the huge theatre at Wilmslow supplemented evening visits to Manchester's excellent Hippodrome and various cinemas. Thus we prepared for war.

On 8 October 302 MSSU assembled to hear the CO issue orders: to proceed on seven days' leave.

Leave became a wearisome pastime. I relieved a feeling of guilt by spending much of my time at the service bench. In restoring aged radio sets to their former glory I convinced myself that my war effort contributed something toward the national welfare.

Lilian worked on a rota basis at the local telephone exchange. When due on a night watch she was transported by police car leaving me to sample the joys of true fatherhood, of which I experienced all too little.

On the final day of that spell of leave Lilian accompanied me as far as Shrewsbury where we took lunch at The George. We saw Gordon Harker in *The Phantom Light* at a local cinema before taking trains in opposite directions.

During the following week Monty's armies opened fire in a big way. The Battle of El Alamein marked 'the end of the beginning' of the war. Lilian's brother, at the ripe old age of twenty, drove a tank in that battle whilst I remained landlocked at Wilmslow.

We marched, we drilled, we fired pistol and rifle. We listened to lectures on music by Dobson and Young, on gas warfare by the Gas Officer, on how to get VD by the MO, on secrecy by the Intelligence Officer and on a host of subjects by self-appointed experts. In other words we passed the time away until further leave seemed appropriate.

On 31 October I arrived in Hereford for weekend leave. On 1 November two events of major importance were recorded: a telegram brought notification that my leave was extended by eight days and secondly 'Yanks landed in Algeria and Morocco at 2.00 a.m.'.

Only the latter of the two events surprised me. The surprise was universal. It was anticipated by laymen and Russians that a landing in Europe would be undertaken, but the North African invasions were logical as well as surprising. The souvenir vendors of Morocco were surprised to receive an inflow of prospective clients by the thousand. The American forces were agreeably surprised by the amicable reception, which was just as well, for to be expected to terminate a trans-Atlantic crossing in pitched battle was unkind. Whilst landings on the Algerian coast met with a degree of hostility the whole operation 'Torch' under the command of General Eisenhower was applauded as a great American success. The British contribution, though considerable, went furtively about its business for fear of arousing the further wrath of the Free French leader, de Gaulle.

It occurred to me that I might get a look-in at the war before it finished. Rommel was retreating into Libya and moving towards further trouble from the west. Meanwhile, Lilian and I saw *Gone with the Wind* at the Ritz and Charlie Chaplin in *The Gold Rush* at the Odeon. Then I called in at Wilmslow to collect another rail warrant for onward transportation to Thirsk, for what turned out to be my last meeting with my parents and sister until after the war was done.

Back at Wilmslow the bush telegraph was alive, but news of our destination must remain deadly secret. The Germans moved into hitherto unoccupied France. Maybe 302 MSSU would land in opposition, via Southern France?

FFI followed kit inspection, tent-pitching practice began, aircraft recognition exercises proved to be an interesting diversion from PT, mass drills, gas drills and games. Activities intensified and when I was permitted to meet Lilian at Shrewsbury on 18 November I knew we must part company for an indefinite period. Tears flowed into the River Severn, then dribbled out of the carriage window as I waved her train southward.

With renewed vigour 302 MSSU drilled and marched, usually without LAC Allen who by this time had perfected the art of evanescence. Our club-footed airman had been assigned the post of permanent room orderly and guardian of our possessions.

On 20 November we competed in an inter-draft football match, practised march discipline and completed two rounds of the arduous Wilmslow assault course. On the 21st we undertook and completed, with full packs, a twelve mile route march. We considered ourselves fit for service anywhere in the world. On Sunday 22nd the order 'Stand-off' came and in the dead of night we boarded trucks for the railway station, entrained and steamed north to an undisclosed destination.

The unmistakable throbbings of two lusty engines on full power indicated clearly that we ascended Shap Fell before daybreak. Grey daylight revealed our progress toward Clydeside.

As we filed up the gangway to board the good ship *Stephan Batory* a lusty-voiced stevedore shouted: 'Ye'll no need yer winter woollies when ye get t' Algiers'. We who had listened to lectures on the need for strict secrecy of troop movements ignored the joke; we were too engrossed in the business of finding our quarters. For us officers of commissioned rank these were beyond my wildest dreams of luxury. The four-berth cabin which I shared with three of my colleagues was constructed of high grade timbers finished to the standards of a stately home. The first-class dining room with waiter service matched the specification of a 5-star hotel. I settled in immediately to my new home.

Loading of the ship was completed after the second day aboard. We moved out to a convoy assembly point off Dunoon. The OC troops called a general assembly at which it was revealed that we were, as predicted, bound for Algiers. Rules were laid down for our safety. First and foremost no refuse, not even a cigarette stub, must be cast over the side during the voyage for fear of revealing our course to the lurking U-boats.

A complete roll call accounted for the whole of our company including LAC Allen. Now was my chance to take that reprobate in hand. He described to me the lucrative taxi service he had provided from his base at Wilmslow. His clients had been American airmen at Burtonwood who were prepared to pay Allen's fees for introductions to special addresses in Manchester and Liverpool. The service would be continued by a confederate.

'How did you manage to enter and leave the compound at all hours?' I asked.

'Oh,' he said, ''ole in 'edge, Sir.'

'Well, now you are on board this ship I shall have to see you don't slip over the side.'

He promised to remain within bounds.

Chapter 31

The Dry Battery Club

The OC troops called for volunteers to organise entertainment aboard. A surprising galaxy of talent attended the inaugural meeting. 302 MSSU made a great contribution. Sergeant Snee, our MT expert, had a fine tenor voice. He had performed in the Harry Korris show at Blackpool. His rendering of '*Le Rêve Passé*' was a certain guarantee against depression. Bob Adams had brought his clarinet on which he played first-rate jazz. A drummer and a pianist were not hard to find among the mass of troops aboard so we had the basis of a concert party anxious to begin rehearsals immediately.

A series of lectures, proposed by our unit Adjutant Flying-Officer Napier, opened with a talk by that very gentleman. Bill had been in Africa during the first world war, handling wireless equipment carried by mules. After his service in the Army he joined the BBC outside broadcast department and had much to say in a very pedantic way. One positive statement was to rebound upon him shortly after our introduction to Algeria. He said:

'You will find that in Africa there is an everlasting glow after sundown. Even on the darkest night it is always possible to see your way about without a torch!'

We became accustomed to seeing Dunoon across the water but on the sixth morning of my awaking in my berth I was aware of a subdued hum from the engine room. The ship was steady as she goes. I turned out at 07.00 hrs. I expected to see Dunoon receding into the background. The first thing I noticed from my favourite viewpoint on deck was a Sunderland flying boat on escort duty. The sea was choppy. The skies were grey but visibility was good enough for me to count fourteen ships in the convoy. Some were bigger than our 14,287 ton *Batory*, none appeared much smaller, except the diminutive looking corvette which oozed up and down with the waves. This little escort vessel never left us although at times she disappeared into a trough in the sea as though preparing to tunnel through the next roller.

My amateur reckoning put us somewhere off the north coast of Ireland. When I looked over the side I judged our speed through the water to be a good 14 knots but my greatest surprise was to observe the ejection, through a porthole of the galley, of a brace of cardboard boxes, a few tins and assorted garbage. The track of our convoy was plainly marked upon the ocean! Clearly

185

the safety regulations meant nothing to the Polish staff *de cuisine.* Otherwise our Polish crew displayed both discipline and courtesy.

Each morning I was out on deck by sunrise and during the walkabout I met some very interesting Army officers. I took delight in listening to their conversations on subjects concerning the conduct of war. They ranged in rank from Lieutenant up to Brigadier. A far-reaching discussion was concluded by a learned Lieutenant-Colonel who stated simply: 'We are a queer lot, we British. Some things we do so well and other things so badly.' His comment fitted the foregoing debate; I have recalled it countless times. It can be fitted at the end of every day.

Whilst I enjoyed my life of luxury on the *Stephan Batory,* existence for the airmen and soldiers was far from comfortable. I visited our own lads as often as possible and listened attentively to their complaints. Conditions below were fuggy to say the least. Some had preferred to curl up on deck. Some had found refuge in the lifeboats. That seemed highly irregular but I gathered that crew members had not discouraged the attempt to seek superior accommodation. I sought out LAC Allen. He had no complaints whatever. He assured me that his nest aft of a ventilator tube was both warm and airy.

The OC troops was informed of complaints but there was little the poor chap could do. We were in the hands of the crew who were trained to carry transatlantic tourists by the hundred, not invading troops by the thousand.

PT exercises were regular features of our daily activities, weather permitting. These ceased on 1 December when the Bay of Biscay welcomed us with a tremendous battering. It was rumoured that the sailors welcomed a good storm because of its deterrent values against attack by U-boats. There must have been something in this judging from the manner in which the corvettes disappeared for minutes on end and even big liners rose and fell like hobby horses on a merry-go-round.

Even the concert party was abandoned until the sea settled. One big ship made a 360° turn during the storm. It was frightening to see this monster roll during the manoeuvre. Some spectators considered that it was avoiding a torpedo; others said it was searching for a man overboard. We never knew the answer. No other ship deviated in like manner. The storm abated. When we sailed silently by night through the Straits of Gibraltar the amazing sight of the illuminated city of Tangier brought forth a concerted call of: 'Put that light out!'

Our concert party gave its final performance before a packed audience which 'rolled out the barrel' long after the curtains collapsed.

On the following day all aboard were issued with a small supply of British Military Authority money in the form of ten shilling notes. It was then that the 'Dry Battery Club' was established. Each officer who had taken part in, or helped organise entertainment on, the *Stephan Batory* signed a ten shilling note and passed it around for signature by the other score of members. For reasons of 'secrecy' it seemed advisable not to mention the *Batory* so we entitled ourselves members of the 'Dry Battery Club'. Rules of the club were simple. If a member was recognised in the street he must be challenged by producing the signed note. Failure to go snap called for the challengee to pay ten shillings. An exclusive club indeed. I treasured my note for over twenty years until a light-fingered citizen of Gloucester pinched my wallet from the pocket of a jacket I had momentarily hitched over a chairback.

On the sparkling afternoon of 6 December we broke away from the convoy and steered towards one of the most noble prospects in the world: the Algiers waterfront, a meeting of Mediterranean with Africa and the Orient. Palace, mosque and *souk* intermingle. Architectural masterpieces of Turkish, Arabic and French origins amalgamate to an eye-pleasing panorama. The Notre-Dame d'Afrique stands sentinel on the cliff-tops in constant survey of City and harbour. Neither to the nose was Algiers offensive. As our liner slipped to the quayside the scents of musk, incense and spices overshadowed whiffs of diesel fumes and unflushed sewers.

It was announced over the ship's Tannoy that we would disembark in orderly fashion and wait for directions to a point where it was planned that we should connect up with our equipment and vehicles. The gunfire had ceased. Ours would be a bloodless invasion according to plan. The plan was excellent.

Chapter 32

Hussein Dey

Our compact unit of forty-five comprising six officers and thirty-nine other ranks stood patiently at ease on the Algiers quay, our great ship towering alongside casting over us a welcome shadow. It was, to our English complexions, hot. The sun shone brighter than we had ever known, the sea sparkled. Heat danced off the buildings. Our tropical clothing was packed in our kits. Though the temperature was a mere 60-odd F°, our winter woollies accumulated a lot of calories.

Squadron-Leader Page had abandoned us temporarily to search for one of the most important departments of the Army: Movement Control. Nobody moved, whether airman, soldier or sailor, when on land, except by express instruction from Movement Control. I called the unit to attention when our CO reappeared, in step with an Army Captain who announced himself as the Movements Officer. He made no apology for his following announcement:

'The ship which carried your vehicles and equipment was struck by a torpedo on its approach to Algiers. She has been towed to a berth but it will be some days before your equipment can be recovered from below the water-line. One Bedford truck has been allocated for transportation of your kit-bags only. You must march to your camp at Hussein Dey, about four miles along the waterfront. Tonight you will bivouac on the sands. That's all!'

Naturally enough, Squadron-Leader Page adopted the truck for his personal transport with he of the club foot as personal driver. With full pack, gas mask and all we formed some semblance of an infantry unit. Only recently we had successfully completed an assault course and a twelve mile route march. In my opinion we were a match for any unit which might be destined to undertake a similar progression along this portion of the Algerian coastline.

Our valiant Warrant Officer Overall, an older campaigner, headed the column whilst I marched alongside, the better to discharge my responsibility for the safety of the flock. Thus I fended off vendors of oranges, dates and offers of services unfamiliar to the average Britisher. The boys enjoyed the exchanges of conversation, brushed up schoolboy French and picked up a smattering of Arabic. Ours was a light-hearted militarism but the heat began to tell. At midway I called a halt. We fell out for a rest, 'smoke if you wish' and a pull at the water bottles.

The idle chatter which pervaded our foot-sore throng was interrupted presently by a rhythmic clatter of marching boots. A platoon of the Welsh Guards approached at a pace well above the respectable 120 strides per minute recommended at Wilmslow. Furtive glances at us from the leading soldiers, sarcastic smirks from the middle ranks and disrespectful raspberries from the tail of the column left us with no doubts of their opinion of the RAF as a marching force. Thus revitalised we made the second half of our task in little more time than the first.

Top marks to the Army lads who had set up a neatly aligned bivouac camp on the sands at Hussein Dey. As the colour of the canvas matched the colour of the sand it must have been considered that we would be not more easily identifiable as a target for enemy aircraft by virtue of the symmetry. In any case the Heinkel which approached low over the glass-like sea concentrated its attention on the ships lying out in the bay. The bombs dropped into the water, missing the ships by a mile. The anti-aircraft fire punctuated the blue sky by puffs of brown smoke and the German turned away hurriedly to the horizon well in advance of a threat by our fighters. At last, were we to see action?

Load by load our kitbags (airmen) and trunks (officers) arrived from the docks and we settled into our bivouacs, one per officer; half per airman. Our activities attracted the attention of the local populace in the form of beggars young and old. Guards were appointed with rifle and bayonet, to look determined and establish some kind of understanding by making a variety of shooing noises. Centrally placed in our camp was a temporary kitchen where our two cooks enlisted the help of men of other trades with the preparation of our first self-supportive meal. The Army had provided us with boxes of standard rations complete with toilet paper. A deep hole for the basis of a latrine became speedily a reality directly owing to the extraordinary skill of Goddard, one of our Despatch Riders. He enjoyed his freedom from his normal duties down a Northumberland coal mine. Digging a hole in the Algerian sands was child's play to Goddard. Within minutes he could create a perfectly formed grave, he himself below ground level, only spadefuls of sand shooting out of the depths as though directed from an automatic machine. Goddard was one of our greatest assets.

In the interest of hygiene a bucket of boiling water was set aside in the kitchen for washing up our dirty cutlery. Once emptied, the bucket remained in position to be used as a convenient short-range rubbish bin.

Having satisfied the inner man, we prepared for the African night. A duty roster of guards ensured our safety. Many of our number, including our worthy Officer Commanding, felt in need of rest and therefore retired to bivouac. A group headed by our Stores Officer, Bertie Spragge, and myself directed our steps towards the village of Hussein Dey, drawn by curiosity and the desire to sample the local wine. We had been warned by OC Troops on the *Stephan Batory* that dangers lay ahead not only from the gun barrel but also from the wine barrel. Spraggy and I stepped apprehensively into a candle-lit bar-café, replete with red and white chequered tablecloths. A friendly, smoke-laden atmosphere pervaded.

Capitaine Jonville of 153 Batterie de DCA expressed immediate and sincere delight in welcoming two officers of l'Air Force Royale. He spoke excellent English and declared himself starved of intellectual conversation. As Commander of the local Ack-Ack battery he was finding life tedious and saw little prospect of business in the foreseeable future. Following a few tentative bursts of fire during the invasion by an unknown enemy and wondering which France he was supposed to defend at the time, he was now convinced that he could depend on *l'amitié des Anglais*. Would we please take a glass of muscatel?

Unceremoniously three demi-tumblers were delivered to our table. They were filled to the brim with Algeria's most delectable product. We expressed our appreciation by establishing a new *entente cordiale*. Both Spraggy and I became more fluent in French as the level of wine in the glasses diminshed. We offered one of our British Military Authority notes in payment for another round. Le Capitaine intervened by calling over the proprietress with whom he conversed at a speed beyond our comprehension. Shortly Madame brought a tray containing four champagne glasses and a bottle of *le plus beau*. Jonville removed the cork without fuss or spillage and filled four glasses. Madame joined us at the table, indicated that she was very pleased to meet *les Anglais*, disliked Pétain and Darlan, wished us '*Santé*' and indicated that this one was '*sur la maison*'.

The last drop drained from the bottle as our new friend requested that we adjourn to his private quarters on the outskirts of the village. '*Vive la France et l'Angleterre*' was pronounced at frequent intervals along our joyous path.

Le Capitaine occupied a cosy portion of a private villa. He regretted that food supplies were limited but pointed to a pile of enormous oranges and we must help ourselves to those as well as to the plumpest dates we had ever seen. At this juncture we were warned not to buy oranges from the street vendors. Many of the trees which provided supplies to those retailers were grown on a small-holder basis and were fertilised by domestic feculence. That was how we understood our friend's description. The dates came from a specialist palm farm; further supplies available for the asking.

I thanked Jonville for his hospitality and begged to be directed back towards our encampment. 'Ah, *mon Capitaine*, you must not yet proceed. *Le café* must be taken *avec le cognac*.' I glanced at Spraggy who considered we 'ought to try a drop of that'.

After promises of further meetings we emerged from the villa a few minutes before midnight. Jonville pointed us in the right direction. We knew that we must cross the main railway and by heading north would reach the seashore. Stage one was negotiated in a series of 'S' bends but we struck the rails without mishap. The aromatic night air now blended with wine, cognac and dates. We glowed within but there was no evidence of the 'everlasting glow' described by Bill Napier. True, the polished lines were dimly visible but beyond all was very dark. We sat down on the rails trusting that no train bound for Constantine would pass at night. Our discussion of proposed angles of further progress was overheard mercifully by one of our vigilant guards who made no haste to come to our assistance. We stood up for fear of falling asleep on the line, stepped over the track and stared into the darkness. The wily guard had moved noiselessly to within a few yards of us before shouting:

'HALT . . . Who goes there?'

'Coo, bloody hell,' said Spraggy.

'Friend,' said I.

'Password?' demanded the guard, rattling his rifle bolt.

'Oh, ah – Blackpool,' I recalled.

'Pass, friend,' said the guard. 'Follow me, Sir.'

As we followed his torchlight through the sand-dunes I complimented him on his perspicacity.

'Enjoy yourself?' I asked.

'Not really,' he said. 'It's creepy out here and I just thanked my lucky stars that I recognised your voices. I didn't see you until I got really close. That everlasting glow the Adj. talked about doesn't seem to apply to this part of Africa.'

'You put the fear of God in me,' said Spraggy. 'Now, find my bivouac, I'm feeling unsteady.'

Further along our track we met a couple of intemperate NCOs whom we were obliged to caution not to awaken our abstemious Commanding Officer. With extreme care we crept into our respective tents and fell into blissful unconsciousness.

At 03.00 hrs. I was aroused by a clatter of buckets and the unmistakable voice of Bill Napier: 'Who the devil was stupid enough to put a bucket in the middle of the flaming footpath?'

Chorus of under-canvas airmen: 'What about that everlasting glow you were on about, Adj.?'

He never lived down the indiscretion.

At break of day a further rattling of a bucket was accompanied by a lively cockney call of: 'Wakey, wakey.' This heralded the arrival of 'nice cuppas' served in person by none other than Driver Blisset, ex-Billingsgate fishmonger who was obliged by force of habit to arise before cock-crow. He was one of the most cheerful chaps I ever met, never a cross word and willing to turn a hand at anything. Also he had a remarkable aptitude of procuring necessities from space. If he hadn't got 'it' he knew where to get 'it'.

Thus roused to activity we prepared for our first day's work on foreign ground. Information received from Movement Control confirmed that 302 MSSU would be immobile for several days. We must transfer our personal belongings by Shank's pony to more permanent accommodation. This was found to be a group of stone-floored barrack rooms, recently vacated by Algerian troops. Our own Army Medical Corps was disinfecting the place by swilling it out with Jeyes' fluid. The Sergeant in charge of the operation assured us that it would soon 'dry out in this heat'. No sooner had he spoken those comforting words than the Algerian equivalent of the monsoons broke upon us.

We six officers of the unit set up our camp beds in one room and would enjoy reasonable comfort. All other ranks were committed to the standard palliasse. One Wireless Operator complained that no good would be done to his arthritis by lying on a damp stone floor. He was in his fifties and had tried to avoid overseas service. He did not wish to cause embarrassment by seeking special treatment, nor did he wish to encumber the unit with a permanent invalid.

My brain searched for a solution to the problem until the indomitable Blisset approached with an armful of wood.

'What now, Blisset?' I inquired.

'Just going to knock myself up a nice bed, Sir.'

'Got enough wood to spare for Fenwick?'

'Cor blimey, Sir, there's enough wood rarned the back for a 'undred beds.'

I made a discreet withdrawal from the scene but before the day was far advanced I noted that every man in the unit was equipped with a makeshift hammock-like structure. Nobody would sleep less than six inches above floor level. I blessed the lads for their ingenuity and trusted that the loss of timber might remain for the rightful owner a mystery.

Latrines of the 'Napoleon's Footprints' type were a permanent feature of the barracks as was a division set off for cooking. A Bedford 3-ton truck had been extricated from the damaged ship so no time was lost in collecting the NAAFI issue of cigarettes, sweets, and, for officers, half a bottle of gin and half a bottle of whisky each. Boxes of rations: type 'B' and 'C' promised tasty meals ahead. Type 'A' rations were reserved for front line troops; they contained luxury items such as Australian tinned peaches.

We had mixed feelings over leaving our bivouacs on the sands, until the rain started. Thankful to have a roof over our heads we stood in the doorways and watched rain heavier than we had seen in *Angleterre*; it swilled down all night and our barrack yard turned to quagmire. We could do nothing but insulate ourselves from the outside world until someone came to direct otherwise.

The someone came in the person of the Movement Control Officer. He was desperate for drivers to shift stuff from the docks; any volunteers? I said I could drive anything and had no difficulty in rounding up a truck-load of chaps anxious to do something towards the war effort. Half an hour later Flight-Sergeant Luke of our Radar Section and I took charge of a Bedford articulated vehicle carrying four elongated coffins, each of which contained a torpedo bound for a Royal Naval Air Squadron of Swordfish aircraft stationed at Blida. These torpedoes would disturb ultimately the Italian Navy at Taranto.

At Blida, about 40 kms. inland from Algiers, in the foothills of the Tell Atlas Range we found a well established air field with a fine set of buildings arranged around a most impressive barrack square. Within the square a geometric arrangement of ornamental trees enhanced the elegance of the architecture. It is regretted that my inexperience in the reversing tactic required by the driver of an 'artic' resulted in some adjustment to the geometry of the orangery. Nevertheless, by sharing the driving and not sparing the petrol we managed to deliver three loads of torpedoes to the RNAS.

On 10 December the rain stopped suddenly, the sun shone brightly and to great rejoicing it was announced that all our vehicles awaited collection on the quayside at Algiers. Not all were in fit condition to be driven away. Sergeant Snee cast his expert eye over each one. Those which had been standing in seawater needed more than a change of sump oil and were towed to Hussein Dey for overhaul. While our small MT Section worked on the vehicles we specialists in Signals Equipment examined the contents of the mobile transmitting stations. It became very clear that power packs which were located in the base of the transmitter racks were quite unserviceable owing to ingress of water. At a short conference it was decided that all the heavy transformers and chokes must be completely dismantled and rewound.

The sun continued to shine on us. Flight-Sergeant Lyons, a man of wide experience in the civilian radio trade, took charge of the open-air winding factory. With endless stretches of golden sands for a workshop we had ample space for the unwinding and rewinding of the coils. One man held a coil on a rod whilst another walked backwards towing the wire until the whole coil lay stretched in the hot sun. With four parallel production lines running, rapid results were achieved. Chiefy Lyons inspected every single coil, not giving the order to rewind until he was satisfied that not a trace of moisture remained. Each wire was wiped with a soft cloth or toilet paper and sun-dried. Rewinding slowly and methodically under close supervision by officers and NCOs was a painstaking process but we won in the end. The RAF Maintenance Manual made no mention of our methods but the cheers when our first message was acknowledged by Gibraltar must have been heard far out to sea.

By 13 December, all our wireless sets were operationally fit. I was at a loose end. So when Movement Control paid their respects to the CO and requested my services as a temporary convoy commander I was delighted. The CO took a dim view of the Army at the time. He was reluctant to release his No.2 together with the majority of the unit's drivers for more hazardous duties away from his command. However, Sergeant Snee was far from happy with his magnetos and dynamos. They would require more drying days. 302 MSSU was immobile.

I don't know what we delivered to Setif. There was a lot of empty space on the quayside after our dozen trucks set forth on the 200 km. journey to that upland aerodrome. I was pleased to have Goddard as a despatch rider to look ahead for possible hold-ups. He counted us as we passed through villages and over level crossings. I chose to ride in a Thornycroft at seventh place in the line, thus enabling me to keep an eye on vehicles both in front and to the rear. Progress was slow as we climbed steadily. It was essential that a sharp look-out be maintained for nimble-fingered members of the peasantry. Clearly it could be seen that any vehicle which fell behind and stopped for a moment would be the subject of Islamic scrutiny.

Goddard had sought and found a suitable halting place for elevenses. He guided our drivers onto firm standing in an emaciated olive grove, already occupied partly by a company of gunners. Hastily I set an armed guard to watch over us but the Sergeant in charge of the artillery assured me that any local felons had departed the district ten minutes previously on being threatened with the business end of a Bofors gun. We were invited to conserve our rations by joining his special regimental tea-making ceremony, which began when an enormous iron kettle was set upon a pile of stones. In the next alarming move a firing cap from a shell was ignited. In a short, searing burst of white heat the kettle boiled furiously. An outsize clay tea-pot was then swilled out with hot water, charged liberally with the appropriate quantity of tea-leaves, brought reverently again to the kettle and filled with just-off-the-boil water. A suitable brewing time having been observed, Army and Air Force queued with great respect to fill our mugs and loudly acclaim the high quality of the Sergeant's special prescription.

The gunners sped ahead of us along the highway whilst we renewed our leisurely, though reinvigorated, progress. As the evening drew nigh our carburettors sensed the fall in barometric pressure at increased altitude. It would be unwise to attempt completion of the journey after dark. I ordered Goddard to seek a satisfactory parking place on which we would spend the night. We stopped on a mountain top a little east of Berabjerid. I took first turn on a two-guard rota with my driver at the same time supervising the setting up of a make-shift kitchen. Ample rations of M & V piping hot direct from the tin fortified us against the iciness of the mountain air.

The driver of my Thornycroft knew all the tricks of survival. As soon as our guard duty ended he started up the engine, brought the cab up to a comfortable temperature, switched off, crossed his arms over the steering wheel, rested his forehead on the self-constructed pillow and fell soundly asleep. At length the temperature fell uncomfortably low whereupon my companion would wake up to restart the engine and repeat the performance. I envied him the ability to drop off at will. He had trained himself in the art during several years' experience as a long-distance lorry driver. I made do with numerous catnaps between which I spent time inspecting the guards and making tea.

As dawn broke we prepared to move again but the Thornycroft jerked only a few yards before stopping dead. It was hitched to an already heavily laden Bedford and towed for the remainder of the distance to Setif, where we arrived belatedly just after mid-day. It was a pleasure to sit down to a meal in the mess, before our consignments were off-loaded and the inevitable documentation completed. It was then far too late to contemplate an immediate start on the return to Algiers so we accepted the hospitality offered: dinner in our respective messes and sleep in our own trucks.

Though much less impressive than that of Blida the station at Setif was adequately equipped for routine maintenance of aircraft. Further we found willing hands in the MT section. A cleaning of plugs, setting of points and check of timing revived our ailing Thornycroft. The easy run back to the capital allowed some time to appreciate spectacular mountain scenery. As a grand finale the sunset glow around Algiers Bay welcomed us home.

Chapter 33

Le Mezloug

Good news: Orders came for 302 MSSU to move to a forward post east of Setif. The bad news: half our vehicles, particularly those laden with heavy technical gear, were unreliable. Sergeant Snee needed more time to certify fitness for a long haul.

It was decided that I should take charge of an advance convoy carrying tents and domestic equipment together with all personnel not involved in mechanicals and electricals. The CO stayed to look after the shop whilst I renewed my acquaintance with the route to Setif.

D/R Goddard performed his 'guided tour' in exemplary fashion. We struck target in mid-afternoon. Our new home was to be established on the village 'green' at Le Mezloug. Wisps of emaciated herbage would be preserved to remind us of our British heritage. We had neighbours, too, in the form of an Air Stores Park as well as the natives of the village. The benevolent ASP donated to us a wooden hut, vacated by them in favour of a brick building alongside the railway line. Our hut would develop as office and workshop in due course but for one night served well as Officers' Mess, Guard Room and ammunition dump.

Erection of tents in a semicircle commenced immediately. The invaluable Goddard excavated immaculate holes at points selected for the latrines. A kitchen took shape at the back of the railway station which provided shelter from the prevailing mountain breeze. We took to Le Mezloug like the proverbial duck to its pond.

Within twenty-four hours the place looked and felt homely. Bill Napier, Adjutant and brilliant manipulator of men, was in his element doing nothing but ensuring that every other member of the unit was fully occupied in useful activity. Bill had established amusing rapport with LAC Allen who, divorced from his lucrative taxi service and more recently from the seedy bars of Hussein Dey, was employed as handyman in the kitchen. P/O Barlow, our 'Radar' expert, found difficulty in adapting his expertise to such mundane duties as adapting a small marquee for use as our Officers' Mess. P/O Kemp, Assistant Signals Officer, accepted his misemployment as aide-de-camp to Bill, a position which ensured that the Adjutant need never lend a physical hand to anything.

Spraggy established contact with the rations supply depot at Setif, organised filling of the 'Bowser' with fresh water and began checking the Equipment Officer's delight: his inventory. Having satisfied myself that all was under control I returned to Hussein Dey, in two stages. First I took a lift on the ration truck as far as Setif, then hitched by courtesy of the British Army.

As a non-paying passenger I was better able to appreciate the splendid Algerian scenery, the scrubbery of the mountains giving way, as we descended, to the fertility of the coastal plain abounding in olive, orange and lemon trees and date palms. Beyond it, the Mediterranean in one of its blue and pensive spells set a scene of peace and beauty. To remind us of the war, khaki Dodge trucks of the US Army dashed by at breakneck speeds driven by men who had discovered a new freedom from New York and New Orleans, careless of life. Little children waved to us at every corner of every village. Away from the built-up areas women of loose virtue offered services by waving loose garments. We waved in reply.

Sergeant Snee had made some progress in servicing our salt-soaked engines and axles. He was suspicious of brake linings and operating mechanisms. He forecast completion of work on Boxing Day. Squadron-Leader Page made up his mind to transfer himself, his personal belongings, office and records to Le Mezloug on Christmas Day. I was to accompany him on the journey during which we must rendezvous with the Air Officer Commanding our Group, for the purpose of receiving direct orders for our future activities.

On Christmas Eve I paid a visit to my friend Jonville. Security rules forbade me to wish a formal goodbye but I wanted to renew my stock of dates and oranges. Our meeting was clouded by the news he had just received from Algiers. The poor chap was in a dreadful quandary. Admiral Darlan had been assassinated and once again Jonville was not sure which France he was to serve. I tried to comfort him by telling him that I would expect to be on his side whatever the outcome. I never saw him again.

Our small party ate Christmas dinner seated in the Bedford 15 cwt. truck in a splendidly isolated alcove formed by rocks which had tumbled from the overhanging cliffs a few centuries ago. Not a soul in sight, the engine stopped, here was peace. We were doing ourselves proud. A box of 'A' rations had been acquired by special arrangement between Sergeant Snee and an old friend of his who, quite by chance, he had found to be employed in the quartermaster's stores.

Our scent must have carried beyond the rocks. I had opened the tin of peaches and was about to pour the contents into a billy-can when a plaintive voice whispered: '*A manger, Capitaine, à manger.*' The little scruff held out his hand. This was the decoy. His accomplice, big brother, had crept up behind the truck to see if there were easy pickings inside. He received a sharp surprise when the fourth member of our party appeared from behind the cargo and yelled: '*Allez*, you thieving bastard!' Both violators of our Christmas reverie vanished at lightning speed to their lair behind the rocks. We completed our repast, yet conscious of a mystic supervision of our presence on the mountain. As we renewed our eastward progress two figures were seen to examine the vacated site in search of remnants.

Shortly after the incident we were alarmed when overtaken by two Dodge 'Six-by-Six' trucks going at a speed estimated to be excessive having regard for the narrowness of the improperly edged roads. Each truck carried a load of cheering Americans who gave us what may best be described as 'the bird'. They looked down upon us from their lofty vehicles. On our rounding the next sharp bend we observed one of the trucks to be inverted at the bottom of a steep embankment, its front wheels still revolving. Some of those who lately had signalled derisively their disrespect for our caution were now crawling from their vehicle. A few were vertical already, others were extracting themselves from the spiky discomfort of a prickly-pear patch.

Our offers of help were ridiculed. Amidst uproarious laughter the truck was righted. We departed. Before we had covered two further kilometres we were overtaken by the same truck going even faster than hitherto, in pursuit of its companion. We were pleased to see the back of it.

The day ended well! Because our conference at Setif lasted beyond sunset we accepted an invitation to stay the night and partake of a second Christmas Dinner. It was a good one: turkey, Christmas pudd. and all the gubbins.

On Boxing Day morning our CO seemed well pleased with his new encampment at Le Mezloug. A respectable office was established in the hut and Corporal Waller settled down to play upon his beloved typewriter. Paddy Lunney, our batman-cum-cook, had got the hang of his oil-fired oven. Domestically we were as good as organised. All we needed were our technical vehicles. Within 24 hours I was on my way back to Hussein Dey with the Bedford and the hope of expediting their movement.

On 28 December at 10.00 hrs. all engines were running. Sergeant Snee was concerned mainly with one of the Crossleys which had been so thoroughly immersed in water that had it been in UK he would have written it off. He elected to ride as passenger in it, with Corporal Dick at the wheel. They would set the pace at the head of the convoy. D/R Caddick would ride well ahead and endeavour to clear the roads so that we might run non-stop through built-up areas and take an unobstructed course up each incline.

From my seat in a Commer VHF Direction-Finder van I could see five vehicles ahead and seven following. The sun shone from a clear blue sky; the blessing of the Almighty might be upon us. Progress was steady through the surburban maze of Maison Blanche, on through the vineyard country towards Bouira which I was hopeful of reaching before sundown. It was not to be. As soon as we started to climb I could see puffs of white smoke and then tell-tale bangs from the ailing Crossley. She was running hot. She cooled off whilst we discussed tactics. It seemed we could run in spurts of about five kilometres.

Thus we made Palestro where a suitable tree-lined street was selected for the night stop.

Of course the local populace lost no time in gathering round us and we took less time to mount guard. We did feel more secure, however, with the small gendarmerie in sight and water for the Crossley was available from a reluctant fountain. Our drinking water was too precious to waste on the topping up of radiators. The night passed peacefully enough but the morning dew settled around our ignition systems, reactivated residues of sea salts, and not until 11.00 hrs. did we leave Palestro.

The mountain air was good; the sun shone and we were signalled a clear run through Bouira by Caddick who had performed his task, so far, with a showing of common sense. I waved to him my compliments which action must have gone to his head. Beyond the town he shot ahead and, seeing a herd of cows straddling the road in a vain attempt to find succulent grass, he raised his pistol, fired a series of shots into the air and screamed incomprehensible words in the manner of a Wild Western cowboy. I was not so concerned at the stupid waste of ammunition as I was alarmed that Caddick failed to observe the level-crossing immediately ahead. True the red and white pole stood upright; the gate-keeper stood upright wearing red fez and white burnous to match the pole and a vacant stare to match the occasion. I could see the train bearing down from Boudjellil as my vehicle crossed over the lines. I leaned out of the window, my hair standing on end as the Arab dropped the pole over the tail-end of the last truck of our convoy. I ordered our secret hooting code to be sounded and the convoy stopped, firstly to allow all drivers to recover their equilibrium and secondly to divest Caddick of his motor-cycle.

It was great to be back on a bike again. I had not ridden one since selling the Enfield Bullet. The telescopic forks of the Matchless I rated to be a distinct improvement over the old girders. I conducted my own convoy escort duty as far as Beni Mansour whereafter I selected a slightly downhill lay-by for the second night stop. That would enable us to start away more easily the next morning.

As the sun went down behind the mountains willing hands and empty stomachs caused rations to be spread and tea to be made. I made a systematic check of each vehicle starting at the tail of the convoy, listening for any complaints from drivers and passengers regarding mechanical performance and to ensure that no vehicle would be left unattended during the night. Rations were ample but unexciting.

Approaching the foremost Crossley, crewed by Sergeant Snee and Corporal Dick, I became aware of a most appetizing smell. When I tapped the door of the trailer it was clear that I had disturbed a clandestine school of cookery. A short discussion dealt with the embarrassment brought upon them by my not entirely unanticipated intrusion. Snee opened the door:

'Ah, we were just preparing a snack, Sir. Would you care to join us? We did a deal for a few fresh eggs in Palestro and they'll go well with a nice bit o' ham.'

'I can't resist the temptation,' I said. 'I'll nip back and get my knife and fork.'

'Bring a spoon as well,' said Snee, 'there's peaches for afters.'

Ham and eggs never tasted better and conversation never flagged. Snee told of his training as an RAF apprentice, how it stood him in good stead when he was later employed in the service department of a large garage in Sheffield. He possessed skills beyond the capability of the average garage mechanic.

'Give me a few files,' he said, 'and I'll turn you out a plain bearing as near round as makes no matter. I'll swear there's no better training in basic mechanical engineering for a young man than in the Air Force. The couple of so-called mechanics I have on this unit are typical products of the motor retail trade. They've had not training in fundamentals; they diagnose by guesswork. Anyway, we shall get where we are going tomorrow as long as the weather holds dry.'

I offered a tot of whisky from my flask.

'No, thank you, Sir,' he replied, 'I acquired a bottle from a friend of mine in the "Redcaps" – served with me in Palestine many years ago. They have ways and means, you know.'

I didn't know, but was learning. The three of us concluded a most convivial evening by drinking the health of the Military Police.

As dawn cracked we prepared to tackle our first five-kilometre section of the day. Neither Crossley wanted to rush away. We tow started. The Thornycroft which had earlier been a source of frustrations now seemed to have cleared its tanks, pipes and entrails of the last vestige of salt deposits. It developed enough power to make light work of pulling Crossley and trailer. At 08.10 we advanced. By judicious use of clutch and brake the two Crossleys headed our arrival at Le Mezloug in afternoon sunshine. The tumultuous welcome must have equalled in noise the applauding of a 'six' at Lord's.

To further enrich the excitement of reunion, the mail truck arrived. Discipline flew to the winds; season's greetings and packets of gifts were received, opened, shared and swapped. At last we were together in a family unit of forty-five members, each with his allotted space in a ridge tent, each with his personal thoughts of the news from home, each with the hope of doing something towards ending the war and returning to his native land.

Once the furore had died down we parked the vehicles in predetermined dispersal points, set guards, satisfied hunger and settled down to living together. Tilley lamps were lit, mail read over and over again, family secrets exchanged. A new life began.

Squadron-Leader Page was entitled to a tent to himself. He was a loner, anyway; bachelor, teetotaller – he drank only water – fastidious in dress, keen disciplinarian in an amateurish way. He tried hard to be hard but failed because he was kind of heart. Bank cashier in civilian life, his hobby was amateur radio. His patriotism had prompted him to join the Auxiliary Air Force. In common with the majority of members of the Radio Society of Great Britain he was well versed in radio theory. In addition, Cecil was a fine technician.

My own mechanical and electrical engineering background has shown me how to detect a craftsman. When I see a man pick up a hammer or a screwdriver I know instinctively whether or not he will do good or damage when using them. When I see a man wield a soldering iron I know whether he will perfect a joint or create a pimple of potential trouble. Cecil Page was a perfectionist in the use of small tools; too gentle and kind to use a sledge hammer or raise his voice in anger, he left it to me, as second-in-command, to perpetuate activity when there really was nothing to be done. 302 Mobile Signals Servicing Unit had made its last move for some time to come. 'They also serve who only stand and wait,' said Milton. Personally, I was not designed to stand and wait.

We established a continuous training scheme. We had numerous wireless receivers in operation so that Wireless Operators could practise their trade; we had transmitters but dared not transmit, so we made dummy transmitters for connection to the Morse keys. We created faults on equipment to provide exercises in diagnosis, we erected aerial masts and dismantled them, we organised PT classes, we route-marched, played football and formed brains trusts. We were highly trained for immobility.

Bill Napier gloried in the organisation of indoor games which did wonders in passing the time on the long, dark evenings. He was expert in the art of involving even the most bashful of us. His rapport with LAC Allen became a feature of these events. It was unusual for Allen to be unheard for long periods. When the Discussion Group chose for its subject: 'Is there Virtue in Early Rising?' the silence of Allen for more than thirty minutes caused Bill to question whether that garrulous fellow had any opinion on the subject. Back came the answer:

'I don't know what virtue means but I know it's a bloody good thing to get up in a mornin'.'

What we yearned for was some real work towards the war effort. Our telephone remained silent. Evidence of wartime activity could be seen as the odd aeroplane flying to or from Tunisia; some days a troop train would stop at the station, its occupants happy to exchange greetings and supply snippets of information direct from the outer world.

Spraggy enjoyed the luxury of a regular weekly ride to the Army Supply Depot for our rations. He and I shared a tent and we discussed the relative merits of sitting back and letting other folk get on with the war. He had to admit that his regular weekly outing satisfied his desire for action. He couldn't find a lot to complain about at the moment; if the worst came to worst he would deal with it when it arrived. Meanwhile, he checked and rechecked his inventory and accounted satisfactorily for the loss of a bucket during my convoy's two-hundred-kilometre-in-three-days marathon. Unusually enterprising for a bank clerk, Spraggy told a good tale of his running a book shop as a side-line and he was working on the idea of hawking salt in attractive small packages. He considered that door-to-door selling of electric light bulbs would be lucrative. We talked of forming a company 'when it was all over' and that's as far as it got.

My first mail had brought a letter from Lilian with news from the home front. In addition to that came another pleasant surprise, the second lesson in my course of 'Pelmanism'. I had signed up during my stay at Wilmslow; a special offer for members of the forces seemed too good to refuse. A better way of spending £4 I cannot imagine. The little booklets reached me regularly; the contents proved to be very helpful in the exercise of memory and appreciation of literature. I became conscious of serious gaps in my education and endeavoured to reduce them by expanding my scope in reading. During my infrequent visits to Algiers, whilst based at Hussein Dey, I scanned the book shops for bargains and struck one. For the payment of ten shillings in British Military Authority money I bought a jumbo sized hardback of Tolstoy's *War and Peace*, in English. That book saved me a lot of money and time for, having read it from cover to cover, I 'went off' novels for years. I cannot claim to have read every word because pages 26 to 30 were missing but what could I expect for ten bob?

I have never learned to 'skip-read'. For month after month I found refuge in Tolstoy. When it was all over I looked at the world with a more tolerant eye. I picked up the odd novel to find boredom on every page; Tolstoy had dealt with the subject more adequately. I turned to biography permanently.

My big problem at Le Mezloug was a constant battle against boredom. I revelled in military exactitude so long as it was interpreted with good humour. The 'falling-in' kept everybody well aware of our warlike purpose; the subsequent 'falling-out' relaxed us as a cohesive unit. Friendliness prevailed above any differences, opinion-wise or otherwise.

We six officers took our meals in a small marquee, at a common table. Paddy prepared our meals in an annexe to the main kitchen and served us at table in an informal manner. He was a willing lad and carried out standard RAF routine cookery practices which gave us little to complain about until boredom with the repetitive menus introduced the odd snide remark about Paddy's lack of enterprise. P/O Barlow was head of our Radar Section, which consisted of himself, Flight-Sergeant Luke and one other. We possessed no radar equipment whatsoever so they had plenty time to think of other things. Barlow thought it should not be difficult to introduce variety into our diet. He offered no suggestions as to practical application.

A short round-table conference concluded by my being appointed unofficial Catering Officer. My first offering, jointly prepared by Paddy and me, appeared on the menu as 'Hamburgers Argentina'. These consisted of corned beef chopped into little bits, mixed with 'smashed' potato, tomato sauce and powdered 'Army' biscuit. Served with veg. of the day they were an immediate success. The news filtered inevitably through to the NCOs and airmen's mess. Demand escalated.

On a corned beef base our variations included meat balls, rissoles and cottage pie. Our crowning achievement was affectionately named 'Le Meggloug' inspired by memories of the world renowned Scotch Egg. From the local smallholders we obtained ample supplies of eggs, fresh-laid, in exchange for used, dried-out tea leaves (mixed with a sprinkling of unused). Hard-boiled eggs, shelled of course, were wrapped in one of our standard mixtures, then rolled in biscuit crumbs. They received the highest accolade and were reserved for Sundays.

Similar concoctions woven round Spam were not popular until we sharpened them up with curry powder. Occasionally we decorated meat cakes with a slice of orange or lemon. Food preparation from limited resources became an exciting pastime, an interesting subject for discussion at table and a great antidote to boredom.

Barlow, as a highly trained radar specialist, did not respond over-enthusiastically to our culinary treatment. He and the rest of us were more than delighted when Group HQ directed him to operational duties at a forward station. We never saw him again. I was sorry to see my erstwhile lorry-driver mate, Flight-Sergeant Luke, go, together with the quietly dependable Sergeant Stewart. That marked the termination of 302's involvement in radar.

For the rest of us life continued to revolve around the village 'green' whereupon we were provided one sunny day with a remarkable piece of spontaneous entertainment. After lunch a period for siesta was being observed in customary fashion. Many of our number were horizontally disposed upon their palliasses, to be drawn abruptly to the vertical by the cheers of those of us who stood at the entrances of our tents, in exhortation to witness the flight of Abdullah. He was three years of age, stark naked except for his tiny red fez, running from the station building in a beeline toward his grandmother's house in the village. The more we cheered, the faster he ran. The faster he ran the more did the bobble on his fez bobble up and down; the other thing which bobbled, I will leave to the imagination of the reader. Abdullah played a leading part in brightening our irksome existence.

Then one day came an urgent telephone call from Flight-Lieutenant Marsh, Assistant Signals Officer at Setif: Did we have a spare aerial for a mobile VHF/DF? Certainly, we would be delighted to supply. Should we deliver it? No, he would drive the vehicle over to Le Mezloug and have it fitted on the spot. Splendid news. We were in business at last.

Marsh himself drove the Commer, its aerial array in a sorry state. He had 'caught it on the hangar door'. Our CO recommended the employment of a Driver MT: 'It is not your job to drive technically equipped vehicles. Our purpose is to service equipment damaged by enemy action. We have only one spare cross-bar.'

Chiefy Lyons organised the replacement, efficiently as usual. Marsh, somewhat reduced in ebullience, departed with the direction-finder as good as new.

An hour later the 'phone rang again:

'Marsh speaking. I'm afraid I've had an accident.'

'Don't tell me you hit the hangar door again!' I said.

'Yes. If I come over again, do you think you could pinch the aerial off one of your Commers?'

'You stay where you are, you twit. We will do what we should have done in the first place. We are the mobility specialists around here; we're on our way.'

When Chiefy had completed the operation to his satisfaction he returned to Le Mezloug smiling like the proverbial pussy. He looked forward to some real work; making one good aerial array out of two damaged ones.

The sun was high at mid-day. We all began to turn colour but the nights were very cold. It was necessary for night guards to wear their greatcoats. Mittens on hands were standard protection when carrying Sten guns which were known to 'go off' at slight provocation. Lack of care in the handling of one of these temperamental weapons very nearly caused the death of a Wireless Mechanic. All concerned agreed that the lad was saved by a genuine miracle.

An ingenious guard duty roster based on a '2-on and 4-off' principle ensured that every man got a fair ration of sleep, sufficient to enable him to stay alert on patrol. By using two adjacent rooms in our wooden hut two guards could enjoy four hours undisturbed slumber in one room while guard-changing took place on the other side of the partition. Using the hut as the guardroom obviated annoyance to occupants of tents, providing that every guard conducted himself in gentlemanly manner.

Officers and NCOs took turns as Guard Commander. On the night of the dreadful fright I was carrying out that noble function. At 02.00 hrs. I entered Room 'A' and shook awake the on-coming pair to prepare for duty. Meanwhile the pair in Room 'B' were half-way through their '4 hours-off' and fast asleep, purring sounds vibrating through the woodwork bearing evidence. My refreshed pair followed me outside holding Sten guns correctly, that is, pointing downwards. An unspoken changing of the guard was effected. The off-going pair, carrying Sten guns pointing correctly at the ground, entered the hut. I prepared to take a turn round the camp with the new guard, when from within the hut came a burst of gunfire.

I took a running jump into Room 'A' to see two ashen-faced airmen gazing with horror at a series of bullet holes in the wooden partition. Next door, two airmen sat up in their beds, looking mightily surprised at being alive. In the light of my torch two bullet holes in Harman's pillow! Between those holes was impressed the hollow where his head had been resting.

One of the off-coming guards had knocked his gun against the edge of a shelf, so letting loose the fusilade. The Tilley lamp was lighted, the CO arrived, followed by the Adjutant who kept at bay a retinue of sightseers. Amazement having been expressed, inquiries completed and calm restored, Harman turned his pillow t'other way up and went back to sleep. He knew he was at peace with his maker.

The amazing escape of AC Harman was a subject for discussion by the philosophers for a day or two, after which the weather turned nasty. Winds shook our tents, rain turned the village 'green' into a gritty mess but when the sun returned we felt its sting. Blades of what might be called grass appeared for a brief period but the heat came hotter and the colour of our tents matched more closely the surrounding terrain. Our camp moulded into Africa. Not only our equipment but we ourselves toned into the scene. We wore khaki battledress and could have been mistaken for pongos but for our blue caps and pistol holsters. From a distance it was not always easy to distinguish between airman and soldier.

I accompanied Spraggy on one of his business trips to Setif and while he attended to the important matter of collecting rations I walked along the main street. Turning a corner quickly I came face to face with two debonair khaki-clad figures who banged up salutes to match their appearance. A few paces further, I glanced round instinctively and the Warrant Officer I had recognised was on his way back to greet me. I had not seen Harry Rowe since my Dishforth days when I was a humble LAC and he a Sergeant. He had been reluctant to welcome the new breed of volunteers into his empire; 'jumped-up fuckers' they called us in Harry's language. Here we were, the tables turned; I could see his thoughts in his eyes: 'He's jumped up even further' . . . We shook hands. When we met again, years later, we were good friends.

Though we spent most of our time trying to kill it, we maintained a cheerful demeanour largely due, I think, to the climate. Personally I found the country to be ideal, in that respect, as a holiday haven and wonder it has not become a popular target for the package tour operators. My first winter in Algeria passed without any annual attack of tonsilitis; it is a fact that I have never suffered a sore throat since landing there but have not sought an explanation. Suffice it to say that none of us troubled the medical branch. Deep snow was reserved for the Monts du Hodna which lay to the south of us and were much higher. When it rained it belted down for short periods, then back came the friendly sun. The odd black cloud would appear, drop its greetings and pass eastwards.

On the occasion of my being called to Setif aerodrome on a technical matter I chose to borrow one of the Matchless motor-cycles. The distant black cloud didn't concern me; I wore adequate waterproof clothing, should it turn my way. It did. Halfway across the wild, open plateau I was under it receiving, not rain, but high speed hailstones the size of moth-balls. The physical pain as they struck hands and face was not acceptable. I propped the bike on its stand and sheltered below tank level. The hail ceased suddenly but so deep were the hailstones on the road that steering a straight course was difficult. I had not gone far before a second bombardment began. At a roadside refreshment house

I joined a cosmopolitan group of fellow shelterers. As we gazed in wonderment at the ferocity of the storm an Army Despatch Rider, head down, rode at good speed, straight as an arrow through hailstones inches deep. His despatches must have carried the 'Most Urgent' label. For his courage I would have mentioned him in his own despatches. Never do I see a hailstorm without recollecting the phantom rider of Algeria.

By mid-March the weather settled. We were resigned to our untroubled life. Then, one day, Goddard brought the message from Group HQ: '302 MSSU to move to Ain Beida' immediately. We packed up as light-heartedly as if we were going on holiday.

Chapter 34

Ain Beida

Blisset never failed to rattle his tea bucket at any hour by request. I had decided on 06.00 hrs. for take-off so asked Blisset to raise the alarm at 05.00. When the call came it sounded like Big Ben. Spraggy and I had dropped round to say farewell to our friends at Air Stores Park before turning-in. They were sorry to lose us, they said and did we like Irish whiskey? They didn't. Spraggy said: 'I'll drink anything.' I nodded agreement, then found I didn't like Irish whiskey but having embarked on the session I supported my colleague. We supported each other on the way back to our tent and collapsed in a heap. So when Blisset rattled his can at the appointed time my head filled with Big Ben Bangs.

I was pleased that daylight was a mere glimmer when I stood in front of the parade. I am sure I looked quite unfit to wear His Majesty's uniform. Somehow I managed to give final movement orders and climbed up beside the driver in the Thornycroft. Sergeant Snee had promised a trouble-free run, his time at Le Mezloug having been sufficient to tune every vehicle to perfection. He didn't let us down. I threw my pipe out of the window and vowed never to smoke again. It was a lovely pipe with a bone stem. I had bought it in Algiers for ten shillings (BMA). I dropped off to sleep for an hour or two.

When I woke up we were running into Constantine, a city to be seen to be believed. From my advantageous seat in the 'Thorny' I was captivated by the sheer phenomenon of the Rhummel gorges. As we crossed the Sidi Rached Bridge, 175 metres above the river bed, an unforgettable spectacle imprinted itself into my visual memory. It is a natural acropolis. No wonder the French found it a tough nut to crack; heroic defenders held off the invaders until 1837. Its history is a book unto itself.

After a hitchless journey, guided cautiously by Caddick and Goddard, conducted at a moderate pace set by Sergeant Snee, we arrived at our new home, on a stony desert, before tea time. An advance party headed by Squadron-Leader Page himself had marked out in patterns of stones, parking points and tent positions. Goddard set to with pick-axe and shovel to create two deep cavities: one with small square aperture to accommodate the officers' single-seater to be enclosed in wooden hut of telephone box dimensions, the other an elongated trench above which would be erected a parallel pair of horizontal bars, the spacing between the two being laid down in Air Ministry Instructions.

Suspension on the horizontals did not guarantee an airman the idyllic state of contemplative solitude. A vindictive individual or a careless one racing to a call of nature might, inadvertently or otherwise, tip the balance of a sitting soliloquist.

Senior NCOs made their own arrangements. Sergeant Snee was not the only experienced 'regular'. He and his colleagues devised a semi-private affair.

On the contrary we commissioned officers enjoyed the luxury of complete privacy provided that sensible use of the 'in/out' label was observed. Through a peep hole in the door the incumbent could view a distant and emaciated olive tree, sole survivor maybe of a neolithic plantation. I resolved to examine it.

In those vast open African spaces even experienced hunters may misjudge distance. I never reached that tree. Nevertheless it gave endless pleasure. To this day whenever I see a peep-hole I look through it and see that same tree.

At our new location we were denied the security of a building of any sort. We erected the minimum number of tents for our domestic use. All equipment was stored in the vehicles. At Le Mezloug we had enjoyed good relations with the natives. I like to think that our conspicuous affection for little Abdullah earned us the respect of the Mezlougians. At Ain Beida we adopted procedures of greater vigilance.

The town lay a few kilometres east of us. To the west a couple of dwellings were mere dots on the barren landscape. Our setting up of camp on the hitherto unoccupied wasteland was monitored only by the odd Arab on ass or mule on his leisurely jaunts 'twixt town and country. As events unfolded it became clear that observations had been more than casual.

The drill for erecting a ridge tent had been well practised. After marking positions where tents were required to be placed, the materials: canvas, pegs and poles, were laid out scientifically to facilitate final erection. On our first evening at Ain Beida two kits were left out pending erection the following morning. The guards for the first night used a truck as their sleeping and changing room. Our excellent '2-on and 4-off' routine of changes operated as at Le Mezloug.

We failed to recognise the greater cunning of the truly rural populace. One roofing canvas could not be accounted for by the erection party when work was resumed.

Doubly certain that nothing of value was left lying around we retired with confidence on the second night, guards patrolling as usual. In the early hours of the morning AC Adams woke up feeling chilly. No wonder! – his blankets had gone and the tent flap was flapping.

A council of war agreed on a plan of action put forward by Sergeant Hopperton, founded on his experiences in Egypt, where he had suffered personal losses in peacetime. The scheme held real promise. A ridge tent kit was laid out on the north side of the camp near the track used by passers-by. A Bedford 'Four-by-four' with canvas cover, but open rear was placed so that a continuous guard watching from its elevated station inside the truck would apprehend, inevitably, any person approaching the decoy. All through the night silence was maintained while at least one pair of eyes looked directly at the component parts spread out on the ground. Not a sound was heard, the bait lay undisturbed.

At dawn the vigilantes jumped from their mirador to discover the loss of the tarpaulin which had been strapped to the very vehicle in which they had spent the night!

We were up against professionalism. We must look around our encampment for routes by which the thieves might approach and arrest them from their rear. There was only one hiding place. Immediately to the north of the track which skirted the camp was a gully, deep enough for intruders to lie low until they thought it safe to move forward. We must post our detectives behind the gully.

At sundown Sergeant Snee and Corporal Dick with well prepared rifles lay in wait beyond the gully, which nobody could enter or leave unseen by one or both of them. A line of washing was suspended between two tents near the track. Two armed guards walked side by side, circumscribing the camp at regular ten minute intervals. In due course two ghostlike figures were seen to creep into the gully and lie low. They verified the routine of the guards. At what they considered a well-judged moment they crossed the track and began to appropriate the laundry. To their astonishment the villains found themselves confronted by our special constabulary, rifles pointing menacingly:

Snee shouted: 'Eryupp!' in steely Sheffield accent.

Dick yelled: 'Gotcher!', which they had.

Already dressed in anticipation I ran from my tent in a flash to supplement the firearms with my pistol. The two guards hurried from the other side of the camp. The two quivering locals were bundled into a truck and off we set for Ain Beida. Instinctively we took them to the *gendarmerie*. I could think of no other course of action. At least I could sharpen up my schoolboy French.

'*Nous avons deux voleurs.*'

The officer was most unimpressed.

'*Ah! oui, mon Capitaine. J'en ai beaucoup déjà. Regardez!*'

He unlocked a heavy door, shoved it open with his boot and repeated: '*Regardez!*'

The room was about the size of the village hall at Much-Binding-in-the-Marsh. Down the centre of the stone floor ran a channel sloping from either end to a hole in the middle. One electric light bulb of economical wattage dangled over the hole. The walls were bare, except for peeling plaster. The smell was nauseating. Our two prisoners were pushed unceremoniously into the cell to join thirty or forty other wretches, men, women and children. I was sorry the moment the door was closed on them.

'*Que faire?*' I asked.

'*Quatre jours, vivre de pain et d'eau.*'

Did I have to make a report? Certainly not. I gathered that after the four days on bread and water our captives would be released and probably back again within a week. It was up to me to safeguard our property and deal with intruders as I thought fit. The gendarmerie didn't want to know about it.

I have never forgotten the sight of those poor people in that slum of a prison. My colleagues and I discussed the subject on our ride back to camp. We resolved never to make further arrests. We must adopt a severe campaign of determent.

Spraggy was uneasy over the deficiencies in his stores. His monthly return was about due! We had an idea that the tent canvases would be found in one of the distant dwellings along the track to the west. Thence we took a truck with the intention of recovering our property under a modest show of force. One call was enough to satisfy our curiosity. At the entrance to the unglazed bungalow stood a wizened woman whose age it was impossible to guess. A few hens pecked at the ground around her feet, a goat stood beside her in the doorway. I tried: '*Bonjour, madame,*' to which there was no response. '*Comment ça va?*' was pointless because any fool could see that she was living in a miserable state.

If any of our property had been absorbed into the household utilities it must be inside the dwelling and neither of us would have dreamed of crossing the threshold for fear of infection. Concluding that communication was impossible we were about to depart empty-handed when the woman croaked: '*Oeufs?*' '*Ah, oui,*' I nodded. We could always do with a few eggs. She shuffled to the darkened interior and reappeared in a moment with half-a-dozen healthy looking samples. I offered a few coins but she said: '*Non, manger!*' – and she pointed to her mouth, displaying at the same time a set of teeth which would have delighted a progressive dental student. We didn't carry food with us but an even number of Craven 'A' cigarettes settled the deal.

From that day forward we were never without eggs. A young lad would turn up at frequent intervals with a basket containing the day's layings. A few sweets, biscuits and cigarettes were very acceptable in exchange. Of such commodities we held ample stocks for at Ain Beida our rations were supplied from the American stores in Constantine, about 100 kms. westward.

The weekly run to Constantine was extremely popular. Spraggy, as Stores Officer, undertook justifiably the personal supervision of the outing. A leave rota was drawn up permitting a small group to ride on the truck to enjoy a few hours in the City. A time of departure from the American stores must be observed strictly. The cargo was valuable and a constant guard had to be maintained over it once loaded on the truck. An enormous advantage to us was the fact that a minimum issue of rations from US sources suited a company of fifty persons. Our numbers were now down to forty-three. We lived like fighting cocks, but knew nothing of the fighting.

Not only did we receive sumptuous food supplies from the Yanks; a bonus came in the form of their 'P-X' issue of sweets and tobacco, chewing gum and peanuts.

The British Army had been relieved of the responsibility of feeding us, yet by some quirk of fortune we continued to receive our NAAFI issue of Senior Service and Craven 'A' cigarettes, Rowntree's clear gums, razor blades and toothpaste.

Hitherto I had eschewed the smoking of cigarettes on economic grounds and had denied myself the pleasure of the pipe by throwing it away in disgust. Now stocks began to pile up at my bedside. I opened a packet of Lucky Strike, sniffed it, lit up and found the taste to my liking. From non-smoker to chain-smoker I converted myself within a week. The Camel brand became a firm favourite, too. I swapped my English cigarettes for American. Then some bright lad began manufacturing pipes.

The Algerian briar roots were reputed to be the world's best material for pipe-making. The craze caught on in quick time. Ingenious designs of bowl appeared and even more ingenious designs of stem. The stems were made from any kind of tubular material which might become available. We tried strips of macaroni, electrical sleeving, bored-out chicken bones, bamboo and any likely vegetable artery.

It came to my notice that the Parker Pipe Company offered prizes in exchange for any unusual design of pipe which would be suitable for addition to the firm's museum. I turned out a square-bowled pipe, with side entry for a curved stem. The objective was a pattern for the ultimate dehydrated hookah to be smoked by a person resting horizontally on campbed or sand-dune. Such was the efficiency of the Army Postal Service and the kindness of the Parkers that within a couple of weeks I received in exchange for my invention, a brand new Parker Clubman. That proved a great joy and the instrument by which I became an inveterate smoker of expensive pipe tobacco, principally Gold Block. As the years went by a barrier of empty tins accumulated, useful as containers of odd screws and nails but a constant reminder of my fiscal frailty.

On the alcoholic front we were envied by the Americans who were very partial to sharing our Scotch whisky. Each British officer was entitled to a half bottle per week each of gin and whisky. It was there to be consumed so we drank it, usually in company with visitors. The CO maintained a strict abstinence. Hence a small stock could be held in a diminutive 'bar' comprising a disused ammunition box in the corner of our mess tent.

In larger formations a sufficiently large surplus of Scotch might be allowed to accumulate to form a basis for barter. A very good friend acquired a Jeep in exchange for a bottle of Johnny Walker. He retained the vehicle as his personal transport to the end of his military career.

The superior quality of food and its great variety did much to dispel the threat of boredom which hovered over us through lack of work. The American rations introduced us to sweet corn, tinned chicken, chilli-con-carne, protein-laden hamburgers and vitamin-laden guavas.

Though we were near enough to the fighting in Tunisia to hear the occasional crump of heavy artillery or bombing we remained unmolested. Our camp stood out like a sore thumb, a prominence exaggerated by our own tidiness. Our venerable commander, punctilious as ever, insisted very rightly that we maintain discipline in habit and dress. It seemed to me going beyond reason to arrange for pathways to individual tents to be marked out by having the boys build lines of stones in scientific order. Fortunately our forward defences deterred the German bomber pilots from selecting us for target practice.

As our weeks of idle luxury drifted by we began to wonder whether we had been forgotten. Hope was renewed when a despatch announced a forthcoming visit by the Chief Signals Officer, Group Captain Grundy. Here was the opportunity for Squadron-Leader Page to exhibit us as a highly tuned company of Wireless Mechanics. In good time the lads were lined up on parade, inspected and instructed, corrected and re-inspected. The sun was burning, the air was still and clear. The approach of the CSO was heralded by a distant cloud of dust which grew rapidly in dimension. A Ford Vee-8 shooting brake could be discerned. The parade was brought to attention, with as snappy a clicking of heels as might be expected of a platoon of the Guards Brigade. The cloud of dust entered the camp enclosing the Ford in its envelope. It stopped, swirled and out popped the Group Captain, his pilot's jerkin flopping from his youthful shoulders. He smiled, wagged a return of our immaculate salutations and said: 'Very good, Page. Dismiss the chaps and let's have a drink, I'm parched!'

A convivial lunch followed during which the G/C gathered information about our facilities and our latent expertise. In return he brought us into a picture of developments across the border.

Rommel had taken charge of all German and Italian forces in Tunisia and might be expected to break into Algeria via the Kasserine Pass. He would have an eye on Tebessa, not far down the road from us. If he could win the airfield at Youx-les-Bains he might still be in with a chance of staying in North Africa. We must not relax our vigilance. Business was in the offing.

Our excitement reached unprecedented heights when, a few days later, an urgent demand for a replacement power unit for a T.1131 transmitter came from an American Air Force unit. With the utmost promptitude, Chiefy Lyons set off with a new unit, his tool kit and an assistant mechanic. The customer had specified in his message that only a replacement unit was required, but our purpose in the war was to carry out the work of fitting and testing. Fitting was a simple matter of unsoldering the many wires from a long strip of terminals, taking out the faulty unit, fixing the new one and resoldering the wires to its terminals.

To the horror of the assiduous Chiefy, the cable loom had been hacked to pieces, quite beyond recovery. Within two hours of his departure from base he was back again to collect his own decorum as well as enough wire to build a new loom. Total time over the task: eight hours. Yet we had executed our first emergency operation. It did not, however, presage a run of business.

On 25 February the German attack ceased. Rommel moved north and began a new offensive along the coast from Tunis. He reached Djebel Abiod, thus securing the port of Bizerta through which he hoped to continue to bring troops and supplies.

We, at Ain Beida, reverted to our customary amusements. I decided to conduct a detachment of the boys on a route march. In the western distance there lay what appeared to be a lake. Fortified with food, drink and cigarettes we set off to investigate.

It was the vast open space which deceived. The 'lake' moved away as fast as we approached it. The wide valley which sloped gently downwards towards our objective appeared now to be disappearing underneath the 'water'. We were looking at an optical illusion or call it a mirage, according to fancy. Fancy it was; there was no lake marked on the map.

We had marched far enough. We fell out of formation and demolished our rations. Everybody knew everybody; I loved being among the lads some of whom were blessed with a higher IQ number than my own. Discussion ranged over any subject which arose spontaneously; nothing was barred by me in this godforsaken hinterland; religion, politics, peace and war could be churned over in good humour and in mutual trust. Back at camp it would be 'mum's the word'. Out in the 'blue' we created our own University.

Not that we proceeded without interruption. A scarab might disturb us with its powerful buzz or demonstrate its skill in rolling itself into a ball of donkey droppings. Our indiscriminate movement of stones uncovered scorpions and pretty lizards. It was not apparent readily to see their sources of food in this hardened terrain. Yet a search among the stones revealed a host of tiny plants just waiting for a sprinkling of rain to bring forth a show of colour. Among them lived a variety of insects.

As we turned our back on the imaginary lake a lone black stork, poised on one leg, gazed from a safe distance. Its sighting raised a few wry comments. Back at camp my mail included an airgram from Lilian forecasting arrival of a fourth member of our family in the coming August. Cheers rang round the tents as the news spread.

Spraggy's weekly ration run to Constantine never failed to attract a few anxious trippers to that spectacular city. The rule of observing the prearranged time of departure for the return trip had been broken once only by no less troublesome a person than LAC Allen. The penalty for holding up the truck for more than an hour was banishment to permanent washing-up duty in the cookhouse. Allen distinguished himself at the task, conducted himself in cheerful manner, bore no grudge and after a month of impeccable behaviour I heard the CO and the Adj. agreeing to allow Allen another day out by ration wagon. I held my reservations but, not being asked for my opinion, I crossed fingers and wished the project well.

The truck returned that evening, much later than usual and without Allen. Nobody had seen or heard of him from the time of arrival at Constantine. Despite a diligent search he was reported to the Military Police as 'missing'.

It was my turn to have the telephone by my bedside for the night. At 03.00 hrs. the bell rang.

'302 MSSU?' asked the voice.

'Correct,' I said. 'Flight-Lieutenant Reddin speaking.'

'This is Military Police, Constantine, Sir.'

I could have guessed the next but the voice continued:

'We have apprehended your LAC Allen, Sir.'

'How is he?'

'Drunk, Sir, and has been disorderly. However, we've dealt with the latter condition. He's in our cell.'

'Shall I come and collect him?'

'No, Sir. We want you to know he is safe and we will bring him to you in the morning. It'll be a nice ride out.'

So it happened. The redcaps delivered. Allen went happily back to the cookhouse. We couldn't be bothered with charges and all the paper work involved. The policemen enjoyed our modest hospitality and returned to a city more peaceful without our prodigal airman.

Domestic chores continued to be our main preoccupation. Though the battle of Mareth raged during the third week in March and only four hundred kilometres away, we heard about it on our wireless sets no sooner than folk back in the old country received the news. Monty's main forces held the Mareth line while Le Clerc took a left hook to the west of Matmata, where the cave dwellers must have thought their homes were indeed a gift of Allah. The indefatigable Freyberg made for Gabes. All hell let loose up and down Tunisia. The Western Desert Air Force made incessant attacks on the enemy which clung desperately to Wadi Akarit. The US 2nd Corps bore down on them from the recently captured Kasserine; Monty's men had broken through Mareth, and on 6 April his big artillery blasted the Germans from the Wadi.

The allies took Sfax on the 10th and Sousse on the 12th April. As they advanced northwards, unrelenting attacks were maintained by our Tactical Air Forces on the northern landing fields, thus preventing reinforcements by aircraft from Italy. On the 18th a great air battle was fought over Cap Bon. After that no German aircraft approached Tunisia carrying men or equipment by day.

Rommel was cornered, but the corner was a big one and his troops highly experienced. Monty's 8th Army had reached Enfidaville on the east coast and knew how to hold it.

General Alexander, as Supreme Commander, decided that Tunis City should be taken from the west, the heavy left hook! The 1st Armoured Division was, therefore, transferred from the 8th Army to the 1st Army. On 22 April the planned attacks began. The high-pitched battles raged for five days before the

German forces began to break. Tunis was entered on 7 May and the fighting in North Africa was ended at last. Package tourists may care to count the crosses in the cemetery at Enfidaville; pocket calculator recommended.

None of the dreadful turmoil disturbed us in our holiday camp at Ain Beida. As the news filtered through of attack and counter-attack, fighter sweeps and bombings, we stayed put waiting for the call which never came.

Though the land-fighting ceased the Air Force must be vigilant. Convoys making for Malta needed cover by fighters and anti-'U' boat patrols must be maintained.

In May, because the fighting had ceased on our continent, new priorities demanded moves of forces to Europe. Whilst major formations would move there would, inevitably, be a few small ones left in position to take part in communications with the convoy patrols. One such was a small wireless station on the north coast near Djidjelli.

Temporarily stranded, parentless, this station was required to be serviced by 302 MSSU. In the absence of any urgent work the CO decided that I should accompany him. We loaded up supplies of spare batteries, playing cards, chess set, mosquito netting, DDT, lamp oil, cans of petrol, cigarettes, dartboard, food, beer, dominoes and wireless sets. Off we set in a Bedford 15 cwt. with the faithful Kirby at the wheel.

Estimated distance to our destination being 300 kms. we reckoned that starting at 06.00 hrs. we could reach it by 16.00, allowing time for sightseeing. Nobody could resist a leisurely cruise around Constantine; we took our time in gazing into the incredible gorges, viewing the Bridge of the Falls and the panorama over the Hamma Valley.

We scrounged a lunch at Setif aerodrome and at 13.00 hrs. set course for the coast. We entered the Col des Cigognes ahead of time, breathtaking scenery to be admired at leisure. In a cleft of the Babor Kabylie Mountains the Kherrata Gorges measure 8 kms. long. The road, constructed by French military engineers, for much of the way is carved out of the rock face high up the east side of the gorge. At certain points it seemed possible to reach out of the truck and touch the west side. The road surface was good but wide enough only for one-way traffic. Any lack of concentration by a driver could result in straight-line descent of several hundred feet to the rocky bed of the river. The occasional passing place was provided where a northbound vehicle would enter a cavernous refuge in the cliff face. Into one of these we were obliged to reverse when confronted by a much beflagged scout car.

It was indicated by the sergeant who stood purposefully in his 'look-out', that we should be prepared to wait until a convoy passed. Kirby switched off his engine and we took liquid refreshment while a number of gun carriers, troop carriers and personnel carriers hurried south. When a pause came in the flow of traffic we decided to venture forward but were confronted by two motorcyclists who ushered us back into our hiding place.

'More to come?' I inquired.

'A lot more, Sir. This is the 51st Highland Division pulling out; afraid you can't go for a long time yet.'

Off they rode and the procession followed in a quick succession of military assortments. We ate half our rations, preserving the remainder in case of a long siege. Periodically I halloed a speeding officer, thus picking up some idea of the extent of his following. By lip-reading, sign language and some shouted remarks I gathered we would not be released from captivity for periods varying between: ''arf-an-hour' and 'God knows'. It was exactly 3 hours and 45 minutes before the final scout car pulled up and informed us that the road to the coast was clear. The 51st was on the first stage of its way to Normandy. We continued to Djedjelli.

It was good to see the Mediterranean again, calm and blue, turning to gold as the sun shone low. The road continued as a shelf cut into the sheer cliffs, popping in and out of short tunnels, now hanging over the water fifty metres below.

We found the wireless station tucked in a valley where the mountains opened up to allow for elementary farming. The men had established their living quarters in an outlying building of the farmstead; a nearby stable housed mules; mules and their deposits attract flies. I have never seen flies in such numbers per square metre or of such individual obesity as the flies of Djidjelli. They attacked anything edible, *en masse.*

The lads were pleased enough to receive visitors, accepted our offerings with gratitude and invited us to join their supper party. One man was on listening watch, the Corporal and the other two members of the crew co-operated in preparing the meal, a lesson in scientific presentation.

The dining table, an integral component of the farmhouse fittings, had been scrubbed clean as a new pin. A mosquito net, cunningly suspended from the roof, dangled over the table. Flies trapped under the netting were dealt with, prior to the start of the meal, by placing on the table a saucer of a sugary mixture which ensnared the offenders. Each individual plate of food was brought to the table under cover of a net. When all six were seated the Corporal advised us newcomers of two alternative methods of eating our supper with the minimum of risk of infection:

1. Each person may operate independently. By raising the main, overhanging net, snatching his plate, withdrawing it, lifting the edge of the individual net, taking the required morsel and popping it in the mouth ere the fastest fly lands on it.

2. The co-operative method of opposite pairing. All six members dive head and shoulders under the net. The three members on one side of the table uncover their plates and eat while the three persons opposite waft the flies, hopefully in the direction of the sugary bait.

System No.2 proved the more suitable for meals involving the use of knives and forks.

Technically the station was in good shape. After a game of darts when quite a number of flies got themselves pinned to 'double-top' we bedded ourselves down for the night hummed to sleep by the buzzers on the other side of the mosquito net.

Following a fly-blown breakfast we engineered some double netting over doorways and left the lads in good heart. We promised to recommend a resiting of the station if operationally feasible and an early visit by a medical officer.

By the time we reached 'home' the sun was nearing its relentless burning period. Corporal Waller greeted us with a handful of mail. We loitered outside his Orderly Room tent glancing at the despatches. The temperature had increased by many degrees since we had left two days ago. Looking down the valley to the 'lake' the shimmering air simulated waves of hot water. Then we saw the whirlwind, a twisting spiral of dust marking its onward haste; then we heard it whistling wickedly. It whipped off the cover from the airmen's latrine, severely disrupting the reverie of an occupant of the horizontal bars; it advanced through the camp picking up everything in its track. We jumped aside as it veered in the direction of our group. It scored a direct hit on the Orderly Room. It picked up the tent and flung it down but took with it papers, books and files.

Air Ministry Instructions, leave passes, Stores Records, 'two-five-twos' and 'two-five-nines', ins, outs and pendings: all could be seen a hundred feet high swirling round in a cloud of dust. The immaculate and painstaking Corporal raced after the tearaway phenomenon collecting up his beloved documents as they returned indiscriminately and spasmodically to earth. A cherished and most amusing memory of 302 MSSU: a score of its members from Squadron-Leader to AC2 garnering its precious case-history from an Algerian wilderness. It marked the end of my sojourn with the unit.

The incoming mail included the call for my services in MACAF as Station Signals Officer at, of all places: Blida. It sounded and turned out to be not only the start of real work but the beginning of my métier.

Mediterranean Allied Coastal Air Forces co-operated with Naval Forces to protect shipping. Wellington and Hudson aircraft fitted with Radar equipment sought U-boats, dropped depth-charges on sitings and reported positions to base stations. Spitfires, under the control of Fighter Sectors, eagerly pounced upon enemy aircraft which might interrupt the task. Memories of Wick and Leuchars awakened as I set forth to use, at last, some of the knowledge I had gained in Coastal Command.

Though parting from my colleagues in 302 was touching, I was happy to break from the ever-threatening boredom. I would have been happier still to be driven to Constantine, where I was to stay the night, by a Driver M/T. However, for some reason known only to himself, my chauffeur turned out to be none other than Squadron-Leader Page himself. We had never enjoyed a convivial relationship; I could not imagine that he intended giving me an emotional send-off. If he were sad at my going it might arise from the feeling that his unit must be about to be disbanded. Maybe he envied my selection for an operational posting, a selection on which his advice had not been sought. Our journey proceeded in uneasy taciturnity. He inhibited my natural searching for humour out of any but the most serious matters of life. I respected him as a first-class technician and admired his inordinate pride in the wearing of the King's uniform. I was more than delighted to be leaving his company.

The hotel which had been commandeered as the Officers' Transit Centre represented the ultimate in hygiene. I was shown to a private room with a most inviting bed, spotless white sheets recalling memories of home sweet home. I resolved to retire early; an undisturbed night was overdue. I had a long train journey to look forward to in the morning.

I was at peace with myself as I switched off the light, sank my head into the pillow and entered paradise. How long I remained in paradisial detachment I know not for after being awakened by strange choral sounds I lay in the dark trying to identify beauty in their content, at the same time hoping they would not be of long duration. Alas! At length I switched on the light to check the time; it was midnight. The cantillation continued unabated into the small hours and beyond. It continued in a monotonous wail. Revel or requiem?

The steward brought tea at 06.30 hrs.:

'Sleep all right, Sir?'

'No, I'm afraid not. What went on next-door? Wedding or funeral?'

'Don't know, Sir. They all sound the same to me – painful!'

My train was due to leave for Algiers at 08.00 hrs. I was pleased to find that my reserved seat, by a window, was on the north side of the compartment. The weather had settled for hot and though I had changed to tropical uniform I anticipated, correctly, a claustrophobic encapsulation in an unventilated compartment.

The enormous, smoke-blackened engine coughed out spark-laden fumes even as it stood in the station. The windows remained closed, not only as a safeguard against soot but as a deterrent against rubber-necked youngsters who sought alms for poor relatives.

The purpose of the numerous armed soldiers, standing at intervals along the platform, was not clear until the engine gave a whimpering bleep, a weary belch of steam and the train began slowly to move. That was the signal for a multitude of prospective non-paying passengers to leap aboard. As fast as they ran and clung to the carriages so ran the Algerian troopers into action. Rifle butts thumped into backsides, mantles were grabbed, flung aside complete with occupant or sometimes torn asunder, soldiers were kicked and railway officials assaulted, but the train moved on, trailing chaos with it and retaining a number of free-riders. As we gathered speed I took my last view of Constantine and turned my attention to my fellow travellers.

A mixture of civilian and military occupants made an interesting study. Opposite me sat a venerable Frenchman who was anxious to communicate his affection for the English race. It seemed that he had established friendships with examples of the breed during the First World War. His wife took up more than her legitimate share of the seat not only by reason of her o/s dimensions but largely because of a substantial hamper which she insisted on keeping on the seat between herself and her neighbour. Fortunately, the latter was a slim young lad who rested his left elbow on the hamper and gave to his grandmother periodic glances of anticipation that it might be opening time. The boy's mother completed the company on the bench. Next to me sat a priest, a nun and an officer of the French Army.

No sooner did the train work up a good turn of speed than it slowed to a standstill, whereupon certain non-paying passengers alighted to be replaced by others who crawled out of the cacti. I was anxious to follow the scenery but for much of the journey I was prevented from seeing out of the window by burnouses flapping against the glass, or by grinning Islamic faces glorying in the rush of air.

Whenever we stopped the outriders vanished. Such were their numbers that it must be assumed that many more rode on the roof or on the buffers than clung to the sides of the carriages. I witnessed no accidents but the law of averages must be obeyed. I concluded that casualties could not be avoided.

Lack of sleep overcame me at an early stage of the morning. When I woke up it was time for snacks. I opened my little box of surprises, withdrew a Spam sandwich, ate it and then took a swig from my water bottle. My action drew smiles from the old lady, who earlier had nodded approval of my amity with her husband. Now the hamper was opened to the obvious delight of the grandson who was accorded first service. Out popped the inevitable *petit pain et fromage, saucisse et saucisson*. She offered me a share in all these delicacies. I refused politely, indicating that I had ample stocks of food. However, when she withdrew, from her larder, a bottle of *vin ordinaire* I accepted a good measure.

A party developed. Though the atmosphere was stifling I remember the occasion as the most sociable rail journey of my time. I was able to point out to my new friends the village 'green' at Le Mezloug, now unoccupied, freed from the threat of foreign encroachment. The train rumbled from one stop to another, never moving without a coating of parasites, until we approached Algiers station when they all dismounted to avoid apprehension by the police. It had taken fourteen hours to cover 400 kms.

I accepted a lift by RAF truck to a transit camp at Maison Blanche. Accommodation was in a marquee erected over a recently cemented base. The blankets on the bunk-bed were coated with a liberal sprinkling of cement dust. Another painful night put final touches to my parting from 302 MSSU.

Chapter 35

Enter the 'Penguins'

On the final stage of my transfer to Blida I travelled in style. A Ford Vee-8 shooting brake whisked me along the road which I had last travelled by articulated torpedo carrier. After four months in the stony wastelands the fertility of the coastal belt presented a picture of Utopia. Shadows of the eucalyptus trees bespeckled the roadway, citrus trees coloured the background, date palms and mosques punctuated the blue-yellow sky, ploughmen and camels animated the foreground.

A peremptory introduction to my new post was conducted by my predecessor: Wing-Commander Fair, elated by his very recent promotion, clearly evident in the newness of the triple stripes decorating his epaulettes, spoke fast, his ginger moustache twitching excitedly. Joining a group intent on invading Sardinia he was taking with him his protegé, Fl/Lt. Dennis Leroux whose fluency in French must have been helpful to Fair in his dealings with local bureaucracy. He carried with him the rank of Acting W/C, renouncing the establishment rank of Squadron-Leader appertaining to the post I was inheriting as Station Signals Officer at Blida. This was not mentioned to me at the time, nor did it concern me. I was only too pleased to have been appointed to the job.

To give credit where due this whiz-kid of a Signals Officer had established a very workable system in the organisation of the section. It struck me that it was at variance with the practices in operation at Wick and Leuchars; it did, in fact, put an extra measure of responsibility on the Duty Signals Officer which should have been handled by the Duty Controller. From the start I felt that the routine did not conform precisely with Air Ministry Instructions but it had worked well to date. I had no intention of altering anything in the mode of new broom sweeping clean. I assumed, quite wrongly, that the unusual arrangement was approved by all concerned. As things turned out I was to live to regret not deviating from Fair's innovation. A terrible disaster, for which I bear some responsibility, will be highlighted at an appropriate point in this history.

Meanwhile, I accepted the situation as it had been established: Overall control of aircraft in the Western Mediterranean area rested with a Senior Controller in Algiers, who acted in close co-operation with Combined Operations Headquarters. Blida was only one of the stations from which aircraft took off and landed.

Yet for some reason Blida functioned as W/T (Wireless Telegraphy) control station. How that came about I do not know. There may have been an historical reason, dating from the early days of the 'Torch' invasion. Certainly Blida was well placed at the foot of the Atlas Mountains but our transmitters were far less powerful than those at the permanent bases of Malta and Gibraltar. We called frequently for their help when conditions were difficult. I had the feeling that my predecessor had hung on to W/T control as a status symbol in his empire. It was not until after the disaster that Algiers took control.

I could not complain about going in at the deep end. I was well aware of what the Wing-Commander explained to me in our brief meeting and I was indebted to the Warrant Officer, Jimmy James, for his advice. Jim was an old-timer who had worked under Fair since the inception of the system. He took his turn as Duty Signals Officer in the ingenious three-watch rota. He never complained of being over-worked, which he most certainly was until I had got a proper hold on the reins. The third member of the watch list was my Assistant Signals Officer F/O 'Cab' Calloway, another new arrival. Fortunately, we were blessed with some experienced NCOs who could stand in temporarily when such urgencies as serious calls of nature must be answered.

The system went thus: Watch 'A' 22.00 hrs. – 08.00 hrs.
Watch 'B' 08.00 hrs. – 16.00 hrs.
Watch 'C' 16.00 hrs. – 22.00 hrs.

By taking turns at the 'A' watch in rotation, followed by an 8-hour rest period before going into the 'C' watch, we each enjoyed a whole day off from operational duty every third day. The hours we worked may not have caused more than a moderate raising of eyebrows by a vigilant trade unionist, but there were many other calls on a Signals Officer.

Paper work needed attention, out-stations were to be inspected, personnel problems examined, training programmes arranged, liaison with the French power engineers to be undertaken, visitors to be entertained, schedules to be approved. When the camp cinema projector broke down I arranged for its repair and continued maintenance. In return for that gesture I was appointed, by the Station Commander, to the honorary post of Theatre Manager and Entertainments Officer!

In this last-mentioned activity I was more than ably supported by my rooming mate Eddy Kelland-Espinosa, of the London School of Dancing. Between us we didn't just organise entertainment at Blida; we revolutionised it! Eddy and I occupied one room of a block of apartments, hitherto allocated by the French Air Force as sergeants' married quarters. We formulated plans for a concert party and within a few weeks we were playing to crowded houses. That was understandable enough for there was no other live entertainment within miles, disregarding certain establishments indicated by red lamps. Nevertheless, our shows proved immensely popular even with selected members of the local citizenship who attended at the Group Captain's invitation.

Eddy started his day in a most entertaining way. Our room was unfurnished except for our own camp-beds, the colourful, tiled floor extending beyond the room along a corridor to the bathroom. Eddy said I was likely to catch pneumonia if I walked to the bathroom in bare feet. Unfailingly, he solved his own problem by walking on his bare hands, directly from bed to bath and back again. I thought of him as the original live-wire until I read a biography of his illustrious father.

What with work, duty and my hobbies at the theatre a minimum of time was left for eating and sleeping. I had changed from an idle life in the wilderness to one of intense excitement at an aerodrome handling hundreds of take-offs and landings throughout each twenty-four hour period. Not only did Blida handle operational aircraft but a big contingent of American Army Air Force personnel lived amongst us. They maintained and flew, with great frequency, Dakota aircraft of their Transport Command. The principal tenant of the hangars at Blida was No.156 Maintenance Unit which overhauled and repaired casualties in engine and airframe. The whole place was a hive of industry. Personally, I was fully committed, thoroughly enjoying myself.

With the dedicated support of my colleagues, things were running very smoothly. Then the 'Penguins' arrived!

From our Signals Office we looked north across the airfield. Aircraft came and went all day and some at night. We were accustomed to noise. Air crews reported to the Control Room and to the Signals Office for debriefing, thence to quarters for rest and refreshment. Sure enough there were jollifications at the bar in the evenings but all in all Blida was a well-disciplined station, much to the credit of Group Captain Strugnell. Struggie, as he was affectionately known, was reported to have joined the Air Force when Pontius was a pilot. Proud of his establishment he monitored it by making surprise appearances at the most unlikely places of work. Thus, Blida pursued its varied missions with propriety.

When No.36 Squadron landed, a change came over the place. Their Wellingtons raised unusually large clouds of dust on the way to dispersal points, engines revved more audibly and the crews sang bawdy songs on the way to the office buildings. They clattered up the stairs and violated the sanctity of the Control Room. Their Wing-Commander Piercy, ex-dirt track rider by trade, burst into the Signals Office, introduced himself as the head 'Penguin', hoped he could depend on my co-operation and swept out again before I had a chance to ask if he had any particular problems.

It was my turn for 'A' watch. I took dinner at 20.30 hrs. and looked in at the bar for a glass of orange juice before walking to the office. The song rang out at a rousing tempo:

> 'We're the outfit for prangs; you will always hear bangs
> If you're ever near Thirty-six Squadron.

We've been out in the rough and we're all very tough
We're the boys of the old 'Penguin' Squadron.
We can shoot you a line about the girls in Singapore,
We've been all round the clime from Bengal to Bangalore.
We've been out in the rough . . .'

and so on, ad lib.

Our local muscatel and vermouth appealed to the new arrivals. Available at less than moderate cost; none but the most abstemious could resist the flavours, nor fall victim to the effects.

Following an uneventful night watch I walked towards the mess for breakfast, having handed over to Cab. I met a distraught Station Padre.

'Seen my bike, Red?' he asked. 'Those bloody "Penguin" fellas rode it around the anteroom last night, pushed one of them down the stairs on it and I haven't seen it since – looked everywhere.'

'You haven't looked on top of the fountain, have you?'

'Well I'm buggered,' he said, 'there it is too. How the hell am I going to get it down?'

'Your problem, Padre. Why not try a prayer?' I suggested. 'I've been on all night and I need some shut-eye.'

The morning passed peacefully enough while the 'Penguins' overcame their hangovers. I woke up when I heard some of their numbers, who had been allocated billets in the same apartment block, nattering away about the affairs of the previous evening. I made their acquaintance whilst shaving and later joined them at lunch in the mess. Harum-scarum they might be but it struck me that they showed tremendous loyalty to one another. Somewhat disgruntled with their leadership, they hoped to find an improvement and better maintenance facilities at Blida. It seemed that Struggie had made a brief observation of their high-spirited behaviour in the Officers' Mess and entered the name of No.36 Squadron in his little black book. Maybe their Commanding Officer was due for a long rest period; in due course he was replaced.

Wing-Commander D. Prince Marvin DFC wasted no time in reshaping the squadron as an efficient unit which would play a major role in ending the U-boat menace in the Mediterranean. A veritable tower of strength, 'Dee-Pee' set an example to all around him. He could drink without getting drunk, wise-crack with any budding comedian, fly a Wellington with exactitude, reprimand without offending, praise without condescending; nurtured in the Palestine Police Force the new chief 'Penguin' cut an impressive figure.

Without much persuasion I found myself taking a special interest in No.36. Their Signals Procedure lacked precision. I spent a lot of time with their Wireless Operators who responded to my entreaty for compliance with the high standards used in MACAF. Idle chit-chat over the wave-bands was forbidden.

To the uninitiated the Morse Code will appear to be a quite impersonal language. This is true enough when information is being transmitted by means of an automatic machine, but when two or more operators send messages to one another by tapping their individual Morse keys then personality becomes very much involved. After only a few hours an operator on a network of three stations will identify certain characteristics of the touch on the key of the other two. The next time he takes over his watch he will be able to detect any change of personnel on the network.

A very close fellowship develops on a triangular D/F (Direction-Finding) network. Each station can 'take a bearing' on an aircraft asking for assistance. If all three stations pass, by telephone, the bearing to a central control room the position of the aircraft can be 'plotted' on a map. In this way rescue services may be directed to an aircraft in distress. It is easy to imagine the spirit of community between these unseen confederates. On taking over a watch it was customary to check whether all was well on the 'net'. The first call of the day, if all is otherwise quiet, may well include: '--· -- --- --' which translates as 'G M O M', an abbreviation of 'Good Morning Old Man!' It made a nice little touch of friendliness to the isolated vocation of manning a D/F station; it may have confused the enemy into the bargain. On occasions when I spotted this irregularity in a log book I seldom commented on it. The practice was never abused, even by No.36 Squadron, once my views on the subject had been made known to their W/Ops.

Prior to taking-off for convoy escort patrol the air-crews assembled in the Control Room for briefing, all except the W/Ops, who came next-door to the Signals Office where the DSO issued 'REKKO' cards, letter of the day and any special instructions regarding Signals Procedure. On the blackboard, almost a duplicate of that in the Control Room, was a coded list of shipping and convoys in the area. Separate columns showed aircraft on duty by letter, name of W/Operator, time out and ETA. There was some logic in briefing the W/Op separately from the other members of the crew; we could discuss signalling problems intimately. In retrospect, I wish I had expressed my opinion that it would have engendered closer team spirit if the whole crew could be present at the full briefing. Nobody had objected to the status quo.

At debriefing the same segregation applied. The W/Op reported to the DSO, handed in his defunct 'REKKO' card, log book for examination and signature and described any signalling difficulties without his captain being aware of any problems. It was not unknown for a captain to pop in for a chat with the DSO but it was not a recognised practice. The Wireless Operators carried the rank of Sergeant or Flight-Sergeant and might play the role of gunner too, then known as W/Op-AG. We in Signals adopted them as members of our élite family of communicators. We came to know their characteristics of performance and attitude. Over the wave-bands judgements were made by our Wireless Operators in the W/T room. The aircraft band receiver was manned by selected operators renowned for their efficiency. They passed messages to the Supervisor who catalogued his own assessment of airborne operators. He, in turn, would pass his comments to the DSO who could bring anomalies to the notice of the W/Ops at debriefing. In this way our joint efforts resulted in improved operating efficiency between air and ground.

With Rommel out of the way in Africa more power could be brought to bear on the U-boats which still roamed the western Mediterranean. No.500 Squadron joined us at Blida with their Hudson aircraft, beautifully equipped with Bendix radio gear. Their Engineer Officer, deputising for the Signals Officer who had been killed in action, presented himself in my office, whipped up a smart salute:

'Warrant-Officer Collingwood! . . .'

Before he could continue I interrupted:

'George Collingwood! Well, well – the last time we met was in the Boy Scouts' hut at Sowerby and you flattened my nose in my one and only boxing match.'

George had entered the RAF as an Apprentice on leaving school. His achievements to date had culminated in his appointment to care for the fine aircraft of No.500, which were to join the growing force of U-boat chasers. The performance of their W/Ops was monitored as usual and measured up well enough.

I was of the opinion that signalling from our Blida-based aircraft must be as good as any in the RAF. Any tendency to complacency was quenched dramatically when, one hot and sticky morning in the middle of July, a course to steer was requested from an aircraft of No.617 Squadron. 'The Dam Busters' were on their way to Blida. I was DSO at the time. The watch superintendent called me on the telephone from the Wireless Room:

'Would you care to come down and hear a bit of air-operating as it ought to be, Sir? It's like music!'

The Lancasters parked around the perimeter; the crews were collected and brought in trucks to the Control Room. I sought the much-photographed features of Wing-Commander Gibson. He was not there, having been ordered to rest. An outrageous moustache identified Micky Martin; of the other original 'busters', I knew of their fame but not their faces.

When the W/Ops came to me for debriefing I was astonished at the elegance of their handwriting. Truly the selection of crews for this famous squadron had been undertaken with the utmost care. A new standard had been set for Blida!

Though '617' had been built up to strength it had not been called upon to operate since their outstanding attacks on the German dams. It is surprising, therefore, that they were rushed off to North Africa without being issued with tropical kit. Blida was running up to full summer heat. Stepping out of an aircraft recently cooled by a crossing of the Alps, into a dusty atmosphere exceeding 100°F must have been a shock. There were some sweaty bodies around for a few days, especially for those who could not be fitted by 'Stores'. Some very peculiar modes of dress appeared in the mess, much against the Strugnell grain, but borrowed misfits relieved some of the suffering.

Two comforts were enjoyed by our illustrious visitors: wine and oranges. The navel oranges of Blida are unsurpassed in size or taste. Consignments were prepared for addition to the bomb-load to be carried on the return flight, bombs to be dropped on the harbour at Livorno, oranges to be landed at Scampton.

Some of the Lancasters had landed at Maison Blanche. I motored over there to deliver the Signals briefing prior to the flight. All the crews gathered together. Group Captain Clark described the target and detailed the flight plan. I did my little bit about frequencies and IFF. Then a hush fell over the gathering.

A quiet little officer now advanced from the corner. It was possible to count the stripes on his epaulettes. It was not possible to count the number of medal ribbons on his jacket. We strained to hear his words of encouragement. He thanked the boys for what they had done and wished them well for the present operation. Nobody had announced him; we could only guess: So this was Air Chief Marshal Tedder. He concluded his address with the wry emphasis:

'Don't warm up your engines in this climate. They are already warmed.'

I was back at Blida to see the take-off of the contingent waiting there. Even though the sun was sinking beyond Gibraltar the heat thrown up from the baked earth was stifling. Anxious to get home the Lancasters started up and filed out to the east end of the runway. The first one took off and the second one followed very quickly on its tail. There was a short delay while the third and fourth lined up on the runway. Meantime an Engineer Officer on the ground was signalling frantically to pilots of aircraft at the back of the queue to switch off their engines. Too late: from two of them came a dreadful screeching of seized machinery. Two aircrews were destined to spend a few more days in the dustbowl, awaiting repairs.

Right at the end of July, '617' called at Blida again, having dropped leaflets over Milan. That mediocre task displeased the great warriors and they fell upon the wine stocks with gusto. A request for a bulk container for transportation of muscatel to Lincolnshire came to my attention. I informed the Stores Officer that a distilled-water carboy should be written off, owing to unforeseen circumstances. It took off, filled to the brim with the finest product of the local vineyard.

Meanwhile, the convoy protection operations continued uninterrupted, with the 'Penguins' playing a leading role. The pressure on the U-boats intensified when No.14 Squadron added their Martin Marauder aircraft to the strength of the Blida armament. They ventured on long range reconnaissance flights, were very quick but difficult to land. It was because of this that I found myself in prison.

Chapter 36

Matters of Recreation

You never knew when, where or how Struggie would appear. He lived in private quarters somewhere in the town. He came rarely into the Officers' Mess. Surprised I was when he sat down beside me at breakfast one morning. Our mess was an informal affair. We sat on benches at long wooden tables. There were neither tablecloths nor serviettes. Semi-self-service was the best way to describe the system. Italian prisoners-of-war served us cheerfully by cleaning up, washing up and topping up cruets, bread baskets and marmalade bowls. Always we had loads of marmalade of high quality.

The Group Captain was no snob. He had drifted in, joined the queue for sausages and a mug of tea and took his place, waving aside any tendency for those of us seated already to rise in deference to his exalted rank. He wished us the time of day and entered immediately into the general conversation. His wit was a match for anyone.

'What have you got on today?' he asked a Met. Officer sitting opposite. 'Any startling developments in the heat wave?'

'Pleased to say it's somebody else's problem, Sir; it's my day off today!'

'Jolly good show,' said Struggie. 'The weather can look after itself, no doubt.'

'Coo, I wish I could have a day off,' interjected the Armament Officer who sat to the CO's starboard side. 'I'm so busy, I can't see any chance of it.'

'Then you are either under-staffed or inefficient; which is it?'

A stony and embarrassing silence followed. Spraule, my Canadian friend, a pilot resting from operational duty, broke the spell;

'If anybody fancies a day out with me they are welcome. I'm taking a Blenheim back to Setif in half an hour's time.'

'Back tonight?' I asked.

'Sure to be something to come back,' he said.

The Armament king didn't pick up the hint so I said:

'Well, if it's OK with the Group Captain I'd like to take up the offer, so long as I'm back before about 19.00 hours.'

Spraule and I excused ourselves. I dashed off to collect my parachute and called in the office to advise Cab that I was off for the day. I expected to be back before the ENSA concert party arrived at the theatre. I could depend on Spraule to bring me back on time.

227

The Blenheim had been well prepared by the MU. Spraule declared it 'a good one'. This meant he could participate in one of his favourite skylarks of 'shooting up' any unwary pilot of an American DC3 transporter doodling his way through the valleys. He could identify a DC3 at a distance from which I could scarcely pick out a dot in the horizon. The gesticulations from the American crew as we peeled away from our 'attack' clearly indicated their displeasure.

My pilot executed another immaculate landing at Setif where Chiefy Whittaker cast an appreciative eye over the Blenheim.

'What have you got for me to take back to Blida?' Spraule asked.

'That Marauder,' Chiefy replied, pointing to the nearby aircraft which showed distinct signs of having been affected by enemy gunfire.

'Oh, I can't take that,' said Spraule, 'not with a passenger. Nothing else?'

'Nothing else today.'

I declared my willingness to go in the Marauder, but my friend would have nothing of it.

'Too dangerous,' he said, 'not enough wing area.'

I knew what he meant. I had witnessed more than one pall of black smoke rising from the Blida runway, fire engines and rescue teams racing desperately to try and save the lives of the crew of another Marauder of 14 Squadron.

After lunch and a decision that further argument was useless I set about making alternative arrangements for my return to Blida. Flying Control couldn't help, the MT Section knew of nothing going west. I 'phoned Cab, explaining my predicament, knowing that he would hold the fort. I approached the Guard Room where the police Sergeant instructed a guard to hail any west-bound vehicle. Nothing came except nightfall. I shared tea and wads with the police. I accepted the offer of a night's accommodation in the cell and so I found myself in prison until dawn when came the joyous cry:

'We've got a lift for you, Sir, if you make it snappy.'

The guard had hailed an American Command Car. There was no time for breakfast but I was prepared to endure a modest fast if I could reach Algiers by eventide. I hopped into a rear-seat alongside an attractive young lady wearing French military uniform. The driver bore the rank of Major and the front-seat passenger that of Lieut-Colonel. The three of them had a common interest: Intelligence Service.

I thanked the senior officer for his kindness in promising my delivery to Algiers. From that moment they paid scant heed to my presence. I feigned sleep.

I imagined the French girl to be an interpreter. She spoke excellent English but had a poor opinion of the English people. Her summation of us as hypocrites cut me to the quick. As a guest in the car I checked an impulse to voice a protest. Thinking further on the subject, I found myself tending to agree with the description but it would have been improper of me to mention any disapprobation of the French.

The roads were unsuitable for any but moderate speeds. By mid-day we had completed but half the journey and hunger pains commenced. My companions had travelled from beyond the Tunisian border and must have themselves felt the pangs, for when a roadside restaurant was sighted we halted. Such establishments were few and far between. I wondered whether the place could, in such isolation, offer anything beyond bread and wine. Hey, presto! The jovial aubergiste clapped his hands with glee:

'*Pour les visiteurs nous avons des oiseaux! Très bon!*'

Well here was a turn up for the book. He must have knocked off a couple of chickens: The chequered table-cloth was spread, the filled bread-basket set down and a pot of *vin ordinaire* stood up, *à la* France. We did not wait long for the main attraction. *Un grand creux* was placed in the centre of the table. It radiated heat and when *le patron* raised the lid there revealed were *des oiseaux*; hundreds of them, sizzling hot.

'Ah!' said the Colonel, 'must be quail.'

I was not in a position to argue for I had never seen a quail.

They looked more like sparrows. I suspected the landlord had netted a migratory flock and set the family on the tedious job of defeathering.

The Colonel picked up one of the poor little things by a clawed foot. It came away in his fingers. The French lady came to the rescue by scooping out ladlesful and filling our respective plates. There was little to eat on each bird but the gravy was good; I fancied its base was *vin ordinaire*. Together with the bread we were satisfied. Followed by the inevitable oranges and dates we all agreed we had enjoyed a meal fit for kings.

The Command Car seemed to run better after lunch and the journey was completed in comfortable time for me to arrange onward transportation to Blida.

In future I would confine my days off to activities of a more local nature. Cherchell, a pretty port just west of Algiers, attracted people who needed a breath of sea air as a change from the smells of a busy airport. Daily leave trucks carried eager beach lovers. During one of these excursions one of my senior NCOs fell in love with a very comely French girl whose grandparents lived in a bungalow near the town and she with them. I was conned into the pleasure of visiting the family.

One afternoon Chiefy called at my office and asked me a favour. Would I care to take dinner with the girl's grandparents? He thought that my presence would help him cement his relationship with them. He was, of course, winning a free alternative to the normal leave truck's routine visit. It sounded a reasonable proposition. He had set up the date in advance, banking on my agreeing to take him. I enjoyed the use of a Bedford 15 cwt., officially attached to the Signals Section.

We arrived in good time. After formal introductions, a walk along the seafront aided the appetite. Grandfather had settled in Algeria following service as chef to a prosperous group of hotels in France. Chiefy said I might expect a complete change of menu from our service-styled meals. He did not mislead me.

From meagre resources the old gentleman concocted a most appetising repast. The apéritif set the frame of mind in the right direction. The soup was a variation of gazpacho andaluz compiled mainly from vegetables grown in the shaded garden at the rear of the bungalow. The main course centred round a pile of whitebait which, later, the Flight-Sergeant assured me must have cost a fortune on the black-market. The bottle of Chablis must have been a legacy from the hotel business. A spinach and cheese sauce accompanied the fish, along with cunningly fashioned blobs of potato, gently browned under the grill. A date and fig gateau finished the feasting. When the café came I withdrew from my pocket a half bottle of whisky, proudly presented it to the chef and he promptly turned it down! He left the table. Maybe I had offended him. Chiefy assured me that was not so and when Grandpa appeared he held up a whole bottle of Johnny Walker Black Label. At this I was astonished, truly. It was explained that the bottle had been brought up from the cellar where large stocks were held in anticipation of the grand-daughter's marriage to the Flight-Sergeant. Things were moving fast.

Should I care to visit again, it was made clear that bottles were not acceptable. If *le Capitaine* could oblige with a bar of soap . . . ooh la la! Circumstances did not permit my calling again. The Flight-Sergeant brought *'Merci bien'* in return for a couple of blocks of Lifebuoy which he delivered on my behalf.

Another pleasant diversion from office work was to take the zig-zag road to Chrea, a village high up in the mountains above Blida. This was not purely a pleasure trip but it was extremely popular with any member of the Signals Section who could persuade me to consider it their duty to visit our small out-station there.

Difficulties had been experienced in communicating with aircraft patrolling at low level along the coast towards Bone. The metallic content of the high mountains which came down to the sea absorbed the transmissions. The relay station at Chrea solved the problem. Keeping the boys up there supplied with comforts and necessities meant that a list of volunteers to 'assist' became a permanent feature of my pin-board.

Corporal Firth was in charge at Chrea. His fluency in French aided his acceptance into the village scene. Air Marshal Tedder and his lady occupied an apartment in the village, a splendid place for peaceful planning of operations. They were not infrequent visitors to the wireless station. I had hoped that the marshal might take up the question of Firth's lack of promotion, but there was no such luck. The worthy Corporal was a long-serving member, a most excellent fellow in every way. He had missed the promotion boat so many times in his career that his reserves of patience were fraying. When a vacancy at Blida did arise I dashed around to see the CO, and he agreed to put the matter in hand.

The result was the posting to my section of a Sergeant W/Op-AG who was resting from flying duties. He had no experience of running a busy W/T centre; Firth got the onerous job of showing him the ropes!

During one of my visits to the mountain, Firth and I went on through the Valley of the Monkeys. The most ardent Darwinists have failed to explain how this isolated colony developed here. Nor is it clear how the village of Medea comes to be populated by a mixture of tribes who live in close communion, reputedly resentful of foreign visitors, but Firth and I entered, boldly walking through narrow pathways between stalls where craftsmen worked. The leather workers sewed and stitched, the pewter workers tapped and hammered. There was no pressure to buy; suspicious eyes peered at us below the shrouds and our few small transactions were conducted with very few words being exchanged. When we spoke French we felt the response lacked bonhomie; but we found a French bar!

In we went and ordered drinks from a very beautiful barmaid. She was about twenty-six years of age, chatted freely about life in the village and, though she did not solicit other forms of business, it was revealed that other services were available beyond the bar, outside normal shopping hours. She was conducting very profitable operations with officers of the United States. A typical charge for a Major would be £25 inclusive of breakfast. The war had brought an enormous increase in emoluments. Her fiancé, who worked in Algiers, kept the books; a recent calculation gave hope that they might advance the date of their wedding by twelve months.

Having thus enriched our understanding of the world we returned to our war effort; Firth to his wireless station and I to the base of the mountain, from fresh, cool air to the burning dust of Blida.

That was the night a ball was held in the Officers' Mess. A five-piece band had been formed from talent which answered my call to organise a concert party. The problem of finding ladies to partner all the officers who had entered the lists presented some difficulties. There were a few nursing sisters in the camp hospital and a few local French females who had befriended certain of our number. Someone had the bright idea of contacting the British Embassy in Algiers. We were surprised to find a number of girl clerks who hastened to the call, from within the hallowed walls. They knew friends who would like to meet the RAF; Combined Ops. heard about it and we reached overload conditions.

The mosaic floor of the ante-room accommodated about thirty couples, chatterers filled the passageways, the band played in the annexe, the bar stewards ran out of glasses and started serving muscatel in mugs, the atmosphere ran out of oxygen and windows were removed from their hinges. The cooks had excelled themselves in providing snackery and a good time was being had by all. It was gone midnight when Struggie looked in to check up whether his rules of mess discipline were being respected.

I could see he was displeased.

In Struggie's mind, any breach of the rules was most likely traceable to a 'Penguin'. He made straight for Dee-Pee:

'Marvin,' he snapped, 'follow me. You too, Reddin!'

Though organisation of the ball was not my responsibility, Struggie assumed that in my voluntary capacity of camp Entertainments Officer I must be involved. I knew better than to argue the mistaken identity. Meekly I fell into line behind my superiors, wondering what calamity could have clouded the happy scene. As we descended the stairs I could hear the Stationmaster grumbling: 'Absolutely disgusting . . . appalling . . .'

We continued outside, down the path to the fountain and there lay, in the gutter, an officer flat on his face, dead drunk.

Struggie pointed with his cane to the head of the senseless body saying, simply:

'Look at this!'

Dee-Pee bent down, raised the head, turned the face towards us, recognised a Met. Officer of Headquarters, put the face back into the channel and said, simply:

'Not one of mine, Sir; one of yours!'

Turning to me, Struggie ordered that the body be disposed of rapidly. The two senior officers then went their separate ways.

The recumbent Met. man slumbered heavily. He was a big fellow, too. I could not have lifted him in sobriety, let alone in his present condition. I raised the head. From beneath the handle-bar moustache came a moaning sound.

'So you're still alive,' I encouraged.

'Where am I?' he moaned.

'In one of your deep depressions,' I said. 'You've been reading too many five-figure codes.'

The fountain was dry as usual but water must be obtained. I was about to set off in search of a supply when a junior 'Penguin' appeared with a jugful. Dee-Pee had not abandoned me. His delegate sloshed water into the ashen face of the weather man saying:

'Try this for a lousy forecast, mate!'

The effect was dramatic. The meteorologist raised himself on all fours and said:

'Christ! It's raining!'

'You see,' said the 'Penguin', 'he can't even forecast a deluge! Let's take him home, out of the wet.'

We loaded him into my Bedford and dumped him in his quarters.

Weather forecasters were not habitual boozers. On the contrary they tackled their work scientifically and seriously, yet always prepared to counter ridicule with wit. They adhered strictly to their craft of forecasting as distinct from foretelling. One of their number illustrated the point when he described how he had forecast fine weather for his wedding day in Chesterfield. When the happy couple emerged from below the twisted spire the guests had run for cover. 'There's no telling!' he declared.

It was inevitable that the case of the horizontal forecaster should deter any further suggestions of another Blida Ball; Struggie would not be approachable on the subject. He was very sensitive to public opinion of his beloved Air Force. He did, however, send for me one day over the booking of the theatre for a concert by the Blida Symphony Orchestra. Civilians from the town must be included in the audience. He would issue personal invitations and see that prominent personalities were properly served with cocktails in the Officers' Mess prior to entering the theatre.

One of my Wireless Operators was a shy little Lancashire lad called Richard Seed. His highly creditable performance as a concert pianist had been brought to the notice of the conductor of the local music society. I had seen to it that Richard had ample opportunity to attend their meetings.

The concert was a huge success. The orchestra filled the stage. The audience filled the house. Naturally, the solo pianist received a standing ovation, much to Richard's embarrassment. Even though the piano was suffering from an over-exposure to drought conditions and some instruments in the orchestra were mishandled, the soloist did us proud.

I had great hopes of promoting Richard to the world of professional entertainment via the good offices of Squadron-Leader Ralph Reader who was charging round North Africa in search of talent. He agreed to attend a performance by our Concert Party, but telephoned me from Algiers in the morning to apologise for his inability to keep the appointment. I made it very clear to the famous organiser of Gang Shows that he was missing a golden opportunity: not only would he be enthralled by the classic pianism of Richard Seed but a new version of the 'Tiger Rag' by Taylor and Thomas was a sure winner. Ronnie Taylor was one of my VHF/DF operators whose hobby was the writing of songs and sketches. His father had set him on the road to success when he gave him a sixpenny ukulele at a very early age. He studied Noel Coward's technique, developed his own style and went on to become one of the best producers in the realm of radio and television. Gracie Fields' Working Party, the Al Read Show, Candid Camera were only a few of Ronnie's hit shows. Maybe it is just as well that Ralph Reader didn't get hold of him.

Meanwhile, at Blida, 'Espy' shaped our own Concert Party which gave pleasure to crowded houses not only locally but on occasion to other military audiences. Before a big gathering of naval personnel in a theatre in Algiers we did, however, experience our one and only flop. Our 'Raf' parlance was not appreciated by the navy wallahs. They sat quite unmoved by our efforts at amusing them. My own Joe Butterscotch, 'The Lad fra' Yorkshire' turn, guaranteed to fetch the house down elsewhere, fell like stones on damp grass. I have heard some of the old time Music Hall artists speak of the heartless reaction of Glaswegians to an opening act. I know what they meant.

Of the famous we welcomed many to Blida. Not only was I in regular touch with ENSA, through whose good offices I booked British shows, but our huge American population entitled us to receive stars from the States. When Marlene Dietrich appeared the boys went crazy, especially when she declared her silk stockings were causing discomfort in the heat. She sat down at the front of the stage and removed them, very gracefully. The supporting orchestra that evening was that of our own Maurice Winnick who was introduced by the American compère as 'The Guy Lombardo of England!'

Ralph Reader's No.11 Gang Show was a rousing success, bringing us, among others, Leslie Hatfield, the leading violinist and Will Haye Junr. with 'The Fifth Form at St. Michael's'. I had seen 'The Fifth Form' under Will Haye Senr. many times and found that his son's voice was indistinguishable from that of his father. They had each made recordings of the act and themselves could not tell one from t'other.

ENSA sent us some wonderful shows. After each performance the artists were invited to the Officers' Mess for refreshments. It was there that I had the pleasure of meeting Wee Georgie Wood who had turned his disability of lack of height into an admirable demonstration of courage against misfortune.

Al Podesta and his Gypsy Band were favourites whom I had seen at the Lewisham Hippodrome and Holborn Empire. Though I was disillusioned by learning that Al was a born and bred Middlesbroughian his Hungarian music had lost none of its enchantment.

The Western Brothers, Kenneth and George, gave us a spontaneous 'out of bounds, you cads' turn, in appreciation of our hospitality. It would not have passed the morality examiner at the BBC.

There was something on at the theatre every night. I held in reserve a film called *North Sea*. Of high drama in the trawler fleet, it contained some very fruity language, which brought forth many a laugh at the first few showings. Regrettably, circumstances necessitated the showing far too often. On my weekly visit to Algiers I endeavoured to book a new film. I was dependent on the staff of Entertainments Branch and they in turn were too often dependent on American sources. I had been promised *For Whom the Bell Tolls* on more than one occasion. When I advertised it as 'Coming Next Week' and it didn't materialise out would come dear old *North Sea*, much to the disgust of my expectant non-paying clientele. At length I secured a definite promise and made a joyous approach to the office in Algiers.

It was not to be one of my better days. Harry Davison, one of the off-duty Controllers, accompanied me in a 'Chevvy' truck. The weather was at its hottest. We took a swim at Hussein Dey *en route*. An Algerian jellyfish took a swipe at me and by the time we arrived in the City the sting had worked up a temperature.

Harry went into the office whilst I waited in the truck to guard our swimming togs. When my companion hadn't appeared after five minutes I decided to investigate the cause of the delay. I stuffed our towels *et alia* under the seats of the truck and entered the office. Harry said there was some difficulty and 'they' were on the 'phone. I stood in the open doorway so that I could keep the truck under constant surveillance. Thus I observed the small child peering over the door of the truck, extracting my towel from under the seat and scarpering with it in the direction of the Casbah. Without thought for any loss of dignity I went after him. Spurred on by the sting of the jellyfish I found myself gaining on the diminutive larcenist. The crowd cheered; a tyreless taxi rattled alongside the chase. It was when the taxi driver blew his horn in a spirit of enthusiasm that the kid dropped the towel; the race was run. Honour had been restored. I beckoned the child to come for a coin but he was having none of that.

Back at the Entertainments Branch I was informed that General Eisenhower was 'in town tonight' and had invited guests to see *For Whom the Bell Tolls*. Back at the theatre at Blida I faced a full house and laid full blame upon the Commander-in-Chief Allied Forces for yet another showing of *North Sea*. The booing echoed in my ears for days; that helped in ignoring some of the goodnatured though well-directed comments. When, a week later, I succeeded in presenting the great classic the house was only half full; I had not dared to advertise in advance.

My intention of pleasing everyone for some of the time brought inevitable trouble for my pains. I advertised a 'Brains Trust'. A wealth of intellect could be called upon for the panel. I selected an historian, an accountant, an artist and a doctor. Doc Sligo declared that he could extend his range of advice far beyond the field of medicine and should any political questions arise he excelled in representing any colour of view. Such flexibility would be invaluable ammunition. I took the chair with confidence. I had not reckoned on the presence in the audience of an airman named Harry Flack.

As expected, the theatre was packed and questions were invited, not prearranged. For half an hour or so I had cause to be delighted with my choice of panel and with the quality of question and answer. Then some wag asked whether the use of bromide in his tea would have a lasting effect on his sexual behaviour. Doc was in his element, introducing a much appreciated sense of humour into his answer. Regrettably, he made mention of a drug manufacturer and that drew flak from Aircraftman Flack. Bromide was a profit spinner; sex was being sacrificed in the interests of shareholders.

Flack showed himself worthy of a stand at Speakers' Corner, complete with red flag flying. He was singularly reproachful of the big insurance company which held a major stake in the drug company. I had lost control of the panel. Doc had a taste for a fight, lapsed into a very basic Irish brogue and adopted a hard right attitude. Eloquence met eloquence in harangue. For a few minutes the crowd was entertained. Sides were taken. Chaos superseded good order. I declared the meeting closed and appealed for calm dispersal. Though no blows were struck I fear many young minds were corrupted that evening.

On the carpet before the Wing-Commander Admin., the following morning, I received unequivocal instruction that any venture bordering on politics was forbidden. Reports on the disturbance had come to the ears of the Station Commander. Lucky for me that Struggie had delegated the reproof of his Signals Officer alias Entertainments Officer to his moderator. It was back to Housey-housey in the theatre, as a regular substitute for any bright ideas which might otherwise have been put into practice.

Certain places of entertainment in Blida town were out of bounds to RAF personnel. One of the duties of the RAF police detachment was to visit these premises with the intention of arresting transgressors. The police came under the jurisdiction of my distinguished colleague Julius Stafford-Baker, Senior Station Intelligence Officer. One of my evenings free of duty coincided with the time for a routine check on the red light district of Blida. Julius asked me if I cared to join the patrol, suggesting that the trip might be educational as well as entertaining. I need not fear any violence. Any rough stuff would be taken care of by the substantially built Sergeant and his assistant.

It was well beyond lighting-up time when we paid our first call, at a small bar on the outskirts of town; the small red lamp above the doorway was the sole giver of light. A sharp rap on the door brought forth a grizzly female who indicated that business was non-existent. The Sergeant begged the woman's pardon, crossed the portals, cursorily surveyed the interior by torchlight, declared it unsavoury and we pressed onward.

Our next call, at a very impressive house with columnated doorway, gave promise of luxury accommodation beyond *l'entrée*. Activity there was a-plenty. The octagonal vestibule was alive with the chattering of flimsily clad females who clung anxiously to soldiers of the United States Army Air Force, language barriers presenting no difficulty.

Julius and the Sergeant were greeted by *le patron* as old friends. They introduced me. We shook hands and furthered the *entente cordiale* when generous supplies of anisette arrived. No questions were asked, no British airmen were present. We were welcome to call and inspect the premises at any time. Business was good and if the English preferred to avoid the august establishment that was all right by the management.

The central conversation continued without interruption even when one of the girls grabbed her client by the hand and whisked him away through one of the eight doorways. A moment later she reappeared carrying a large water-jug, hurrying away through another doorway in search of fresh supplies. Having left the door of her own cubicle open the operational couch was revealed to be overdue for attention by the laundry. However, water supplies were replenished, the door closed and privacy restored to those within. Our inspection party withdrew on the best of terms and on we journeyed to our next and final call, at an Arab brothel.

I was almost inclined to refuse to witness what I imagined to be a more revolting sight than the cattle-marketing of the previous call. I would have missed a rare architectural gem. Mosaic floors and gaily coloured, tiled arches, fountains playing in a discreetly illuminated courtyard, orange bushes and oleanders, hibiscus and bougainvillaea blended into a version of paradise. No cackling females offended the ear; only the gentle patter of the droplets from the fountain disturbed the silence. Were I ever in need of such services it would be to the Arabic world I would turn. It seemed sacrilege to walk round the fountain and peer into the cubicles which surrounded the garden, but the Sergeant and his mate did so and drew a blank. The madam in charge flung open a small wrought-iron gate adjacent to the point where Julius and I had halted. She pointed to the couple in comfortable embrace in the bed. In the gloom could be seen the Algerian military uniform hanging from a wall-hook. The soldier sat up showing natural annoyance at being interrupted in intercourse; the fat wench beside him registered a possible sign of relief from boredom; not a word was spoken.

The Sergeant was satisfied that no RAF uniforms were suspended in any of the dozen chambers. The routine inspection was complete. We bid the madam '*Adieu*'. She responded with: '*Beslémeh*', and slammed the door.

Flight-Lieutenant Julius Stafford-Baker was a great entertainment in himself. Born of an illustrious father, the inventor of 'Tiger Tim and the Bruin Boys', stars of *The Rainbow* comic paper, Julius carried on the traditional artistry. From my vantage window in the Signals Office a common feature of the airfield was of Julius at his easel capturing, for eternal preservation by the Air Ministry, pictures of ground crews busily working around their Wellingtons. He recorded from the turret of a Hudson of 608 Squadron the magnificent sight of ships in orderly convoy. In the Imperial War Museum may be seen his painting of a 'Doodle-bug' being transported by train. His versatility with pencil and paper fascinated me. Within a minute he could recall the thrills of the speedway, Hutton driving through the covers or a tennis player serving an ace; it all looked easy.

Characters such as Julius and Espy added colour to the generally interesting personalities inhabiting the Officers' Mess. Not only did one meet the Blida-based personnel but a sprinkling of visitors could be noted at every meal-time. It was not always possible to engage them in conversation owing to language differences or for security reasons; it was obvious that some of those dressed in casual civilian clothes were members of one or other resistance movement awaiting transportation by special delivery. Their only communication would be with the Intelligence Section.

Our most important visitor was Lord Trenchard, Father of the Royal Air Force. Struggie and he were old friends and the only two officers who carried canes. Though they were many rings apart in rank, their mutual affection was apparent as they strutted around on a thorough tour of inspection. The day temperature reached beyond the magic 100°F mark at the time but his lordship, though seventy years of age, seemed quite untroubled.

It was during that hot season of 1943 that I received the heartening news that my Lilian had walked with her suitcase to Hereford General Hospital and there brought into daylight our second son on 8 August. Though it would be a further two and a half years before I was able to see him, the tidings provided another excuse for riotous celebrations in the Officers' Mess.

The frequency and depth of celebrations depended very much on the state of the weather and the proximity of German U-boats. When flying was out of the question a celebratory atmosphere evolved spontaneously. Though 'Penguins' featured prominently in anteroom games the post of referee would always be fulfilled by Jack Mills, Canadian pilot and heir, reputedly, to a major department store in Vancouver. Jack occupied customarily an elevated seat on the east end of the bar itself. He possessed a good all-round knowledge of any sport likely to be played in the confined space. The restrictions were less severe than might be imagined by readers unacquainted with mess etiquette. With modifications to the standard rules we played cricket, hockey, soccer, tennis, baseball and rugby. This last was played most realistically when Duckie Duckworth, the Adjutant of the 'Penguins', substituted for the ball. I cannot recall a single incidence of violence off the 'field', and Doc Gordon, the squadron MO, was usually at hand in case of injuries on it.

When Jack was not in position on the bar he was either eating or sleeping or piloting a four-engined bomber on special duties. He had completed already four tours of operations but refused to give up flying. His crew was devoted equally to the profession, especially his navigator, an American Warrant-Officer known only as 'Wally'. Warrant-Officers of the RAF did not qualify for residence in the Officers' Mess, but because Wally was inseparable from Jack nobody dared or wanted to invoke any international law which might deny us the pleasure of the American's company. Rumour had it that Wally was under permanent orders to terminate his temporary attachment to the RAF and return to the US Army Air Force, but he remained undisturbed by officialdom. In any case, he was a very quiet chap. While Jack drank and made merry, Wally drank and dropped off to sleep. It was not unusual for his slumbering body to be carried away by his colleagues when the party ended. On the way to their billets they would call in at the camp pigsty to bid a good night to 'Wally-Two'.

On one of their rare visits to Blida town Jack and his entourage had become involved with some local agriculturalists and bought a young pig. It was transported clandestinely to the aerodrome and found temporary accommodation pending the illicit erection, by the camp 'chippies', of a 'pukka' sty. Enormous quantities of culinary left-overs were fed to 'Wally-Two'. He waxed fat and became very strong in no time, strong enough to bear, for a short distance, any of his sponsors who attempted to ride him. The ultimate aim of serving up 'Wally-Two' as a supplement to the Christmas dinner was frustrated by a

French veterinary officer who got wind of the enterprise. He quoted numerous reasons why 'Wally-Two' should not live in close proximity to western Europeans, nor should he be considered for human consumption. In short the animal was 'put down', as the saying goes. The valedictory service, in which the station padré refused to officiate, was conducted in all solemnity by 'Wally-One'. The burial ceremony was followed by a fitting celebration through the whole of which the namesake of the deceased slept soundly.

The absence of roast pork from the Christmas dinner did nothing to dampen our spirits. With wine running at sixpence a pint, drought was impossible. The dessert course included the inevitable pile of dates on each long table, perfect ammunition to fire at the principal entertainer. One of our Italian waiters, a strongly voiced baritone of the Opera di Milano chorus, elected to stand on the top table and sound off a couple of his favourite arias. His gaping, cavernous mouth roundly concluding his love affair with Maria was too much of a temptation for critics of the opera. A hail of dates projected by trained marksmen put an end to the cantata and heralded the reintroduction of the 'Penguin' song.

I left the celebrations early. The spreading of Christmas greetings in the telephone exchange, the W/T room and the out-stations would be a nice gesture. The rotor arm of my Bedford truck was in my pocket, a necessary precaution against the popular sport of grand larceny. Outside my quarters, where I had parked the vehicle, was an empty space! I reported the matter to the police immediately, trusting that my beloved Bedford had been borrowed. I never saw it again. The invitation to pay £1,500 towards the cost was acknowledged with thanks. I heard no more.

Chapter 37

Blazing Blida

Struggie once summarized the continuous activity at Blida, thus: 'We always have something on at Blida; either a concert or a fire!'

That piece of jocular exaggeration typified our attitude to life at Blida. It was not the place where anybody could take a quiet kip at the side of the runway. Considering the amount of traffic we handled, the variety of aircraft and the primitive facilities available, it was surprising how few accidents occurred. Those which did occur were either serious or horrendous.

No.14 Squadron, (heavily populated by Australians), suffered from being equipped with the infamous Martin Marauder. With those Australians it was not easy to join light-hearted conversation. They were Marauder men. I could not help treating them with great respect. The explosions on the runway and the black smoke coiling up into the hot atmosphere are indelible memories. Never any survivors, no W/Op. to de-brief; spare seats in the mess and spare beds in the billets to be filled by replacement crews; the Adjutant to pack the kits and write the letters; not owing to enemy action, could it be said, but because few pilots mastered the problems of landing at the high speeds required by the design.

I was called to the Station Commander's presence to find Squadron-Leader Nelson, the Senior Flying Control Officer, already in conference with the great man. The subject was the suggestion by Nelson of the siting of an auxiliary control point at the east end of the runway. In view of the absence of any form of marker beacon it seemed a good idea to station an experienced signaller equipped with appropriate flags and Very lights in the approach path, to deal with emergencies. The request for a radio transmitter/receiver complete with one of my operators to work on the watch-tower frequency did not meet with my approval. I visualised verbal misunderstandings. However, being strongly outranked, the practical details were agreed.

A few days later the red and white striped hut on two wheels was set up at the point chosen by Nelson. I expressed my opinion that it was too near the side of the runway. The operator climbed aboard, full of enthusiasm, excited at the idea of being so involved in the aeroplane business. Nelson was delighted; Struggie thought it worth trying.

Two days later a Wellington of the 'Penguins' came in a bit too low, caught the hut with its port wing, landed all right but smashed the hut. The next time I saw my young operator he was in the station hospital; one leg had been amputated below the knee. He was a brave lad. When I wrote to his wife I carried out his instructions of emphasising that he looked forward to continuing in their favourite pastime of ballroom-dancing.

Flying control reverted to normal.

For aerodrome control we depended on the antique TR9-F unit as fitted in all the Wellingtons. Interlinked with this was an equally old-fashioned intercom system. Every member of the air-crew plugged in his headphone set so that he could overhear conversations between his colleagues and between his Captain and the watch-tower. It was brought to my attention by some of the 36 Squadron W/Ops that spurious and intermittent raspberries, originating in the IFF transmitter, were also being carried into the headphones. The matter was serious enough to be investigated.

W/O Howe, the squadron Signals Officer, joined me in a diligent examination of the wiring diagram of a Wellington. We took it in turns to make physical checks on our researches. Five minutes at a time was all we could suffer inside the fuselage with temperatures over three figures in the shade, but we came up with the answer to the problem. It would involve moving the IFF set and its supply cables to the opposite side of the airframe. The necessity to drill holes and relocate the grey box needed the approval of the Engineering Officer. When the work was completed we could boast 100% success.

A detailed report was despatched to Headquarters at Algiers. There my good friend Squadron-Leader Jacob studied it, passed it for approval by the Chief Signals Officer, Group Captain Vickers, and onward it went to whoever it might concern in the United Kingdom.

About six weeks later there arrived in the despatches a copy of an instruction from RAF Farnborough detailing 'modifications to Wellington aircraft for the elimination of IFF interference on the intercom'. Though no mention was made of the source of the 'discovery' both Howe and myself were quite 'chuffed' over the affair.

W/O Howe was not overworked on the squadron. Because of the growing intensity of the anti-U-boat campaign I enlisted his help as a Duty Signals Officer to give some relief in our arduous watch system. Jimmy James had been called to other fields. His place was taken by W/O Bob Heritage, a quiet godsend to any Signals Section. Without fuss he maintained excellent discipline. We never had any 'charges' in Signals. Cab was still with us, as unflappable as ever. We nearly lost him during the 'Great Fire of Blida'.

Corporal Trigg was Duty Wireless Mechanic that evening. He was in the Signals Workshop busily engaged in vetting a receiver. I had called in for a chat, when at fairly close proximity there was one hell of a big explosion. Before the building had subsided on to its foundations, Trigg and I were outside taking stock. A huge ball of smoke ascended, driven by searing, yellow flames.

Very lights shot out and about, bullets crackled all over the place. The sun had gone down but there was plenty of light. My first thought was to beat it to the telephone exchange, located underneath the watch-tower block. As I ran bullets spattered the walls of the building. I could see airmen silhouetted against a background of inferno, desperately trying to extricate aircraft from the spreading flames.

In the exchange I was gladdened to find all under the control of a capable supervisor who informed me that every available fire-engine was already either at the scene or on its way. Continuing my impetuous tour of inspection I hopped over broken glass and tiles and climbed the stairs to the Signals Office where Cab was on duty. There he was, bless him, as cool as a cucumber. The shutters were smashed, the window gone!

'You all right, Cab?'

'Oh, yes, thank you. That thing just missed me!' He pointed to the stub-axle of a Hudson, embedded in the wall of the corridor. That 'thing', consisting of a few kilos of high tensile steel, had cut through the wooden shutters which had been closed against sundry insects, whistled over Cab's starboard shoulder, passed through the open doorway and split an opening in the opposing wall. My friend must have been destined to live to a ripe old age.

Through the gaping hole where the window used to be we viewed the terrifying fire. At least a dozen aircraft were ablaze, constantly fed by petrol from bursting tanks. Water jets did nothing to quench the furnace. All the fire-fighters could do was to protect surrounding buildings and themselves. A number of aircraft had been dragged to safety. Eventually the fire settled into a distorted pile of twisted, molten metal. The wonder of if all was that not a single life was lost. A total of twenty-five aircraft suffered either total loss or damage. The cause could be blamed directly on that controversial device, the Leigh light, recently introduced to No.36 Squadron Wellingtons.

The Leigh light was fitted in a retractable turret in the underbelly of the aircraft. For inspection purposes a hole had been dug in the ground adjacent to the perimeter track outside the 156 MU hangar. To put it in popular parlance: 'One would have thought that the hole would have been covered over or clearly marked or made inaccessible.' We can only report the events as relayed from eye witnesses, bearing in mind the fast fading Mediterranean light: 'A Hudson of 608 Squadron, piloted by the charming young Flying-Officer Knight returned from patrol, was taxiing around the perimeter under guidance. One wheel dropped in the hole, the Hudson caught fire. The crew escaped unharmed, raising the alarm for the area to be cleared. The aircraft was still carrying enough explosive to blow up a U-boat. There was not long to wait. The blast projected blazing petrol and burning oil in a hundred-metre circle; metal parts sped to all points of the compass.'

A Court of Inquiry would be held. Subdued talk in the mess embraced the subject of blame. Who gave orders for the digging of the hole; why was it dug so near the track; who guided the pilot? Ultimately must the blame be put squarely on the Captain of the aircraft, the pilot?

It takes time to set up a Court of Inquiry. The key subject would never be called. Poor young Knight and his crew went down in the sea when venturing a subsequent operation.

Two of my favourite 'Penguins' lived in the next door apartment. Scott was the archetype of tall handsome young Englishmen. His navigator and constant companion, Bray, was of medium height, stocky, blond and quietly jolly. Cartoonist 'Jon' created 'The Two Types' of Desert Air Force fame. Only a first rate portraitist could have done justice to the immaculate Flying-Officers Scott and Bray. They called me into their room one morning with a request to keep a watch over their property whilst they spent a couple of weeks in UK. Their Wellington was to be converted for Leigh light operations. They bade me farewell and I wished them *bon voyage*; a fortnight in UK, by jove!

Walking down to the office half an hour later I saw the Wellington. It had just lifted off the runway. It was less than thirty feet off the ground. I knew it wasn't high enough. I lost sight of it behind the hangar. A dull thump sounded from the olive grove and up curled the tell-tale cloud of black smoke. There would be another inquiry. I helped the Adjutant clear the next door apartment to make room for replacements for the irreplaceable. We developed a callousness over people 'getting the chop' as it came to be termed; there were so many of them. The war must continue. Yet of all my mates now dead I retain a vivid picture only of Scott and Bray setting out on their *bon voyage* to UK.

The rains came on 11 September 1943, at 10.00 hrs. as predicted by M. Lafayette, the French electrical engineer. It was lovely to walk out and get soaked. Then came the steam and the 'Metmen' started forecasting fog. With it came tragedy of a most agonizing kind.

F/O Reg Stannard, a dashing young pilot of the 'Penguins', had married a pretty nursing sister of the camp hospital staff. In due course the dear girl suffered a miscarriage. The camp hospital was not equipped to deal with this eventuality so she spent some days in the major establishment in Algiers. It so happened that on the afternoon of her telephoning to inform her husband that she would be returning to Blida he was briefed for convoy escort duty. She would be waiting to greet him on his completion of the patrol.

The weathermen studied their charts and, as usual, conferred by telephone with their colleagues up and down the coast. Though take-off would be in clear daylight there was a very distinct possibility of fog after dark, at the ETA of 23.00 hrs. If the fog materialised, instructions would be transmitted for the aircraft to land at Reghaia, a fighter base on the coast east of Algiers. All members of the crew were made aware of this detail. I was Duty Signals Officer that evening and personally discussed the matter with the Wireless Operator, an experienced Sergeant.

The Captain made clear his intention of returning to base where his wife would be waiting to greet him. The Controller was equally insistent that should fog descend upon base the flight would be diverted to Reghaia. By 22.00 hrs. visibility at Blida had closed to a few metres. The HF/DF station answered a request for a course to steer, by transmitting in plain language: 'Land at Reghaia.' Repeated requests for bearings were given the same reply on the instructions of the Controller. It was obvious that the young pilot was determined to attempt a blind landing. Nothing else was possible for as the aircraft approached at low level the landing wheels snapped the main power overhead lines. The whole aerodrome blacked out but we could hear the Wellington in circuit.

My mechanics had reacted like lightning in starting up the stand-by power generators. The D/F station continued to tap out the 'Land at Reghaia' message. We waited anxiously. The Captain's wife stood on the steps at the doorway of the Sick Quarters hoping and praying. For the second time the Wellington swept across the fog-bound airfield, missing the watch-tower by a very few feet. It crashed into a building at the centre of an adjacent orange farm. The crew of six died instantly as did several Algerian soldiers who were billeted in the building. Fire completed the destruction.

The first question asked whether the W/Op had received the instructions to divert to Reghaia. At crack of dawn I began a search of the wreckage. Debris was scattered amidst broken and burned orange trees. There seemed little chance of a log book being found but away from the seat of the scorched area stood a tree which had suffered only a slight drying of its leaves. Hanging from a branch were pieces of human remains, part of a flying-helmet and a glove. On the ground beneath lay a half-burnt log book. My quest was over; the unburnt part showed clearly the plain language message: 'Land at Reghaia', not once but several times. So at least one widow knew exactly how her husband died, needlessly. The Adjutant would despatch five more letters to next of kin. The Algerian Commander would have some explaining to do, also.

Naturally, such a terrible accident on our doorstep cast a more than unusual gloom over us. We had scarcely recovered our equilibrium when, during another spell of bad weather, three aircraft crashed within an hour. The first one overshot the runway, hit the trees and burst into flames. Visibility was very poor at the time. Whether the orange glow of the flames was mistaken for the runway approach lights will never be known. It was late evening when it all happened. A group had assembled in the anteroom when the windows shook. We looked out to see the dreaded flames lighting up the filthy night, silhouetting the black shape of the hangar. Away went the fire-engines and rescue teams; nothing we could do except leave it to the experts. We carried on with our habitual guessing: 'Who is it this time?' talk. Maybe strangers? It was not unknown for UK-based bombers to run short of fuel while attacking targets in Italy or southern France and seek refuge at Blida. Only officers on duty were aware of the minute-by-minute expectation of arrivals. One crash at a time was enough for our rescue services to handle; when two more followed they were overstretched beyond human endurance.

At length the flames died down, the scurrying of ambulances ceased and fire-engines returned to stand-by. Talk in the mess strained to recover a degree of normality. I began to tinkle a quiet tune at the piano; the level of conversation rose to a steady buzz when into the room swept Doc Sligo. He pushed me off the piano-stool: 'Let me have that!'

We were treated to a full scale outlet of nervous tension in the form of extemporisation at high speed and maximum loudness. I drew a double whisky at the bar and stood beside this extraordinary pianist until, after ten minutes, he felt able to stand up and say: 'I think that just saved me from going completely round the bend.' He took the whisky and drained the glass at one go. We all said: 'Good old Doc!' We asked no questions.

Chapter 38

Matters of Communication

One important duty of the Station Signals Officer was the supervision of the use of priorities in messages. Topmost priority was 'Emergency' which was reserved for use by Captains of aircraft in distress or on the sighting of an enemy U-boat. Transmission of an 'Emergency' from a ground station could be authorised by no other than the SSO.

When the W/T supervisor brought to me a message form categorized 'O' and signed by the Station Commander I recalled the appropriate Air Ministry Instruction and telephoned the originator accordingly.

'Your request for boots, Sir.'

'Oh, yes. What about it?'

'I am obliged to reduce the priority to "Routine". You will remember from your flying days that "O" means life is endangered.'

'Quite right, my boy. I wanted to know whether you remembered your Cranwell training!'

'Fortunately for us all, Sir, my W/T superintendent remembered his.'

The Sergeant enjoyed the joke. Between us we altered the text of the message to read: 'Request urgent supply . . .' Within five minutes the information would be in the hands of the Stores Officer in Algiers. What action he took was not our business.

In the business of U-boat hunting, the 'O' in the preamble to a signal from an aircraft on patrol meant that all stations on the frequency would pay very special attention. Sightings were transmitted in a non-secret code consisting simply of the Figure '465', followed by the grid reference of the position. The information was passed to the Navy at Algiers, for onward transmission on their own frequency to the destroyer group cruising in the area. Meanwhile the spotting aircraft would have dropped a depth-charge in the hope of damaging the U-boat, if not sinking it, marking the position in anticipation of the arrival of the ships.

The three-cornered signalling method seemed to me to be a waste of valuable time. I said so. My friend Squadron-Leader Jacob did not agree with me, arguing that any short cut would result in loss of control. I could see no reason why aircraft and ship should not communicate with one another directly.

I put my suggestion to the head 'Penguin' who talked the matter over with his Flight-Commanders and with Squadron Leader George Williams, the inventor of Operation SWAMP, an ingenious plan designed to destroy U-boats. The discussion carried to the ears of the Chief Signals Officer, who considered my idea worth a trial. Jake came on the 'phone:

'Harry boy,' he said, 'kindly let me have a paper on your notions of improved communications. You know I don't see eye-to-eye on the subject but the CSO has decided to study your proposition.'

In anticipation of a favourable reaction my paper was ready for despatch. Within a few days a new Signals Instruction covering the subject of Direct Communication between Naval and Air Forces on the sighting by aircraft of a U-boat, was issued by Headquarters Mediterranean Allied Coastal Air Forces. I was over the moon.

Meanwhile, Dee-Pee had organised a trial run during daylight. He drove the Humber shooting-brake with a couple of 'Penguin' observer types and myself as passengers. Another party followed us to Algiers harbour where we boarded HMS *Cleveland*, a Hunt class destroyer commanded by Lieut-Commander Tyson. Our first task was to descend to the ward-room and accept a liberal dose of pink gin. A submarine would proceed to sea to function as target in the search.

Glasses in hand, we gathered around the table on which was spread a chart of the central Mediterranean. Making frequent use of his favourite expression: 'There we were chaps, steaming ahead,' the Commander traced courses steered during a recent sortie. He then indicated the course to be taken on today's exercise in which he hoped to find it beneficial to be in direct communication with the co-operating aircraft. Inwardly, my pride swelled; I couldn't wait to get to sea.

The invitation for two members of our party to join the submarine crew was received with qualified enthusiasm. 'Not on your Nellie,' was the response of one intrepid airman but on the assurance of a submariner that his career was far safer than that of a flying man, two volunteers left us for underwater experience.

Next we were conducted on a tour of the ship, paying particular attention to the elaborate radio and radar equipment. Further pink gin being dispensed before sailing, we sighted the open sea in high spirits. For me the thrill of riding the waves was enhanced by the sight of HMS *Catterick*, sister to the *Cleveland*, sailing in company. The roar of the big guns in firing practice added spice to the experience. Then it was down to the ward-room for a light lunch in preparation for the exercise proper.

Meanwhile the submarine had plunged ahead to its secret position. From time to time we observed the Wellington of 36 Squadron pursuing its square search and eventually to start circling around a point on the distant horizon, when it dropped a flare. It was time for our miniature armada to investigate. Our Commander gave the 'Full steam ahead' and shortly we saw the submarine waiting to be 'sunk'. It would be inappropriate to commence radio transmissions for fear of enemy intervention in our exercise. On such occasions the good old Aldis lamp came in handy. The first signal from the aircraft to us could best be interpreted to mean: 'Where the bloody hell have you been?'

The ship's wireless operator had no knowledge of a sighting report. I was in no doubt that the transmission had been made. It was not for me to explore the probability that the naval operator was not correctly tuned to the aircraft channel. The glaring truth was that the exercise had failed. We returned to port. I drank another pink gin because everybody else took one.

We dined well and during the evening a group of submariners joined the company. Dee-Pee invited them to visit Blida and take a ride in his beloved Wellington. The general opinion was that flying was altogether too risky. They preferred the relative safety of the deep. Nonetheless, the invitation to take a close look at our monsters of the skies was accepted. In due course a few of the mariners did undertake a few circuits and bumps. Their faces showed relief on returning to *terra firma*.

Jake telephoned me the following morning:

'Well, Harry boy?'

'You told me so. I bow to experience. No doubt you received the sighting report.'

'We did indeed and we waited in W/T silence to see what would happen next. We had no intention of beginning an acrimonious inquest over the ether. Not wishing to make a pun of it I regard those naval wallahs as riding on a different plane, if you follow me. They have their family of wavelengths and operators and we have ours.'

'I see the point of each controlling its own operations and passing information via Combined Operations HQ; lesson learned.'

'However, we are going to give it a run for a week under operational conditions. It will do no harm providing we also pass sightings to the Navy as before, for onward transmission to the ships. There may be a significant saving in time; we shall see.'

Aircraft-to-ship communication did not prove satisfactory in the circumstances. It could have been developed but as it called for two operators at a time on duty on the ship my idea was unacceptable. We reverted to the old Signals Instruction.

Our closer personal relationships with the sailors augured well for future and more extensive application of operation SWAMP. At least one naval historian attributes the concept of SWAMP to Air-Vice Marshal Sir Hugh Pugh Lloyd, popularly known as 'Huff-Puff'. I prefer to think of it as the brain-child of Squadron-Leader George Williams.* Whatever the source of the theory, in practice this operation was ideal for our purpose of sinking U-boats which were

---

*George Williams, CBE received no award for SWAMP. The CBE is a recognition for geological work in the oil industry. He is the writer of the Foreword to this book.

a continuous menace to our coast-hugging shipping. No matter what precautions were taken by escorting ships and aircraft, a daring U-boat captain might succeed in placing his vessel near the shore and await an on-coming convoy. Ironically, once a ship was attacked, the U-boat captain had signed his own death warrant. We pinpointed his position. He was obliged to leave the coast eventually but in the short term he must surface for battery-charging even when staying 'in-shore'.

Whenever he emerged an aircraft fitted with ASV would be conducting a square search of the area. Our experts knew the maximum speed of a U-boat and its time of endurance below the surface. First a square search covered the area surrounding the point of the attack. As time went by further square searches were added to SWAMP the whole area of sea in which the U-boat was bound to come up for air. When it did, even if just a schnorkel projected, our ASV radar would detect it. The objective then was for the aircraft to drop a depth-charge in order at least to damage the victim until the naval flotilla arrived to complete the destruction. By night the aircraft might have the option of switching on the Leigh light to aid final sighting. Though technically intricate and interesting for all of us involved, it was at the same time terribly dangerous for the air-crews and for the mariners, both allied and enemy.

The importance of rigidly correct W/T procedure was brought home to me on a fateful stormy night when, as Duty Signals Officer, I had briefed a W/Op of No.14 Squadron prior to his departure on a long distance reconnaisance patrol. Atmospheric conditions were particularly bad and the aircraft suffered a severe battering in the turbulent air. The aircraft channel was always manned by one of our top-class operators who could understand the difficulties of working in an unsteady aircraft.

When the W/T superintendent, a thoroughly experienced Sergeant, brought for my examination a copy of a signal received from an aircraft, I knew there was real trouble. Normally, such messages were passed directly to the Controller for action. Our function was to accept and deliver messages correctly, not to act upon the content. This particular message did not make sense. The Sergeant sought my advice.

That it was a sighting report there was no doubt but it was not of a U-boat. The object located was described as either: 'HSP ship' or 'HSL ship'. Neither of these apparent abbreviations were official code words although 'HSL' was a commonly used anacronym meaning: 'High Speed Launch'. The difficulty arose because of the similarity between 'P' for which the Morse symbol is '·--·' and for 'L' which is '·-··', a mere difference between one 'dit' and one 'dah'. I called for a further repeat in plain language and for two operators to listen to the response. Still there was uncertainty. I took the message to the controller myself explaining the problem in detail.

Of course, we at Blida were not the only receivers of the signals from the aircraft. Algiers, Gibraltar and Malta all joined in the trial by wireless. Incredible though it may seem none of us imagined the fellow was trying to tell us that a *Hospital* ship had been sighted, but that is what it was. So, the order went out for whatever it was at the position indicated to be attacked. The Beaufighters and their torpedoes made short work of it. Herr Hitler screamed quotations from the Geneva Convention.*

When the patrolling aircraft returned I examined the W/Op's log book. It was clear that he had transmitted the word 'hospital' in full. The bouncing of the aircraft and adverse atmospheric conditions could be blamed for the misunderstanding.

Of course there should have been no signal in the first place. The Captain of the aircraft should have acknowledged the inviolability of a hospital ship, observed W/T silence and mentioned the matter only on return to base. Such courtesies tended to be overlooked in the urgency of war operations. For my own part I think of the incident, even half a century later, as regrettable and avoidable. I should have asked for further repeats.

I was not disappointed when Algiers assumed responsibility for W/T control. My days at Blida were numbered. Struggie telephoned me one morning to tell me that he had been examining the establishment of his station. The post of Signals Officer should be occupied by a Squadron-Leader and he was taking up the matter of my promotion with HQ. This invigorating news was followed shortly by counteraction. It appeared that the establishment of Squadron-Leader was still held nominally by Acting-Wing Commander Fair at his post in Sardinia! No doubt, under Air Ministry rules there could be found some small print to cover the situation. In any case my move to Reghaia was in the offing. There I would join 338 Wing which would embrace my old friends of 36 Squadron, the 'Penguins'. The Spitfires and Beaufighters were operating already from Reghaia but the metal runway would need to be extended to take the Wellingtons.

Most of the HQ staff of Blida would be transferred with me: Controllers, Met. Officers, Intelligence Officers, Codes and Ciphers, Wireless Operators and Mechanics. The family was moving house, from town to country, from bricks and tiles to canvas and ropes, from mountain to sea, from winter to spring.

---

* A very brief mention of the incident was made in a BBC broadcast. It would have been of no comfort at the time to recall the sinking of the allied hospital ship *Talamba* off Sicily when fully illuminated on 10 July 1943.

Chapter 39

After the U-Boats!

Not that U-boats were the only menace to our ships. When 338 Wing established its rustic headquarters amongst the trees at Reghaia only three U-boats were active in the Mediterranean. A good many more were confined to their base at Toulon where they received devastating attacks by American bombers. So whilst escort vessels equipped with asdic and aircraft with ASV listened and watched for the U-boats, the other menace came from the skies.

JU88s dropped torpedoes and wireless bombs. There was no plain sailing for our shipping along the North African coast. However, an umbrella of fighter aircraft took toll of the Germans. After an attack we never failed to listen to Lord Haw-Haw's report of the event. On one notable occasion a small convoy was attacked off Algiers. His 'lordship' announced the sinking of fourteen ships. That particular convoy consisted of nine ships only! Though one ship was damaged they all reached port.

Subsequent to the taking of Sicily, Sardinia and Corsica, convoys *en route* from Gibraltar, Oran and Algiers were encouraged to hug the coast before turning for the islands. In that way they were assured of better protection.

I had experienced nothing of the operations by our fighter aircraft until I arrived at Reghaia. There I was to observe their coming and going more or less as a spectator. My immediate responsibility would continue to be the provision and operation of signalling facilities for the U-boat hunters of 36 and 500 Squadrons.

The post of Wing Signals Officer called for an officer of Squadron-Leader rank. I had half hoped that this would fall to my lot but it was not to be. Somewhat apologetically I was greeted by my new boss, Squadron-Leader E.R.L. 'Bob' Lewis, a first-class academic who was thoroughly versed in Fighter Sector Operation. He had tried to hang on to his old posting at Bone, where he had been very happy but owing to some personal differences in the regime he was moved sideways. Bob was a gem of a man with whom to work. I worked with him, not under him, for a year. At our first meeting he declared his lack of experience in the business of U-boat hunting; he would leave that to me and he would take care of the fighter operation. This was compromise at its best, shared responsibility without rancour. Together we saw the end of the U-boats in the Med. and built a lasting friendship into the bargain.

It was good to be back under canvas, especially in the holiday camp atmosphere. I shared my ridge tent with Harry Davison, who was good company during the infrequent periods when we were together in daylight. At night our friendship became endangered by his bouts of snoring; he would wake himself up thinking a Wellington was taking off and then light a cigarette. Fortuitously, owing to our respective watch-keeping rotas, I was subjected to these irregularities only one night in three.

Group Captain Scott commanded the Wing. He lived on the premises. Thus, a very close family atmosphere developed. The large wooden hut which served as Officers' Mess and bar-room was big enough to accommodate our party-throwing needs. The big marquee which served as Airmen's Mess incorporated a stage at one end. I needed no pressing to take on the buckshee job of Entertainment Officer. Espy had moved on to take his very professional 'Malta Knights' on tour but Ronnie Taylor, bless him, stayed as my right-hand man. His preparations for a brand new show entitled 'Airborne' were so advanced that rehearsals began within a week of our setting up camp.

Bob and I shared a Nissen hut Signals Office. The Duty Signals Officer occupied a desk in the Operations Room close to the Controller's switchboard. One regular inhabitant of the switchboard was Charley, a praying mantis which never missed a briefing. When no aircrews were present he would pop inside the box, reappearing with military precision to wish the boys luck in their next sortie. He would sit there wagging his little head from side to side as if to emphasise the Controller's words of wisdom.

Necessarily, we were self-sufficient for electricity. The faithful Lister engines plonked away day and night. Whenever the need arose for them to be stopped, the Meadows engines acted on stand-by. The Meadows started easily and ran smoothly but not for long. The valves objected to the use of high octane fuel and top overhauls were required all too frequently. Repairs were carried out very efficiently under the discerning gaze of the excellent Sergeant Snee who came to us on the disbandment of 302 MSSU. Naturally, he joined 'Airborne' to thrill us with his fine tenor voice.

> 'Airborne – free and easy
> Airborne – bright and breezy . . .'

So opened our new show to Ronnie's latest opening chorus. We played to a most appreciative audience with a galaxy of scrambled eggs in the front row, chief of whom was Air-Vice Marshal Lloyd. Struggie had come over from Blida for the occasion plus a group of staff officers from Algiers. Except for a few WAAF Officers there appeared to be none below Squadron-Leader in the first three rows. I made reference to this in my Joe Butterscotch character act which I inflicted on everyone prepared to endure it. Topicality being an essential ingredient in any such entertainment I brought up the subject of 'sweatin' on promotion'. The air temperature in the marquee hovered around the 100°F.

mark and with a suitable gesture to emphasise the point my remarks were greeted with roars of approval. Struggie was seen to rock in his seat. It was such simple turns of humour which kept us all sane.

The masterpiece of the show: *The Court Martial*, an operetta for four parts, written and produced by Ronnie Taylor. This was Ronnie at his very best. Though, of course, he demonstrated his proficiency in numerous post-war radio and television shows, I never enjoyed anything more than *The Court Martial*.

We were all in good spirits, domestically established, operationally fit and ready for business. Maytime in Algeria: The sea was calm and blue, the vines were green and frogs croaked in the bog beyond the airfield. All we needed was action and we got it.

All three U-boats were patrolling the coast and made their positions evident by torpedo attacks. Operation SWAMP began with the first sighting and developed in intensity until all three were destroyed. For three days and three nights aircraft took off, searched, bombed and landed. During the whole period I supervised a non-stop signalling bonanza. Log books filled up faster than could have been imagined.

Excitement through the camp left nobody unaffected. The cooks turned out better sandwiches, tea urns simmered continuously, snack meals were snacked, sleep was snatched, the air vibrated with the slap of propeller blades and the clatter of runway planking. Square search upon square search built up until the whole of the Western Mediterranean seemed to be swamped. There was no rest until the third U-boat was sunk. Anticlimax settled on us.

Our mission was complete. Thoughts of unemployment scarcely deserved a mention. Meantime we would sleep for a day and a night. Then came a day of recuperation followed by an evening of celebration. Group Captain Scott was apprehensive of being drawn into a 'Penguin Party'; he made a discreet withdrawal after dinner leaving Wing Commander Marvin the senior officer responsible for the preservation of order.

From that moment, disorder reigned supreme. As chief 'Penguin' and choirmaster, Dee-Pee conducted the 36 Squadron Anthem. At the conclusion he asked if anybody knew the 'Road to Mandalay'. Some unsuspecting outsider said: 'Yes,' and got the stock answer: 'Don't sing it, take it!'

When the choir drifted into some of the more revolting parodic madrigals, a group of non-vocalists started an impromptu darts tournament, the shove-ha'penny experts shoved and a most entertaining character chewed a wineglass. A dispute developed in the Canadian poker school over the rightful ownership of a five-pound note, satisfaction being gained by the incineration of the said note; my Yorkshire upbringing tempted me to offer a pound for the sacrificial document but I was too late; the serial number had vanished.

As the bar stocks lowered, so spirits heightened, Dee-Pee was defrocked and for a few brief moments I wore the insignia and wings of my reverable friend. It was obvious that he would be promoted very soon. He had led with distinction his 'Penguins', to be kings of the U-boat conquerors. When I handed back his shirt he thanked me for my interest in 36 Squadron. Then in uncustomary confidential tone he said:

'Look, Red – why don't you apply for a permanent commission?'

'Never thought of it,' I replied.

'Well,' he said, 'it's a great life, you know. It suits me. I'm a lazy devil!'

'Do you think I'm a lazy devil?'

'No, but think about it. You've done very well in the short time you've been in and if you go back to civvy street you will have to face a rat-race. Vickers thinks well of you. You stand a good chance of being accepted. You would go to the Staff College at Malta and become one of us.'

I said: 'I'll make a bargain with you. I will apply and if I am accepted before my demob date, I'll stay. If not, I'm out!'

As we celebrated the demise of the U-boats the allied armies captured Rome. It seemed logical that the services of 338 Wing, as a mobile fighter unit, would be required in Italy. Meantime we must bide our time at Reghaia. The excellent bathing beach lay a hundred metres from the wooded encampment, the weather was perfect and the mosquito menace bearable. We were, however, about to be invaded by another less pleasant insect – the locust.

I borrowed the section's Bedford and with Harry as passenger we set off in the late afternoon for Algiers. As we joined the main road we picked up a couple of American GIs who jumped in the back behind the canvas awning through which was a peep-hole enabling us to keep an eye on passengers and contents of the truck. A kilometre or two along the road we were hailed by a pair of Italian hitch-hiking soldiers. I pulled up as soon as possible but noticed the road looked dark and slippery. The Italian ex-POWs, now co-belligerents, were obliged to run a little distance to reach the back of the truck. Seeing the Americans aboard, the potential passengers cheered, saying: 'Ah! Americano, very good. Inglese – not so good!'

I peered through the peep-hole and said:

'Italianos no good, Italianos like walkies? Si?'

'Ah! Inglese very good. *Capitano bonito! Molte grazie.* Inglese very, very good.'

The American boys enjoyed the joke, helped the 'Ities' aboard. We didn't hear another word from them.

Looking behind us we could see distinctly dark purple tracks left by our tyres. Ahead the road was smothered in reddish-brown dancing insects. The beautiful green young vines on either side of the road were coated with the pests. None of us had seen anything like the phenomenon and didn't know what to expect. The seething mass bubbled two inches deep on the road; our tyres now squelched juicy bands of corpses by the million until we entered the outskirts of the city where the vegetation was insufficient to attract the invaders.

On our return journey, with replacement films, the road was an evenly distributed slimy mess resulting from the passage of vehicles. The sun behind us cast long, long shadows and those insects still alive had settled into the succulent plant life, intent on destroying it.

Back at the camp I described our experience to the Wing Adjutant, a heavily bronzed Rhodesian. 'Ah!' he said, 'The locusts are here. They will strip the vines overnight and grow to a full size in no time. We shall see them here among the trees within a couple of days. They haven't been this far north for years. Because of the war the French people haven't been able to carry out their annual crop spraying beyond the mountains.'

The Adj. was right. Like whopping big grasshoppers, four or five inches long, they rained upon our domain, flying over us and round us, close enough for the draught from their flapping wings to be felt, but miraculously avoiding contact with human beings. Bob and I took sadistic pleasure in standing outside the Signals Office, each wielding a suitable piece of timber, lashing at the offenders and scoring one point for each 'definite'.

Constantly flying, the locusts stayed around for a couple of days, seriously interrupting flying of aircraft. In all directions they flapped and hovered, dived and swerved, never colliding with one another. At night they settled in the trees, having stripped the vines bare, slept on tents and guy ropes, not moving until dawn. When they were satisfied there was no more food it seemed a master controller gave the signal to move and in one enormous swishing cloud they departed south.

After that excitement we devoted our time to fighting against boredom. Air mail from England reached us regularly and our forces newspaper, *Union Jack*, kept us informed of progress in the war, albeit under censorship. We learned that the Island of Elba had been taken by French forces on 16 June, making extensive use of mules in the process of unloading!

On 20 June the intrepid Commander R. A. Allan RNVR, from his base in Bastia, led his flotilla of MTBs on a daring raid on German shipping in Leghorn harbour. On 19 July when American forces captured Leghorn they found the harbour littered with wrecks. The town had been bombed. When the Germans retreated from it they sewed mines in every street. These pieces of news seemed insignificant at the time I received them. In due course Leghorn was to be my next home.

The U-boat chasing done, a great change came over 338 Wing. Our Spitfires hotly received any German intruders. The 'Penguins' prepared to leave the theatre and return to UK. A new Commanding Officer arrived to take over from Dee-Pee. George Williams, inventor of Operation SWAMP, deserved well his promotion to Wing Commander. The handing over ceremony called for special effects.

A grand Sports Day raised morale to new heights. The boffins of my Signals Workshops built a Public Address system over which I revived my pre-war function of announcer. Uproarious three-legged races, mock battles using dates, oranges, olives as missiles, tipping the bucket (of water) and every conceivable form of impromptu competition released a lot of tension. A successful day rounded off in theatrical style when Espy turned up with his second gang show. After the show, starting around midnight, a terrific party in the mess marked the end of Dee-Pee's command of 36 Squadron. He would go to Taranto as Group Captain, 242 Group.

During a year long association with the 'Penguins' I had been privileged to enjoy the friendships of a rare assortment of characters. Few decorations had been awarded; but that of Canadian George Abel was particularly meritorious. During the Blida days when his Wellington caught fire on landing, George got out safely but was horrified to see the rear-gunner trapped in his turret. Without hesitation George, with his bare fist smashed the perspex and dragged his mate clear. George showed me his fist the very next day; it showed no sign of a bruise. Appropriately, George was awarded the George Medal!

George Williams received a cordial welcome. I had met him more than once and in particular on our day of exercises with the Navy in Algiers Bay. I asked him how he had enjoyed his voyage in the submarine. He said the pink gins had knocked him out and he didn't know whether he had submerged or not!

One day of relief from relative unemployment came as a result of my being appointed Officer-under-Training on Court Martial duty. Wing Commander Kemp of our Beaufighter squadron transported me to Oran for the occasion; he presided over the court. I had not flown in anything as quick as a Beaufighter and my young skipper was noted for not loitering. At little above nought feet we sped over Cherchell where hosts of sunbathers of the Blida day-leave party rose as one to shake fists of protestation and shout unheard profanities at us.

Over the intercom my pilot said:

'That'll remind them that the war is still on!'

On we swept, took a look at Oran harbour, then turned inland to do a couple of circuits around the French Foreign Legion HQ at Sidi bel Abbès, albeit at a respectable height and radius for fear of drawing their reputedly accurate rifle fire.

The Court Martial was a very dull and, in my opinion, a very unnecessary one. This opinion proved to be quite erroneous. A young Corporal, with a wife and two children at home, had been charged with the disgraceful habit of relieving his bladder in the cactus garden of the local cinema. Considering that the local populace seemed to have no objection to their male members paying minor calls in less secluded places, it may be wondered why the charge was brought at all. The reason was that this chap was British. Further: he failed to observe the approach of a brace of WAAF officers who saw the whole thing!

Somebody should have warned me to look up my Uxbridge notes on Court Martial procedure. The only thing I could remember was that as Junior-Officer-under-Training I would be called upon to suggest a suitable sentence.

The case for the defence, eloquently put by a young Canadian lawyer, touched my heart strings. I thought that 28 days in detention would be adequate. I said so and the Chairman nearly fell off his seat. He said: 'His CO could have given him that! If he had found it possible to do so we would not be here today.'

Then it was revealed that the prisoner had committed a number of offences. Regrettably, his wife and kids must suffer a drop in income, for the Corporal would be reduced in rank. As that was one of the hazards of misbehaviour in public I was obliged to accept the decision of the Court. Having thus added to my store of knowledge I was 'Beaufightered' back to Reghaia.

Thenceforth, time-killing being a feature of our lives despite numerous recreational pursuits, a score of us began to delve into religion. Our padre was a devoted Evangelist, quiet in the extreme but intensely persuasive by way of a very few words. Desmond K. Dean taught simply, quoting appropriate passages from the Holy Bible to illustrate that the only advice he could give was to follow the Scriptures. Desmond could listen intently to any tale of woe for as long as his applicant wished to ramble. The answer was to quote a Chapter and Verse and say: 'Shall we look it up?' There was no need to look it up; Desmond knew the Bible backwards. I fell under his spell. He believed everything in the good Book to be truly the word of God.

I had to agree that the writings of St. Paul constituted a second-to-none guide to moral behaviour; the story of the resurrection was exciting and provoked deep thinking. In trying to come to grips with the Old Testament I became bogged down in one family tree after another, like looking up a name in *Who's Who?* and being absorbed in succeeding pages. Several times I have resolved to read the Bible from cover to cover, which I understand has been done by many an enthusiast. I look for inspiration in every line but tend to lose interest when I come to such passages as:

'Then Zipporah took a sharp stone, and cut off the foreskin of her son, and cast it at his feet, and said, Surely a bloody husband art thou to me. So he let him go; then she said, A bloody husband thou art because of the circumcision.'

Now there's a thing to say to anyone. Pondering over such verses, wondering 'Who *is* who?' takes up so much time that I fear I shall never get through the lot.

Bob Lewis, an arch disbeliever, treated Desmond with respect until one night, after most of us were abed, a disturbance developed. The padre occupied the next-door tent. As the party of inebriated officers lurched by, one of them tripped over a guy rope. I heard clearly the ecclesiastical voice opine that if some people must get drunk they might have consideration for those who have no need of such diversion.

Even more clearly I heard the reply from Bob:

'You should complain. We subsidise your mess bill, don't we?'

So life jogged along for many weeks. Elsewhere the war continued without 338 Wing. On 29 September Admiral Hewitt relinquished his command at the successful conclusion of the invasion of Southern France. Control of the naval forces had been centred on Bastia. Now it moved to Leghorn.

That was when we received the glad news that we would pack our gear and cross over to Europe. By the time we assimilated instructions for the transfer, another month passed. The majority of personnel would fly to Italy and set up Headquarters in Leghorn. The vehicles, all forty-five of them, would follow by sea, all in one shipload.

The day before we were due to vacate our country seat at Reghaia I was called before Group Captain Scott to receive a new instruction. He had considered that the Transport Officer should fly to Leghorn with his HQ party to arrange parking lots for the vehicles when they arrived, locate sources for petrol and oil, establish an office and select a site for a workshop. That should keep him busy for the few days whilst the vehicles were at sea. Therefore, he chose me to take care of the vehicles and drivers in transit. A brief trip across the Med. seemed like just what the doctor ordered.

'All you have to do,' said the G/C, 'is marshal the convoy at 06.00 hrs. tomorrow morning and conduct the 45 vehicles to Algiers Docks. You will be met by Army Movement Control at the gates. From there you will be under their orders. They will arrange the loading onto the ship. Your function is to supervise the drivers and look after their welfare during the voyage. Have a calm crossing and I look forward to seeing you at Leghorn in a few days' time.'

So, I set about loading my personal equipment into the Signals Section Bedford. The Stores Officer heard the news that I had been appointed to take charge of laden vehicles and approached me in the hope that I could take personal care of the residue of the stocks from the Officers' Mess. I agreed to accept a few cases of gin and whisky, put these in the back of the Bedford, fastened down the canvas and parked outside the Signals Office prior to retiring therein for the night. Our tents having been dismantled, Bob and I had erected our camp-beds in the Nissen hut where electric lighting was still available. My mammoth copy of *War and Peace*, purchased in Algiers for ten shillings, occupied most of my reading time. I was immersed in a chapter of it when a scuffing sound diverted my attention. It reminded me that between the corrugated layers which formed the roof of the hut there dwelt a family of rats. They had never troubled us during our working days, nor ever were seen inside the office. I chose to ignore the noise. When Bob came in he was in the ideal state for falling into bed and lost no time in doing so; I switched off the light and went to sleep.

When I woke up, in pitch darkness, I was aware of having company on the pillow behind my head. The rat was chewing something. I lay still except for a slow and dexterous withdrawal of my right arm from beneath the blanket. With clenched fist I intended dealing the animal a deadly blow. The animal, quick to realise the danger, took-off over my face. I felt a pin-prick in my left eye. I shot out of bed and switched on the light. The rat had gone.

Bob woke up and grumbled: 'What's going on?'

'A rat ran right across my face,' I said.

'Oh, put that light out and let's have some sleep.'

Those were the last words Bob spoke to me at Reghaia except, when I left the hut early in the morning, he murmured:

'Make sure my Jeep gets there, won't you?'

Chapter 40

Wheels over the Water

I entrusted the Signals Bedford to a competent driver and headed the convoy myself, driving Bob's Jeep.

At the dock gates, just as planned, the Movements Officer checked my documents against his loading tickets and directed me to a parking place on the quayside. Sergeant Snee, as Senior NCO, made sure that all the vehicles lined up as neatly as could be. They were a mixed lot indeed, ranging from the Jeep, through an assortment of trucks, Crossleys and Austins with trailers, a Coles crane, Commer D/F vans and a couple of water Bowsers. They would be loaded in a carefully arranged order.

Loading began at 09.00 hrs., heavy vehicles first. Not without trepidation, we saw some of our prized transmitter carriers swinging at the end of a single steel rope. As each vehicle went aboard so followed its driver. Everything proceeded according to plan, until the clock approached mid-day. About half of our consignment was in the hold, towards the stern of the vessel.

Numerous pieces of British Army equipment were being taken into the forward hold. A Churchill tank rotated in mid-air.

The call of the muezzin carried across the harbour from an adjacent mosque. The tank plummeted to strike the ship's rails as well as the quayside, so pushing the ship outwards far enough for the tank to drop into the harbour. It was all over in five seconds. We adjourned for lunch. The Movements Officer said I need not worry about security of the vehicles. The Military Police would look after them.

Sergeant Snee, my trusted No.2 i/c, confided that in his lengthy experience of military life he had not found the 'Red Caps' themselves to be beyond a trifle of misappropriation. I gave the order that no vehicle should be left unattended. We ate our rations where we stood, while those of our colleagues already aboard spoke highly of a change of diet available in the galley.

When the Movements Officer returned he showed much concern for the state of affairs. The ship must be taken out of the harbour to allow manoeuvring of equipment required in the recovery of the tank. Good-natured banter passed between those men leaning over the ship's rails and those of us still landlocked. My own apprehensions grew as an even more frustrated Movements Officer appeared to say that his higher authority had dictated that the remainder of my charges would embark on another ship, in another dock. The Military Police would conduct us to a new starting point. I must confess to falling into a trap of false security.

The police had watched over us during our long wait and had ample time to size up what we carried in each truck. I insisted on being the last vehicle to leave and so ensure nobody would be left behind. As I hopped into the passenger seat of the Bedford the last remaining 'Red Cap' came alongside and said:

'I'll jump in the back, Sir, and keep an eye open until we leave this dock.'

I nodded my approval and signalled the driver to chase after the other vehicles. At the dock gate a 'Red Cap' on point duty halted us and made great play of waving on a few passing trucks. Meanwhile we were stationary just slightly ahead of the guard-room. We seemed to wait an inordinately long time for the traffic cop to satisfy himself that all was clear. Finally, as we received the go-ahead gesture our rear-mounted 'guard' said:

'I'll leave you now, Sir. Just turn left and keep going, you're all clear!'

Undoubtedly, it was at that point that a couple of cases of whisky were added to the stocks of that guard-room. It was some time later when preparing the Bedford for shipment that I discovered the loss. When I mentioned the matter to the Movements Officer he expressed no surprise and would I hasten aboard to introduce myself to the skipper of the *Empire Rock*. With that worthy gentleman I leaned against the rails and observed the scenes of activity on the quayside. The Signals Section truck was hoisted up complete with my personal kit and what remained of the whisky. Several more 338 Wing conveyances successfully reached the hold; five more including Bob's little Jeep and the Coles crane which presented a problem for the hoisters remained on the ground.

'We're full now,' said the skipper.

'What about that lot? They're mine.'

'Won't go on here. Leave it to Movements and don't worry! They'll be put on another ship.'

After two days of activity within the harbour we joined a convoy of about a dozen ships in the bay and set course along the coast. I consoled myself with the knowledge that all my vehicles and men were in the same convoy and looked forward to meeting them all in Leghorn. When I expressed my satisfaction on this point to the Skipper he corrected me: 'We're not going to Leghorn. I am to off-load you at Taranto!'

'That's a hell of a long way from Leghorn. What about the other two ships which contain some of my chaps and vehicles?'

'I can't tell you that but I will try and find out for you when we call at Augusta!'

After an excellent dinner with my new friends I turned in early, feeling less enthusiastic about the task ahead.

During the night I was awakened by a loud-hailed American voice from the escort vessel:

'Ahoy there! You. *Empire Rock* – can't you get that old tub to move faster?'
Voice in reply: 'No – she's flat out!'
'You're supposed to do nine and a half knots minimum.'
'Sorry, can't oblige. We've got barnacles up to the gunnels!'
So we dragged along behind the convoy for three days and nights. We had no need to worry about U-boats; German bombers would have a long flight from Northern Italy but it was comforting to see the odd Beaufighter take a look at us. We put into Augusta harbour on 7 November early in the morning. The sea lay postcard blue and calm; Mount Etna sparkled in the dazzling sun. An aged farmer sat side-saddle on his donkey, surrounded by piles of carob cuttings. There was no sign of war, only of peace. Over the wireless the Radio Officer picked up the news that the Germans were putting up a stiff resistance in the Lucca and Viareggio region to the north of Leghorn. I prayed that Group Captain Scott and his merry men could hold out until our arrival.

The Skipper received more documents and was able to advise me that one of the other ships in which I had an interest was bound for Brindisi and the third would dock at Bari. It could now be said that 338 Wing was widespread. With another day's sailing ahead I had time to work out a plan of how to reassemble my scattered flock.

Sitting up in the bows of the *Empire Rock* I sighted the mainland of Italy, conscious of a prickling pain in my left eye. The rat of Reghaia had left its mark!

The bleary waterfront of Taranto was presided over by a huge, neatly assembled pile of bricks, either the Town Hall or a monument to Mussolini, untouched by bomb or torpedo. Beyond it stretched poverty.

Our skilful skipper brought the ship to the quayside without a tremor. Officials came aboard, papers were examined. I was given directions that my convoy of vehicles, at present in three portions, should assemble as a unit at a Staging Post near Foggia. The *Empire Rock* could not be unloaded until the following day. Several hours of daylight remained for our further examination of the delights of Taranto. The lads were keen to stretch their legs.

I recalled that 242 Group Headquarters was established in the area and thither I made my way, in search of my good friend Dee-Pee. I found him in great spirits, his uniform embellished by the four rings of a Group Captain. He was truly the Captain of the Group. A major achievement, since taking over that responsible post, was to order the sinking of the Italian crack liner *Rex*!

Dee-Pee had been taking a noggin of wine in the mess when the Duty Controller telephoned:

'The boys have sighted the liner *Rex*, Sir. What should we do?'

'Sink it,' said Dee-Pee and returned to the bar.

That was on 7 September. Though Beaufighters found the 51,000 ton ship an easy target, 100 rockets were pumped into it before it was to burn its proud heart out and beach itself. There it lay on a northern Adriatic shore, an early post-war tourist attraction. In Dee-Pee's scrap book, below a photograph of the wreckage, was a copy of a signal from Air Ministry. It read:

'No co-belligerent shipping to be attacked without express Air Ministry approval.'

Beneath it was written: 'Too late, chums!'

That was my last meeting with Dee-Pee. He reminded me to apply for a permanent commission. I informed him that I had sought and received my wife's approval and had made the application. With a promise to keep in touch I returned to the *Empire Rock*.

One of the first vehicles to be off-loaded was a Chevrolet 15 cwt. truck. It was but lightly loaded. I would discover the reason by-and-by. I appointed a Senior NCO to supervise the unloading to completion, gave him the map reference of the assembly point near Foggia and instructed him to wait there until the rest of us arrived. Thereupon, I adopted the Chevvy as my personal transport and set off alone for Brindisi. The weather was good and I was pleased to have the heel of Italy to myself. The engine revved freely; being quite unacquainted with the make of truck it did not occur to me that the clutch was slipping like mad. There were few hills until I reached the outskirts of Villafranca when a sharp rise in the ground brought the Chevvy to a standstill.

By great good fortune the local school was turning out. Its up-and-coming academics gathered round. Laughing and with tremendous enthusiasm they pushed Chevvy to the top of the incline. As it gathered momentum down the other side I sighted my guardian angel. A Polish mechanic was busily packing up his tools in preparation to journey north in the wake of his unit. He had no intention of carrying out any major repairs but promptly produced from his mobile workshop, a can of paraffin, a pint of which pungent liquid he poured into the fly-wheel housing. The effect was magical. The clutch gripped and as I moved off with the remainder of the paraffin in reserve, the cheers of the youth of Italy ringing in my ears, I prayed for easy roads ahead.

After two more applications my supply of paraffin was exhausted and so was my supply of rations. I was more than delighted to crawl into the dockyard at Brindisi and find Sergeant Snee collecting together Part Two of my responsibilities. He was none too pleased to have to take the Chevvy into tow, pending attention to its clutch. Bob Lewis's Jeep was included with the Brindisi assignment and this I adopted as my personal transport for the trek to Leghorn. I deemed it advisable to carry a companion on the next stage of the journey, selected a useful looking airman, and set off for Bari, leaving instructions with Snee to meet me at Foggia.

It was quite a treat to drive the spritely little Jeep. We made Bari in time to catch the boys brewing up tea on the quayside. They had enjoyed a comfortable voyage and were not short of rations. The tea carried a distinct flavour of Scotch whisky. The Army Movements Officer had been taken by surprise at the sight of a detachment of the RAF coming ashore. I explained the situation and assured him we would not ruffle his paper work unduly so long as we could spend the night on his waterfront.

Two days later we took a count of heads and vehicles at Foggia. Nobody was missing and all vehicles were in working order except the Chevvy, for which spares were unobtainable until we crossed the mountains. It would be towed. Speedy travel was out of the question. Sergeant Snee insisted on the big Crossleys and trailers heading the convoy and implored the drivers to 'walk 'em up!' I would bring up the rear in the Jeep to make sure nobody conked out unnoticed. A despatch rider was ordered to maintain communications between front and rear.

We were under the supervision of Army Movement Control and must not start without permission, otherwise we were likely to become involved in a major traffic jam. I was assured that our whereabouts would be reported to 338 Wing HQ at Leghorn. It was obvious that we were behind schedule. I think Group Captain Scott visualised our making a glorious landfall at the port of Leghorn. I must confess that I had that in mind when I boarded the *Empire Rock*.

The weather continued fine, though the rains must be approaching. The signal to commence our mountainous venture came at daybreak. All engines started and Sergeant Snee set the pace. Our objective was to complete the tortuous route to the next Staging Post at Maddaloni near Naples, a distance of some 125 kilometres, by mid-afternoon. Theoretically we had time in hand. We bowled happily along for about an hour; then we started to climb.

Many of our vehicles had survived the heat of the Western Desert and in doing so had become war-weary. The mountain pass presented a new terror. Bottom gears sounded irritable, clutches emitted warning odours, axles growled notification of old age. Sergeant Snee stuck to his principle of 'walking up'. He dared not stop in case he could not start away again on the steep gradients. We made painful progress. Engines over-heated and then the worst happened: LAC Green, ex-Midland 'Red' bus driver, revolted against the walking pace, gave an extra burst of throttle to his Crossley and the clutch failed to stand the strain.

I instructed the despatch rider to guide all the other vehicles to continue past the immobilised Green, except the Coles crane, a most useful device in almost any emergency, and one of the good old Thornycroft trucks which could be hitched up to the trailer. The Coles would haul the disabled Crossley to the top of the pass.

By the time we arrived at Maddaloni both vehicles and men needed rest and reparation. We parked on good firm ground in a clearing surrounded by myrtle bushes. In this ideal camping ground I decided to settle down for a couple of days. After digging the necessary hole, setting up a temporary kitchen, showering under the water Bowser and satisfying hunger we drew lots for leave. Half the gang went off to Naples for an evening of adventure on the strict understanding that the NCO in charge would be held responsible for any misbehaviour. I found that condition to be a guarantee of co-operative loyalty.

Meanwhile Sergeant Snee and I reviewed the situation regarding serviceability of vehicles. A list of essential spares would be presented at the nearest stores depot and from appraisal of availability a decision would be reached upon how much work could be tackled on site.

Snee worked on the postulate of the difficult being ordinary and the impossible taking a bit longer. He used his powers of persuasion on the store-keepers to the extent of procuring pretty well all he wanted in the way of spares. He organised the work, directed here and assisted there. The Coles crane lifted the engine out of the Chevvy which received a new clutch plate. Brakes were adjusted, wheels changed, tyres checked and magic adjustments to the Crossley made it fit to continue. The run up the west coast avoided steep hills; we anticipated no further serious trouble. It was agreed that we stay put for an extra day to clean up and double-check the vehicles. The second half of the party took leave for the evening. That additional day was very welcome. I checked up with the Movement Control Officer who approved the change. Our route ahead was clearly marked with Staging Posts; notification of our estimated time of arrival at all points ahead had been signalled. We would start at daybreak. We retired into our respective caravans or trucks in good spirits with the stars twinkling merrily.

The rains began at 02.00 hrs., steady at first. Then the wind rose to a siren-like scream. Pieces of myrtle bush cracked against my Brockhouse trailer. Now the rain increased in quantity and quality. Waterfalls streamed down the windows to swill, soak and swirl across our parking plot. Inspection was pointless. At least we stood on level ground and must await dawn for realisation of the worst.

With the rising of the sun our predicament was clear. Our vehicles stood in red-brown soup. The occasion called into use the pair of thigh-length rubber motor-cycling boots which I had carried in my kit for more than two years. Thus equipped I toured my company. Our first priority was to ascertain whether many engines were affected by flooding. Barefooted airmen raised bonnets and mopped up surplus water. Tea was brewed, spirits raised, water receded. In the steamy heat a systematic withdrawal from the bog began.

Four-wheel driven vehicles would drag the trailers out to the main road. The Bedford 'Four-by-Fours' were invaluable for pulling out their two-wheel-drive brethren. It was inevitable that one or two throttle-happy drivers should spin rear wheels to inextricable depths, necessitating the slow and painful extraction by Coles crane. The combination of ingenuity, stupidity, enterprise and brute force saw the convoy lined up, muddy but mobile. It was mid-day when we left Maddaloni. I went ahead in the Jeep and located a suitable stop for a decent meal.

We were not short of rations and the efforts of the morning called for rest and replacement of energy. Our travels had involved us in chance contacts with armies both British and American. Thus we had acquired Type 'A' rations and numerous 'P-X' goodies. When we resumed our journey we came shortly to Cassino, scene of intense fighting during the previous May. The monastery on the mountain top stood in silent testimony to the folly of man. The village below it lay as a gigantic pile of rubble on the top of which some highly competent sign-writer had erected a huge board pronouncing: 'HOTEL REALE – OPENING SHORTLY'. The humour behind the message was not lost on my companion and me but it was tempered by the spectacle of a Churchill tank resting on its side in a roadside pool of deep, clear water. I have wondered often whether the tank was buried where it lay.

Our mechanical disabilities allowed of only very modest speed. We were less likely to attain the latitude of Rome that day when a minor mishap caused us to take advantage of hard ground on the outskirts of a village. A spring broke on Chiefy's workshop. Luck, on a Western Desert trek, had brought the 338 Wing Signals Section upon some discarded German equipment, amongst which was a wooden hut on a two-wheeled trailer chassis. The perspicacious Flight-Sergeant had adopted it as his personal workshop. It became an accepted feather in 338 Wing. A glance inside the hut was sufficient to convince any non-technical observer that he was being permitted an insight to advanced technology. Undoubtedly some first-class work had been conducted in the hut, most of it unofficial, nevertheless in the interests of the general welfare. If a watch-strap broke or a spectacle frame snapped, a precious book fell out of its binding or a favourite pipe disintegrated, it was worth a visit to 'Chiefy's' workshop. Ten to one he could fix it. The hut and he were inseparable.

By repacking loads and transferring from one to another we made enough room on one of the trucks to take the hut minus its chassis. The hut itself was raised aloft by the Coles crane; the chassis prised away and dumped on the roadside. A passing cyclist made a cash offer for the tyres and secured possession of the whole chassis in exchange for a pile of lire. This I converted into sterling at an early date and despatched a contribution to St. Dunstan's.

During the labour of shifting loads it became more and more apparent that an appreciable quantity of stores had been rifled. A lorry load of clothing aboard the ship which suffered damage from the falling tank had received the attention of thieves during the night when the ship stood away from the quay. It was impossible to count the losses because I had no idea of the contents of some of the vehicles. My orders were to conduct the convoy!

We by-passed Rome the next morning with one more Staging Post to go. The Army Movement people flagged us down and directed us into a parking lot. Priority must be given to a fighting unit making for trouble at the foot of the Appennino Tosco where German forces were putting up more than a fierce resistance. We were only too willing to allow them preferential use of the highway.

When could we go forward? Might I communicate with my unit? Army Movement control would see to all that, not my problem. Just follow the instructions. Everything according to plan. I must not worry but I did. Our nomadic life did good to nobody. We were homesick for our parent unit, lost to the war effort.

After two days we received the signal to move. As soon as the Jeep got up speed I felt the draught in my left eye. Tears began to fall, grittiness set me blinking and I knew that I must get to hospital at the end of my present mission. We struck lucky with the weather and entered Leghorn in triumph just fourteen days behind schedule.

The streets of Leghorn appeared to have suffered from measles. The retreating Germans had mined every roadway and placed booby traps in every building. One poor chap received dreadful injury when he sat down to play a piano. 338 Wing HQ was located in a square apartment block overlooking the harbour. The building had survived the shocks of war extremely well. The staff enjoyed considerable comfort.

My gang of road-riders received a rapturous welcome from their sedentary colleagues. Bob Lewis greeted me with a jovial: 'Where the bloody hell have you been?'

Group Captain Scott said: 'You should have let me know where you were!'

I said: 'I was not sure where I was half the time. I understood that Army Movement Control were passing information to you as we progressed.'

I reported the loss of some equipment but had no idea of the value of it. I requested permission to seek specialist attention to my eye at the American hospital which I had noted on my way into town. Permission granted, I dumped my kit in an appointed room in HQ and left for the hospital immediately. Bob took me there in the Jeep which he was pleased to repossess.

There were no half-measures at the 64th General Hospital. I was treated as a front-line casualty. My eye was inspected by Major Haik, a specialist of high repute of the New Orleans State University Hospital.

Within ten minutes I had been issued with new pyjamas, ordered to take an overdue bath and glowingly settled in a comfortable, spotlessly clean bed. I fell asleep.

Chapter 41

American Hospitality

My name, rank and number were entered in the records of the 64th General. Certainly there was no reluctance to accept me as a patient. I was so exhausted by my recent experiences that I took scant notice of my surroundings before dropping into the oblivion of sleep.

How long I slept I do not know but when I stirred I was conscious of being watched over by a number of people. Somebody said: 'The Cap'n's awake, nurse.' Henceforward I was known as the Cap'n. The nurse, a cheerful little blonde from Albany, introduced herself whilst surrounded by a small crowd of curious onlookers. She said:

'You are to go on milk shar—ts, Cap'n.'

The whole company cheered.

'You'll like those, Cap'n' added one of the viewers. 'They make you feel real good.'

'What are milk shar—ts, Nurse?' I asked.

'You'll find out soon enough, but first you have dinner.'

'Am I staying here for the night, then?'

'You'll be here about two weeks, I reckon. You'll get a milk shar—t every third day and penicillin every third hour. That's what the Major says.'

It passed through my mind that I might be guilty of desertion from the RAF. I had no option but to do as I was told. Not that I was the only Britisher in the ward of twenty patients. A young Captain of the 8th Army had suffered a severe injury from shrapnel in the side of his head. He described how Major Haik had saved his sight. His left eye had recovered from surgery but settled out of alignment. That was no problem to the Major who contrived a shortening of the muscles on one side to bring it into line. There was no doubt that I was in capable hands.

After a very palatable dinner the nurse appeared with a tray which held a syringe full of a white liquid. A cheer went up: 'The Cap'n's taking a milk shar—t.' The boys gathered round. I was ordered by the nurse to lie face down, trousers down, while all 10 cc. of the contents were injected into my right buttock. The pain was excruciating to say the least. I gripped the bed-head during the prolonged agony. The continuing chorus helped enormously. I fell asleep again and started dreaming.

The dreams developed into nightmares. Flight of fantasy were interrupted at the prescribed three hour intervals when penicillin shar—ts were administered to an upper arm. Such realisms were portrayed during the long periods of delirium that I welcomed the return of daylight to confirm that my fellow-men did exist as I remembered them before nightfall. My neighbour to starboard, a bearded Jew, Sergeant Clark, was first to speak:

'Had a bad night, Cap'n? You talked a lot – don't know what you said but it sure sounded like you had trouble.'

'Sorry if I disturbed you but I feel very feverish.'

'That's the milk shar—ts,' he said. 'The Major's speciality. Sets up a fever and the penicillin knocks out the germs.'

'Is it really milk?'

'Sure is, Cap'n. Real Carnation milk, straight from the tin!'

I resolved to check my friend's statement in due course. Meanwhile, I enjoyed first-class meals in spite of difficulty in sitting up to eat them. Muscular discomfort in the nether regions discouraged any tendency to take exercise. Any inclination to feel sorry for one's own predicament faded to naught when I, as a new boy, was inspected by other occupants of Ward 8. All had suffered damage to eyesight in one way or another. Some had been blinded totally; some had lost limbs. Rank, colour or creed entitled no person to distinction.

Johnson, black, blind and legless, conducted himself cheerfully by wheelchair, crashing from one bedframe to another inquiring into the welfare of the incumbents. He was an inhabitant of some long suffering, well known to patients in neighbouring wards as well as his own. He was due for repatriation and looked forward to it with glee:

'When Ah gits home to Memphis, Cap'n, mah ole' lady's goin' to git the surparze of her life when she fands Ah got two legs missin'. Jarhson, she'll say – don't tell me you lost anythin' else!'

He acted as a porter on Thursdays when the P-X issues came around, assisting the nurse in distributing cigars, cigarettes and goodies. He knew the likes and dislikes of each patient.

P-X day was the one time when the British residents were treated differently from their American brothers. The little nurse called out:

'Arl you British guys collect your Pee-Ex issoo!'

Those of us who were reasonably mobile shuffled along the corridor to return triumphantly with ten Craven 'A', a packet of 'Monkey Brand' matches and a tube of Rowntree's Clear Gums. The matches were popularly known as 'Three-in-One', it being normal to strike three before getting a light. Anyone unable to walk could depend on Johnson's delivery service. He knew his way around. Anyone careless enough to leave anything out of place in corridor or ward would receive a fearful dressing down when Johnson crashed into such an obstruction. When distribution had been completed surplus requirements were pooled. Non-smokers gave their cigar rations to the impoverished Britishers.

American hospitality was typified when a huge cake arrived from Sergeant Clark's parents in honour of his birthday. He cut the cake into twenty pieces. Everyone received one slice including the Sergeant himself.

The days passed happily. I received a succession of visitors from 338 Wing. Among them came the Wing Medical Officer who pointed out, justifiably, that I should have sought his advice before entering the hospital. Ethically, I had shown discourtesy, but being very appreciative of my eyes I did not hesitate to make straight for what I considered the best source of expert treatment. Frankly, I was not fond of the MO.

Major Haik examined my eye daily. He did not vary the treatment. The nights continued to be spent in nightmare land with wheels falling off lorries and sparks flying out of exhaust pipes. At times I longed for the nurse to shoot me instead of injecting more penicillin. My arms continued to be punctured every three hours day and night, the nurse finding it more difficult to select a soft spot. The second milk shar—t was administered to the left buttock, the audience witnessing and cheering the event as before. Thereafter I stiffened up to such an extent that I thought I would never walk again.

Nevertheless when the nurse announced that my third milk shar—t was due I managed to shuffle along to the dispensing room.

'Please do show me what it is you are going to inject.'

'It's milk, Cap'n, just plain condensed milk with distilled water.'

With that she punctured a small tin of Carnation milk, drew some into the syringe and topped up with distilled water to make 10 cc.

'Right,' she said. 'Now to bed, face down for your last shar—t.'

The boys gathered round and I grasped the bed rails, thankfully for the last time.

Thenceforth, the dramatic content of my nightmares lessened; the three-hourly squirts of penicillin scarcely disturbed my sleep; the pain in my eye ceased. The Major declared satisfaction with the results of the treatment but directed that, as a precaution against another possible source of infection, I present myself for dental inspection at the appropriate department. An appointment was made for 14.00 hours on the following day.

It so happened that the following day was the fourth Thursday in November: Thanksgiving Day. The 'Goodies' arrived mid-morning. Again, no distinction was made of rank or nationality. Each bedside table was laden with first-quality fruit, chocolate, sweets and cigars, cakes and biscuits. Luncheon included tinned turkey and all the trappings of an abundant Christmas dinner. Alcoholic liquor was prohibited in the ward.

The Department of Dental Surgery reminded me of an up-market hairdressing salon I had once patronised during a short spell of affluence in London. I was ushered by an orderly to one of the chairs in a long row. The arrival of the surgeons from their own lunch was heralded by a high level of jovial laughter. It was clear that they had not been subjected to prohibition. The officer who inspected my teeth breathed odours of Bourbon but was inoffensive otherwise. The occupant of a neighbouring chair was less well-pleased with the white-overalled gentleman who attempted a similar inspection but slithered to his knees, spatula in hand. He was promptly picked up and dragged away by two of his colleagues, much to the relief of his patient. I was thankful to be given a clean bill of health and made my way back to Ward 8.

In passing a noticeboard I glanced at a list of religious services. I resolved to pass away an hour at an advertised time, in pursuance of my faith. Therefore, on the Friday evening at 19.00 hrs. I took a seat in the centre of a row some comfortable distance from the altar. I sat, in silent contemplation, for several minutes, alone. I selected a chapter from my pocket edition of the New Testament. Quite content with my lot, it did not occur to me that I had misread the time of commencement of the service. I carried on reading. After twenty minutes had elapsed a host of worshippers poured through the doorway. The rows of seats were fully occupied. I thought nothing of it when Sergeant Clark bid me a cheerful hallo and sat beside me. All of my fellow pietists wore the standard hospital garb, a dressing-gown. That much we had in common. On further observation I realised they all wore hats. That feature I did not share with them. I had gate-crashed the synagogue!

Hemmed in as I was, it seemed discourteous to create a commotion by extracting myself from the predicament. I decided to stand it out. Sergeant Clark was kindness itself, guiding me through the ritual. The officiating clerics – there were two of them – were dressed in the uniforms of US Army officers. Thus attired they held me in less terror than had they donned mystical robes. The senior of the two, whom I regarded as the Rabbi, addressed the congregation in simple language. Pointed reference to the Crusades of the British seemed designed to prick the conscience of the intruder; if so, the effect was to assure my indifference to the subject for evermore. As we filed from the hall I thanked Sergeant Clark for his help, explaining my error in the reading of dates and times. He made no further mention of the matter but did insist on my acceptance of all his Thanksgiving Day cigars, cigarettes and pipe tobacco.

My final week at the 64th included the saddest of days; we said our farewells to Johnson. The great humorist was at his best. He whizzed his wheel-chair at breakneck speeds from building to building and ward to ward thanking everyone for the help he had been given in overcoming difficulties! Yet it was he who had inspired hundreds to fight problems.

Anyone who could walk came to see Johnson wheeling himself to the door of the coach which was to take the returning heroes to the Flying Fortress which would carry them home. He couldn't see a thing but he waved us goodbye and left us all in tears. America would be a better country for his presence.

Bob Lewis came and collected me from the hospital when the Major set me free, after prescribing new spectacles!

338 Wing had been operating satisfactorily without my assistance. I was delighted to be assigned to inspections of out-stations. These included the aerodrome installation at Rosigano from which our Spitfires operated, a VHF/DF and small W/T outfit in the vicinity of a remote mountain farm near Volterra and D/F facilities at Pisa. In addition to these were certain responsibilities on the island of Corsica, to which fair land the most convenient means of transport was to be provided by the Royal Navy.

Chapter 42

Diverse Diversions

The Transport Officer said:

'Take this Ford V-8. It's just the job for storming the mountains up to Volterra – same size as the Bedford, more or less, but a lot more poke in the engine.'

I was delighted with the soft purr of the motor as I turned south along the coast road to Rosigano. Mercifully the macadam on that stretch was undamaged by the passage of track-laying vehicles. The scenery, well deserving mention in the travel guides, added to the pleasure of my mission.

I parked the Ford near the riggers' tent and walked across to the Flying Control cabin, found everything working well and everybody happy. I checked the log books, joined the lads in a brew of tea and went back to the truck.

The engine lumped over a few times but didn't fire.

'Always the same, those things,' said the Flight-Sergeant Fitter. 'Six-volt battery, you know – no good. You'd think the Yanks would've got round to twelve-volt by now, wouldn't you?'

Disagreement was pointless.

'There's a knack, you know,' he said. I didn't know but I waited to hear about it:

'Let it go "Yuh" twice and switch off. Let the battery rest a few minutes. Next time, press the starter button but release it just before the peak of the second "Yuh". That gives you the best spark and if you're lucky, she'll start. If not, keep trying!'

I was lucky, she started. The engine ran silky smooth as I headed up the Cecina valley, following the precise instructions given to me by Bob to locate the out-station. Along the rough track, past the farm house, down the steep bank, ford the stream, climb the opposite bank and look for the aerial mast. The boys were pleased to see me. They were low on cigarettes, welcomed extra blankets. I delivered petrol for the generator, batteries and rations. They had established good relationships with the farmer and his family, enjoyed home cooked spaghetti dishes and fresh eggs in exchange for samples from the ration boxes. I stayed for tea. The Ford fired on the second 'Yuh' and I set course for Leghorn in good spirit.

The engine conked as I changed into bottom gear to enter the stream. It refused to restart. From the lonesome silence in the bottom of the narrow valley

I could neither see nor be seen. Whilst pondering my next move, there appeared, silhouetted against the evening sky, the head of an ox moving along the ridge towards the farm. I called out '*Prego*' and a few words which were recognised as meaning that help was required. The genial farmer and his son came to the top of the hill and looked down upon me.

'*Assistenzi, prego, Signor*,' sounded about right. It did the trick. Cigarettes were accepted as I explained: '*No motori, batteria caput*.' I indicated that if the vehicle could be towed to the top of the hill I could start with a push down the other side.

Pronto the boy ran up the hill and reappeared a minute later leading two oxen. 'Oh, *grazie, grazie*, Signor!' Hitched up to the two animals, all that was needed was for the *bambino* to slap one of them over the hindquarters and we mounted the hilltop with ease. More cigarettes, a push down the slope and the V-8 came to life. As I accelerated away I heard: '*Ancora, ancora Capitano!*'

The Transport Officer listened to my opinion of his Ford V-8 and promised me a Bedford for my next trip. However, my connection with the Signals Section of the Wing was to be interrupted yet again.

At some layer in the hierarchy a decision had been reached to hold a Court of Inquiry into the loss of £1,500's worth of equipment in the process of moving from Algiers to Leghorn. My presence, as Officer i/c convoy, was required at Caserta, the MAAF headquarters near Naples. Thither I was transported in the Piper aircraft of Communications Flight. At first I thought my leg was being pulled. It was clear that a quantity of boots, socks and shirts had been pinched from the ship damaged by the fall of the tank in Algiers harbour. I expected to be questioned, exonerated and returned to Leghorn within 24 hours. On the first day I was called before the Court which consisted of four Group Captains. I was not alone. I recognised at least two officers of Army Movements but there were others unknown to me. One was a Stores Officer from HQ and another an Accountant. They detailed the losses which were exaggerated to sound terribly detrimental to the war effort.

After the initial meeting came a very respectable lunch. I learned that my attendance would not be needed during the afternoon. I was allocated a comfortable room and then explored the palace. I found my old friend Squadron-Leader Jacob established in his new office. I told him about the Court of Inquiry and of my experiences on the move. He thought it was a joke which would end the next day. We spent a most hilarious evening together in the Officers' Club.

The 'joke' did not end next day, nor the day after. As time went by I met my fellow 'criminals' who took the matter very seriously. The Army, it appeared, were very upset to have received a complaint against them by the RAF. I was not called again until the afternoon of the fourth day. By that time I was inured to any form of reprimand. I was surprised when one of the four G/Cs invited me to sit down.

'We've been here four days now, Reddin, and have got nowhere.'

'I'm not surprised, Sir. There were too many people involved to lay blame on any one or group of persons. It was my responsibility to watch the shipment of the convoy onto one vessel at Algiers and, I imagined, to see it off-loaded at Leghorn.'

'Tell us what happened.'

I outlined the move from the day the tank damaged the ship. My audience showed more and more amusement as the story unfolded. Finally, my opinion was sought: I suggested that boots, socks and shirts might be found in the Kasbah at Algiers, a case of whisky in the care of the Military Police. One Arab crane driver, beyond British jurisdiction, started the chain of events. Investigation should be terminated. At that the Court disbanded and nothing more was heard of it by me.

When I arrived back at Leghorn a grave emergency arose. A crack Panzer unit had been reinforced, and was not only defending the entrance to the Serchio Valley but was fighting out of it. The best of the American troops had been transferred to Southern France. Ahead of us were assortments of allied forces of no repute. Group Captain Scott issued orders for us to prepare ourselves to defend ourselves and to fix detonators to our lovely wireless sets in case a withdrawal became necessary. I polished my pistol and wondered whether I might after all be obliged to fire a shot in anger.

Not for the first time did General Freyberg despatch New Zealanders across from the east coast to straighten the line. They arrived just in time to repulse the German attack. We relaxed and reverted to our role of helping to contain the Arno plains while the serious business of a breakthrough to the Po Valley was being planned by our forces, at Rimini.

Our Spitfire pilots made regular reconnaissance runs up north every morning at daybreak to photograph enemy movements. On the return flight they made a habit of livening up proceedings on a German parade ground. In spite of being daily shot up by a swooping Spitfire, the Sergeant-Major, with characteristic Teutonism, adhered strictly to his timetable!

The weather was not conducive to enthusiasm for fighting. As Christmas approached attention was turned to entertainment. Our latest Concert Party took on the title of 'The Oversears'. Ronnie Taylor wrote a whole revue called 'Get On Parade'. It went with a swing and received a flattering report in the Wing Magazine, a monthly publication devised and produced in the W/T room.

Christmas Dinner was an outstanding success, largely because the cooks had gained a lot of experience and were making good use of the more abundant supplies available since the demise of the U-boats. As usual the Officers acted as waiters in the airmen's mess; when mince pies and trifles were handed round for the fifth course it became apparent that earlier courses had been over-liberal.

So much good food was left over that we organised a Boxing Day treat for local Italian children. Never was so much eaten by such little ones in so short a time. That was a Happy Christmas, that was!

Great changes came about in the New Year:

Rear-Admiral Morse moved his Headquarters from Naples to Leghorn, the better to deal with the German naval forces in Genoa. Co-ordination between Air Force and Navy intensified, not only militarily but socially also. Whenever inclement weather prevented operations by the Motor Torpedo Boats it was customary for a group of mariners to patronise our comfortable mess. There was, too, a good deal of sharing of transport in the interests of sightseeing and searching for alternative forms of entertainment.

As a water-borne force the sailors had difficulty in procuring wheeled transport but one vessel carried its own Jeep! That vessel was the dredger which daily toiled to keep the harbour clear of sludge and wreckage. At the end of each working day it was tied up at the quayside whereupon the derrick swung into action and from the hold the Jeep was extracted to be delicately lowered ashore. Four or five of the crew would be seen to drive away in pursuit of evening recreation. In the small hours of the morning the whining of the winding gear indicated that the Jeep was being returned to its portable garage.

Army co-operation, too, was evident for we relied on the ever-dependable Air Formation Signals chaps to install and maintain our land-line facilities. Therefore, never a day went by without one or two 'brown-jobs' milling around the Wing.

Generally speaking, it could be said that inter-service co-operation was both friendly and fruitful. In the least expected way it broke down: Our beloved padré, Desmond K. Dean, had left us to spread the gospel elsewhere. His replacement, Squadron-Leader Cook, drew even bigger audiences. Whereas dear Desmond had spoken quietly and with utmost sincerity Cookie was able to make himself heard over great distances yet with equal conviction. He was a businessman who, after reasoning out his belief, had turned parson. He had the natural gift of explaining the Testaments Old and New in language we could all follow easily. The result was that men from all the services came from far and wide to join us at the RAF chapel. We turned nobody away and were obliged to move to the theatre to accommodate the expanding congregation.

After hearing Cookie at his best and finishing up with a stirring hymn, I and a group of fellow officers returned to the mess in joyful mood. There we saw trouble in the form of two melancholy chaplains, one each Army and Navy. On that particular Sunday neither of them had attracted a single worshipper to his respective chapel. In concert they came to protest.

I nipped smartly downstairs and waylaid the offender:

'Padré,' I said, 'there is trouble ahead.'

'What's up, Red?' he asked.

I explained the situation in a few words. His reply was:

'Then we must bear in mind Corinthians 12, Verses 5 and 6: And there are differences of administrations, but the same Lord. And there are diversities of operations, but it is the same God which worketh all in all.'

The acrimony expressed by our two visitors seemed unbecoming of men of the cloth. They were nettled but our man remained unstung. He listened to their inference that the men should 'support' their respective chapels! Then he introduced his masterstroke:

'I will direct no man away from his preferred place of worship,' he said. 'I do suggest that we take advantage of the great theatre we have available across the road and hold a combined service next Sunday. Let us confer during the coming week, agree on the part each of us shall play in the conduct of the rituals. Here I see a wonderful opportunity of bringing together ever-increasing numbers in brotherhood.'

There was a short pause for thought. Soldier and sailor had no option but to agree to a meeting. Thenceforward Songs of Praise, on Sunday evenings in Leghorn, could be heard far beyond the confines of the theatre.

The weather was bad enough to deter the Germans from trying out any further sallies from their hideouts in the Apennines. Commander Allan and his flotilla of torpedo boats were ready to tackle any breakout by their counterparts based in Genoa.

I took the opportunity of taking, along with half a dozen colleagues, a rather special form of leave. We attended a Christian Leadership Course in Rome. For accommodation the RAF Chaplainship had taken over a small hostel, the Impero. Therein, we listened to our tutors under the direction of Wing-Commander Ireson. Our meals were taken a sharp march away at the 'Bon Gusto', a few strides from the Trevi Fountain. Some fifty of us, drawn from all over Italy, ranging in rank from AC2 to Squadron-Leader, enjoyed one whole week of education in religion, architecture and opera.

Our lecturers represented a cross-section of interpretation of the Bible. When I suggested that Desmond K. Dean would have extended the range of thought into the fundamentals of Christianity I was rebuffed by the director: 'Dear old soul, Desmond, but you know he is far too bigoted!' That unkind remark put me off formal religion for life. I still think of Desmond as the most sincere believer I ever met.

However, my week in Rome was a grand experience. We visited every major Church and the catacombs. We attended an audience of the Pope, Pius XII, a man of genuine humility. He spoke in numerous languages, opening his address with: 'Brothers and Sisters of Jesus Christ . . .' From there his listeners were spellbound. Those who so desired might queue to kiss his proffered hand. This practice seemed to me none too hygienic but the hand appeared unaffected by multitudinous abrasions. The bronze foot of St. Peter, in the great Cathedral, had fared considerably worse over the years. Its toes had vanished.

We ogled at the ceiling of the Sistine Chapel, wondered at the 'wedding cake' of Victor Emmanuel and marvelled at the immensity of work by Michaelangelo.

The course organisers had arranged for us all to see opera in the Reale. I knew nothing of opera but a few popular arias. It was a privilege to start near the top with *Il Trovatore*. I tried hard to enjoy it but didn't succeed. The highlight of the show came when one of the round dozen soldiers, in a march-past, turned to glance at the audience, tripped and fell flat on his face to the accompaniment of clattering armour.

Two evenings later a few of us elected to have another dip into the opera pot; this time it was *La Bohème*. Puccini got things moving fairly early in the proceedings; I began to enjoy the music until the engineer in me emerged to examine the structure of the building. I looked up to the 'gods', wondering whether anyone sitting up there could see the stage. Taking leave of my colleagues I decided to resolve the problem. Climbing one staircase after another I arrived at the top deck to find half-a-dozen rows of seats, few of which were occupied. I descended the steep stairway and selected a seat near the centre. Peering over the balcony I could just see part of the stage where miniature performers sang their pieces. The volume of sound reflected from the domed ceiling was adequate. On further observation it became clear that the front row was not popular. I noted that all other occupants of the gallery lay in their seats further back, with eyes closed. Now the penny dropped; that was the way to enjoy opera!

I moved four rows to the rear up hill. There it was impossible to see the stage. I lay back in my seat, closed my eyes and determined to become a lover of opera. I began to appreciate the music when I was gently tapped on the shoulder. The usherette beckoned me to follow her. Believing that I might have transgressed against the codes of etiquette I followed the woman. We descended to the next lower level. Now it dawned on me. The good soul was inviting me to enjoy a seat from which I might see the stage, but nay . . .! She stopped, opened the door of her broom cupboard and indicated that therein could be enjoyed other forms of entertainment! I muttered an ungrateful '*grazie*' and hastily rejoined my friends in the safety of the stalls.

So ended my flirtation with opera. Subsequently, I have found the lively humour of Gilbert and Sullivan more to my taste.

Back at Leghorn I was questioned by Bob Lewis on my experiences in Rome. He applauded my appreciation of the magnificent architecture, disapproved my opinion of opera and was in no mood to hear anything approaching a Christian mission. He didn't believe in the virgin birth, for a start, so we never got any further!

'Anyway,' he said, 'you are off to Corsica in the morning. I've booked a berth for you on the *Hornpipe*, sailing at zero seven hundred. I'll tell you all about the project after lunch. So pack your kit, you'll be gone for a week.'

Chapter 43

More Maritime Matters

HMS *Hornpipe*, commanded by Lieutenant-Commander de Lys, was bound for Bastia on the special mission of escorting an old-fashioned, long-funnelled tramp steamer, *Cardinal Richlieu*. Normally, *Hornpipe* headed the Leghorn flotilla of mine-sweepers. With the intimate knowledge of channels cleared by their own efforts the crew was well qualified to guide the uninformed.

Flight-Lieutenant Collins, the Wing Equipment Officer, accompanied me up the gangway to be welcomed by the skipper. Daylight was still an hour away; a cold wind blew down from the north and we were delighted to be shown below where hot coffee awaited us in the ward-room. It was explained to us that the painfully slow *Richlieu* would cause the voyage to take seven hours instead of the usual five. We were to 'make ourselves at home', the steward would see that we would not want for food or drink. A roughish crossing was anticipated. There being not much room to move around, it would be better if we stayed below, leaving the crew unimpeded by our presence.

We stacked our personal kit and document cases at one end of the long settee, leaving enough space for Collins to stretch himself at full length. I occupied a comfortable armchair adjacent to the pile of our belongings. We settled down to read.

A rumble from the engines, a few nautical terms heard above; we were on our way. The second officer looked in to say we might take air if we wished. Collins, immersed in his book, stayed put. I emerged from the hatch to nod farewell to Leghorn. As the *Hornpipe* emerged from the shelter of the harbour wall she started to heave. The *Richlieu* followed and began to sway, her tall funnel describing a wide arc against the clouds. I hung on to a sturdy rail, an integral part of the wheelhouse. We rolled and pitched alarmingly. This I thought is normal, so why should I worry? The ship must have withstood worse than this. As we approached the island of Gorgona I glanced behind to see the old *Richlieu*'s funnel oscillating like a drunken semaphore signaller.

As the oilskin-clad skipper forged past me he shouted something about a gale warning. I clung tightly to my bar, not daring to move and feeling very unwell. One minute I found myself staring at the rain-laden clouds, the next down into a cavernous sea. Too ill to be sick I began timing mentally the sequence of the motions. The clouds gave comfort; I visualised the blue sky beyond, there was hope there; through them in an aeroplane was Paradise. Then we rolled over to stare again into the deeps. Now I felt so ill that I contemplated letting go of my anchorage and ending the journey, but over we heeled again to view the clouds. The skipper pressed by again shouting: 'That Frenchman refuses to turn round!'

It was time for me to go below to avoid the temptation to give up sailing altogether. With cat-like care I eased myself backwards down the stairway to join Collins. He continued reading, seemingly unconcerned for his safety. I clamped myself into my armchair.

'Rough, is it?'

'The skipper looks worried,' I said, 'not so much for ourselves but for the *Richlieu*. Half the time you can see nothing of it but the funnel. We've been going for more than an hour and we haven't yet reached Gorgona.'

'You'll have to read this book, when I've finished.'

I was about to ask the title when our relationship to the horizontal altered suddenly and excessively. The ship rolled to port so steeply that our baggage fell from the settee and crashed to the opposite side of the ward-room. Collins followed.

The *Hornpipe* resumed propulsion in less violent mood. It was obvious that we had turned. Within the hour we were back in the sheltered harbour at Leghorn. I asked the skipper how he had managed to persuade the captain of the *Richlieu* to turn:

'I signalled "Minefield immediately ahead". That did the trick. I think he shipped a drop of water down the funnel in the process!'

'Is that what you call a really bad storm?' I asked.

'Never known worse,' he said. 'Picture postcards of the Mediterranean are very misleading. It comes up and goes down in ten minutes whereas the Atlantic takes time about it.'

As I waddled back to the Officers' Mess I felt thankful to be back on land, yet yearning to return to sea. The wind blew itself out during the night. My presence in Corsica being urgent, I contacted the Navy with a view to re-joining the *Hornpipe*. An alternative and more speedy vessel was available. I accepted a lift on a Motor Torpedo Boat. Its rudder was bent; a replacement was available in Bastia. In spite of the damaged steering gear which tried to turn the boat northwards throughout the voyage, we cut through the water a good deal faster than the *Hornpipe* could move. After we cleared Gorgona the waves improved in quality, causing the boat to adopt a different attitude. It cut through one wave, dropped into the subsequent trough and slapped its hull into the forthcoming wave. Thus we progressed; woops, pause, slam. The young skipper, clad in white polo-necked jersey, blond curls wafting in the wind, looked the picture of health and happiness. We roared along at about thirty knots.

'Can't go any faster,' he apologised, 'rudder's bent. Are you enjoying it?'

I confessed to feeling a bit queasy.

'Go with the swell,' he said. 'Don't try to resist the motion, that's impossible. Just clamp yourself to the boat and go with it.'

I took the advice and found it very beneficial. I began to enjoy myself. After all, here was I cruising at the King's expense. The steward joined us at the wheel: 'Breakfast's ready, Sir.'

I followed him down the few steps to the tiny ward-room which was a cavity surrounded by fuel-tanks laden with high octane petrol. The powerful smell overshadowed the odours of cookery. Two bowls of baked beans in tomato soup had been set on the table for starters. I took one look at the mixture swilling about in concert with the movement of the boat, retraced my steps and stayed aloft to face the wind and the spray for the remainder of the trip to Bastia. We weaved through the wrecks in the harbour. I set foot for the first time on the magic island of Corsica. Collins was to follow in less haste in HMS *Hornpipe*.

Meanwhile I located accommodation for the pair of us and set about the business of establishing a centre of communications for 301 Air-Sea Rescue Control Unit. Hitherto, activities in Corsica had been very much the domain of the American Forces and the British Navy. Landlines were to be transferred to the care of the French PTT; a 'secret' wireless link was to be established with Leghorn. A reliable network for the passage of information to and from ASR bases at Calvi and Ajaccio and the radar station at Cap Corse was essential. The Northern Mediterranean continued to require the vigilance of both RAF and Navy over the German Naval Forces in Genoa.

Collins was fluent in French. When he arrived we got down to serious negotiations with our allies. Lieutenant Denny, their Intelligence Officer, was wonderful company. He knew every inch of the island and gave graphic descriptions of how the local populace had suffered and survived under German occupation.

On our second day we began a tour of the island. Collins acquired a Jeep. Denny acquired a French companion of equally enchanting personality. Lieutenant Grofotteau, veterinary surgeon, was responsible for the health of the island's mules. Our first stop would be at Ajaccio, more than a hundred kilometres away on the west coast. The roads needed repair, the spectacular mountain scenery invited numerous stops, but we managed to present ourselves in time for lunch at the hotel which, Denny promised, would provide food and accommodation. It was run as an international officers' transit depot. The American administration had moved to the mainland. The French filled the vacuum. Regrettably, nobody had thought of continuing or replacing the American food distribution system.

Lunch consisted of dates, oranges and a slice of bread. Coffee tasted as though made from powdered tree-bark. Denny thought the stops would be pulled out for the evening meal. Meanwhile I had business to attend to at the airfield.

Flight-Lieutenant Fletcher, the Flying Control Officer, governed the simple aerodrome facilities. Ajaccio was now little more than a staging post. Fletcher was king. He had fallen in love with Corsica, had made arrangements to settle there as soon as he could be done with military service. I envied the lad. High on the hillside overlooking the seductive bay stood the MF/DF station and thither I was conducted by the engineer-in-charge, Lieutenant Touhémont, who occupied, with wife and family, a pleasing bungalow a stone's throw from the four red and white masts. His garden, the subject of picture postcards, contained not only flowers but a wide selection of vegetables. The view from the patio embraced acres of orange groves, sea, sand and harbour, airfield and town. No wonder the Lieutenant did not seek promotion. He and his dependents had survived the war in relative luxury.

At the hotel we gathered in anticipation of a meal of more substantial proportion than the lunch. We were to be disappointed. The thin soup, tasting possibly of cabbage and garlic, gave promise of more to come. What arrived, in lonely sublimity on each plate, we identified as a rissole. Then, with a great flourish, a waiter added a dessertspoonful of stewed spinach. *Le café de* tree-bark completed the meal and we left the table more hungry than before we started. It was obvious that the local populace was undernourished. Grofotteau was a big man. He complained bitterly. Denny bade him, '*Fermer la bouche*,' and suggested it was time the vet should sacrifice a mule or two.

Denny's further contribution to the well-being of mankind was to lead us to a 'nice little restaurant' he had heard of down by the harbour. The flaking green paint on the door was loosened irrevocably when Grofotteau beat a tattoo with his enormous fists after the gentle taps recommended by Denny elicited no response. The door remained closed but via a tiny peephole came a voice questioning our purpose. It was explained that a minimum charge of what amounted to one pound sterling was payable for a meal. We accepted that necessity is the mother of extortion, the door opened and we followed the voice up a narrow stone staircase. The room at the top was quite cosy with whitewashed walls, lights flickering and red and white chequered cloths on the tables. In an adjoining room the bar displayed a modest stock of bottles. A few customers had preceded our admission. We joined them in apéritif and conversation. The whole company deplored the lack of sustenance available through normal channels. The proprietor regretted absence of a formal menu but could offer us fresh lobster and salad. A chorus of approval included a call for refills of the apéritif.

At length we were called to be seated. A basket of bread appeared and a large carafe of *vin de maison* became a central feature of our table for four. Things were looking good. From snippets of conversation drifting through from the kitchen it seemed there was difficulty in dividing the catch of the day among an unexpectedly large number of clients. The portions of lobster served would have been better appreciated when viewed through a magnifying glass. Uncovered from liberal layerings of greenery they were at least fresh and tasty. No sooner had we started upon this rich repast than another thundering at the outer door could be heard. Denny said it would be the local gendarme calling for his peace money. That was not so.

There entered the Captain and four of his officers from an American Liberty ship. Thank goodness they were not in search of food, otherwise we would have feared for a cut in our lobster rations. They were investigating the night life ashore. What happened forthwith culminated in the establishment of a new set of standards in *entente cordialité*. The Yanks joined us in the consumption of another carafe of *vin ordinaire* and sampled the extremely well matured piece of local cheese. The tree-bark coffee was unbearable without cognac, supplies of which were soon exhausted. *Le patron* then offered crème-de-menthe and a number of liqueurs. The level of liquid in each bottle indicated that stocks were low; our combined efforts finished them off and the bar closed.

As we helped one another down the stairs the US Captain expressed his appreciation of our company in a most cordial manner; he invited us to take breakfast aboard his Liberty ship at 08.00 hrs. the coming morning. The offer was far too good to miss. It met with the especial approval of our French confederates who had survived on meagre rations long enough.

At 07.45 hrs. the four of us presented ourselves at the dock gates. The French armed guard refused ironically to allow his fellow-countrymen to enter. There was no problem *pour les Anglais* but *les Français* needed a special pass to go beyond the gates. Argument proved useless. It was all very embarrassing for Collins and myself. Our friends insisted that we go ahead and they would search for some authority where they could obtain the necessary permits.

We two RAF officers strode up the gangway of the ship to be greeted by a seaman who had been briefed to welcome us. He promised to look out for our French companions.

Not having any idea what to expect, we were surprised to find ourselves directed to a table in what can best be described as a first-class cafeteria. The open-plan kitchen boasting stainless steel fittings was staffed by chefs dressed in spotless white uniform. A handsome black waiter handed us each an extensive menu, plus a glass of fruit juice. He awaited our commands. Collins thought toast, marmalade and coffee was all that could be handled. Hangover or no hangover I could not resist an omelette.

That 'Liberty' omelette wasn't made; it was created by an artist in omelettery. It arrived on a stainless steel oval dish. Shaped and bulging like an outsized Cornish pastie, done to a turn and surrounded by grilled tomato slices and delicately cut crispy bacon, it presented a picture worthy of the front page of a glossy magazine. Collins bet I couldn't eat it but I was determined to show my appreciation of top-rank cookery. I cut off one end of the omelette and out poured blackcurrant jam. Now that has always been my favourite preserve. Truly I had never considered eating it together with bacon and egg; a combination I recommend to anyone who delights in gastronomic experimentation.

I was midway through my most enjoyable breakfast when Denny and Grofotteau arrived beaming pleasure at having obtained passes from the Town Major. They settled for gigantic portions of eggs and bacon. Our host, the Captain, joined us at the table, taking for himself a similar breakfast to that of Collins. He had regretted the unfortunate mixing of crème-de-menthe with vermouth. He did say that my appreciation of the 'Liberty' omelette had raised morale in the galley. We returned to shore feeling better fitted to continue our respective duties.

At that point we left Grofotteau to inspect his mules and Denny to do whatever a French Intelligence Officer must do. Collins and I visited the skipper and crew of the Hants and Dorset launch at the Air-Sea Rescue base before driving up the west coast of the island. The journey was not one to be hurried. From the winding road one breathtaking scene followed another. At Piana we were favoured to observe the mountains running deep down below the surface of the green-blue sea, the coloured rocks mixing pink and grey and yellow with the water. The gentle waves glistened in the sun as they lapped the cliffs to set up a kaleidoscopic fantasy of unsurpassable beauty. All the way to our destination at Calvi wonders of Nature provided continuous entertainment.

We spent the night at Calvi in the hospitable company of the Air-Sea Rescue Unit, taking note of its requirements. It was important that the boys were kept supplied with recreational facilities as well as operational necessities. Their life could entail long periods of inactivity, yet they must always be prepared to put to sea whatever the weather. The RAF was very proud of its ASR.

Following our return to Bastia we spent a day driving up to Cape Corse where the Radar station continued its vigilance over the Ligurian Sea. The American Signals Corps had established a simple landline between Bastia and the Cape. Theoretically it was so simple it must be trouble-free. Account had not been taken of Corsican sheep. They broke poles, pulled them from the ground and chewed them. If wires were buried they dragged them out and snapped them. Almost daily a repair party had to inspect and repair the line. Eventually I negotiated with the local Poste-Télégraphe-Téléphonique engineers to take over the maintenance of this line on the understanding they could adopt it for their post-war use. I promised also that RAF transport was available. The PTT chaps were delighted. I was pleased not to have my Wireless Mechanics wasting time chasing sheep.

It was fortunate that HMS *Hornpipe* should be in harbour at the conclusion of our business. What is more she was making ready to return to Leghorn. Again the cheerful Lieut.-Commander de Lys welcomed us aboard, this time to enjoy a relaxing cruise beneath a cloudless sky.

Chapter 44

Intelligence Off-Guard

In a fabulous villa situated south of Leghorn lived an expatriate native of North Yorkshire, a Mrs Carter. With rooms to spare she had been pleased to provide luxurious accommodation for Group Captain Scott as well as Captain Mackenzie RN.

Scottie phoned through to the Officers' Mess and gave me instructions of surprising originality. Normally of cheerful but disciplinary manner, on this occasion he chattered in prankish mood.

'We have a Captain King of Naval Intelligence staying with us. He is engaged on an extensive tour of fields of conflict to enlighten the troops on the course of the war in general. We, that is Captain Mackenzie and I, have decided to pull his leg. I want your co-operation.'

Always ready for a bit of tomfoolery I listened with keen interest.

'The weather has turned sour and tonight's planned raid on Genoa by the MTB boys has been cancelled. So Commander Allan and some of his chaps are calling round to pick you up, by which time you will have thought up some outrageous plot.'

My mind worked quickly enough to tell him to expect a call from a group of shipwrecked civilians, in search of accommodation.

'I'll leave it to you,' he said. 'Expect you in about an hour's time. By then we shall have finished dinner and be well charged with drinks. Oh, I must warn you that the Admiral will be joining us for dinner. He has no knowledge of this little lark.'

I commandeered a fellow member of the Concert Party. By the time the naval detachment arrived we had selected a quantity of civilian type clothes from the theatrical stores. Half a dozen of us disguised our military bearing by dressing in ill-fitting garments which would pass off hopefully as war-time civilian utilities.

Allan, too well-known to escape detection, appeared in normal uniform, as conductor of the party. One MTB skipper, wearing customary white polo-necked jersey, purported to be the Captain of the minesweeper which had rescued the occupants of a ditched aircraft.

As we piled into an estate car and drove to the villa I outlined the most unlikely tale of our misfortunes. I would make it known that I was Harold

Arkwright, head of a delegation bound for Turkey to disseminate advanced technology of the textile industry. I was MP for Heckmondwyke. My grandfather had invented the self-doffing spindle which had revolutionised the weaving trade. I was considered to be the doyen of the Yorkshire woollen industry.

Group Captain Scott welcomed us over the door-step at which point I warned him rapidly of the theme. He had primed already the unsuspecting guests, all of whom were internally warmed by alcoholic refreshment to the point of not being more than idly inquisitive.

Drinks were served to all newcomers; discussion groups thrived on incredible versions of our rescue. I found myself being questioned closely by the Admiral who was anxious for news of what life was like in England. He soon fell to reminiscence of his younger days in the navy, how he had enjoyed his sea-going days, how he yearned to be out there with his boys tonight battling with the waves and Germans. Dammit, he had become a parasite!

'It's those lads out there at sea, as I speak to you, who are fighting the war.'

He looked directly at one of 'those lads', a stocky young Lieutenant disguised as a shipwrecked civilian.

One group picked up snatches of conversation from another. Exaggeration added to exaggeration; incredibly our stories were believed and enjoyed. Even Captain King, the visiting Intelligence Officer, direct from UK, seemed delighted to hear yarns of Yorkshire.

With superb timing, Scottie took me to one side, suggesting that it was time for the 'civilians' to be taken to safe accommodation for the night. Things had gone far enough; any more acting and the bluff would be called. We accepted the good wishes rained upon us and retreated into the rain.

Back at the RAF headquarters we restored our civilian wear to storage and celebrated our success in appropriate fashion.

I was at my desk in the Signals Office when, at 09.30 the following morning, the 'phone rang. It was a very concerned Group Captain:

'I'm in hot water,' he said. 'Captain King came down to breakfast a very worried man. He has castigated himself severely for not checking on the identity of "those damned people" who invaded our privacy. I have been obliged to explain that I am responsible for the joke. That made matters worse. He, as a Senior Intelligence Officer, is supposed to be a spy-catcher!'

The harbour-side theatre was filled to capacity by soldiers, sailors and airmen. Captain King prefaced his lecture on 'The War in the Far East' with the following remark:

'Good evening to you all. I am afraid the RAF got at me last night. I was hoodwinked good and proper. In the front row I recognise perpetrators of the practical joke for which I fell. With one eye on these people I remind myself of the well-known words of wisdom: Careless Talk Costs Lives!'

The venerable Captain proceeded to deliver his well-prepared talk, unmolested and in masterly fashion. Valued information on the war in the Far East broadened our vision beyond our necessarily limited horizons. It set us wondering also whether some of us might be called further afield in the very near future. It was obvious that the end of the war in Europe must be no more than weeks away.

Some of our number had arrived at Leghorn only just in time to embellish their uniforms with the 'Italy Star'. It seemed logical that the latest arrivals were at a Staging Post for Japan. Captain King was not to be drawn into discussion of such possibilities. Whatever the object of the amiable Captain's visit may have been, his subject did set the machinery of rumours in motion. To his own vast store of experiences he admitted to be adding memories of an embarrassing encounter with the Royal Air Force.

Chapter 45

Italian Priorities

The valley of the Arno collects water in abundance from predominantly mountainous Tuscany, so much of it that the Arno delta country is a veritable bog. The roads run straight and narrow between bends and bridges.

On a solo journey to Pisa airfield I was overtaken by an American army truck going at a speed which rendered it incapable of negotiating safely the forthcoming right-angled bend. I did not see the accident. When I arrived at the bend the scene of disaster was distressing and at the same time amusing. The donkey lay dead and its aged owner lay equally mortified beside it. The wrecked cart, strewn over the roadside, had carried large containers of Chianti which now flowed in streams of various intensity from the damaged vessels. Screaming women from nearby cottages wielded jugs and other domestic utensils capable of retrieving some of the precious liquid. Men stepped over the corpses determined to salvage some of the bulk supplies, as yet unspilled.

The US army vehicle had not stopped, yet its driver must surely have been aware of the impact. There was nothing I could do to aid the dead and certainly nothing I would do to help the clearing of booty. I circumvented the chaos and drove on towards my objective. The road being devoid of further traffic and my mission being of no great urgency I pulled into a side lane with the intention of meditating over my recent experience. The engine stopped to enhance a peaceful rural setting. A lone worker paddled about in the reeds at the edge of the watery waste searching for I knew not what. True, there came over the mountains to the north a few puffs of distant gunfire, otherwise the war seemed to be over and done; the sun blazed from a pink-blue sky. My thoughts turned from the dead man and his donkey to poetry and the forthcoming peace.

A single high-flying Spitfire appeared from over the Garfagnana range. It hovered, its engine spluttered, it accelerated vertically to plunge into the marshland. The parachuting pilot swung gracefully suspended by shining white strings. Calmly he surveyed the uninviting quagmire below. I lost sight of him as he plunged amongst the reeds half a mile away. I was powerless to do anything toward immediate assistance but the peasant was seen to climb into a flat-bottomed boat and punt away for all he was worth. I wondered whether he would have exercised himself equally strenuously had the unfortunate aviator been a member of the Luftwaffe. The general cry of the Italian proletariat was now: '*Inglese* – very good; *Tedescho* – no good,' perpetuating a remarkable affinity for feigning allegiance to an occupying force of any persuasion. I felt confident that the pilot would eventually be delivered to friendly villagers on the distant side of the broad marsh.

The whole of the Arno valley including Pisa was now secure in allied control. Hard fighting continued around Rimini where the mountains meet the sea. The narrow gap presented a natural barrier to the efforts of our forces whose objective was to break into the Po valley. On the western side of Italy we enjoyed immunity from further attack by the Germans. Fraternisation with our co-belligerents was encouraged to the extent of our organising a joint social gathering in the Officers' Mess at Livorno. In conversation with Lieut. Brugiatelli, an accountant with an exceptional knowledge of languages, I broached the subject of priorities by asking what he thought the Italians would do to celebrate the eventual proclamation of peace. He declared quite seriously that they would organise motor-cycle races throughout the land. It would not be many months before I witnessed one such hair-raising event.

Chapter 46

Napoleon's Island

The intrepid Commander Allan RN and his daredevil torpedoists repeatedly attacked the German naval forces at La Spezia and Genoa. Yet the enemy continued to threaten our shipping in the northern Mediterranean. The radar station at Cap Corse must maintain constant watch. Furthermore Air-Sea Rescue services were required around Corsican coasts. American land forces had transferred their presence to southern France. Whilst a small French contingent remained on the island the main occupying power was the Royal Air Force.

I considered myself fortunate to be appointed Signals Officer to what was formally known as No. 301 Air-Sea Rescue Control Unit. For two happy months I reigned almost as uncrowned king of Corsica. A couple of Squadron-Leaders floated about the place sharing the duties of Senior Flying Control Officer. There was little flying to control and they never interfered with my responsibilities. I regarded Jake, at Naples, as my immediate superior.

I acquired luxury accommodation in a bombed building which served as cookhouse, Ops. Room, Officers' Mess and Leisure Centre. The weather turned up trumps. From my bedroom window I looked down upon the wreck-strewn harbour of Bastia. Way out across the sea the high points of Elba added interest to the horizon. The church spires of Pianosa served as compass checks. Altogether a holiday setting.

My first priority was the establishment of a secret wireless link with 338 Wing HQ at Leghorn. Thus sightings of German raiders might be transmitted without the enemy being aware of counter-attack.

In conference with my senior NCOs the decision was made to erect a 'Zambesi' aerial in a narrow valley, the mouth of which faced our target seventy-odd miles north-east. Theory went into practice. The design called for careful siting of poles in the rocky ground, the stringing of seemingly endless wires to include a precision-built transmission line back to the little T.1083 transmitter in the Ops. Room. Completed with great enthusiasm by the technicians, our masterpiece required proof of efficiency.

Bets were taken on degrees of success. I prevailed upon the men of wings to provide a Wellington aircraft to be flown up and down, round and round on planned flight-paths. For much of the time the Wellington was in sight so that the ground staff could take a direct interest in the experiment. It became clear that we would have reason to be proud of our well-executed system. We celebrated the result: a beam no greater than 2° in spread, a result which received favourable comment from the upper hierarchy. All the participants in the construction of our 'Zambesi' proudly claimed a modicum of credit for a part in the final demise of the German Navy in the Med.

I devoted considerable effort to provide entertainment for the chaps. Taylor and Thomas came over from the mainland and visited the various units around the island. Wherever a piano could be found, Ronnie Taylor could amuse audiences which often included members of the swarthy Corsican populace. Many of our airmen had been established on the island long enough in time to make personal friends in town and village.

One day the mess Sergeant came to me asking whether I was ever likely to use again the pair of Dunlop thigh boots which had accompanied me on my journeyings. I had used them once only since landing at Algiers. He said he could sell them to a local fisherman who would put them to good use. I agreed and away went the boots with a promise of cash to follow.

The next day the Sergeant presented me with the princely sum of £5 worth of francs. I said:

'Well, that's splendid, Sergeant. They cost me thirty-four shillings in 1934 – a handsome profit indeed. Let's split it down the middle, shall we?'

'Oh, no, Sir,' he replied. 'I can assure you I saw myself all right at point of sale!'

Black marketing was rife on the island. There was a lot of money about and not much to buy, except fish, eggs and oranges. The British Army was responsible for feeding us, a small supply boat coming over from Naples at unscheduled intervals. There being only about a hundred of us scattered around the coast we could not be classified as 'high priority'. Our diet lacked variety. Surprised we were then, when one lunchtime we were served rice pudding and prunes. This called for great rejoicing. The sweet course at dinner-time included rice pudding and prunes. For breakfast on the following morning rice pudding and prunes were available. The popularity of both waned at the succeeding lunchtime when inquiries were made of our venerable Mess Sergeant as to the expected duration of supplies.

It appeared that a small shipload of prunes and rice had been delivered to Naples, so small that the authorities there considered it quite inadequate for normal distribution. Bastia was chosen as a suitable destination for the whole consignment. So rice pudding and prunes constituted a major part of our diet until VE day.

On that glorious day of May when victory in Europe was officially announced I found myself to be the senior Officer on the island. No Squadron-Leader could be found. The Town Mayor sent a messenger calling for the representation of the Royal Air Force at his Victory Parade in the town square. At the head of the parade I was photographed, garlanded and kissed by many maidens and elder womenfolk.

Overcome by the importance of the occasion and its embarrassments I was grateful to return to my office for a rest. There I found a signal instructing me to return to Leghorn immediately to take up a new appointment. Though all aircraft were 'grounded' officially to allow celebrations to be conducted in greater safety arrangements were made for me to fly back to Pisa in the ASR Walrus. I had not flown since leaving Algeria; what a thrill it was to take to the air again, especially in this fascinating machine. When the Flight-Sergeant pilot started the engine a vibro-massage effect emphasised the din; open-air flying is my favourite way of getting about and with the propeller out of sight behind the wings the magic carpet sensation is unmistakable.

We took off from the Bastia airfield and saluted the celebrationists still cavorting on the quaysides. Then, buzzing only a couple of hundred feet above a glass-like sea, my attention was drawn to the sight of half-a-dozen mines floating green and safe at anchor. The position being noted we flew on to report the matter at our destination. My desire for a 'landing' on the water could not be fulfilled. My pilot indicated that his orders were to put down at Pisa; time being of no importance, however, he did provide me with advantageous views of the Leaning Tower and the great Cathedral.

Chapter 47

Peace in our Time

For five and a half years we had been organised for war. What were we to do in peace?

Celebrations were inevitable. All ranks were called to a mighty gathering. The cooks produced an incredible variety of snacks. Barrels of Chianti provided a plentiful supply of liquid refreshment. A kind of thin beer was available to satisfy the few abstemious participants.

Wireless operator crews from our outstations joined us to renew old friendships. The crew from Elba included a Glaswegian named Middleton. Prior to his despatch to Elba three months previously he had not spoken a word of Italian. During the height of the merriment my friend Brugiatelli inquired: 'This fellow called Jock. How does he come to speak Italian with a Bolognesian accent?' I explained Jock's sojourn in Elba. Brugiatelli said he would report this extraordinary marriage of languages to his literary college. Jock was very impressed and said he would, on his return to his native land, consider resigning his job as a railway truck driver and explore the possibilities of entering the academic world.

Talk turned generally to the subject of demobilisation. Opinionated colleagues advised me that as a member of a Technical Branch I was most unlikely to be demobilised for years. My application for a permanent commission was on its way through the various channels of officialdom. When my father wrote to me inquiring whether he should sell the family business or hang on to it for my ultimate home-coming I replied by advising him to sell it. It seemed probable that I should find myself being despatched to the Far East where the war continued with unabated fury.

Another important subject to be discussed amongst my fellows was the political situation at home. When the results of the general election, held on my birthday, 26 July, indicated a clear victory for the Labour Party a great cheer came up from the Wireless Room. Our Chief Superintendent, Sergeant Jacques, an ex-employee of the Birmingham Gas Board, joyfully entered the Signals Officers' sanctum wielding a copy of the news from London. He boldly proclaimed 'the dawn of a new era'.

The north of Italy took on the mantle of a true holiday region, the prime attraction being Venice. Our military authority, with an extraordinary stroke of

293

wisdom, set up an Officers' Club just round the corner from St. Mark's Square. Together with a select company of other ranks from the Signals Section Bob Lewis and I made it convenient to visit the priceless city. The army provided motor launches to establish a veritable water-bus service which conveyed anyone free of charge between convenient points of the city and out to the Lido. Gondola services fitted in between the great waves churned up by the hurrying power boats. Everybody was very happy. Shopkeepers set about the new era with eyes upon future profits. People rushed about on foot or bicycle, with or without tyres. There was no need for a rush; it just seemed to be the right thing to do.

One enthusiastic sergeant-pilot of a water-bus opened the throttle with such determination that three nuns, not yet seated in the stern of the vessel, were alarmingly caught off balance. The gallant rescuers, including the sergeant, expressed sincere apologies for inconvenience caused to which the ladies replied by giving thanks to the Holy Preserver.

Relaxations in our freedom from the threats of enemy action brought about the uneasy feeling that we were now all redundant. What did the future hold? Japan or UK? Individual discussions delved into flights of fancy. Still, it seemed that my own services would continue to be required. Indeed I hoped so, for I had no definite civilian employment to return to in UK. Relieved I was, indeed, on returning from Venice to Wing Headquarters to find instructions for my transfer to Bologna.

Immediately I was provided with a driver and a Bedford truck to take over command of 301 Mobile Signals Unit from a Flight-Lieutenant Hopper. Further, I was to set up a new organisation to be known as Aircraft Safety Centre (Northern Italy) using as a nucleus the equipment of the MSU.

By very good fortune our approach to the city was obstructed by troop movements. Hazarding a guess at a diversionary route my worthy driver steered a course along a narrow and picturesque lane, passing between two very desirable-looking residences. On the closed gate of each driveway a notice proclaimed the presence of a Polish regiment which I knew had moved from the area a few days earlier. I found 301 MSU wallowing in a smelly farmyard. The horrifying sight of flies battling their ways under mosquito nets incensed me into being extremely curt with Mr Hopper. I interrupted his well-meaning introduction to the administration of the unit. Though he was posted to a transit camp for onward movement, he hoped to UK, he would, he said, be prepared to see me settled in at the farmstead. I thanked him for the offer but assured him that I had no intention of staying even one night in such an unhealthy location. He would, I requested, despatch himself with all haste to his new appointment. Selecting two capable senior NCOs to accompany me, I drove into Bologna.

The Town Major had no objection to my taking over the two buildings I had observed on the outskirts of the city. Thence my small inspection party drove to ascertain the suitability of the properties for our use. We were well satisfied.

One building had the appearance of a small 'palace'. The other comprised what must have been servants' quarters and dairy. Beautiful gardens surrounded the complex. The 'palace' would function as Officers' Mess, Operations Room and Signals Office. Whilst I checked the dimensions of the main rooms Sergeant Higgins roamed the grounds and outhouses. He summoned me to inspect an underground passageway. At the end of the passage a brick wall had been breached within the past 24 hours. Through it we passed and beheld a store fit for a king. Hams, carboys of *vino*, bottles containing the better wines, cheeses galore plus a variety of delectables which had quite obviously been sealed beyond the reach of prying Germans for the past few years. We touched nothing but withdrew in silent contemplation, hurrying back to the unwholesome farmyard.

All hands of my new unit set to with a will, packed the vehicles and made a thankful retreat from their awful camp. When they saw their new abode great rejoicings rang across the gardens. Their new CO was automatically accepted as a reasonable sort of fellow.

I had selected my own sleeping quarters and conjured up the compliments I would receive from my superiors when they came to examine my organisation. My reverie was disrupted by Sergeant Higgins who announced: 'Some bastard has sealed up the wall again.' I confirmed his observation. The mortar was still wet! Our arrival must have been monitored. We had been served a dirty trick, which may have saved us some measure of embarrassment under Italian Civil Law. Comforting ourselves that 'what you never have you never miss' we emerged into the evening twilight to come face to face with the rightful owner of the property and his very attractive wife.

We were in luck. The lady, of Welsh birth, was a professor of languages at the University. Her frail husband had suffered in prison at the hands of the Mussolini regime. A skilled surgeon, he was unlikely to be able to continue in his delicate work in the near future. They expressed the hope that we would take care of the premises as the Poles had done. I assured the charming couple that their wishes were as good as fulfilled. I was invited to dinner at their apartment in the city the following evening. I shall never forget that dinner. I got the impression that my hosts and their friends – I think ten people in all were at table – had ample stocks of food and liras tucked away. Some looked exceptionally well-fed and struck me as recent collaborators with whatever regime may have been in power. The dear old surgeon had been unlucky enough to reveal his true colours and had gone 'inside'. I did not care to go into too much detail, enjoyed a sumptuous meal, drank far too much wine; no mention was made, by either side, of the hidden treasure.

Early in August the Japanese people were rendered dead or impotent by the atom bombs. Aircraft Safety Centre grew into a thoroughly efficient peacetime utility. My own command did not last long for 301 MSU was disbanded. German prisoners of war built for us a very substantial transmitter hall at the top of the hill above the palace. We removed the transmitters from the vehicles and installed them in the new building. A receiving station was housed in a room of the palace. My Signals Office looked out on the garden. The indispensable Air Formation Signals unit came under the command of the efficient Major Dangerfield. The speed with which this unit connected transmitters to the receivers, the outpost Alpine rescue parties and our own Air-Sea Rescue Units to the Operations Room was not short of magic.

Redundant, tour-expired, time-expired, cheesed-off and thoroughly tired ex-pilots were available to fill any odd job whilst awaiting repatriation or demobilisation. A Wing Commander took up office at Bologna and there were enough Squadron-Leaders milling around to fill any vacancy which could be created. My favourite of these was 'Dinger' Bell who occupied the essential position of Chief Flying Control Officer. He and I got on famously. Within three weeks Aircraft Safety Centre became an operational reality.

Our purpose was to keep watch over the northern Mediterranean and the Adriatic. Any aircraft transmitting a distress call would be sure of our attention. It was a grand set-up with ASR launches strategically located round the coasts, direction-finder stations at the alert on mountain-tops and homing stations listening at the airfields.

The final testing of the HF/DF station at the end of the runway at Bologna brought to light a serious problem. The Wellington aircraft provided for the calibration was piloted to perfection. It circulated time and again but the calibration chart showed consistent inaccuracy towards the north. Nothing geographically could be blamed so we called the patient pilot to abandon the test. When questioned he could throw no light on the reason for such discrepancy.

In my wisdom I had included in my working party the invaluable Jock Middleton, he of the Bolognesian accent. It was clear that there must be some metal deposits within the vicinity of the airfield. Whilst my NCOs checked and rechecked the installation of the four aerial masts and the cable connections, our Jock wandered off to chat up a peasant working on his vines. His inquiries revealed the cause of our problem: during the days of heavy fighting a German bomber had plunged to earth in a high-speed dive and hit soft ground in the vineyard.

Jock's new-found friend burst with excitement. To be in the important position of principal informer broke the monotony of endless weeding. He described how local metal collectors had taken anything portable from the wreckage yet had left huge chunks of *Tedesco aeroplano* to be buried under layers of his valuable soil. He pointed out the recently planted stock which marked the precise area required to be explored. Our engineers produced a Coles crane, a tractor and a group of burly German prisoners of war. Merrily did the Germans set to work in search of their lately own property.

Within a few hours the Wellington renewed its orbital test flights whereupon a highly satisfactory calibration chart confirmed that Bologna HF/DF was ready to offer navigational aid as a vital service to any aircraft which chose to call us. The gleeful vintager was permitted a brief viewing and hearing of our procedures inside the hut. A rare tale he would take to his family and compatriots.

Though Wing Commander MacDonald reigned as titular CO of Aircraft Safety Centre (Northern Italy) it was I to whom everybody turned for information about the set-up. After all I had discovered the fabulous quarters in which all personnel dwelt in veritable luxury compared with the conditions in which some of my colleagues had survived during the past five years. Most of the airmen were ex-301 MSU and known to me. My Wireless Operators were experienced and efficient. The Senior NCOs supervised the technology and my Signals Office Clerk, LAC Pragnell, formerly an Insurance Agent from Exeter, conducted, in exemplary fashion, the day-to-day running of the office. I was lucky beyond expectations. Free to roam as technical inspector I acquired a Model 16H Norton motor-bike, making good use of it for business and a modicum of pleasure.

It was on the Norton that I entered the exclusive circle of the Bologna Motor Cycle Club. This enterprising organisation included among its membership the great Omobono Tenni, winner of the 1937 Lightweight TT Race in the Isle of Man. (Not only did he win the race; he broke also the lap record at 77 m.p.h. at the same time entertaining the spectators with a superb demonstration of neatness in cornering. Tenni promised me he would be back in the island as soon as conditions permitted. He did not disappoint; in 1948 he entered the Senior race on a twin-cylinder Moto-Guzzi and showed the way round four out of the six laps whereafter the engine revolted and Tenni finished ninth. Sadly he died a few weeks later whilst practising for the Swiss Grand Prix.) At Bologna I was introduced to Tenni's protegé, Ferdinando Balzarotti, who offered me a ride on his Moto-Guzzi. Of course the 16H Norton was no machine to enter the sport and one look at the crowds massed for the most advantageous view deterred me from trying out a Guzzi. The course followed the tramlines around part of the city. The spectators stood *en masse* in the road and parted just sufficiently to leave a gap for the speedmasters to pass through; the gap then closed so that the fast disappearing machines could be observed from the rear. My in-built safety factor predicted trouble. The ambulance service did a roaring trade, not because of motor-cycle accidents but in rescuing crushed pedestrians. When the supply of ambulances proved to be inadequate some wise official called off the event, much to the relief of Tenni and his colleagues.

Very few calls from aircraft in distress disturbed the tranquillity of Aircraft Safety Centre (Northern Italy). Nevertheless, our sphere of operational facilities continued to be expanded. Group Captain Vickers, Chief Signals Officer, inspected our assemblage, expressed his approval and announced that an additional responsibility to be added to our repertoire would be the establishment of communications with and operational control of the Italian sea-plane base at Venice. Forthwith our worthy Wing Commander took up temporary residence at the Italian Naval Station on the Lido. He would discuss broadly, with the base commander, the objects of combined services. Within a few days a small contingent of specialist officers would join him to 'tie up' the details.

To fulfil this last requirement four of us set forth in the Piper, piloted by 'Sammy' Sampson who knew his way around Italy like the back of his hand, as the saying goes. We landed on the small strip within the naval barracks area. Twilight descended as we alighted from the plane, to be greeted by a naval rating who required us to move off immediately. We were informed that no accommodation for officers was available at the place, neither was safe haven for our little Piper possible. He insisted that we must take off for Mestre. Sammy took a dim view of this and as we circled in the darkness he said he wasn't quite sure where Mestre was, but I was happy to recognise that he was pulling our respective legs. We got down all right and found a few RAF 'bods' about the place, even a transportation officer who provided us with a truck and driver. So we arrived at the Venice terminus where we were lucky to board a water-bus which delivered us to Piazza San Marco.

The cooks at the Officers' Club (officially known as a Transit Camp) had mastered yet another disguise for bully beef and army biscuits. The main course was followed by fresh peaches from Verona of which unlimited supplies were available; then the inevitable Chianti by the tumblerful to restore our faith in our fortunes. I checked the time-table to ensure that we could take a water-bus across to the Lido where we were due to meet the 'Wingco' and the Italian Naval Captain at 10.00 hrs. the following morning.

We boarded the water-bus at 09.00 hrs. for the twenty-minute run across to the Lido. Leaving its moorings in great haste the vessel turned towards the Grande Canale. I was not perturbed, believing the manoeuvre to be a navigational necessity. When Santa Maria di Salute appeared to our port side, however, I sensed we had problems of my own making. I inquired of the sergeant at the helm whither we were heading. He informed me that a new schedule came into operation from this very day. Service to the Lido was discontinued. I had failed to read the small print! There was no alternative to completing the round voyage to the terminus and back.

An hour later we found ourselves at the San Marco quay hailing the stoutest gondola proprietor in sight. Never mind the price, nor the weather (it had turned decidedly choppy). The gondolier protested that it was most unusual to attempt the passage under present conditions. A few extra lira and we set course. Encouraging words directed at the stalwart fellow's left ear assisted him in his arduous task. Business being quiet, the taxi driver sitting in his tyreless vehicle on the slipway smiled at our discomfort. Rattling and clattering on the rims we made the rendezvous just one hour late. The Wing Commander's blood pressure could be measured at a distance. His Italian companion, superior in rank, grinned sympathetically. Following a successful conference we four participants, having played our parts in the cementing of Anglo-Italian relations, returned to Marco, there recovering our respective equilibria. The vermouth was good and cheap.

Sammy piloted us safely back to Bologna the following morning. I was prepared to receive a rollicking from the CO for my mismanagement of the transportation. However, such had been the hospitality of the Italian naval forces that when finally he returned to the 'palace', he was in extraordinary good cheer. Naples HQ had complimented him on the success of our negotiations. Aircraft Safety Centre (Northern Italy) was a vital and thriving element of the Royal Air Force.

Happily, our services were rarely called upon and now that the excitement of building up the organisation was over and done I began to feel underoccupied if not redundant. Even visits to Venice began to pall. As a diversion a foursome took the Ford V-8 shooting brake to view Lake Garda where the rain was in the process of topping up the water level. On the outskirts of Verona we were invited to inspect a peach farm. The proprietor distressfully conducted us between rows and rows of dripping trees. Rotting peaches lay on the ground over which we splodged. The fruit had been offered gratis to the RAF, the offer being refused regretfully though it would have been very acceptable to a ration-starved Britain. Transportation would have interfered with our normal services.

Though quite bored with the lack of urgent work, I had to admit to a sense of achievement. Surrounded by friends and living in comparative luxury, master of the technical organisation built up under my own direction, I started a fight against complacency. The RAF had invested a lot of money in my training. I felt worthy of promotion. Yet my world began to disintegrate. Many of my fellow officers were being demobilised. My administrative superiors assured me that my membership of the Technical Branch assured my retention into a distant future. The thinking was logical. The politicians were not. At the end of October I boarded a train at Milan bound for an uncertain future as a civilian. The termination of 'Lease-Lend' had caused a great determination in government circles to cut expenses. My little empire at Bologna must function without me – for how long I would not know. I have never returned to that beautiful city.

Chapter 48

Route to Uncertainty

The fabulous scenery of northern Italy did much to dispel the chagrin of sudden departure from my comfortable life at Bologna. The splendid tree-covered mountains surrounding Lago Maggiore and the sparkle of Alpine snow together formed paradisic landscapes as the train climbed to Domodossola. There we stopped in a deep pocket of the foothills whilst the Swiss railways took us in hand. Immediately we felt the benefit of the special steam-heater attachment at the rear of the train. We entered the Simplon tunnel in style.

Our emergence into Switzerland brought us into yet another panoramic galaxy. The unforgettable sight of electric trains winding through snow-laden forests banished all worries about the future. Our own track meandered down to Brig. Onward we sped beside the scintillating Rhône to the shores of Lake Geneva; a brief but magical sight of the Chateau de Chillon before halting at Geneva. There the train was boarded by numerous officials whose primary objective was the encouragement of tourism. Samples of chocolate were gratefully received.

Night began at the French border where we lost the benefit of the steam-heater. Precious whisky rations aided our passage through freezing France. Dawn broke at the outskirts of Paris. The distant view of the Eiffel Tower did nought to raise our spirits. The train stopped in the middle of a marshalling yard. Hundreds of war-wearied folk begged for any goods which might be spared. Exchanges of blankets for bottles of wine improved *entente cordiale*. The train chugged away to the cheers of the crowd; through a rain-soaked wilderness to Dieppe where the November fog heralded our nearness to Blighty.

The faithful old *Isle of Thanet* appeared grossly inadequate to bear so large a number of troops. Her paddles churned deeply into the English Channel as the engines gave of their venerable best.

Regardless of rank, the mass of passengers huddled against one another, behind bulkheads, coils of rope, any item of deck machinery which afforded a modicum of protection from the mist-laden draughts. We represented a miserable example of society. Memories of sunny Italy and Swiss trains contrasted with the murky outlook from our struggling ship. Few words were spoken until some unwise but comparatively alert observer on the starboard bow yelled:

300

'Look: Beachy Head!'

An immediate wholesale shift to that side of the aching paddler caused a serious list. The port-side paddle being relieved of duty caused upset in the engine-room. A stern voice implored instant return to larboard of those who had bestirred themselves from stupor. A dramatic levelling of the deck gave promise of a safe arrival at Newhaven.

Though unpicturesque the railway platform was dry and solid. Our arrival coincided with that of the London Symphony Orchestra, fresh from a concert tour in Germany. Members and their instruments underwent a lengthy and thorough examination by His Majesty's Customs and Excise Officers. Not surprisingly, we militarists were instructed to wait.

A young Flight-Lieutenant of our company was recognised by a member of the local RAF Police. Leaving his kit on the platform he strode away with his friend to the comforts of the guardroom.

All in good time the musicians and their gear boarded a train which steamed away to the Capital. Another train arrived. The Customs wallahs ushered us aboard. They were desirous of terminating their day's work, had no wish to inspect us or our baggage and clearly wanted us out of their way without further delay. With rising hopes we willingly cleared the platform except for the kit of the wayward Flight-Loot. He was found to be somewhat under the influence of alcohol. He received the especial attention of the Customs Officers who expressed their displeasure by searching his kit before the eyes of the now curiously interested passengers on the waiting train. Numerous items were counted as contraband and the unfortunate officer was obliged to relinquish a collection of souvenirs of his wartime experiences. Happily fortified by impounded Scotch whisky supplied by his friend he bore no grudge; he slept all the way to Brighton.

We looked forward to spending our first night on our home ground in the Metropole Hotel. This hostelry displayed severe signs of wartime wear and tear but the beds looked inviting enough. We lost no time in turning in, expecting to get a good night's kip. Alas, we were disappointed. Earlier in the day the Australian company which had resided in the Metropole awaiting embarkation had been moved to Southampton pending their shipment home on the troopship *Orion*. Conditions on the ship were less than satisfactory to the Australian warriors. They revolted. Refusing to stay even one night on the ship they were transported back to the Metropole. The noise of their invasion of our privacy was reminiscent of a cavalry charge.

My own bed was one of twenty in a room designed to take two or three in normal times. The door was burst open by half a dozen irate Aussies who announced their intention of setting up a card school to which we were all invited. Protests from a bunch of Pommies would have signalled full scale war. We agreed to accommodate them at one end of the room if we could be allowed to remain horizontal and physically undisturbed. Truly, these two privileges were allowed but sleep was out of the question. Gambling stakes of high orders, placed upon the table with tremendous audible firmness, grew throughout the remainder of the night. Any sign of an objection from any member of our party drew forth the most outrageous descriptions of the British heritage. When a sergeant of the Army Movement Control gave us an early call we Brits made haste to Brighton station, greatly relieved by our release from the company of our Antipodean allies.

It was disclosed that we were now destined to be demobilised officially at Hednesford, where we would be provided with civilian clothing. *En route* we changed trains at Waterloo where a fellow officer expressed his satisfaction at once again observing the behaviour of personnel in a well-ordered city. Thereupon I took note of the smooth actions of the station porters, the unflappable demeanour of the guards, the indifference of pedestrians to the noise around them, in short, characteristic British stoicism. Such contrast, all this, with the unpredictability of the Italians and the dire indiscipline of the North Africans with whom we had all been acquainted in varying degrees for the past three years. Thenceforth, I began to appreciate, more than thitherto, my Englishness. I recalled the enthusiastic outburst of Sergeant Jacques. I would enjoy being witness to 'the dawn of a new era'. Forward into socialism with the newly elected Labour Government.

Reintroduction to civilian life began at Hednesford. Row after row of suits, trousers, jackets and coats hung temptingly from hangers. Under the helpful supervision of civilian attendants we were at liberty to choose from the vast array of 'Utility' garments. In haste to be away home I made the unfortunate choice of a blue pin-striped suit and a fawn overcoat, both ill-fitting; neither was to be approved by my wife.

Happily, we were allowed to retain our uniforms during three months of paid leave following 'demob'. After handing over my unused pistol and my gas-mask I signed off, thus absolving the government of responsibility for my welfare. Rail passes in hand we joyously scrambled through a chaotic round of back-slapping farewells: 'Keep in touch.' 'Well, that's that.' 'Let's hope it's the last one.' 'Where are you going?' 'Got a job lined up?' 'What happened to old Fuckdust?' 'Pity old Willie got the chop, nice chap.' 'Best of luck, old man.' 'Got to find a house first.' 'You'll be lucky!' 'Must buy a car.' 'They say the dockers are coming out on strike.' 'Don't be stupid. We've got a Labour Government now, so they won't strike against their own.' 'They bloody well will, you know.' 'Unions will have a whale of a time, you see.' 'Don't believe it.' 'Going to Birmingham?' 'Right, I've got to go that way. I'll join you.'

At Birmingham I telegraphed to Lilian my expected time of arrival in Hereford. I found time to pop into a sweet shop intending to buy an assortment for the family. Selection complete I inquired the cost. Then came the unexpected question: 'What about coupons?' An explanation of my ignorance in the matter cut no ice with the shopkeeper.

Unequipped with peace offerings I alighted at Hereford. Lilian looked more beautiful than ever as mother of the two boys. Michael John, the blonde, curly-headed laughtermonger now four years old would have welcomed me whatever my shape and size. Philip Gordon, born during my absence and now two-and-a-half years of age, was dressed in a bright red coat (how Lilian loves colour), dark-haired like his Dad. This was my family. I must lose no time in finding a means of supporting them. With overseas allowances *et al.* my income had reached the incredible heights of £13 per week. This would now diminish and, after three months, vanish.

Meanwhile we walked, all four of us, the youngsters seemingly delighted to have this new addition to their entourage. Arriving at Lilian's parental home, a council house in Ledbury Road, the welcome could not have been more sincere. Mum and Dad (ex-Durham Light Infantry of World War I) expressed genuine delight that I was home again safe and sound. Lilian's brother welcomed me too. Uncle Basil, at the age of nineteen, had found himself driving a tank in the 8th Army, had 'done' the lot from Alamein to Knightsbridge, from Mareth to Sicily, from Reggio to the Sangro River where he celebrated his 21st birthday by stopping a German explosive with his war machine. Discharged as 'psycho-neurotic' he currently walked around Hereford clearly labelled: 'Please return to . . .' He was 'getting better' but it was apparent to me that the seven of us could not live together in harmony once the joyous days of reunion lost novelty value.

The next move took us to Thirsk for a reunion with my own family. My father yearned for me to 'go into business' with him. I knew that could not have been an agreeable partnership. With two hands on the steering wheel the vehicle would have crashed. Nevertheless, once the niceties of the homecoming had been overcome I left my family in temporary care of my parents and set forth in search of, quite frankly, I knew not what. An infinite number of indefinite possibilities titillated my fertile mind.

Father had indicated that limited financial assistance could be made available should I decide upon a renewed venture into retailing. He continued to hope that I could find a suitable ironmongery shop to which I could attach a radio department and in which he could participate. In deference to this I did look into establishments as far apart as Wigton in Cumberland and Wigston Magna in Leicestershire. Neither place attracted me, nor could I suppress my memories of Bologna, Ajaccio and the clicking of cicadas in oleanders and the slopping splashes of the waves against the banks of the Canale di San Marco. I must think again. Oh, God, perhaps I was not a settler. I was born to be a traveller – but then I had undertaken to find a home for my own family – a commitment of the greatest importance.

It did not occur to me to seek advice at any such organisation as a Rehabilitation Bureau. I planned exploration of three possible sources of income: employment in the retail trade, manufacturing, or self-employment as a retailer.

First I arranged an appointment with Mr David Robinson at Bedford. His one shop in the city displayed lampshades and a few electrical appliances; radio sets were difficult to obtain. Likewise his motor business lacked stock. He impressed me greatly with his systematic approach to business, said he aimed at expansion. He asked me to join him on a three-month trial basis to see how we worked together. I agreed this to be advisable. Had I been able to find accommodation for my family I would have taken up the offer. The local estate agents could not assist; I wondered how they made a living. So I left Mr Robinson to get along without me, which he did. Robinson Rentals and Rentaset became one of the success stories of the century, enabling Sir David to buy Kempton Park racecourse and donate huge sums to hospitals and universities.

My next call at Cambridge gave promise of employment with accommodation. Mrs Wilkinson, very much in charge of Miller's of Cambridge, was inclined to offer me the post of Service Manager but expected three other applicants to turn up within hours. Quite reasonably she wished to interview them all. She thought the flat over her branch at St. Ives would be suitable accommodation, temporarily at least.

Still floating, I renewed acquaintance with Murphy Radio Ltd., at Welwyn Garden City. I asked the perspicacious Sales Manager if I might join the firm as a Sales Representative.

'So, what makes you fancy the job?' he asked.

'Well, you know that I have a great affection for Murphy and for motoring. Five years of wartime activities have left me wondering whether I can cope with other than a mobile occupation. I would enjoy trotting around the countryside meeting people.'

'And I'll tell you something,' he said quite bluntly, as was his wont. 'You are a self-employed person. Don't kid yourself or anybody else otherwise. Now I have a proposition. I am looking for a dealer at Glastonbury in Somerset. Our retailer there has just committed suicide.'

'Well, that's a bloody good recommendation, I must say.'

'Let's not go into the why and wherefore,' Bill said. 'Glastonbury is a charming little town. Do go and have a look at it.'

With that we parted. When I arrived home, father showed me a copy of *The Wireless Trader* and there in the small ads. I read the following:

'Radio business for sale in Glastonbury. Well established Bush Dealer. Owner retiring.'

The game of chance was being played by the 'Upper House'. This must be one of those opportunities which, if not taken, would be regretted ever after. I lost no time in meeting Reginald N. Webb who traded as 'The Newtown Radio Service' at 73 Manor House Road. Over the neat little double-fronted shop was a sizeable bedroom. To the rear the tiniest of lounges gave way to a narrow staircase, access to the aforementioned bedroom and another one somewhat smaller. Certainly sleeping accommodation adequate to my small family's need could be arranged. The rear downstairs annexe comprised a very small dining room and a greenhouselike kitchen. The WC hygienically occupied a prime position a few steps into the garden area. There was no bathroom. A substantial wooden hut contained Mr Webb's service bench and stocks of valves as well as spare parts in great variety. He assured me that the business was most lucrative, £50 being a not unusual figure to be achieved for a day's work at the service bench. Subsequent examination of his invoices confirmed that by gross overcharging he had adjusted his income to suit his needs. At the bottom of the garden a corrugated iron building provided coverage for the Morris Ten van to be included in the asking price of £5,000 for lock, stock and barrel. The immaculate Wolseley Ten saloon was exclusive. Rows and rows of shelves were occupied by hundreds of 2-volt accumulators which gassed merrily in the process of being recharged. A substantial income resulted from the battery rounds. Prospects were, in my view, favourable and I promised serious consideration of purchasing the place.

Chapter 49

A Family Affair

'There is a tide in the affairs of men, which, taken at the flood, leads on to fortune.' I decided that the tide was in my favour. Taking the words of Brutus to heart I stepped into the deep water.

No sooner had I announced my intention of going into business on my own account than a complication arose. My sister, now officially engaged to a handsome young soldier, mentioned my intentions to her potential father-in-law, a wealthy Manchunian Estate Agent. Malcolm was at the stage of being released from military service. His father, not desirous of taking his indolent son into the housing business, seized the opportunity of off-loading him onto me, offering as juicy carrot the whole capital required to purchase 'The Newtown Radio Service' with no strings attached. He was prepared to trust my judgement but I insisted he accompanied me on a further exploratory visit.

The network of the British railway system embraced Glastonbury. Thus the pair of us journeyed to stay at Ye George and Pilgrim Inne.

When we asked Mr Webb for a sight of his ledgers he withdrew from his pocket a small diary in which he had noted his own estimates of profits from the various subdivisions of his fiscal enterprises: sales of radios, cycles (few), cigarettes and tobacco (largely to himself), batteries, servicing of radio sets. From this list he compiled a return to Inland Revenue, annually, never to be questioned.

Malcolm Senior summed up the situation to his satisfaction and signalled to me that he would be prepared to settle the deal without further question. At £1,000 he considered the premises to be a snip; £5,000 for the lock, stock and barrel seemed to him 'about right'. Meanwhile I had taken a keen interest in the stocks, mentally devalued them by £1,000 and suggested that £4,000 for the lot would be more in keeping with the size of the package. At this point my distinguished adviser recorded by change of visage the fear that I has scuppered the deal. On the other hand, Mr Webb, anxious to leave the district, promptly accepted!

Legal business being set in motion, Malcolm Senior and I opened an account at Lloyds Bank, where I was pleased to meet the manager, Tom Jefford. I made it clear that capital would be supplied on a fifty-fifty basis, I depending on my father to advance £2,000 as a loan to myself. From that point I swept along in the flood of events.

Mr Webb revealed that, for personal reasons, he wished to make a clean break from Glastonbury. His modern detached house on the Isle of Avalon was for sale. Malcolm Senior agreed to purchase it as soon as it could be vacated. This did seem to present a wonderful opportunity for my sister to begin a trouble-free, idyllic marriage. I was sure that my Lilian would accept the basic living accommodation 'over the shop'. She was more than anxious to be set free from her parental home, convenient though it had served as a wartime refuge.

All parties agreed that a roseate path lay ahead; all except my father. Never quick to part with money, when asked for £2,000 at one go, he succumbed only under pressure from my mother who was heavily intoxicated by the flavour of romance. My sister's pre-marital ecstasy urged the payment along. I felt sure that the old man held reservations over the advisability of my entering into a partnership with one so young and untutored.

Lilian and I, together with our two young sons, moved immediately. Mr Webb stayed with me for a week principally to introduce me to all the customers on the battery rounds, a most lucrative source of trade. On our first day together in the flat wilderness of the Somerset marshes, the weather did its very worst to dampen my enthusiasm. The dismal sight of reed-blocked rhines and peat bogs brought on a dread fear that I had 'done the wrong thing'. My thoughts strayed to sun-soaked Corsica, twitterings of Morse code signals drifting across the garden at Bologna, the view of Florence from the Futa pass, the constant bonhomie of Air Force colleagues.

I got through my first week at Glastonbury in large measure because of Lilian's willingness to cope with domestic chores, serving in the shop by applying her natural charm to strange customers, generally working wonders.

By working late into the nights I managed to connect up the accumulators to the charging boards, repair radios and electric irons, inaugurate a simple book-keeping system, pay the bills, order spares, answer correspondence, fix the stair carpet, replace tap-washers, kiss the lads good-night and forget my depressions. At the end of the week I was whacked, very thankful for Sunday. Together we could cope, just.

Only two letters came in the Monday morning post: the first from the Air Ministry offering me a permanent commission in the Royal Air Force, the second from the kindly Mrs Wilkinson expressing deep concern that I had not accepted the post at Cambridge, the flat at St. Ives now being ready for occupation. The Air Ministry letter, graciously allowing 28 days for my consideration or rejection, was immediately consigned to the coal fire. To Mrs Wilkinson I could do no more than regret the non-arrival of her kind offer. She was good enough to respond by wishing me luck in my new venture and to apply to her again should my fortunes turn unbearably against me.

It benefited me greatly when Webb the younger offered his services to me as battery roundsman. Terence was a most pleasant boy whom the customers adored. Would that this born salesman could have stayed with me. Destined to leave the district with his family I was obliged to part with an ideal business partner, the like of whom I would never again see. He helped me through the first three months of acclimatisation.

My mother and sister stayed for a few days at Ye George and Pilgrim Inne, long enough to measure for new curtains at the house as yet still occupied by the Webbs. Returning north they talked of bottom drawers and wedding cake.

At length Malcolm, released from the Army, took up residence at a local hostelry on a bed and breakfast basis. Lilian, the indefatigable, added much of his further nutritive requirements to her responsibilities. It became immediately apparent that he would find far greater difficulty than I in adapting to civilian ways. Only twenty-three years of age, fundamentally weak, he failed to resist the temptations of the flesh and the devil. I admit to encouraging him in the purchase of a 500 cc. Ariel Red Hunter motor-bike. Hopefully it would enable him to work off some of his pent-up emotions. He and the Ariel combined to attract a fair maiden of the parish.

Scandalmongers were quick to sense drama. I countered small-town gossip by calling Malcolm to account, pointing out the unwisdom of his actions. He promised to desist from frivolous activities, to concentrate on learning his trade and further the aims toward a happy union with my sister. On the strength of his promise I undertook not to mention the matter further, trusting the affair would 'blow over'.

Malcolm proceeded to take over the Morris Ten van from Terry and, as far as I could see, conducted the battery rounds in a promising manner. A well-meaning neighbour informed me that the aforementioned maiden had been observed in fond embrace in the van, with the driver, between successive calls on the battery rounds. Without hesitation I telephoned Malcolm Senior in Manchester to advise him that his son was 'not playing the game'. The venerable gentleman lost no time in taking up temporary residence in Ye George and Pilgrim Inne.

The triangular discussion, held after closing-time in the shop, was far from acrimonious. Malcolm, too weak to put up a defence, seemed barely to understand that I was not prepared to allow my sister to begin her married life in an all-pervading environment of unsavoury small-talk. His father asked him the pertinent question: 'Was this local girl providing him with forms of amusement denied by a respectable fiancée?' 'Oh, nothing like that,' replied the son, sheepishly. Unconvincing though the answer sounded I did feel it may well have been true.

Malcolm the elder then asked me to suggest a way forward. Unwittingly I delivered a block-buster. I directed that Malcolm must set forth to Yorkshire and present my sister with details of the unhappy affair. She would decide the outcome. If she opted to go through with the wedding in the circumstances I would stand by them in the face of any form of scandal-mongering.

Malcolm Junior accepted willingly these terms. On the contrary, the father firmly stated:

'In that case the wedding is as good as cancelled.'

I could not understand the significance of the declaration. My mother explained to me, in due course, that on one of her visits to Malcolm Senior's home she had made a surprise emergence from the bathroom to find herself interrupting a romantic entanglement involving the head of the household with his sister-in-law, a spinster who shared the hospitality of the establishment.

As Malcolm Senior predicted, the wedding was called off. I received a solicitor's letter requesting the return of £2,000 plus 10% interest within six months. My response was to offer £2,000 nett or to relinquish my half of the business in return for the same money. I guessed correctly that neither Malcolm nor his father would want a radio shop. I heard no more but set about collecting funds.

Relieved of the burden of a useless partner, I became a fully-fledged workaholic. Misgivings vanished. Aided and abetted by Lilian and by Tom Jefford at Lloyds Bank I determined to pay the £2,000 precisely at the end of the year. The solicitor was informed accordingly.

Lilian proved to be a born saleswoman. She charmed customers, scheduled her shopping, dealt with household chores and fitted in the comings and goings to school of the two growing lads, generally fitting into the Glastonbury scene.

By scrupulous management the bank balance grew at a satisfactory rate. Suppliers received payments in time for us to take advantage of discounts. Further, I declined to discount manufacturers' list prices. Customers accepted my view that makers' guarantees could be honoured only if the full list price was paid. Those who couldn't pay cash were at liberty to buy on HP which incurred interest charges. Nobody ever argued with me over these terms.

Postwar shortages of supplies into an economy bursting with wartime profits could be likened to selling buns to elephants. Stock turned over rapidly; obtaining stock was the problem. To make headway I worked long hours at the service bench. Many of the pre-war radio sets were in a deplorable state of decay. Ingenuity, innovation and even invention must be applied to restore some of the antiques to acceptable working order. It was the work at which I excelled. Customers came from far afield. A supplementary form of income came in the form of Public Address engagements. One of these resulted in an unexpected boost to the bank balance.

Included in the assets of the business was a very fine Public Address amplifier built by a Mr Phillips of Weston-Super-Mare. The quality of music from the equipment left nothing to be desired. However it had the disadvantage of weightiness. Two healthy persons were required to lift it into the van. Add batteries for the power supply, two large loudspeakers constructed of pinewood, and the Morris Ten sank ponderously on its springs and tyres. I attended a fête at the neighbouring town of Street when Charlie Heal's fun fair occupied one side of the grounds.

The magnificent sound of a Sousa march attracted the attention of Mrs Heal who introduced herself to me by saying:

'What a lovely set, Mr Reddin. Would you sell it to me?'

Quite taken aback, I declared truthfully that such a move had not occurred to me. In any case the price for so robust an outfit might appear to be astronomical.

'How much?' she asked.

Suddenly I became uncontrollably bold:

'Six hundred pounds,' I said. The figure came to mind as a substantial contribution to the dispossession of my late partner. The sum caused no disconcertion to Mrs Heal. Her only query that the electrical supply available on the fun fair might not suit my amplifier could be answered by a demonstration. The fun fair would next appear in Wells Market Place.

It was Sunday. The congregation, on leaving the ancient Cathedral, were enthralled by the rich voice of Bing Crosby drifting through the arches. Mrs Heal showed her delight by opening a cupboard inside her sumptuous caravan, disgorging wads of bank notes and counting out £600. I refused a request to reduce my price and as nonchalantly as I might contain my excitement I stuffed the notes into my various pockets, took my leave and returned to Glastonbury. Lilian and I checked over the notes three times, placed them in a parcel, put the package under the mattress for the night and slept on our rising fortunes.

Flushed with success, yet feeling the strain of overwork, conscious that my young wife could not be expected much longer to endure excessive pressure, my thoughts turned to engaging additional staff. It came unexpectedly. It set off a chain of events which raced towards calamity.

Chapter 50

Profit and Loss

Robert, with cultured accent, introduced himself as the nephew of one of my most respected customers. His watch strap had parted company from the watch. Aunt Emily recommended my services. Though I declared it to be outside my normal sphere of work I felt obliged to effect a satisfactory repair. He expressed his delight; then asked me if I could give him a job. His ebullient approach persuaded me that he was a born salesman. When I offered him £5 per week to start as van-driver-salesman he was overjoyed. Driving was his hobby, passion, fulfilment.

When Aunt Emily called to thank me for my attention to the watch-strap she registered reservations over my decision to employ her nephew. Ebullience was one thing, outright impetuosity another. She would have a word in the ears of both father and son.

My new salesman made a promising start. Sales of new accumulators took a sharp upward turn. It took a while for me to recognise the cause of the apparent success. Inherent clumsiness combined with haste resulted in breakages galore. Robert then turned on his charm in persuading customers that replacements were necessary as a normal course of life. Accumulators could not be expected to last for ever!

The seriousness of the amount of damage being done to clients' property became clear when Robert was obliged to take a few days sick leave. The poor chap was allergic to the effects of sulphuric acid on the numerous abrasions to his hands. Fingers swelled to alarming proportions, further exaggerated by copious bandaging.

We soldiered on for several months. Mutual discussions on moderation aided understanding but did nothing to curb Robert's love of speed. The inbuilt urge to go from A to B, no matter how short the distance between the two, at maximum velocity began to tell on the trusty Morris Ten. It developed a distaste for longer journeys. A more suitable vehicle for our family outings was sought.

New cars were obtainable only on the black-market. The second-hand car business was run, in the main, by racketeers. Robert had contacts in the backgrounds. When he turned up with a blue Standard Nine open tourer at £105 I jumped at the bargain. Whilst the side-screens were in good shape the canvas hood needed expert replacement. A firm in good old Weston-Super-Mare supplied and fitted a complete new canvas for £12. Family joy rose to new heights.

Never did an engine sound so sweet as that of our little Standard pulling us up the Bristol Road out of Wells, on our way to Hereford. It was August Bank Holiday 1946. We crossed the River Severn by way of the Aust Ferry. It made a pleasant and exciting change from the usual drag up to Gloucester. The run up the Wye Valley, sun shining upon us in our open tourer, is remembered as one of our most satisfying motoring experiences.

I left Lilian and the two lads in Hereford to enjoy a holiday. I set forth alone on the Monday with the car running perfectly. I drove through Bath on that occasion. Halfway up the Wells Road an ominous clatter from beneath the car warned me to proceed no further before investigation of the mechanism.

Removal of the floorboards took just a few minutes. The trouble was revealed. Only two sets of nuts and bolts remained out of the four originally fitted to the coupling in the drive shaft. Short work with a couple of spanners saw us roadworthy again. I replaced the floorboards and enjoyed the rest of the trip in comfort.

By removing the rear seats from the Standard this fine little car functioned as a battery carrier while I arranged for major renovation of the Morris van. Hamilton's of Bridgwater rebuilt the engine to a high standard of engineering. It sounded and felt like new. I cautioned Robert, stressing Mr Hamilton's instructions to 'run-her-in' gently. I looked forward to running into a period of profit.

Robert found the extra power of the skilfully refurbished engine irresistible to his throttle-happy foot. When Mr Grenter, the milkman, informed me that he had been overtaken by my van travelling at what he described as an alarming speed I resolved to speak sternly to the driver on his return from his rounds. He returned at the end of a tow-rope. The engine had seized. I explained to Robert that I could not afford to have him around any longer. We parted good friends; for my part with genuine sorrow, for his with customary courtesy. On balance, during his period of employment I reckoned he had increased sales by £250 and expenses by £500.

Now without van or driver I fell to dependence on the Standard tourer. When S. G. Bartlett, the experienced proprietor of a local garage, heard of my experiences he recommended a solution:

'What you want is a big Yank.'

'Find me one,' I said.

So I came into possession of an ex-Canadian Army Ford V-8. 'They never wear out,' said Mr Bartlett.

Equipped with corpulent tyres designed for use in North African deserts and estate car body the Ford did look and sound promising. The engine purred like an outsized cat.

The arrival of the Ford coincided with another chance engagement of supporting cast. Francis Figgins, the very antithesis of Robert in his approach to business, was a skilled electrician. We quickly came to an agreement. He would divide his time between operating the battery rounds and venturing gradually into the expanding business of house-wiring. Outside the urban area the majority of our customers were not connected to the electric mains. As the supply lines extended so would we expand our business.

Meanwhile, Francis introduced the Ford to the petrol station. Both 12-gallon tanks were filled to the brim, enough energy, I thought, to cover the battery rounds for at least one week. At the end of the first day and 50 miles one tank was empty, the other nearly so. Horrified, I sought the advice of the advocate of 'big Yanks'. After much twiddling of the carburettor the consumption improved to about 8 m.p.g. – about right, thought the advocate. With petrol at three shillings per gallon there was a chance of running, long term, into profit.

A further disadvantage of the 'big Yank' showed after it had covered 2,000 miles, using 800 gallons on the way round: all four knobbly tyres showed canvas. The 'advocate' fitted a set of replacements at the bargain price, he said, of £36.

Prompted by one of my strokes of sheer genius, I saw a possible way out of my difficulties. I posted a letter to Mr William Rootes (later Lord Rootes) of the Hillman Car Company. In it I described the problems of an ex-serviceman with wife and two kids battling against intolerable odds. Unless I could buy a new vehicle I felt I would succumb to overburdening expenses.

To my immense delight I received a response from the Cathedral Garage Ltd., Bristol. A new van could be supplied immediately but if I was prepared to wait a fortnight I could have the very first of a new post-war model. I telephoned my preparedness.

During that fortnight the Ford behaved itself and distinguished itself in an emergency by acting as a temporary hearse. It happened thus:

The day's work was done. Brent Knoll stood clear as a pyramid against a reddening sky. I was about to turn the Ford into the garage when of two figures approaching from the western end of the back lane I recognised one to be the local undertaker, Charlie Oldis. He introduced his companion as the Station Sergeant from Street.

It transpired that a London bus driver, shortly after arrival on a visit to relations at Butleigh Wootton, had died of a heart attack.

'As you will know,' said the burly Sergeant, 'Charlie doesn't have a hearse and it's my job to see that the body is delivered into the Street mortuary as soon as possible. If you could oblige us in the matter, I am sure the Coroner will defray your expenses.'

I waived the matter of expenses. I was on the best of terms with the local police and would be happy to oblige Charlie as a point of courtesy to a customer. Advising Lilian that I would be away on a special mission for an indefinite period, I bade my passengers take up positions in the Ford. Charlie sat in the passenger's seat on my left. The Sergeant made himself uncomfortable on the left side wheel arch. There was no dividing partition in the Ford so all three of us could communicate without difficulty.

I parked the van in the driveway of the beautiful gardens which surrounded the stately home, now converted into flats. My companions made their way into the building, reappearing after a suitable period carrying between them a long board on which lay the corpse covered by a black cloth. The two men without my assistance slid their charge into the back of the shooting-brake and regained their former positions in the vehicle. The engine started willingly, purred away as does any well cared-for V-8. I regarded the occasion as one of inviolable solemnity. No word was spoken but Charlie made subdued champing noises as he sucked away at a large boiled sweet. It became obvious that he was deep in thought. As a fellow retailer, though in a quite different trade, I could imagine his thoughts were focused on costs.

'Well, this is going to cost a bonny penny, Sarge.' Charlie was formulating a plan of cost recovery.

'That's your problem, Charlie. So long as I get him into the morgue I'm finished for the night.'

Charlie continued his ruminations. 'As far as I can see, it's going to cost somebody seventy-five quid to get him to London and I don't know these people from Adam.'

Only the engine could be heard for the next three minutes. The boiled sweet having been ingested, Charlie's masterly alternative proposition came:

'Of course we could always run him up to Bristol for cremation and send him on by parcel post. That would save a bit.'

The Sergeant mumbled disinterest. I was not sure whether Charlie was serious or not. He certainly had never struck me as a fellow with any sense of humour. I recorded the incident in my mental catalogue of jokes, have related it many times over the past forty years or more, always with some measure of incredulous response.

The Morris was too good to be scrapped. Hamilton's worked wonders on the engine. In good working order I sold the van to a local greengrocer whom it served for a number of years.

When I collected the Commer from Bristol I could not believe my luck. Hitherto, headlamps of cars usually were appended to the wings; not on the Commer. They were fitted within the wings, giving the vehicle a very upmarket, streamlined effect. LAE536 became an object of admiration throughout the Somerset countryside. Francis returned from his first trip in it asserting that it could in no way be bettered by a Rolls-Royce.

The ex-Canadian Ford stayed around. Costs of advertising it for sale reached double figures. Finally I took it to Cannard's Grave car auction where it fetched £100 after extraordinary efforts by the auctioneers. That was the first of at least half-a-dozen cars which I have owned but which I heartily wish I had never seen.

The Commer was a delightful van to drive, so much so that it begat my one and only fine for speeding, the speed limit on vans being 30 m.p.h., a quite unrealistic figure. I carried no goods at the time of the offence, only Lilian and her friend. Out in the open country, carefree, I did not see the big Wolseley follow us on the road to Yeovil. I persuaded the AA to appear for me and I paid £3. Thereafter, I continued to find it impossible to restrict the cruising speed of the Commer to less than 40 m.p.h. on good roads. It was obvious that the authorities which set speed limits had no knowledge of a modern light van.

Francis developed sales on the battery rounds to a satisfactory level. He was a good timekeeper, a conscientious family man quite determined to avoid workaholism. You could, as the saying goes, 'set your clock by him'. When the Commer did not arrive at base at his usual time on a hot August day I feared he might have met with an accident. I telephoned a few customers and confirmed that he had lunched with the Cox family at Burtle, a regular event. The next call at the Parsons' farm unveiled a clue to Francis' departure from schedule. Mr Parsons had remarked on the extreme heat of the mid-day sun, recommending that a glass of his farmhouse cider would help the traveller on his way. Francis was an abstemious chap but accepted the farmer's kind offer. A few calls further along the road customers reported that Francis appeared to be not his usual self. In fact he had parked the car in a gateway, fallen asleep and stayed that way for a couple of hours. We were all very relieved when he turned up looking no worse for wear.

Trade blossomed at a steady rate. Supplies from our principal manufacturers, Murphy and Bush, improved. My borrowings from the bank diminished. My debt to Malcolm Senior was a thing of the past; I had repaid my father a good part of his loan. It occurred to me that with winter approaching my family would appreciate the luxury of a saloon car as opposed to an open tourer. The Standard Nine was handed over to Bartlett's garage for a check-over before attempting to sell it. The frosts came early that year to Glastonbury. My nice little car was left outside the garage for the night, without antifreeze in the radiator. When I called to collect it the proprietor (advocate of 'big Yanks') was pouring 'Radweld' into the radiator. He apologised for the split in the cylinder head! 'It will be all right now,' he said.

The Standard did serve until I managed to trade it against a smart Austin Ten saloon. Whilst we, the family, appreciated the better protection from the elements of the English climate, the performance of the Austin left much to be desired. For one thing the clutch slipped, making the climb to the top of the Mendips something of an ordeal. Secondly, the rear springing played precedence over the steering. Descent of hills, especially when the ineffective brakes were applied, was frighteningly hazardous. The paintwork was excellent, the seats comfortable when the car was stationary. A neighbour took a fancy to it and forced me to sell it to him at a profit of £4. So went the second car I was not displeased to disown.

Next came one of the best cars I ever had the pleasure of owning, a 1938 Hillman Minx. I bought it from Castrol. A company car, it had been fitted with Rotaflo shock-absorbers. Not only did the family ride in comfort, but the Hillman could be adapted for commercial use in my trade. The windscreen could be opened upwards by turning a handle mounted on the dashboard. The bootlid could be lowered and the back seats tilted forward. Thus, a ladder could be inserted from the rear and project over the bonnet. The private car now functioned as an aerial erector's utility. The Minx earned its keep, contributing greatly to a sustained period of profitability.

Whilst Sir Stafford Cripps remained in charge at the Treasury, the national economy steadily improved. The 'new era' was in hand. It seemed sensible that coal and electricity supplies should be nationalised. Yet Cripps vetoed the same treatment for ICI. His common sense application of austerity could be seen to be steering Britain to controlled prosperity. Bread rationing ended in 1948, clothes in 1949. Then my political hero was, in 1950, obliged to retire owing to ill-health. Successive chancellors have played ducks and drakes, never getting back to the rails of Crippsian evolution.

Though a stranger to Somerset, my straightforward ways of doing business were accepted by a large section of the populace. My principal competitor in the town was a genuine Glastonian who retained the loyal support of those indisposed to trust a 'foreigner'. Much of my trading successes developed around Street where the majority of workers enjoyed steady employment with the gigantic Clark's shoe company. The not always friendly rivalry between the two neighbouring towns caused some of the people to shop in the opposite camp. Overall I felt I was getting a fair share of the cake.

Lilian, a brilliant ballroom dancer, practised her art with good friends. Once each week I put the two children to bed, worked profitably at my repair bench, sorted stock, 'did' the books and baby-sat until mother returned from her frolicking. Both boys, now at St. John's school, became involved in all those activities which boys find essential in life: cubs, choirs, sports and larks.

I joined the Tor Motor Cycle Club, bought a Velocette ('GTP'), even entered a trial. I provided the Public Address system, with the latest Philips amplifying equipment, at scrambles and sports days. Altogether we had, as a family, merged into the Somerset scene, a scene enriched by numerous personalities, some of whom maintained Victorian characteristics.

Chapter 51

Customers

Glastonbury's endowment of characters was as rich in the post-war era as it had been through the centuries. I was privileged to enter the homes of many of them in pursuance of my living. To those unable to change the batteries in their radio sets or even an electric light bulb the Newtown Radio Service was at beck and call, usually at no extra charge. We called it goodwill because it promoted friendships as well as future business.

Undoubtedly, the most distinguished character of the times was the Reverend Lewis, High Churchman, vicar of St. John's, in front of which magnificent church grew the legendary Holy Thorn. His reverence, well over eighty years of age when I met him, captivated me with his academic jargon. He began translating Greek and Latin from the age of four. Ten minutes in his presence was as good as a whole term at school.

His study contained stacks of books, pamphlets and periodicals dating back many decades. His desk, weighted down under correspondence opened and unopened, permitted a small space for a notepad on which could be entered thoughts for the next sermon.

To post an account to the vicar was a waste of time and paper. When he owed money I would pay him a call of an evening, listen to tales of early history and seize a pause in the monologue to request my dues. A delicate hand would slide under a pile of papers, withdraw the cheque book. He would sign a cheque, pass me the book to fill in whatever amount I cared to enter. The withdrawal of the book caused layers of documents to slither to the floor, adding to the oceans already there.

Knowledge poured from Lewis's incredible brain. Every sermon was a nutshell of education. His mind enjoyed a separate existence from his body. Yet he had learned to drive an Austin Seven saloon. He was accorded special privileges by police and public alike. His car, from numerous similar models on the streets, was recognisable by virtue of the yard of ecclesiastical cloth flapping along the road surface. After posting his mail in the High Street he would execute a kangaroo-like three point turn by reversing onto the pavement, stopping only when the vehicle biffed the wall of the Post Office.

Frequent telephoned calls from the vicar to the police reported loss of the car. Invariably the Duty Officer could provide the vital information. Someone obligingly told the police where the vehicle had been forgotten by its owner. There were occasions when the car had remained in the garage while the reverend gentleman walked to town, subsequently reporting the loss. Happily the police were seldom overburdened with reports of crime in the borough.

Customers who complained that their batteries 'didn't last long' invariably added the rider 'we don't use it much – only for the news in the mornings and perhaps a bit at night.' The delightfully eccentric Miss Morris convinced me that there 'must be something wrong' with her Ever-Ready portable. So I called at the Victorian semi on Wells Road and soundly rapped the door-knocker. There was no reply. Yet I could hear music. Raising the lid of the letter box I peered down the marbled hallway, could see the source of music on the kitchen table. 'Good afternoon, Miss Morris,' I said as I met the dear lady emerging from the Post Office. 'The radio sounds very healthy.'

'Oh, dear!' she said. 'Have I left it on again? I must remember to switch it off when I'm not using it.'

On his milk-rounds, Mr Grenter always wore a white smock. Occasionally he added to his accoutrement a bowler hat. Lilian's curiosity questioned such incongruity on first sight.

'Ah!' replied Grenter, 'it's when I'm bearing.'

This extraordinary remark called for further explanation.

'Well, you see; we don't have a proper hearse in Glastonbury so four of us wheels a 'and carriage. We shall be by here about eleven o'clock. You'll see.'

We did and a very impressive cortège it was. Charlie Oldis, the very essence of solemnity, complete with top-hat and Dickensian black tunic, set slow-march. The elaborate four-wheeled carriage equally silently bore the flower-bedecked coffin, under the able exertions of our milkman/customer and his three bebowlered colleagues.

Though I firmly believe that the most important person in any business is the customer, I cannot subscribe to the adage that he or she is always right. The fellow who frequently bought a twopenny battery before requesting the use of our telephone was asked to conduct his horse-racing activities from his own home and public telephone.

The statutory half-day holiday allowed me to probe technical snags without interruption by the shop bell. Lilian and the boys were visiting grandparents in Hereford. In an effort to fulfil a promise to a customer I was annoyed when Lilian phoned to say she and the lads were at Temple Mead station. Could I pick them up? Missed the bus. Didn't feel like waiting another hour.

Priority begins at home. Without much hesitation or dispute I made haste in the willing Hillman Minx. Two hours later I was back at the bench. The front doorbell rang. It was the owner of the Philips, in belligerent mood.

I explained that I was working on the object of his inquiry, had hoped to complete it during the afternoon but had been obliged to collect the family from Bristol.

'If your family is more important than your customers . . .'

I did not hear more of his outburst. I picked up the set, a sizeable console model, and placed it in his arms, saying:

'I am sure you will get better service elsewhere!'

I knew that the man had already fallen out with my immediate opposition. Three months later he reappeared full of apologies, requesting my attention, at leisure, to his problem.

My charges of five shillings an hour resulted in cash settlement in most cases. It was not unknown for the odd customer to protest that I had not charged enough. Immediately prior to the start of an important football match, a neighbour's Ferranti gave up the ghost. He carried the set across the road pleading for instant attention. I pulled out all the stops, cleared a very simple fault in twenty minutes, delivered the patient to him and charged half-a-crown. His delight knew no bounds. He brought the instrument back to me a week later asking me to give it a proper overhaul. He could not be convinced that I could do nothing more to improve performance so I kept it under surveillance for a day, charged him £2 for doing nothing, and he was tickled pink.

Joe Thomas, wealthy scrap dealer of Wells, owned a much abused Murphy A40C with the infamous so-called 'remote control'. The control panel could be withdrawn from the front of the cabinet and rested on the armchair of the user, connection being retained via a flat multicore cable. This disappeared at high speed by virtue of a strong spring-loaded cable drum inside the substantial cabinet, if the user was careless enough to allow the machinery to have free rein. Joe took great delight in demonstrating its behaviour, much to the discomfort of the woodwork. Rectifying all the faults took several hours. A couple of new valves added to the account brought the total to £9. Joe thought the job 'too cheap' and hoped I would 'catch him next time!'

The next time I met Joe Thomas our roles were reversed. I bought from his vast stock of ex-army equipment a small petrol-electric generator set on behalf of one of my customers. The unit was wrapped in hessian sprayed with a water-sealant. It had every appearance of being unused. My client soon found that the big-end of the engine had 'gone'. I returned the set to Joe asking him to exchange it for another. 'Oh, I can't do that,' he remonstrated, 'you takes your pick here. Hard luck you picked a bad 'un. You give me £5 and pick another.'

I selected one which sounded healthy and paid Joe his five quid which he pocketed. He reminded me:

'Don't forget to stick it on next time you see to my wireless!'

A good customer is best described as one who returns to do business again and again because he or she is satisfied with the trader's service. There may come a time when things go wrong to the extent of severance of former good relations. Lilian had established excellent commercial rapport with the effusive fishmonger, Headley Hucker. Headley's expressions of gratitude included the incongruous: 'I am indubitably obliged!'

Customers at the fishery received even more colourful treatment when Mrs Hucker chose to assist behind the counter. She possessed a rare assortment of hats more befitting a meeting at Ascot than the streets of a small Somerset town, let alone the wrapping of cod in a fish shop. Display of affluence by Mrs Hucker could not be attributed entirely to profits from the sale of wet fish. She ran a close association with the occupant of the western half of the semi in which she and Headley dwelt. This neighbour, a well-dressed gentleman of substantial independent means, was known as Monty Porch and to be in some way related to Winston S. Churchill. Be that as it may, he did, on more than one occasion, indicate to me that he subscribed generously to the expenses of the combined households.

Lilian, as my good ambassadress, never failed to detect a possibility of a sale to her suppliers. When Mrs Hucker hinted that her pre-war vacuum cleaner had long since failed to collect dust in quantity Lilian suggested that I demonstrate the latest Bylock machine. Vacuum cleaners were rarities to British homes and still in rather short supply. By good fortune I had purchased several dozen Bylock Classic models which sold like hot cakes at £7 19s. 6d. They were excellent machines but Mrs Hucker wanted no 'popular' or 'common' goods. The 'de Luxe' model at £12 19s. 6d. suited her up-market style. It was bigger, more powerful and sounded expensively smooth. After a short demonstration run over a bedroom carpet I was truly astonished at the amount of fluff collected. Mrs Hucker, Mr Porch and the charwoman observed my actions. Noting the doorway leading through to the adjoining house I emphasised that the process of ridding two houses of the accumulation of wartime dust would call for frequent emptying of the dust-bag.

A week later came the urgent call. The Bylock was getting very hot and very smelly. Not only was the dust-bag full but the tube leading to it was choked with fluff. Patient poking, picking, shaking and probing allowed the machine to breathe again. I repeated the warning that frequent emptying of the dust-bag was absolutely necessary; failure to conform would cause the machine to go on fire.

Seven more days passed before the next call. This time the bag was full, the tube was not only full but exhibited plain signs that it had been used to haul the machine around the premises; it had stretched and contained more than one kink. Mrs Hucker opined that the vacuum was not up to the job and she expected a free replacement. Mr Porch saw reason. I agreed to ask the manufacturer to replace the damaged hose as a gesture of goodwill. We parted on uneasy terms.

I heard nothing from the Hucker households for some weeks. When peace broke, an extraordinary emergency was declared; a major wall dividing the two houses had been demolished leaving an electric supply socket hanging in mid-air at the end of its cable. My immediate attention was demanded. I regretted my inability to oblige:

'I cannot leave my shop unattended and Mr Figgins is working out of town.'

'In that case I must take my business elsewhere.'

'That seems to be a very sensible idea,' whereupon I replaced the receiver on the hook, trusting that would end the kerfuffle.

The following morning a reasonable approach was made. Francis rerouted the cable and located the socket in a position agreed by consensus.

Many of our customers belonged to the farming fraternity who went to great lengths in bargaining. Returning home from one of my evening service calls I dropped in at the Ashcott Inn. A noisy group of agriculturalists occupied the bar-room. Recognising one of them:

'Hello, Mr Willis! May I buy you a pint?'

'No, no,' he said. 'It's my turn to buy a round. You are in it.'

'Thank you,' said I. 'But what's going on?'

'Well, we've all been out looking at some pigs.'

'And did you buy them?' I asked.

'No, we couldn't agree on price,' he replied. 'We got stuck over a fiver and he wouldn't come down, so we left 'un.'

'Oh, dear,' I ventured, 'so you are celebrating your victory, eh?'

'Well, you could say that. Anyway we weren't goin' to budge. So we're spendin' the fiver we saved, on beer.'

Keri Jones, a newly qualified veterinary surgeon became a customer and personal friend. Directly from the Liverpool College, Keri secured an appointment with the Ministry of Agriculture and Fisheries. A stranger to Somerset and anxious to prove his proficiency he became highly elated when during his first week he diagnosed a case of anthrax. Popping his head round the shop door one afternoon he wanted to share his excitement, telling me that he had just despatched blood samples from the sick beast to the County Laboratory at Taunton. With even greater enthusiasm he later called in to announce a positive result. He dashed onward to burn the unfortunate victim. When all the excitement had faded my friend called in with a full report.

We had a wonderfully friendly black cat at the time. Keri examined him, saying: 'He ought to be castrated. I've never done a cat. Would you like me to fix him?'

'If you think it advisable, go ahead.'

'Right,' said the vet. 'I've got my tools with me. You hold him down on the bench and I'll do the trick.'

Tibby, always ready for a cuddle, allowed me to pick him up as I closed the workshop door.

Inverted on the bench the cat's trusting eyes stared at me. Content as usual he allowed me to rub his tummy. Then Keri searched the black fur adjacent to vital parts. With electrifying change of personality the animal rocketed to the ceiling of the hut, looped the loop three times at inestimable speed, scattering packages and packets in all directions. I opened the door. Out shot the tom to the highest roof-top refuge in its sight. There it stayed until nightfall. Keri was astonished at the outcome of his first encounter with a small domestic animal; he said he would refer to the textbook before making a further attempt.

When I told the story to Doctor Evans, school medical officer, customer and friend, he expressed only mild amusement.

'That's no problem,' he said. 'Bring the cat to my place tomorrow evening. My wife will fix him in a trice.'

Mrs Evans ran a cattery. Thither with Tibby safely locked in his basket, I drove in the Hillman Minx. Mrs Evans opened the basket, grasped the cat firmly, wrapped him tightly in an old smock and handed the parcel over to her husband who placed it on a table, unearthed the operable sector of the animal and with a deft snip removed the testicles. Emerging from its temporary strait-jacket, Tibby whispered a faint meow, and licked the painful spot once before settling back in the basket, anxious to return home.

Doc Evans made a practice of visiting my 'surgery' every Tuesday evening. He took a keen interest in my diagnostic expertise. He later became a regular listener on the short wavebands. He may have been the first Somerset owner of an ex-RAF Receiver type 'Eleven-fifty-five' adapted to work on the mains electricity supply. I acquired two for him from a scrap dealer and got one of them to work properly! He was also one of the first viewers of television. I supplied a Cossor with a 9" tube on which we received, albeit occasionally, tolerable pictures from Sutton Coldfield soon after transmission began in 1951.

Much better pictures were fairly regularly received on a 9" Vidor receiver which I supplied to a Mr Davy whose house was well sited on rising ground facing north. One of the most avid viewers of TV was a child from a neighbour-ing house. Michael Hembury was about six years old, so fascinated by the new invention that he would sit for hours looking at the test-card! Although recep-tion from a transmitter fifty miles distant was variable, to say the least, I kept a TV running in the shop almost continuously. It created a lot of interest and caused comments of widely differing opinions. 'Wonderful,' was a popular assessment. 'It'll never catch on, too expensive.' 'Rather go to the pictures,' were not untypical remarks.

Customers came from all walks of life. We, at the Newtown Radio Service, treated them with courtesy and understanding. All were trusted until any doubts were raised. We never asked for references formally, though in the course of conversation a new customer would be persuaded to reveal his life-style and the name of his employer. Anyone employed by local companies was assumed to be trustworthy. Though the majority of customers paid cash there were occa-sions when short-term credit seemed convenient to both parties.

A 'phone call from a chef at Millfield School brought me to the gentleman's apartment in Street. He chose a small Murphy mains 'portable' radio as most suited to his requirement. The price was 14 guineas. He would prefer to settle at the end of the month. He had just joined the staff, had spent loose capital in assisting a nephew with college expenses, so was temporarily embarrassed. I swallowed the tale and left the radio without taking even a token deposit.

The end of the month came and went; several telephone calls were unanswered. I decided on a personal call after dark. There was no reply to my door-knocking so I retreated, to be met in the corridor by the local florist who was owed a fiver. He volunteered the information that the 'chef' was indebted to a taxi-driver for three times that amount and the tobacconist was whistling for much more.

I decided to seek the advice of my good friend Sergeant Boyce of the Glastonbury Police. Lilian and I had the greatest respect for the local constabulary. Sunday evenings when we were relaxing in our miniature lounge behind the shop it was customary for the police to check on our welfare. One or more officers would join us for a cup of tea and a chat. When the good sergeant called he never failed to bring his Alsatian bitch. Vicky's principal contribution to the entertainment was her ability to distinguish between two digestive biscuits. One was described by her master as Churchill's, the other as Hitler's. The two being placed side by side on the floor before the order to 'take' was announced, invariably Hitler's piece remained untouched. No amount of persuasion by members of the gathering induced Vicky to disobey instructions.

It came to light that the 'chef' had been apprehended by the Bristol police in connection with theft from a leading radio dealer of that city. Sergeant Boyce made it convenient to inquire of the destiny of my Murphy portable. It had, said the accused, been stolen from his side whilst he took forty winks during a train journey. On the Sergeant's advice I wrote off the cost of the Murphy against 'experience'.

One of Lilian's favourite customers was the genial proprietor of Godwin's Peat Industries. Long before clothes rationing ended Eddie obliged by sparing a few coupons at intervals from a seemingly endless stock. With two fast-growing lads to cater for she was more than grateful. A great raconteur of Somerset stories, Eddie also took delight in passing on to us hints and tips for the promotion of business handed to him by his late father:

'If you have a good customer, don't hunt 'un;' was a typical Godwinism.

An exceptional character to whom Lilian took a dislike lived in a fabulous manor at Butleigh Wootton, beneath the shadow of the Hood memorial. Local folk maintained that Mr Allen was an off-shoot of the great admiral's family tree. He owned a suitably impressive Dynatron Console radio to the care of which I was entrusted. During a visit to the manor I was attracted by some miniature portraits executed in white paint on brown parchment. Mr Allen noticed my interest and asked me what I thought they were. I could only describe them as precise paintings of faces in a unique medium.

To my amazement, my client told me that they had been accomplished by his own grandmother whilst under the influence of a spiritualist friend. Normally, the grandparent was quite unable to make a rough sketch. One portrait of an

American Indian Chief complete with feathered headgear was so rich in ethos that, forty years later, my visual memory can recall it at will. Inevitably Mr Allen made close contact with a group of fervent spiritualists, sold his beautiful home and moved to Sussex. Lilian was relieved. She had always felt uncomfortable in the man's presence. Certain ladies of Taunton would miss his custom.

On one occasion only Lilian became obliged to patronise a local dentist. She was not well pleased with the service administered. When she related her experience to Mr Grenter the milkman that gentleman confirmed that it was not unusual for Mr Beavis to extend inadvertently the time between injection and extraction. Grenter described how on one visit he waited so long after the injection that its effects were plainly diminishing. Beavis apologised on returning to the surgery: 'Oh, I'm sorry. I'd forgotten about you. I've written a letter and been down to post it. You'd better have another injection!' Superior dental services were, fortunately, available in Wells and Street.

Few customers paid by cheque. So much money had been accumulated during the war years, stuffed away under floorboards and mattresses, that it was wisely brought into circulation in small doses. I offered attractive Hire Purchase terms. A simple payment card, retained by the customer, showed a running account of his indebtedness or, as often as not, a credit balance. My inestimable bank manager smiled wryly when he discovered that I was financing the system on my overdraft. So confident was he that my business was sound that he partook of it by purchasing a Bush radio set on the same terms.

Nevertheless, I was truly alarmed at the extent to which many customers flew into the hot winds of Inland Revenue. One ex-serviceman unfastened a huge wooden box to withdraw £21 in payment of a new radio. He boasted that the taxman knew nothing of his return from overseas service. The situation could not continue indefinitely, of course, but a lot of hay was made before the gentlemen of the Treasury clouded the sunshine.

As the Civil Services welcomed back their returning warriors, so customers and suppliers alike came under increasing scrutiny. The warnings of impending inquiries circulated like wildfire. The amiable farmer Nurse, popularly known as 'Doc' for some unaccountable reason, was charged by the Ministry of Agriculture and Fisheries of the unforgivable sin of killing two pigs on one licence. Immediately Doc's entourage of husbandmen held a meeting at the bar of Ye George and Pilgrim for the purpose of formulating a plan of defence. Fortuitously, the Chairman of the bench, before which the hearing would be held, would be the incumbent Mayor of Glastonbury. The time of the hearing would be arranged to allow for suitable entertainment of the Ministry representative at the aforementioned hostelry prior to the mounting of the bench.

When in due course the case was heard His Majesty's Inspector was in no fit condition to be punitive. It became clear that a simple human error had caused officialdom to misinterpret the rules. Doc had personally slaughtered one pig, his farm manager the other. Neither had been aware of the action by his associate. Besides, Glastonbury was the most hospitable place on earth; the Inspector, being assured that no such misdemeanour was likely to be detected in future, left for Bristol a happier man.

Doc stood numerous 'last rounds' that night at the Crown. The constable on duty made repeated attempts to supervise closing time. When finally the front door was locked he left the tavern comforting himself that the back door gave on to a non-residential area.

Chapter 52

Suppliers

Though dependence on customers is a retailer's linchpin he must of necessity keep faith with his suppliers. Of these there are two species: direct and wholesale. Each of them, by nature, subdivides into varieties.

Our principal direct suppliers were the manufacturers: Murphy and Bush. They were represented, individually, by an astute salesman whose job it was to encourage us to buy more and sell more of their marque. Further, these knights of the road called upon us at regular intervals as a welcome link with the outer sphere of the trade. It is all too easy for a retailer to become bogged down in his niche, often taking on a seemingly unfair share of tribulation. When things were not going too well some comfort could be found in hearing news of those in worse plight. I began to envy these bearers of tidings good and bad.

Norman Davis of Murphy adopted the hard line approach. Little time he spent in small talk. I could detect the influence of Sales Manager Bill Greenwood, a constant cracker of the whip. Imbued with Murphy Madness in my pre-war experiences I was easy meat for Norman's appetite for order-taking.

Much of Murphy success to date could fairly be ascribed to the innovative cabinet designs of Gordon Russell. Contemporary with de Havilland's introduction of 'flying wing' style of aircraft Murphy introduced a fabulous console radio. The walnut veneered cabinet consisted of a large baffle with generous side flarings curving towards the listener. A ten-inch speaker mounted in the centre of the baffle reproduced faithfully the sounds received by the tiny ingenious receiver mounted neatly on the top of the baffle. It was an eye-catcher; in trade terms: a seller.

Unfortunately, production of the A146 began at the new factory at Hirwaun, in South Wales. Newly trained assembly workers were allowed to get away with appalling soldering. Dry joints were to blame for intermittent faults; I was obliged to act as final tester for every set which came from Hirwaun. The miniaturisation of the new breed of radios called for highly skilled soldering work.

Established models coming from the old works at Welwyn Garden City had none of these faults. Regrettably, in the drive to stay ahead the Murphy designers introduced customer-operated gimmicks such as 'flywheel' tuning. By loading the conventional tuning spindle with a heavy wheel a satisfying 'feel' was imparted to the turning of the knob. The overall result was far from satisfactory. Whilst a person of natural mechanical sense could appreciate the smoother running of the tuning dial pointer, the less technically minded user found joy in the spinning from one end to the other. No braking mechanism had been provided. The nylon cord involved in the design was not up to being abused. Frequent service calls resulted, all 'free of charge, under guarantee' at the dealers' expense. One farm-worker in the act of removing his boots at the end of a hard day, let fly with a clod-hopper at a knob-twiddling son, missed the child and smashed the plastic cabinet. The client accepted my favourable part-exchange terms in supplying a more durable model in a strong wooden cabinet.

There was no knowing what the Murphy boffins might next produce in the way of gadgetry. The loudspeaker of one radiogram was surrounded by closely packed corrugated cardboard. This was intended to damp out undesirable vibrations. It succeeded in diminishing the bass notes. The average British listener wanted more bass!

The Murphy scientists' most embarrassing clanger came to light on the introduction of the battery portable known as the B.123. Acclaimed in the press as being the best thing since Marconi straddled the Atlantic it looked, on paper, to be a winner. Clad in a double-sided aluminium 'cabinet' with twin dials at the top it was innovative, certainly. It was also flimsy and top heavy until the batteries were fitted. Extra weight was provided by using a jumbo-sized bell cell to heat the 1.5 volt valves.

Now bell cells, as the name implies, were designed to give long life for intermittent use on door-bells. In the B.123 the required voltage was maintained about long enough to enjoy the six o'clock news plus 'ITMA'. The solution, at the dealers' expense, was to modify the battery connections and supply proper radio batteries.

Murphy Radio Ltd. struggled to exist, largely on the goodwill built up by its founder and that of the numerous dealers who remembered the good old days.

Frank Murphy attempted a 'come-back' in the late forties, under the controversial name 'F-M Radio'. He inaugurated also a factory turning out high class domestic furniture, including probably the most substantial wooden step-ladders ever seen. The public was disinclined to pay for top quality in that field and Murphy Radio Ltd. forbade its dealers to 'sign up' with 'F-M'. The project failed. Unable to obtain financial support for his revolutionary marketing methods Frank took solace in Canada, in the menial task of a hotel porter.

Bush Radio Ltd., under the able and friendly guidance of G. Darnley Smith, never went for the hard-sell. They concentrated on building thoroughly reliable radio sets in unpretentious cabinets. The company was represented in the West Country by a genial Bristolian, Don Wines, a regular and welcome visitor to our little business. He helped us enormously in obtaining extra supplies of the famous dry battery model designated BP90. I was never happier than when I could fill a shop window with BP90s.

Some of our rural customers lived miles away from the main electricity supply whilst the Bristol area rapidly approached saturation point. When the Broadmead Wireless Co. accumulated a surplus stock of battery portables Don arranged an exchange of one mains set from my stock for a dozen BP90s. A friendly relationship developed between myself and the then Managing Director of Broadmead, Ben Turner. This enabled me to negotiate several mutually advantageous deals. Regrettably this caused an eventual breach of faith with Don Wines.

When Broadmead fell prey to the aggressively expanding John James Group, its Bush Dealership was withdrawn. My extraordinary supply line was severed. When Ben Turner appealed to me for just one more Bush mains set to satisfy one of his 'special customers' I fell into the trap. The Bush was displayed in the main Broadmead shop as a bait to attract customers who were then worked upon by a slick salesman practising the obnoxious art of 'switch selling'.

Ere long a perspicacious member of the fraternity of genuine Bush dealerships brought the matter to the attention of the Bush representative. Don's admonition must have overheated the Bristol-Glastonbury telephone wires. As soon as he had completed his outburst I vented my feelings by ringing Ben Turner and terminating a brief but fruitful friendship.

Murphy and Bush were not our only 'direct' suppliers. McMichael was a great name in radio. Ferranti too produced a very attractive range. The Ever-Ready van called weekly with supplies of fresh torch and radio batteries. Vidor approached us through a private agent called Bill Mitchell. In common with myself, Bill's progress was hampered by difficulties in obtaining reliable transport. The first time he called on us at Glastonbury his Ford van was coughing and spluttering, barely able to carry its heavy burden. Bill was more than delighted when I bought three battery portables and a handsome consignment of HT batteries. Our friendship never faltered.

We endeavoured to divide our extensive battery business fairly between suppliers. Exide batteries came via F. O. Coward Ltd., of Bristol and Weston. Their jovial representative Les Philips was a great favourite with the family. We were all very sad when Exide ran into a dreadful production problem which forced me to discontinue buying from Les. Corrosion of the wires connecting individual cells was found to be caused by a female operator in the factory being endowed with extra perspiratory fingers. Once she was replaced on the line, Exide reliability was restored to its former high standard.

Varley 'Dry' Accumulators carried something of a misnomer. When new they were economic of storage space. After weeks of charging and recharging the bakelite cases began to split. Messily they became even less desirable than the conventional glass bodied monstrosities. The Varley agent, named Figgures, was an uncommonly good artist; samples of his work may be found around the Bournemouth area where he lived.

Excellent relationships were established with numerous wholesalers, none better than that with Westradio Ltd. of Bristol. Their accountant, John Davis, lived only a few doors away from us in Manor House Road. On his way to catch the morning bus he would call in for an order and deliver small quantities the same evening. In that way we were enabled to maintain a continuous stock of the famous Morphy-Richards electric irons for which there seemed to be an insatiable demand at £2 5s. 0d each or £2 10s. 0d with chromium plated top! Millions of these excellent devices were sold throughout the world. In their original form they would be a good buy today at £25. John advised me when such a rare commodity as a washing machine was available. For an English Electric or Hotpoint washer I would dash off to Bristol without delay. Cumbersome though these early machines were, with roller-type wringer, war-weary housewives were only too anxious to persuade husbands to part with £45 or so in exchange for one.

John Davis was brother-in-law to Maxwell Crease, managing director, chairman, proprietor, very much the boss of Westradio. Max was one of the most charismatic members of the trade, likeable and roguish. He lived in a fabulously sited house above Wells. He maintained a small warehouse in the city. There we frequently met to do business outside normal working hours. Invariably discussion continued beyond closing time at the Star Hotel. Rarely did on-coming vehicles intrude upon my headlight lonesomeness during my short return journey to Glastonbury. The benefaction of cats' eyes was never more appreciated.

One hot summer night Max and I were abnormally late in concluding our business. He deemed it advisable to phone Lilian in explanation of my tardiness. Similarly I appraised Mrs Crease of the whereabouts of her husband. My homecoming was accepted rather than greeted. Max had taken the romantic precaution of arming himself with a two-pound box of Cadbury's chocs. Max presented his gift to his beloved who lay in bed with window wide open. The recipient took it, flung it far into the rosebeds. Local wildlife enjoyed a rare treat on that occasion.

I was fairly well known in the radio trade. Max knew everybody. When at the 1950 Radiolympia we accepted the hospitality of all those who vied for our orders. We were obliged to charter a taxi-driver to ensure our departure from Paddington on a train destined for Bristol. A friendly guard woke us up at Temple Meads. To finalise a memorable day Max drove us over the moonlit Mendips in immaculate style in his new Austin Somerset.

Lugton's of London were my sole suppliers of gramophone records, difficult to handle economically in small numbers. Their Mr Young guided us skilfully through extensive catalogues. Thus, we made a profit on the best sellers: The Ink Spots, The Smith Brothers, Harry James and Bing Crosby. Orders for the classics would be accepted on payment of a substantial deposit. When the long-playing 33 r.p.m. discs were introduced, response from the public could best be described as 'conservative'. 'They'll never catch on,' 'Who wants to listen to a record for three-quarters-of-an-hour?', 'Far too expensive,' were typical comments. Many a duel-standard pick-up head ground away at the good old 'seventy-eights' before being turned over by some venturesome youth determined to break down family prejudice with a Christmas present LP.

Spare parts for Murphy and Bush were readily available from those manufacturers, often free of charge. The renovation of old and ailing radio sets constituted a major part of my business. For this I obtained components from a variety of sources.

The name of 'Radiospares' came to my notice as a source of silvered-mica capacitors. These were required in particular for the restoration of performance of short-wave receivers. Orders placed with Radiospares came by return of post on a COD basis which suited me admirably. In due course, however, a personal representation of the firm called in the shape of one 'Johnny' Johnson. From a Ford 8 van he stepped into my life, a breezy character, never failing to bring good cheer. His arrival marked the beginning of momentous and far-reaching events in my world of radio.

Chapter 53

A Festival of Upheavals

In 1951 Britain set out to shake itself free of self-denigration. The 'Festival of Britain' would proclaim to the world by a great blowing of trumpets that we no longer had use of the proverbial bushel for the hiding of lights.

Hugh Gaitskell had taken over the Treasury subsequent to the retirement of my hero, Sir Stafford Cripps. Henceforward the general economy would jerk along as a car constantly traffic-jammed, the driver never finding a clear road. Meanwhile the Festival purported to represent 'faith in the Nation's future', a great letting down of the hair.

Infected with the universal euphoria I took the plunge of moving family and business to more commodious premises in the High Street. The combined shop and tiny accommodation at Manor House Road went to a jovial fishmonger for £1,750 which contributed handsomely to the purchase of the three-storey monster with extensive outhouse and garden facilities at £3,000. The apparent bargain brought additional worries, expenses, work and turmoil hitherto not encountered.

Lilian decided to raise our living standards. She had suffered considerable indignity in cramped quarters. Quite rightly she embarked upon her own scheme of expansion. A first floor room, overlooking the garden, was transformed into a spacious kitchen. On the same floor the lounge allowed for the laying out of extensive model railway tracks and the entertainment by our growing family of numerous schoolfriends. Michael, now aged ten, had already set course on a career in Social Science; the first stage being the sympathetic adoption of the least hygienic members of society and the hungriest. Lilian's stocks of biscuits and buns could not be maintained at a level satisfactory to our own immediate needs. Philip, two years junior, distanced himself somewhat from the mob. Taking advantage of additional horticultural space he launched into animal husbandry. An animal lover myself, I gave unstinted encouragement to the activity until Hector proved insufferable.

Tibby, our black cat, well accustomed to his compulsory celibacy, settled into our new abode contentedly. His skill at climbing ladders could now be exercised to the greater heights of a three-storey building. He spent most of his days sleeping on the roof out of the way of Hector. The guinea pigs and hamsters caused no problems, but Hector resented captivity. He excelled in his natural habits of eating and burrowing. He refused to comply with the rules of behaviour laid down in the book on *Rabbits and Rabbit Keeping*. Soundly constructed of substantial timbers, enclosed by stout wire-netting, the cage appeared to cover enough pasturage to sustain Hector for two days, Within the hour the patch resembled a batting crease at Lord's. Furthermore the animal had tunnelled its way to freedom and was well into its second square yard of the outfield. Something had to be done about it.

The main garden, designated for vegetable growing, was unhappily riddled with ground-elder. Hopefully, we set Hector in the middle of the infested area, consoling ourselves that he would be usefully employed. He took an instant dislike to the ground-elder but made a rabbit line for the few remaining lettuce plants on which Lilian depended for domestic consumption.

My staff included at the time two notable employees. Leslie Childs exercised a wide range of skills which set him in the class of the handiest of handymen. His main occupation as a porter at Glastonbury station brought a poor financial return. He supplemented his income by part-time working for us as battery-charger, carpenter, scene-shifter and whatever was asked of him. His hobby of watch and clock repairs could readily be adapted to unravelling the intricacies of Philips dial drive systems.

Maurice Ingerfield joined me straight away after leaving school, studiously adapted himself to fault diagnosis and had become a valuable assistant in the workshop. In anticipation of a call to National Service, Maurice attempted to volunteer for service in the Royal Air Force, his preferred choice. Admittedly with selfish motive I rejoiced when Maurice returned from his interview carrying a notice of rejection on the grounds of some minor ailment.

The three of us set to work on improving Hector's security. A trench to a depth of one foot was filled with bricks from a defective wall, the cage mounted upon the bricks and suitably weighted beyond the rabbit's capability for weight-lifting. A huge cabbage, as well as an assortment of root crops being inserted into the cage, we left Hector contentedly nibbling at high speed. Misguidedly I looked forward to a busy but relatively peaceful existence. A series of events of varying degrees of fortune would have far-reaching effects upon myself and family.

I was approached by members of the local council with a request to illuminate by floodlight Somerset's most prominent landmark, the Glastonbury Tor. Persuaded that my acquiescence would be regarded as my personal contribution to the festivities I undertook to execute the task free of charge.

First I approached a specialist electrical contractor in Bristol, who agreed to hire me four floodlights for a week at a sympathetic charge of £10. My next call at the Territorial Army Barracks at Ashton Gate secured the ready co-operation of the Officer-in-Charge. He seized upon the opportunity of winning unexpected publicity. He agreed to supply a mobile diesel generating set under the surveillance of Sergeant-Major Raine. On due date the generator was towed by a gigantic 'Matador' to a predetermined site at the foot of the Tor.

With the help of all the casual labour I could muster, the four floodlights were set around the ancient tower and connected by His Majesty's cables to the generator. When all was approved as technically safe Sergeant-Major Raine and the Matador driver enjoyed one of Lilian's culinary delights. Hardly had the meal been consumed and table-talk entered common ground when the next-door neighbour appealed for assistance. Hector had started on his second row of cabbage lettuce! A chaotic chase headed by Hector at his quickest, dart-like rate resulted in horrifying damage to the kindly fellow's vegetable plot. When finally the animal was confined to its hutch the godsent Sergeant-Major expressed the intention of acquiring a rabbit for his son's birthday present. Ownership of Hector was transferred instantly. Complete with hutch he was loaded onto the Matador.

At sundown we assembled, together with a host of sightseers, at the foot of the Tor. The generator started willingly and hey-presto, for the first time in its long history Glastonbury Tor could be seen at night from most points of the county. Determined on close examination of our work a group of us climbed the hill. Intense heat accompanied the light from the great bulbs. A shower of rain descended. Furthermore the cold water shocked the glass covers of the lamps; each, a metre square, split to pistol-cracking cacophony.

Such was the excitement that none of us had observed the interest taken by the small herd of cows which normally grazed round the base of the hill. Whilst we mortals examined the state of one lamp the cows put paid to the diametrically opposite one. The outsized bulb exploded. We signalled to the engineers below to switch off the engine. In darkness we moved what was left of the lamps to the inside of the tower. Somewhat despondent, I descended the hill for the second time that day working on a plan for improving our efficiency. It was midnight when we waved goodbye to the Matador, its driver, the worthy Sergeant-Major and, thankfully, Hector.

King's of Bristol apologised for not providing waterproof glasses and made amends without further charge. Sergeant-Major Raine drove over on each successive evening, dined with us, climbed the hill, helped set up the lights and tended the generator until midnight 'switch-off' before returning to Bristol. Seventeen times during that week I ascended and descended the Tor, being much comforted when reports of distant sightings filtered through on the rural telegraph.

When it was all over I received a bill from His Majesty's Territorial Army, for a hundred pounds. This I passed to the Borough Council, stating that I had understood the service to have been provided as a contribution from public funds. From that point I lost sight of the bill and have no knowledge of its ultimate settlement or destiny.

The battle of events was taking a toll. I realised that I was over-working. Feeling the need for a dependable partner I invited the conscientious Francis

Figgins to enter into a partnership with me at no financial cost to himself. I felt it right that he should share in profits in recognition of his loyal service. He promised to talk the matter over with his wife and a wise uncle. Within a week he tendered his resignation, having decided to take up an appointment with the *Central Somerset Gazette* as seller of advertising space. I have never thought other than that a consensus of the family had viewed my offer to be that of a lunatic and that Francis would be better away from such influence. The willing and likeable Leslie Childs took over the battery rounds, a responsibility unsuited to his abilities.

However, business continued brisk and Lilian fitted into the social life of the small town. She made frequent visits with the two growing boys to her parents in Hereford either by train or driven by me in the Hillman Minx. Then it became clear that the ageing parents were ill.

I never considered it as other than my duty to place the welfare of my in-laws high in my list of priorities. They had provided safe haven for my own little family during my absence on warlike activities. Lilian journeyed to Hereford with the children during school holidays. At Eastertide we made a practice of driving to Thirsk to visit my own parents, escaping on occasion to good old Scarborough. My father spent one week keeping an eye on the shop at Glastonbury whilst we foursome revelled in a holiday in Jersey. The benefit fortified me somewhat which was just as well for my cup runneth over when Maurice received his calling up papers and joined the RAF as a Wireless Mechanic, being pronounced fit for service. Throughout his two years in the force he carried the medical report which declared his being unfit!

The next blow came when Leslie reversed my prized Commer van into a cottage wall, doing considerable damage to both. His constitution could not overcome his sense of failure. He, to put it in modern parlance, 'went missing'. He was missing for four days during which time his landlady poured out her misgivings. The cottager let it be known that his garden wall was an important matter of concern. Sergeant Boyce made inquiries, and numerous sightings were reported. Finally Leslie turned up at an old haunt in Bristol. A kindly Police Officer took him in hand, recognised he needed expert medical attention and saw that he got it. A complete rest was ordered.

From Hereford came a cry for help. Both of Lilian's parents were confined to bed. School holidays yet had two weeks to run so wife and family made haste in response to the cry. I battled on in loneliness, drawing solace from sympathetic customers and friends, particularly from the good Doctor Evans and his wife.

During this period of self-pity a passing motorist chanced to be attracted by my new His Master's Voice sunshade. He requested my attention to his car radio, a relatively new invention. He revealed his occupation as that of self-employed business agent. Quite flippantly I said: 'You can sell this one if you like.' He expressed his opinion that radio businesses were difficult to sell at the present time but he would bear it in mind. I solved his immediate problem. We shook hands. He went on his way to Torquay and I forgot the incident.

Meanwhile Lilian stayed dutifully in attendance to her parents, coping at the same time with our two boisterous sons. By way of diversion from my business I made occasional weekend sorties to Hereford, usually via Gloucester, sometimes, when tides suited me, by way of the Aust Ferry. The helmsmanship of the ferrymen of Aust never failed to amaze me. The crossing of one of the world's most temperamental estuaries could have terminated in disaster should the man at the wheel lose his concentration for a second. Such were the powers of ebb and flow that straight-line navigation was out of the question. Passengers might be heard taking bets how far up or down river the ship might be steered before turning for the opposite shore. Yet with miracle-like precision we sloshed to the quay and drove safely toward our respective destinations.

On these journeys I might use the Commer van or the comfortable Hillman Minx which latter developed, on one trip, a severe uneasiness around the rear axle. The accompanying clonking noises prompted me to take the car for professional attention to Elver's Garage at Street. Elver and I were good friends. He had one foot in the radio business but felt indisposed to handle repairs. Hence, he offloaded all his service work onto myself. My charges suited him. We got on famously. I considered it time for me to sample his style of motor mechanicry. He diagnosed, in a short test drive around the premises, defective Hardy-Spicer joints. Within twenty-four hours Harold telephoned to say I could collect the Hillman. I was delighted with such prompt service. Regrettably, on the way back to Glastonbury it was clear the clonking noises were undiminished.

It so happened that, on my arrival home, the motor mechanic employed at Draper's Glove Manufacturing Company waited in my shop to talk business. Gilbert Brice owned an immaculate Riley Twelve-Six, a car renowned for its water-cooled main bearings. I was impressed by his wide-ranging conversation on the subject of motor vehicles. I asked him to give his opinion on the dear old Hillman Minx. Without hesitation Gilbert shuffled underneath the car, confirmed that new universal joints had indeed been fitted but then with loud expressions of sheer disgust he identified the real cause of the ailment. The U-bolts which clamp the rear springs to the axle had worked loose. A few deft turns of Gilbert's spanner restored the car to its former delightful performance!

To those readers who choose to pursue this history to its end I promise to reveal further outstandingly serious samples of appalling ignorance in motor servicing.

In my own trade of radio and television servicing there have operated some thousands of so-called 'cowboys'. Swindlers, fly-boys, sharp-practicers, whatever they may be called, have really taken the public 'to the cleaners'. A badly serviced radio set or television receiver may have caught fire but such potentials of danger cannot be compared with those perpetrated by incompetent motor mechanics. For the short remainder of my time in Glastonbury I depended on Gilbert for my motor maintenance.

As winter approached so Lilian's dilemma intensified. The health of her parents did not improve, yet our boys were established members of the St. John's School fraternity. I began to doubt my own ability to run the business without the constant support of my wife. Especially conscious of the additional technical problems accompanying the onset of the coming television boom, a radical change of strategy was necessary.

A solution began to formulate when a Mr S. W. Baker telephoned to say that the agent in Torquay recommended inspection of my business. Baker and his accountant surveyed premises, stock and books. My asking price for the lot and including goodwill was £7,500. After a few days of his 'thinking it over' I received a call from the buyer offering £7,000. This I refused very firmly. Had I accepted that reduced figure I was informed that Mr Baker would have backed down from the deal!

In due course I received formal notice of intention to buy. By the same post and maybe urged by mental telepathy an equally formal offer came from my pre-war employers C. F. King and Co. of Hereford. This extraordinary coincidence could be classified only under 'it had to be'.

By Hillman Minx I hurried to Hereford and visited a friendly estate agent who declared he was about to sell a house by auction within the hour, the house being in an area much favoured by Lilian. The house was 'knocked down' to 'the gentleman from Somerset' for £2,250. I then declared to the solicitor acting for the agents that I was unable to pay a deposit on the spot. I offered to leave my beloved Hillman as security. This was considered unnecessary. At that point I established an enduring relationship with an incredibly efficient and likeable lawyer, Leslie Charles Phillips Powell. He was to guide me through a number of domestic problems and over the years save me a great deal of money. With a sense of humour beyond compare added to an ability to convert difficulties into simplicities, this highly respected City Coroner held the confidence of a very broad clientèle.

On the following day I appraised my kindly bank manager of the situation. Did I detect a slight raising of an eyebrow? It was to be a sad parting when eventually I said farewell to Tom Jefford at the completion of negotiations. He was soon to retire to the lovely village of Box, there sadly to die but not before he had the great satisfaction of seeing his daughter Barbara well on her way to becoming one of the leading Shakespearian actresses of our time.

When all was cleared with the bank I had about £1,000 in the kitty. Lilian and the boys were already installed in our new Hereford address. I spent an uproarious evening bidding adieu to my many fellow patrons at several Glastonbury inns. Reg Mapstone, the reigning Mayor, paid me his final compliment, inimitably describing me as 'a bloody fool'. He said: 'It takes most people twelve years to become accepted as Glastonian. In only five years you have become one of us. We shall miss you on your microphone calling up the children on Sports Days, organising events at the Con. Club and best of all, lighting up the Tor!' I thanked him for his kind words.

I left the old town the following morning in the heavily laden Hillman Minx, not in the least apprehensive. I looked forward to becoming thoroughly immersed in the technicalities of television without the trauma of balancing the books.

Chapter 54

'Never Go Back'

The novelty of going to work as an employee, unworried by immediate financial risk, I found a relaxing experience. The house in Ross Road stood free of mortgage. The two boys settled into Hunderton School where they joined the Cubs. Lilian could keep watch on her ailing parents. My salary of £11 per week seemed adequate for our needs.

Though structurally sound the house needed extensive decoration to bring it up to Lilian's colourful aspirations. A friendly architect recommended a 'good chap' who would do it right through. I did not ask for a quotation: mistake number one! I paid £25 on account: mistake number two! When the final bill arrived I recognised it as an attempt by the 'good chap' to clear his bad debts. I requested a detailed account. It covered three foolscap pages.

Unable to reconcile quantities with square footage I appealed to my architectural ally. Following rapid calculations aided by slide-rule he declared that the kitchen ceiling must bear a layer of whitewash not less than an inch thick. He suggested an offer of half price to the 'good chap'. I posted a cheque for that amount in settlement and heard no more.

My inexperience in the servicing of television receivers caused me considerable anxiety especially when my first assignment brought me into conflict with the eggheads at Welwyn Garden City. I had caused already some consternation at the Murphy camp when the editor of the house magazine had published my criticism of workmanship emanating from the Hirwaun factory. The local representative, Freddie Beer, lost no time in calling on me to save his company's face in the case of a model V.120 supplied by C. F. King and Co. to a famous breeder of Hereford bulls.

The set had been unsatisfactory from its introduction to the Morgan Jones household. The stage had been reached where the owner threatened to sue somebody for loss of entertainment. At that point the V.120 had been returned to the factory for expert attention. After six weeks it was reinstalled. It exhibited the same fault. I anticipated a hot reception but found Morgan Jones to be a quiet and reasonable man. I promised to clear the fault. In return he promised me a side of pork.

Instead of taking the Murphy to my workshop at King's I took it to my home where my long-suffering wife was enlisted as unpaid observer. Within twenty-four hours she described the symptoms of the fault. These matched exactly the complaints as related by Mr Jones. After twenty-five minutes the picture simply vanished from the screen. After a few minutes cooling-off period the picture reappeared to disappear after a further twenty-five minutes.

I telephoned Johnson, the Service Manager at Murphy, hoping to pick up a clue which might direct me to a solution of the problem which he and his henchmen had failed to find. He was quite 'sure that the trouble was caused by instability in the I.F. stages'. With this useless particle of information at the back of my mind I adopted a different approach.

The Mazda cathode ray tubes fitted to Murphy sets were heated from a 2-volt supply. A quirk of the brain prompted me to connect the heater of the tube to a 2-volt accumulator, thus isolating it completely from the built-in power supplies. Hey, presto, a good picture was maintained for a whole hour. A further test proved the cathode ray tube to be faulty. With new tube fitted I returned the set to its owner who understandably questioned my credibility:

'You seem very confident,' the great man said. 'How is it that all those other people failed to detect the fault?'

I declared that to be beyond my comprehension. I would, however, make my feelings known to the top levels in the hierarchy. With that Jones bid me wait a while, presumably I thought, to procure from his larder my promised side of pork. He reappeared, bearing a parcel wrapped in greaseproof paper saying:

'In appreciation of your efforts here's a pound of cooking fat for the missus.'

I took my leave complete with trophy, never to set eyes on the fellow again. Nor did C. F. King and Co. receive further complaints of loss of entertainment. Nor did the manufacturer comment on my diagnosis.

Freddie Beer must have reported the happy ending to his firm's embarrassment for I was shortly to receive an attractive offer of employment from another Murphy Dealer. This, on account of my inherent loyalty, I could not accept.

Many radio and television traders refused to service sets not sold by themselves. I regarded that as a short-sighted policy. Tackling faults at which somebody else had already 'had a poke' could lead to inordinately difficult diagnoses. On the other hand a tremendous sense of achievement and of pleasurable customer reaction came as reward for sorting out knotty problems.

A surgeon, highly valued by the local hospital management, called in at my workshop to express dissatisfaction over the treatment of his Philips projection television at the hands of one of our competitors who had supplied the set to him. In response to the customer's complaint that the picture persistently 'rolled', the service man replaced the frame output valve. Repeated calls resulted in only temporary cure. The surgeon now boasted of a stock of spare valves. Logic prevailed. The diagnosis was faulty.

Though Philips projection receivers were not 'cheap', the manufacturer had fitted tiny carbon resistors incapable of coping with their function. At a very small cost I replaced all the quarter-watt resistors with one-watt types where desirable. The surgeon was pleased with the result of the operation. He presented me with his surplus stock of perfectly serviceable valves.

Projection television has never become popular for domestic use because of the need for meticulous maintenance. A local taverner expressed horror at fizzling noises and pungent odours emanating from his Phillips. I was myself alarmed to see such a veritable fountain of purple lights playing around the projection unit. Owing to a heavy accumulation of dust coupled with an atmosphere of exceptional humidity the extra high tension set up a corona discharge comparable with the Northern Lights. Delicate use of vacuum cleaner and camel-hair brush, finally removing all traces of grime by judicious application of commercial alcohol, meant normal operation was resumed. The customer declared:

'We've never had such a good picture.'

Whilst his remark was pleasing enough, it was untrue. The set had lacked the regular servicing so necessary for projection televisors. Had the manufacturers insisted on professional attention to their products after sale I have no doubt that Projection TV would be more popular.

A discreet sense of humour was as useful to a radio and television service engineer as his tool-kit and test meter. One needed to be prepared for all manner of descriptions of complaints, symptoms and reasons.

The copper-oxide rectifier had served the radio trade remarkably well for many years. Its relative inefficiency could be excused in deference to its unfailing reliability. The selenium rectifier's superior performance found favour with the manufacturers of K-B Television. It was less reliable, however, and when it failed it did so in spectacular fashion. Not only did it smoke but it emitted an appalling stink.

The rather genteel firm of Heins and Co., administered by the esteemed Mr Leslie and Mr Gilbert, had supplied a K-B to an upper class household on the outskirts of the city. Their likeable Bert King was dispatched in answer to a call for service. A very senior lady of the house opened the door. Indicating that she was very deaf she conducted Bert to the large sitting-room and pointed to the sickly K-B. Bert switched on and the selenium rectifier did its immediate and worst odoriferously.

'Young man,' said the lady, 'I do think you may have left that outside. I shall most certainly report your behaviour to Mr Gilbert.'

No amount of persuasion or gesturing could pacify the lady's displeasure. It fell to Mr Gilbert to telephone the master of the house on that gentleman's return home from his place of work.

Though known to be financially well equipped, our milkman regarded television as 'nothing but a waste of money'. By cautiously enlisting the connivance of his wife I arranged a free demonstration in the home, this to coincide with the showing of a Saturday afternoon football match. My prospective buyer professed no interest in my movements until I switched on the Bush TV12 which displayed with incredible clarity a picture of Stanley Matthews in action.

An extraordinary change came over Mr Armishaw. In a paroxysm of excitement he pointed to the screen. There followed a few seconds of uncanny silence, a paralytic holding of breath; then, as he stared at me in disbelief he screamed at me:

'That's Stanley Matthews . . . that's Stanley Matthews . . .! Look! Look! . . . LOOK! That's Stanley Matthews.'

As if this outburst was not sufficient, to the astonishment of both Mrs Armishaw and myself he promptly called out:

'Get me my cheque book, Missus! You make out a cheque and I'll sign it!' With that he settled into his favourite armchair, the better to fix his gaze upon the footballing.

When he called at the shop with the milk on the following Monday morning he declared himself thoroughly happy with his purchase. He just hoped there would be more football mid-week.

Customers came in all shapes and sizes; complaints came as varied as their informants. The majority expected priority attention regardless of normal working hours. Such luxuries as overtime pay or special arrangements regarding unsociable hours were unheard of in the radio and television trade. We service engineers were indeed a brood of nighthawks. Puzzling symptoms of faults called for keen observation. Exchange of views within the trade evoked widespread comradeship between employers of rival companies. The correspondence columns of trade magazines contained valuable hints and tips often interspersed with touches of humour.

One recently purchased Bush TV12 was reported by its owner to give highly satisfactory results until 7.00 p.m. At that time, without fail, a speckled line appeared across the picture. As described to me the symptom clearly indicated the use in the house of a faulty electric light bulb. On my suggestion the customer checked all the bulbs in the house, even asking the next-door neighbour to co-operate in the research. In response to a further request I arrived at the house at 6.45 p.m. and found everything in perfect order. Settling down to wait for the vital 7 o'clock appearance of the mystic line, I witnessed the despatch of the seven-year-old child of the family to 'a good night's sleep to be ready for school'. Mother returned to the fireside having tucked the offspring in bed. We waited patiently for the phenomenon. Lo and behold, it obliged right on time. I identified the apparition as being caused by a faulty electric light bulb. The happy parents showed signs of doubting my sanity. They obliged by touring the house to confirm that no light was shining. Still I maintained my stance; a faulty bulb must be found. I sensed growing annoyance by the customers when I suggested I be introduced to the neighbours. Reluctantly they agreed to take me 'round the back' to meet the occupants of the other half of the 'semi'. We did not get that far. I observed a light shining from a small pantry window. The problem was solved. Each night after the paternal tucking into bed the lad had adopted the habit of nipping smartly down to the pantry. After pinching a biscuit or two he returned equally silently to bed but failed to switch off the pantry light. The case closed over a nice cup of tea and a good laugh, all free of charge.

On my arrival home a neighbour asked me to inspect his Ekco TV. He was not a customer of King's but of the local branch of Curry's. He had been quoted £15 by that company for the replacement of the cathode ray tube. He could not believe this to be necessary. Would I adjudicate?

Immediately I identified the lack of a picture to be caused by the absence of connection to an aerial. The lady of the house had dislodged the plug from a junction box on the window frame, whilst doing the daily dusting. Without making a charge for my expertise I left the owner to his thoughts.

Lilian was well accustomed to my irregular working hours. I worked as hard as if the business were my own. Many customers assumed that I was indeed a fully fledged partner in it. Truly I was my own master to a great extent. It was a family affair. Charlie King persuaded me to take on the voluntary secretaryship of the local branch of the Radio and Television Retailers Association (RTRA). This served the purpose of a gossip shop for small-minded shopkeepers in which they could vent grievances against the nationalised electricity board and the big multiples such as Curry's and Stone's. These were considered to represent unfair competition.

The Midlands Electricity Board was the principal enemy. As a protest against nationalisation I was instructed by the committee to arrange a meeting with the local MP. Thus, I had the enlightening experience of coming face to face with J. P. L. Thomas, who at the time was our First Lord of the Admiralty. I had often wondered what a cabinet minister looked like. This one turned out to be a very fine example. 'Jimmy' was tall, highly distinguished, patient. With a gold-plated fountain pen he took copious notes of the bleatings of some of the members; the majority were dumb-struck by such elegance. The meeting concluded with a round of hand-shaking. The conclusion drawn by members of RTRA (Hereford Branch) was that nothing would be done towards de-nationalisation, nor was it.

In pursuance of my work on behalf of the RTRA it befell me to organise the Annual Dinner at the Green Dragon Hotel. Numerous captains of the trade attended. Amongst them came one Paul M. Sebestyen, Sales Director of Radiospares. There was a personality beyond compare. Fitted out in a very expensive tuxedo outfit, embellished by a flouncy cummerbund, 'P.M.S.', as he came to be known, resembled, in deportment, an elongated sack of potatoes. His healthy complexion added warmth and sincerity to his radiant personality. Undoubtedly of central European stock, this man possessed a remarkable command of the English language which enabled him to put himself and his audience at ease. His disarming smile magnetised the ladies. Here was no ordinary business man. I resolved at some future opportune time to join him on his upward thrust through the jungle of the disorderly British distribution network.

Meanwhile I settled for the fullness of life in my favourite city. In answer to an appeal for volunteers to join the Home Guard I adopted khaki uniform for a few weekends. I failed to see any sense in the mock exercises dreamed up by an aged retired general. I joined the Royal Air Forces Association (RAFA) to be induced shortly into taking on the secretaryship. I agreed to this at the end of a committee meeting which ended after midnight. One condition of acceptance was that no meeting should stretch beyond 'closing time' of the licensed premises which were used as temporary headquarters. The condition was applauded. From that point forward the branch prospered as never before.

The Halifax Building Society leased a large room to RAFA at nominal rent. Members rallied round to build a bar, furnish the place. Supported in great measure by Group Captain F. S. Wakeham, Officer Commanding RAF Credenhill, we made it known to the general public that RAFA was worth something to the city at large. On Sunday of Battle of Britain Week a full-dress parade to the Cathedral was headed by an RAF band, followed by a column of airmen. The RAFA banner proudly carried by Ted Davis headed a contingent of old-timers and the local branch of the Air Cadets. Broad Street was lined with appreciative citizens. The Dean of Hereford conducted an impressive service to an unusually large congregation.

During the week the flower-bedecked Shire Hall accommodated the Battle of Britain Ball. There was no trouble selling tickets for dancing to Jack Parnell and his Orchestra.

The week concluded at Edgar Street football ground where a highly trained team of airmen from Credenhill gave a thrilling display of commandless drill. An equally stirring performance by the RAF Dog Team highlighted the extensive programme which I compèred over C. F. King's public address system. The overall benefit to the RAF Benevolent Fund gave great satisfaction to all who contributed.

Our second attempt at a supper ball evaded disaster by a couple of whiskers. Bob Thompson, one of the committee members, had taken into his private enterprises an agency for big bands. He agreed to book Lou Preager, reserve the Shire Hall and publicise the ball. Colourful posters appeared all over the county. A week before the event I called in at the hall to ascertain whether all was arranged. The caretaker informed me that the annual flower show was to be held on the date mentioned. In a state of near panic I raised hell, ordered correction stickers for the multitude of posters announcing that the venue would be the Drill Hall, which I was able to book by the kind connivance of my friends in the Home Guard. The Drill Hall, being an out-sized Nissen Hut with concrete floor, needed an abundance of floral decoration. Furthermore a spring floor added enormously to our overall expenses. Lou Preager didn't find the acoustics to his liking but once his brass section blasted into 'Darktown Strutters' bar-takings rocketed. Yet another Battle of Britain Ball could be recorded as a success.

The dear old Hillman Minx had been replaced by a rare and unsatisfactory motor-car, a Singer 1500 cc. saloon. I bought it from a Mr Bill Haynes who had been recommended as trustworthy by a pre-war colleague at King's but who was now very much involved in the motor trade. The Singer could have been mistaken for a stylised London taxi-cab. Its ample seats were comfortable, its bodywork heavy and coloured black. An imposing chromium radiator grille separated two gorgeous headlamps. Under the bonnet a four-cylinder engine with single overhead camshaft provided adequate power. I have never understood why the majority of car makers were reluctant to use this simple basic design. It would appear that a s.o.c. engine must have been cheaper to make than one requiring a forest of push-rods. Singer made it work well enough. The gear-box operated with little noise; the changing of gears was a delight. So what was wrong with the Singer '1500'? The suspension was diabolical and the brakes quite dangerously inadequate for so heavy a car. The wizard gear-change enabled the driver to avoid most hazards. The steering did not help. If the front tyres were set at recommended pressure front springing lacked evidence. A reasonable degree of comfort could be achieved by drastic lowering of tyre pressure; the steering then became tolerable only at speed.

In examining the rear brakes with a view to improving the system I discovered to my horror that a rear-wheel bearing had been replaced by one of much smaller diameter than the housing. After fitting the correct size of bearing I reported the matter to my friend. He supported my suggestion of taking up the matter with the dealer, with a view to claiming compensation under 'guarantee'. Frustration was short-lived. Mr Haynes had died of a heart attack and the business no longer existed! So much for 'guarantees'.

The willing and sweet-sounding engine together with the excellent gear-box endeared me to the Singer for two years. Unaware of the inadequate brakes the family, plus the in-laws, enjoyed many an outing. Fully laden the springs responded well. Four adults, three children and a dog comprised the load on a memorable journey north. In the Staffordshire town of Leek I remembered well, from my motor-cycling days, a steep hill down to a cross-roads. The route lay straight ahead. In bottom gear already I stood on the foot-brake pedal. The Singer refused to slow down. In desperation I turned left. My passengers were unaware of the danger and accepted my apology for taking a wrong turn. Finding an alternative way to the Buxton Road I resolved that the Singer must be disposed of at an early date.

It became urgently necessary to sell the car when Michael John, our elder son, won a scholarship to Monmouth School. A local car dealer expressed willingness to negotiate a sale for a modest commission. The fellow had struck me as being an honest mechanic. Therefore, I requested that he should spot weld a small fracture in a front wing before offering the Singer for sale. He drove the car to his workplace, welded the offending crack and two minutes later the fire started. Damage to the front seats, carpets and to the dashboard was extensive. Years later when I referred to one of the famous Haynes Manuals on Car Servicing I noted in the opening chapter the wise instruction to disconnect the battery before commencing the simplest of maintenance tasks. On the Singer a live wire passed immediately behind the point of welding. The rubber insulation had melted, resulting in a short-circuit and consequent fire. My man was full of apologies, accepted full responsibility and would arrange an insurance claim. He did – on my insurance company! – the Road Transport and General.

The manager of the RT and G in Hereford was a fellow member of RAFA, one Roddy Thomas. It later transpired that the salesman/mechanic was not himself insured against damage to customers' cars. Thomas persuaded him that if he placed all his future business with him the claim would be made against my policy. I was asked to 'sign a form' and did! Repairs to the car were completed only six weeks later. When my insurance premium fell due I gathered that I had foregone my no-claim bonus and on questioning this I discovered the mean trick played by my RAFA colleague.

By the time I was reunited with the Singer its value had depreciated. I managed to off-load it to a dealer in Gloucester for £350, which represented a considerable financial loss. In order to meet my first payment to Monmouth School I was further obliged to cash in my much-prized life insurance policy with the Sunlife of Canada, another sad loss. I had not learned to live without a motor-car. The fawn coloured Morris Ten saloon was notable for its extensive rust. At £145 I could not complain. It served us well for a year or more, economically lively of performance and endowed with excellent brakes.

In the Morris two of us from RAFA attended the 1955 Annual Conference of the Association at Scarborough. This was the second occasion when I came under the spell of Air Marshal, by then Lord, Tedder, President of the Association. His quiet handling of aggressive delegates was a lesson to us all. He would have made a wonderful Prime Minister.

With my heavy family commitments I began to feel concern for the rusty undercarriage of the Morris. When a local watch-maker admired the lightness of the car he agreed to an exchange for his 1500 cc. six-cylinder Rover, which I could not resist. This was what I imagined a real car to be: leather seats, walnut dashboard and door sills, free-wheel, silent running. The Rover had everything except performance. It wouldn't pull the skin off a rice pudding! I decided it needed a re-bore and new pistons. At £14 I thought it a bargain. The performance was unimproved. To 30 m.p.h. the car was a dream. It accelerated smoothly and with great promise but there it ended. The throttle pedal felt limp to the foot and even downhill 45 m.p.h. could not be exceeded. Still, the feeling of well-being gave enormous satisfaction. No amount of adjustment coaxed an atom more power, yet it consumed petrol at a prolific rate.

Increased living costs and school fees dictated a requirement for increased income. It was not forthcoming from C. F. King and Co., where the management showed signs of weakness. When I detected an excess of private drawings and a reluctance to support any expansion in my department I considered it time to leave. I refused two offers from competitors in the city because of my ingrown loyalty to Charlie King. When the Radiospares representative, an uninspiring lay preacher, advised that he would be vacating his post I wasted no time in applying for it. A month later when he called upon me, announcing his resignation, I was able to inform him that I had 'got the job'.

It was only when I left C. F. King and Co. for the third time I realised that I should have remembered: 'NEVER GO BACK.'

Chapter 55

'On the Road'

Three short-listed candidates for a vacancy on the Radiospares Sales Force faced the monstrous personality of P. M. Sebestyen, Sales Director. On my left sat a promising young fellow who did join the company at a later date. On my right a nervous lad from Swansea shifted uneasily from one buttock to the other during the whole of the forthcoming interview, which began in most unorthodox fashion: the opening question brought all three interviewees to a high pitch of alertness:

'Tell me, boys: do you enjoy a good fuck?'

From the Londoner to my left came a stifled chuckle; I made a spontaneous gesture intended to indicate that nothing disagreeable was under question. The Welshman made his first big shift, bowing his head as though recalling a chapel-going background. Following a suitably long period of anticipatory silence 'P.M.S.' continued:

'Well I don't mind who you fuck, so long as you don't fuck my customers.'

The great man had relished his stock joke Thereafter the interview proceeded in serious mode. The periodic interjection of pertinent questions kept the listeners alert though the candidate from Wales answered only by a shift of his bottom.

A master of précis, the interviewer outlined the history of his company. He and two brothers named Wineburg, operating from a hut in the Edgware Road, sold components useful to repairers of radio sets. The highly satisfactory profit of £28 was made in the first month of trading; with this sum one of the Wineburgs sloped off, changed his name to Winter and started the Winter Trading Company. Brother Herbert changed his name to Waring and stayed loyal to his Hungarian partner. From that point they never looked back. Blazing disagreements occurred from time to time, a 'continental' letting-off of steam, quite foreign to the average 'Brit'. Once a decision was reached either way then the course was set for both parties, no deviation. The Sales Force currently embodied 45 men.

Each and every month a new and up-to-date catalogue was issued. About the size of the average theatre programme, the Radiospares catalogue contained numerous illustrations of the products offered for sale, details of electrical performance, dimensions and prices of every single item. Everything was available by return of post, postal charges included no matter the size of the package. With such information and such service at the customers' command it would seem that no personal representation was necessary. So one of P.M.S.'s star questions came:

'Why do we need representatives?'

The silent thoughts of the three interviewees failed to volunteer an answer. P.M.S. knew the answer, of course. He gave it:

'Because our customers are bad business men.'

I did not appreciate the full significance of the statement until I began my task of calling upon them. Then I saw the value of having a monthly debt collector. Prompt settlement of accounts in return for prompt, efficient service – therein lay the secret of success.

I returned to Hereford confident that the job was mine. Confirmation came when P.M.S. telephoned me at King's. I understood that at a not too distant date I would be required to move to Gloucester.

Parting from my immediate environment called for a special celebratory gathering. Six of us piled into the Rover which enjoyed a full load, not that it went any faster but it sat the road with even greater certainty. We, radio technicians all, travelled to Ross-on-Wye to be entertained at the home of an eccentric schoolmaster, one Grant Dixon. He demonstrated to us what was probably the world's first domestically operated colour television. Entirely of his own design but aided by sympathetic industrialists such as Marconi-EMI, this extraordinary character spent incalculable time constructing the apparatus.

Before beginning life on the road I attended an intensive training course in the business methods of the company. Largely under the direct tuition of P.M.S. or his partner Herbert Waring, my eyes were opened to the application of Greek mythology to modern business systems. P.M.S. was a classical scholar from Budapest University. Herbert was a typical arrogant Dutchman, pertinacious, sometimes quite bloody-minded, sarcastic and rude. He and I never met on the same wavelength. P.M.S. and I understood one another to the extent that I never incurred his wrath which could, by all accounts, burst into uncontrollable thunder. I have known people leave his presence wholly demoralised and in tears, yet a kind heart lurked not far below his well-upholstered chest.

I swallowed the Radiospares bible hook, line and sinker.

My initiation to the profession of commercial travelling came under the supervision of my Area Manager, one George Parker. He accompanied me during the whole of my first month 'on the road'.

George, a fountain of hints and tips on Salesmanship, reeled off innumerable adages on life and how to live it. Regrettably he lacked tact. He told me how my predecessor had come to give up the job in favour of a life at sea:

Bassett, the laypreacher, too timid to be a salesman, had tried George's patience beyond its limit. On a visit to Stibbs' radio and electrical shop in Abertillery, George was demonstrating his skill for Bassett's benefit. He was on the point of persuading Mr Stibbs to order a drum of cable when Bassett timorously commented:

'Of course you usually buy your cable on your weekly visit to the Cardiff wholesalers, don't you, Mr Stibbs?'

When, finally, Area Manager and underling left the premises George looked Bassett straight in the face and said, simply:

'You cunt.'

Bassett promptly gave his notice and quit. Hence I came, for one month, to be under George's immediate guidance. We got on famously. My family liked him. Though I found him helpful he seemed uncertain of some particulars of the company's policy. When I questioned certain points he resorted to evasion. I resolved to accept his interpretation of the rules for the time being and apply my own after his departure.

George approved of the comfort of the Rover but suggested I would be better off with a Ford. I took his advice and obtained a 'Prefect'. The winter closed in; we both froze. The only way to maintain blood-heat, in George's opinion, was to accept hot tea at every call and at any snack bar sited in between. George had an insatiable capacity for tea. As a result we irrigated every hedgerow in Gloucestershire and Herefordshire. The snow descended in quantity, the Ford slithered from call to call but as George repeatedly proclaimed:

'Radiospares and the mail always get through.'

That rallying call helped me many times in appalling weather.

George insisted on a 'proper' lunch. At about 13.00 hrs. we made for the nearest cafe, hotel or whatever was the nearest place for refreshment. Transport cafes with sweating windows, serving sausages and beans, egg on toast with extra toast, were as acceptable to George as the Royal Hotel. No alcohol at lunch time; beer at night when we stayed in hotels.

My first months tested my financial resources. Wages at £10 per week and car allowance at £4 per week saw me through. Modest hotel bills were met by the firm at the end of the month. I looked forward to being on my own when I could earn commission. As George departed he made a statement which caused my one and only unpleasant skirmish with the management. He said in front of Lilian:

'I don't see any reason why you should move from Hereford.'

Believing him to speak with authority I cancelled my instructions for the sale of my house and looked forward to a further sojourn in the Wye Valley. It transpired that the Radiospares management did not delegate authority to its Area Managers, instructing them only to supervise. When, ultimately, P.M.S. questioned my continued residence in Hereford it dawned upon me that Parker had not mentioned the subject to him. Not wishing to 'drop George in it' I spent a miserable weekend working over the problem. I 'phoned him and asked him to solve it on my behalf. He told the great man that he had given me 'the impression' that I need not move to Gloucester! His economy of truth glossed over the situation. I was given the option of moving to Gloucester with a promise of a more lucrative territory or staying where I was with a 'marginal' territory. Immediately I set about moving. It was a bad time for doing so.

House prices in Hereford fell sharply whereas a temporary boom in the famous Gloucester aircraft industry caused a rise in that area. I was one of the first to be 'gazumped'.

Meanwhile I acclimatised myself to the life of a travelling salesman. My first night away from home I spent in the Spread Eagle Hotel, a thriving establishment overlooking Gloucester cattle market, the site now occupied by the Central Bus Station. It set a good standard in hotels. I was obliged to stay away from home a dozen nights each month. The Spread Eagle was my measuring rod; I found several hostelries less to my liking, few better.

The commission rates offered exciting possibilities. The first £150 worth of sales garnered no commission, the next £150 earned 5% and anything over £300 attracted 10%. I found no great difficulty in merging into the highest level. George Parker was delighted with the results. He 'managed' ten or more territories and depended on his team to boost his ego, his standing with the grand master and the size of his Christmas bonus. Bassett's feeble efforts had done nothing for George. I gloried in the rising fortunes of the territory.

The Ford Perfect displeased. The engine got through a pint of engine oil between petrol stops. I still wonder why the Prefect became one of Ford's most popular models. The springing did not spring. Back seat passengers suffered spring-jolting discomfort while the driver concentrated on avoiding major bumps. I yearned for the dear old Hillman Minx. However, I chose an Austin Devon saloon, the late property of a Hereford doctor. It was, as the trade delights in describing their used models: immaculate. Lilian loved its olive green paintwork, the interior comfort earned praise from all the family. The A40 rode like a queen of the seas. At 40,000 miles it was due for the fitting of Cord oil-control piston rings. I accomplished the task myself. The results were highly satisfactory. The Devon served well for a couple of years.

Business progressed. Selling for Radiospares could be regarded as running one's own business on somebody else's capital. The monthly catalogue, with its piece of string by which it came to be suspended from a conveniently placed nail in the customers' workshop and office, became an institution in the trade. It comprised an actual stock-list of components and accessories available by return of post. The back-up service operated with precision. There was no better service in the radio or any other industry. Customers so took it for granted that any minor hiccup brought forth outrageously uncomplimentary criticism. If the Radiospares service failed in any way prophecies of impending national disaster were rumoured.

On the occasion when a customer found a tomato sandwich included in a neat package of components he retained the offending morsel, presenting it to the firm's representative on his next monthly call!

Regular monthly calls ensured superb credit control. Bad debts were rare; very bad debts were not permissible. Clients who fell more than two months in arrears were transferred to the COD list. The ever-growing network of highly satisfied customers ensured ever-increasing profits.

The beautiful territories of Gloucestershire, Herefordshire and Monmouthshire were mine to travel and behold. To these must be added the heavily industrialised Monmouthshire Valleys. Amidst smoke and grime I found hearts of gold behind unclean shop windows. The most depressing place in the kingdom was Abertillery on a wet day. The wide main street of Blackwood brought relief from the environmental strictures of Ebbw Vale and Bargoed.

Being no stranger to the Welsh way of life I readily adapted my sales technique to match the language of individual customers. Those who chose to swear at me caused as little embarrassment as those of more genteel manner. Of the whole territory I regarded only Winter's of Newport as a really well-disciplined and efficient business. The vast majority were as 'P.M.S.' had stigmatized them: 'Bad business men.' It became clear to me within the first few weeks of my visitations that the majority of retailers shuffled along on extended credit from wholesale suppliers, paid minimum wages to staff and looked to some sort of accountant to mollify the local tax inspector.

The television boom of the late fifties attracted all manner of unqualified people into the trade. Disgruntled miners left the pits; grocers, butchers, chemists and candlestick makers rushed into the gold mine. The genuine venturers were obliged to fight the 'get rich quicksters'.

Radiospares served them all, large and small, so long as they occupied business premises open during normal shopping hours. How else could we representatives collect the money? We sold switch-cleaner, solder, anti-static polish, nuts, screws, washers, rubber feet, knobs, wires and piles of spare parts, many of which would never be used, to many who didn't know how to use them. It has been estimated that at least half the total of 'engineers' were trimmer twiddlers and valve rappers, sardonically referred to in the trade as 'poke and hope merchants'. Inevitably it became known that my own expertise might be of use. A select few would put a 'sticky' fault to one side to await my next monthly call.

Gwyn Evans, a typical 'p and h merchant', sold McMichael televisors from a small ship in Nantyglo. When I put up at the New Griffin Hotel in Brynmawr, he would stand me a pint before persuading me that the local populace would benefit from my attention to his problems. He cannibalised one set to breathe new life into a faulty one. Thus he accumulated piles of disabled sets to the point where his business approached disaster and he a nervous breakdown.

I missed seeing Gwyn for a couple of months. He had taken a holiday away from the valleys, so his account remained unpaid. He owed my company £12. I caught him by stepping in front of his A35 van in Nantyglo:

'Gwyn,' I said, 'I want £12 from you, now.'

'Oh,' he said, 'here you are. It's all I've got. I've just had a final demand from McMichael. I had no idea I owed them fifteen hundred pounds!'

The next time I saw Gwyn he held down the post of 'Service Engineer' at Blaina Co-op. Undoubtedly, he would consolidate that organisation's long list of dissatisfied customers.

The relentless progress of piped TV installations by Rediffusion restricted the proliferation of inefficient small retailers who moaned about unfair competition. In an effort to survive, a large number of private traders clutched at the extraordinary schemes offered by Pye Radio and Television. This highly respected firm came under the direction of the garrulous Irishman, C.O. Stanley.

Stanley's enthusiasm, unbounded by financial discretion, swept Pye itself and numerous retailers to crash-point. We Radiospares representatives observed from our prime positions on our routine calls the antics of grown men rushing towards bankruptcies. Our job was to sell the best service in the industry and collect the accounts on due date. What the customer did with the stuff once he had bought it was his problem.

Radiospares Limited styled themselves manufacturers by virtue of the fact that every single catalogue item was guaranteed by the company. In fact the great majority was 'bought-in', packed in attractive Radiospares packaging, and marked up to give a very handsome profit.

All orders were despatched post-paid, even during rail or postal strikes, when the company turned to air-mail or direct road services. We never failed to deliver. Backed by such a service and governed by what the management described as a benevolent dictatorship we reps were the best paid in the industry. Surprisingly, not all members of the sales force appreciated their unique position.

After my 'breaking-in period' in the Welsh Valleys, P.M.S. moved me eastwards into more pleasant grounds. I retained Herefordshire and Gloucestershire but my travels now embraced the rapidly expanding economy of Swindon, the Cotswolds, Newbury and parts of Oxfordshire. The harvest improved enormously.

In 1958 the company took a giant step forward. Having built up a nationwide business on the backs of the unsuspecting but gullible retailers we launched into industry with a great flourish. Had the retailers been watchful of the expansion of industry all around them and catered for its obvious need for small electronic components for maintenance and repair Radiospares could not have found the tremendous market open to them. The Sales Force divided its time between retailers and industrial users, only one or two days a week being devoted at first to the new breed of customer. There were two reasons for this: firstly, the range of goods offered for industrial use was very limited; secondly, quite new sales techniques had to be learned by degrees. It was impossible to 'drop in' at a large manufacturing concern, hospital, educational establishment or government experimental station with hail-fellow-cigarette-distributing joviality. The softly-softly approach, more appropriate to the vastly more so-phisticated clientele, paid dividends. We learned rapidly by experience. The increasing number of calls precipitated overload conditions. These were re-lieved by the decision to make calls on industry only two-monthly. That splendid move allowed a more gradual increase in stocks suited to customer needs.

Meanwhile the tendency for the reps to bathe in the sunshine of newly acquired fortune was corrected. The warning not to relax pressure upon the retail sector curtly reminded us of our heritage. Any protestations from the retailers against our venture into new fields, on their territories, were answered by the assurance that our service to their good selves would continue unabated. Not unnaturally, when an employee in local industry, with catalogue in hand, walked into his nearest radio shop asking for Radiospares components at cata-logue prices there arose many acrimonious discussions. Our representation developed new strata of diplomacy.

The Austin Devon had served with unfailing reliability but when I spotted the 'Car of the Week' in a Newbury showroom I satisfied a long felt desire to own a Jowett Javelin. HJB172, in shiny black, had been fitted with a modified engine, the previous owner having failed to pour anti-freeze into the radiator. A bargain struck, money paid, I returned to Gloucester in a machine which performed in a manner quite exhilarating. Acceleration from 0-60 mph in 21 seconds con-firmed the reputation of the Javelin as the fastest $1\frac{1}{2}$ litre car on the road. Steering and road-holding qualities matched the performance. All-in-all the Javelin far outclassed anything of comparable price. It did have faults. The flat-four engine, forward of the front wheels, collected rainwater around its spark-plugs in every downpour. The main niggling imperfections of this thor-oughbred piece of Yorkshire craftsmanship could be suffered only by the Jowett enthusiast, of which select company I continued to belong until the marque was bulldozed out of existence by the Ford Motor Company. Instead of losing millions on their purchase of Jaguar in 1991, Ford could have developed the famous Jowett into a great financial success. Regrettably, the demand for Fords raged insatiably. The last Jowett left the Idle factory in 1953. By a complicated monetary route when I drove for a short time an Austin A40 Somerset, I ended up with one of the 1953 de luxe versions of the Javelin. Its leather seats, wooden dashboard and armrests all made for greater comfort than that of the standard model. The Somerset served a useful purpose in between deals. Thoroughly reliable and comfortable of ride in a straight line the Somer-set knew nothing about road-holding. Cornering called for cautious negotiation, at respectable speed.

During my Somerset ownership I experienced a change of Area Manager. The sage persistence of George Parker gave way to the recently promoted Johnny Johnson with whom I had first made acquaintance at Glastonbury. Whereas George exhibited passion for detail Johnny cared for it not at all. This

carefree attitude to his job certainly allowed me to interpret the company's
rules as I wished. Johnny smoked a pipe, drove a car like a raving lunatic and
spent excessive time cheering himself and anyone in sight through pints of
English ale. His visits to me were uncluttered by bureaucracy. He had no
stomach for routine but I insisted on sticking to it. He did not object. He
preferred to drive my car. On a right-angle bend in Wiltshire he nearly did for
both of us. The Somerset could not take it. Had the road been wet we would
have executed numerous somersaults. The road being dry the tyres, in perfect
condition, stuck grimly to the tarmac; the body of the car creaked and cracked
as though to part company from its running-gear. Books and papers scattered
over the seats. I called for a halt to tidy the mess. Shaking like a leaf I quite
forgot my hierarchically inferior position with the company and addressed my
Area Manager in thoroughly uncomplimentary terms. He was unlikely to fire
me; in the heat of the moment I could not have cared.

I found a ready buyer for the Somerset, a very popular model with the
undiscerning motorists of the times. My de luxe Javelin was purchased from
Jackie Welton of Cheltenham. Jackie could be classed truly as a 'Character'. He
lived at Prescott, site of the famous hill-climb, so he had every opportunity of
putting up some good times in his Cooper Single-seater-Single-cylinder racer.
His wife, Pauline Brock, reigned as Ladies' Champion.

Jackie drove the Javelin on a demonstration run around Cheltenham, on a
dark night. Whilst he extolled the virtues of the 'excellent version' (he had
'personally vetted it'), a rear wheel came off! He had 'personally omitted to
tighten the nuts'. The minor offence rectified, I began an amicable association
with my second Javelin, remembering it to the present day as a highly innovative and successful design, lost in the midst of rampaging mediocrity.

My progress as a travelling salesman had not gone unnoticed at Headquarters. The big chief disclosed the reason for directing my move to Gloucester.
He joined me for one day during my calls upon customers in that city. As he
observed my behaviour on the circuit I had the pleasure and benefit of his
company. Highly skilled in the art of conversation he displayed a remarkable
aptitude for selecting the most pertinent answer to an impertinent question. Our
catalogue clearly indicated that Mr. J. Diamond (later Lord Diamond) acted as a
non-executive director of Radiospares. Now Jack Diamond, as he was well
known locally, being MP for Gloucester, represented the Labour Party. To
many a businessman that seemed incongruous.

One of my favourite customers, the jovial Archie Smith, declared himself a
high church Conservative. Therefore as P.M.S. accompanied me towards
Archie's shop in Worcester Street I warned the great man that he would most
likely be questioned on the advisability of harbouring a Socialist on the board
of management. We went through our business of order-taking before Archie
broached the subject. He chose the question:

'And where does John Diamond fit into your organisation?'

P.M.S. replied: 'Mr. Diamond is a good friend, a most excellent accountant and analyst, but I have no time for his fucking politics.'

We left Archie well satisfied and full of glee. The tale went down well that evening at the 'Con' Club.

At the end of the day P.M.S. offered me the post of Area Manager for Wales, the West of England and (for experience) four territories in North London and Essex. I would not refuse promotion on principle but in accepting it I put an end to a very pleasurable period of my life. Area Managership with Radiospares turned out to be a very hot seat, without responsibility other than supervising the work of the fourteen representatives allotted to my surveillance. I took no part in the selection of staff. P.M.S. took upon himself sole responsibility for success or ultimate failure of an individual salesman. Saleswomen were out of the question. He said he had enough trouble with men!

Chapter 56

View from the Top

Initiation to the duties of Area Manager began with a thorough study of the workings of company headquarters at 4–8 Maple Street. The splendid organisation of offices and stores targeted one aim: service to the customer. All else followed automatically: staff morale, incremental wage packets, higher profits. Departmental managers worked without interference but reported daily the progress of their own particular efforts. Waring kept a watchful eye on the internal machinery of the system. P.M.S. received recordings of number of parcels despatched (the GPO ran a shuttle service), new order intake and news from the Sales Force in the field.

Every month P.M.S. scrutinised his elaborate analyses: customers were grouped in levels of turnover, representatives were notified of their figures in comparison with those of the previous year. Appropriate notes from P.M.S., complimentary or otherwise, served as reminders that the great man took a personal interest in the individual. A complimentary memo from P.M.S. acted like a tonic. His terrorising criticisms to the laggards acted purgatively.

I was treated to an insight of all recent correspondence, thus gaining in a short time valuable knowledge of the idiosyncracies of the members of the team to be supervised by me. I was unable to read reports of my own performance on the road because Johnny Johnson had destroyed them. I did not dare report this to P.M.S. for fear of setting off a civil disturbance. I was taking over Johnny's team. Johnny had been promoted to Sales Manager, a new appointment designed to relieve P.M.S. of some responsibility. I thought P.M.S. should have seen Johnny's limitations but I assumed he chose him for his open mindedness and his command of the English language. Johnny's gift of the gab was a cultured one; it lacked common sense. We spent two weeks together at HQ undergoing our respective initiations. As the days went by I became apprehensive of the new Sales Manager's ability to absorb fundamental principles of management at the level to which he was being introduced. As my Area Manager he had shown scant regard for maintenance of journey books. Wrongly, I assumed that my own penchant for detail allowed him to relax vigilance in my case alone. I would soon be surprised by the truth.

During our training period both Johnny and I enjoyed the hospitality of the Mandeville Hotel. After dinner we resorted to Johnny's favourite London pub, the Seven Stars in Carey Street. There we met many notable journalists, employees of the Inns of Court, traders, punters, assorted personalities of both sexes and several nationalities. Johnny absorbed friendship as he absorbed beer. We never quarrelled. I always enjoyed his company. His promotion warranted a 'better' car. He bought a Sunbeam Mk.III, very expensive and very fast. Johnny in his Sunbeam surely put the Oxford Circus to Marble Arch record far beyond the reach of any future driver. From the comfortable passenger seat a blurred stream of coloured lights denoted our passage through London's principal artery.

As I departed from HQ I espied Johnny kneeling on the floor of his new office, maps spread out all around him. He was endeavouring to come to terms with the complexities of territorial calling schedules. There were signs that he was out of his depth. He was surely a salesman, but not a Manager. Inadvertently I became the instrument of his demise. He had mapped out his own fate in the record books.

My first task as Area Manager was to introduce my replacement on my old territory. Leslie Piercy, like myself, had forsaken service engineering and again like myself found enjoyment in selling the Radiospares service. He sold by charm. He succeeded simply because he was a cheerful chap. The customers took to him straight away. I knew my beloved territory would be well preserved.

My next move took me back to the comforts of the Mandeville on a Sunday night. A good sleep was desired in preparation for my apprenticeship in big city business circles. The novelty of travelling to work by Underground dispelled any nervous tendency. I was forty-five years of age, experienced in the art of selling, no stranger to management of men. I met my first subject at Archway.

Brian Perry, a big chap, ex-bomber pilot, ran a comfortable old Rover. I suggested a preliminary chat before starting the calls of the day. Brian warmed to the idea. Courteous of manner he asked if I objected to a walk on Hampstead Heath particularly for the benefit of Kim, his wire-haired terrier. This, I agreed, was a splendid idea. I had studied the list of calls in my master copy of his schedule calling book. To my surprise his list bore no relation to mine. 'Johnny never told me about that master book,' Brian volunteered.

I directed that we should continue with no alteration. I settled for observation of Brian's method of working, reserving my assessment until the end of the day. The first few calls went well. Brian's quiet, pleasant approach could not be faulted. The customers liked him. It came to me as a bombshell when Brian said: 'Now this next fellow is a right bastard; I hate his guts and he can't stand mine!'

'Oh, dear. That's no way to speak of a customer,' I said.

'Well, I shall be delighted to see what you make of this one,' Brian chuckled.

The shop stood in a side street near Golders Green station. We parked the car near the shop. I glanced at the customer's buying record. There was none!

Determined to demonstrate how to open the account with an order we entered the diminutive premises. Brian introduced me. No handshake was forthcoming. The proprietor opened the conversation:

'I don't do business with German Jews,' he declared.

'My masters are not German,' said I. 'One is Hungarian, his partner a Dutchman.'

'Makes no difference,' came the retort. 'Can't stand bloody foreigners'.

'Very well,' I terminated, 'I wouldn't dream of serving so evil-thinking a person as yourself, no matter what your background. You are forthwith transferred to my "Stop List". Good day'.

As we walked back to the car Brian cleared his throat before laughing: 'By jingo. That's done me a world of good. I've been trying to find a way of dealing with him.'

'Why didn't you "Stop List" him yourself?' I asked.

'I didn't think I had the authority to do that,' he said.

'Then you haven't studied Standing Instructions.'

From that day forward Brian came forth with countless problems concerning the territory. We made a thorough check on his journey book. By the end of the week I had rescheduled his territory and left him a happier man.

My second week in the London area was based on Brentwood in Essex. I booked into the Warley Arms where Stanley Underhay met me on the Sunday night. Over a pint of beer we made arrangements for the Monday. I was horrified when Stanley said he would pick me up at 10 o'clock.

'Good heavens,' said I. 'My first call has always been 9 o'clock without fail, no matter how far from home.'

'Well,' replied Stanley, 'it's up to you. You are the boss but if we start at 9 o'clock from here we shall not be in Edmonton before ten. Traffic, you know!'

'Pick me up at half-past eight, Stanley. There's a good lad.'

At 8.30 sharp we joined the traffic out of Brentwood and were outside our first call at 9.30. Very respectable I thought. The shop was locked. 'Won't open till ten,' Stanley said. 'Let's have a cup of tea over the road.' At 10.15 we entered the shop. The proprietor looked, and was, unhappy. He wanted to order some bits and pieces.

'Before I take an order, Guvnor, I want some money.' Stanley made no bones about it.

The customer cleaned his spectacles, looked at me and said: 'Hard man, your Mr Underhay!'

'I'm hard too,' I said. 'When it comes to money, that is.'

'Business is bad and your firm's got plenty money. You can't be 'ard up for ten quid.'

'We shall be if twenty-five thousand customers all owe ten quid.'

'Well, 'arold ain't come in yet an' he's got the key of the till. I'll get 'im to post you a cheque when 'e comes in.'

'That's no good,' says Stanley. 'The last one bounced. I want nine pound seventeen and six cash before I take another order.'

Two shabby fivers came forth from the inner office; Stanley put down half-a-crown change and booked the order.

As we strode toward our next call Stanley pronounced:

'That was an easy one. They're affluent up here. Wait and see what I've got in Shoreditch and Bethnal Green.' He went on to relate how one client with an outstanding account of twelve-and-sixpence had offered the services of his daughter, Mabel, in lieu of cash! I found the story incredible until I met the horrible subject on the following day. I was to learn a good deal more of life in North London. I found my thoughts drifting back to the charms of Ebbw Vale and Troedyrhiw, where laughter flowed more freely from people who jealously defended their sordid environment.

Londoners readily criticised the powers of authority and honestly recognised corruption. My own naivety exposed itself when in a Walthamstow shop a number of car radio sets were labelled at stunningly bargain prices:

'How ever do you manage to sell at such low prices?' I asked.

'Knawked orf o'cawse,' the proprietor replied.

'Twas truly a different world, requiring a sharp awareness. On meeting the jovial Frank Mozer of Tottenham I inclined to venture on a 'have-you-heard-this-one?' approach. Promptly he said:

'Ah! you down't cam' 'ere to tell stories. You cam' 'ere to collect 'em!' whereupon he reeled off a brace of revolting yarns which cured me of story-telling for months ahead.

Thankfully we spent more and more time searching out more customers in the rapidly growing electronics industry. The name of Radiospares was familiar enough to many of our potential clients in manufacturing establishments. Of the electricians, technicians and scientists employed in schools, colleges, factories and research centres a select number were members of the Radio Society of Great Britain. Others had graduated from the service departments of retailers. Now the monthly catalogue was distributed directly to them in their places of work.

Industry demanded different components and more stringent specifications. The backroom boys at HQ took heed of the requirements. The catalogue expanded, the service never failed. Buyers and heads of departments quickly came to appreciate the value of 'by-return' delivery of the smallest order.

Members of the Sales Force were cajoled and prodded into rigorous searching for new customers. I personally called upon one gentleman who occupied a wooden hut at Llanwern. It marked the starting point for the building of the vast steel rolling mill of Richard Thomas and Baldwin. Within three years Radiospares components were being consumed at the rate of several thousands of pounds worth per annum. What is more, parcels were accepted on a COD basis. The huge accounting system failed to meet our strict standards of credit control.

Any customer who fell behind in payment was transferred to the COD list. If they couldn't pay we didn't want the business. The 'bad debt' list in the Radiospares accounts department did not fill the back page of a small notebook.

The expansion of business was most noticeable in my favourite country areas. I travelled the whole of the West Country and Wales encouraging my team of representatives to explore every village for signs of embryo businesses. It was surprising where they could be found.

It was even more surprising to me to find how reluctant some members of the team were to exercise their own curiosities. When I asked my man in the Torquay area what he considered to be the principal industry he made no mention of tourism. He could not conceive of a use of electronic components in a hotel. Together we visited the Imperial and found the resident electrician fitting up an elaborate sound amplifying system. We took a handsome order for cables and wires.

So Radiospares marched forward relentlessly. The turnover rose to heights never envisaged by the originators. P.M.S. was fond of saying: 'We know where we are going and we are going to get there.' He told me that he had no ambition to be a millionaire. Yet when the outfit became burdensome for private handling it 'went public'. Both P.M.S. and his partner made handsome gains. Changing the name of the company to Electrocomponents it blossomed as a blue-eyed boy of the Stock Market for years on end.

Shares on offer to members of the staff were soon mopped up at eleven shillings each.

After fourteen years of gruelling work and travel, exciting pioneering and living for much of my time away from home, I decided to give my notice to P.M.S. I hung on for eighteen months until he found a suitable replacement. I felt indisposed to work for a public company. I was not a settler. Whilst I had dedicated myself largely to map-reading and motoring, the intensity of traffic began to frighten rather than irk. Motorways were still of the future. The A38 between Bristol and Gloucester consisted mainly of three-lane carriageways. Life in the centre lane courted with death. When eleven people died in a summertime crash at the Mercury Café bend I deemed it time for a change. I was fifty-four years of age and inwardly urging to start something new.

To date I had worked in the retail trade, in manufacturing, owned my own retail shop, served in the RAF. I needed a change. I had a thousand pounds in the bank. I would venture into wholesaling, but that is another story.